Rethinking Anti-Discriminatory and Anti-Oppressive Theories for Social Work Practice

From Christine: To Adi, Frania, Rivka and Shane. Without your support I could never do what I do.

From Trish: For the fabulous Ted and Katie Letchfield; such a great sense of humour, and thank you for your appreciation and support, I am so proud of you both.

Rethinking Anti-Discriminatory and Anti-Oppressive Theories for Social Work Practice

Edited by Christine Cocker and Trish Hafford-Letchfield

First published 2014 by
PALGRAVE MACMILLAN

Palgrave Macmillan in the UK is an imprint of Macmillan Publishers Limited, registered in England, company number 785998, of Houndmills, Basingstoke, Hampshire RG21 6XS.

Palgrave Macmillan in the US is a division of St Martin's Press LLC, 175 Fifth Avenue, New York, NY 10010. Palgrave Macmillan is the global academic imprint of the above companies and has companies and representatives throughout the world.

Palgrave® and Macmillan® are registered trademarks in the United States, the United Kingdom, Europe and other countries

ISBN: 978-1-137-02397-1

This book is printed on paper suitable for recycling and made from fully managed and sustained forest sources. Logging, pulping and manufacturing processes are expected to conform to the environmental regulations of the country of origin.

A catalogue record for this book is available from the British Library.

A catalog record for this book is available from the Library of Congress.

Typeset by Cambrian Typesetters, Camberley, Surrey

Printed in China

Contents

PART III SUBJECTIVITY

PART IV DECONSTRUCTION

Foreword

Helen Cosis Brown

Christine Cocker and Trish Hafford-Letchfield's book, a collection of 14 edited chapters, is a much needed contribution to social work thinking, both in practice and in the academy. Anti-discriminatory practice is a contested area of social work's 'doing', as well as 'thinking'. This book makes a purposeful intervention into this contested terrain to stimulate debate and the development of ideas. The book's value lies in four aspects of its conception and realisation.

First, one of the pleasures, and indeed strengths, of an edited text is that it affords the reader different perspectives relating to a subject. Alongside strengths there are sometimes weaknesses. A potential weakness with edited books is when different perspectives translate into disparate, unconnected chapters that do not come together as a coherent whole. This is not the case with this edited social work text. The structure of this book has mitigated any such risk by employing two devices. The first being the sub-grouping of the book's 14 chapters into four sections related to the postmodern, post-structural themes of: power, discourse, subjectivity and deconstruction. The second being editorial comment at the beginning of each section offering, as it does, continuity and coherence to the whole enterprise.

Second, the contributions are drawn from Australia, Ireland, New Zealand and the United Kingdom (UK). This geographical and political range means that differences in the development of ideas, and how these ideas are applied and explored in practice, are evident. Deconstructing the potential generalised debate about ADP in the UK is enabled by Bernard and Campbell's focus on Northern Ireland through examining the specificity of social work practice in that setting.

Third, the book has a particular theoretical palette, drawing as it does chiefly on the work of Foucault. Although the work of Foucault is fore fronted, there are a range of other theoreticians manifest in the book, including: Derrida, Badiou, Butler and even Althusser, who as a Marxist might have been considered too 'modern' for such a postmodern/poststructural text. This theoretical focus enables theoretical depth, similar to an oil painting with its many-layered profundity.

Fourth, this is a book about ideas informing social work thinking. Because social work is in essence a 'doing' occupation/profession then to be useful these ideas have to be translatable into practice. Here lies one ubiquitous, perennial tension between social work academia and sites of social work activity. However, there are examples of how, what are in effect highly complex philosophical, social, cultural, and political ideas can inform practice in chapters such as Garrett, Turney, Green and Featherstone, and Laird. Cowden and Singh's chapter reminds us of the need to deconstruct and read as 'text' service user involvement, which, like anti-discriminatory practice, has become an integral, established part of the status quo. Social work has to be measured by its ability to both enhance the life chances and quality of life of those it works with, and minimise its potential damage to those involved with its interventions. Carr's chapter denotes the realities of the constructed categories and artificial divides between those that receive or have services imposed upon them, health and social care professionals, social workers, researchers, and academics. The embodiments of each are often not separated, but rather are components of the same person. This realisation reminds us that, firstly, social work is a human activity, working with human experience and emotion and, secondly, that our neo-liberal preoccupation with difference has lessened our focus on sameness.

Social work involvement with individuals, networks and families can, and often does, have immense impact for those involved and the generations of individuals who come after. Social work involvement, for better or worse becomes part of the narratives of individuals, networks and families. As social workers we therefore need to tread with great care, kindness, humility and critical thought. This book offers much to inform that thought.

Helen Cosis Brown is Professor of Social Work, Institute of Applied Social Research, University of Bedfordshire

Acknowledgements

Thanks to the clever, co-operative and well organised contributing authors who all did their stuff brilliantly!

Abbreviations

ABSWAP	Association of Black Social Workers and Allied Professionals
ADP	anti-discriminatory practice
AMPH	approved mental health professional
ANT	actor network theory
AOP	anti-oppressive practice
BME	black and minority ethnic
CPD	continuing professional development
DLA	Disability Living Allowance
DSM	Diagnostical and Statistical Manual of Mental Disorders
ECtHR	European Court of Human Rights
EHRC	Equality and Human Rights Commission
EU	European Union
GSCC	General Social Care Council
HCPC	Health and Care Professions Council
HRW	Human Rights Watch
HSE	Health Service Executive
IASSW	International Association of Schools of Social Work
ICD	International Classification of Diseases
IFSW	International Federation of Social Work
LGBT	lesbian, gay, bisexual and transgender
MPA	Mental Patients Union
NHS	National Health Service
PCS model	Personal, Cultural and Structural model
SiA	studies in ableism
SSD	social services department
TIC	The Integration Centre

Editors

Christine Cocker is a qualified social worker and a Senior Lecturer in Social Work at the University of East Anglia, Norwich, UK. She is a trustee for the British Association of Adoption and Fostering (BAAF) and an independent member of a local authority adoption panel. Christine completed her social work training in New Zealand in the 1980's. She had worked as a social worker and a social work manager in an inner London local authority for 13 years and at a national voluntary sector consultation service as a service development director for three years prior to moving into academia. Her research and publications are predominantly in the area of social work with looked after children, child protection and lesbian and gay fostering and adoption. Amongst her many publications are: *Social Work with Lesbians and Gay Men* (2011) with Helen Cosis Brown, published by Sage and the second edition of *Social Work with Looked After Children* (2013) with Lucille Allain, published by Learning Matters with Sage.

Trish Hafford-Letchfield is Reader in Social Work at Middlesex University, UK. Trish is a qualified social worker, nurse and educator and has worked in both the statutory and voluntary sector as a manager, coach/mentor. Trish has published widely within the areas of leadership, management and organisational development. Her research interests include sexuality and sexual identity in social work, educational gerontology and the arts in social work education. Her most recent publication is with Sharon Lambly, Gary Spolander and Christine Cocker: *Inclusive Leadership: Managing to Make a Difference* (2014) with Policy Press.

Contributing Authors

Claudia Bernard is Head of Postgraduate Studies at Goldsmiths, University of London. Her principle interests are in developing students' research-mindedness for evidence-informed practice. Claudia actively researches the intersection of race, gender, social class, and child and family welfare, and is developing research methodologies that open up new ways for understanding violence and abuse in the lives of vulnerable children from stigmatised and marginalised communities in the UK. Claudia has published widely on child abuse and gender-based violence.

Rachel Burr is a qualified child protection social worker and anthropologist who currently teaches in the Education and Social Work department at Sussex University. She has worked and undertaken research with unaccompanied children in London, Ireland and Vietnam and fervently believes that given the opportunity most young people make a positive and valuable contribution to their adoptive country.

Jim Campbell was appointed as Professor of Social Work at Goldsmiths, University of London in 2012, having spent 20 years teaching and researching at Queens University Belfast. He has published extensively on social work and political conflict and mental health social work.

Sarah Carr is an independent adult mental health and social care knowledge consultant. She previously worked for the Social Care Institute of Excellence (SCIE) as a Senior Research Analyst. Sarah specialises in service user participation, equality and diversity, evidence-based practice, research and policy analysis. Sarah is Co-Vice Chair of the National Survivor User Network (NSUN) and sits on the editorial board of Disability and Society. She holds a number of Honorary academic posts, including Visiting Fellow at the School of Social Policy and Social Work at York and Senior Lecturer at the School for Social Policy, Birmingham. She is a long-term user of mental health services.

Stephen Cowden is originally from Australia and is based at Coventry University, UK. His PhD was concerned with Australian nationalism and the construction of discourses of 'white' identity. His approach to social work is concerned with issues of social justice and social inequality and the social construction of social problems. Stephen's main research interests are in the interface between social work and social theory and how practitioners 'theorise' their work with service users and in critical pedagogy to inform the 'praxis' (theory and practice) of social work. Stephen's latest publication, *Social Work and Ethical Practice* with Annie Pullen-Safascon, was published in 2012 by Pearson Education.

Priscilla Dunk-West is a sociologist, social worker and senior lecturer at the Flinders University of South Australia. She is the co-editor of *Sexuality and Sexual Identities in Social Work: Research and Reflections from Women in the Field* (published by Ashgate) alongside Trish Hafford-Letchfield, the author of *How to be a Social Worker: A Critical Guide for Students* (2013, Palgrave Macmillan) and, along with Fiona Verity, *Sociological Social Work* (Ashgate). Her research is concerned with self, professional identity and gender and sexuality.

Brid Featherstone was born in County Galway and graduated in sociology at Trinity College Dublin. As a community worker in London before qualifying as a social worker, her early practice experience was with young offenders and then as a social worker and team manager in generic teams. In 1992 she became a full-time social work academic at the University of Bradford. She has developed an international profile as a researcher and theorist on gender relations, family support and child welfare. Brid is currently Professor of Social Care at the Open University.

Paul Michael Garrett is the Director of Social Work at the National University of Ireland, Galway, in the Republic of Ireland. His publications critically examine social work/social policy relating to children and families. *Remaking Social Work with Children and Families* (Routledge, 2003); *Social Work with Irish Children and Families in Britain* (Policy Press, 2004); *'Transforming' Children's Services?* (Open University/McGraw Hill, 2009). His work has also appeared in academic journals across a range of disciplines and he is a member of the editorial boards of *Critical Social Policy*, the *European Journal of Social Work* and is a consulting editor for the US-based *Journal of Progressive Human Services*.

Lorraine Green lectures in social work at the University of Nottingham and has research interests in social divisions such as gender, sexuality and social class and in applying ethics, life-course theory and sociological and social theory to social work. She has also written widely on children, child abuse and child sexual exploitation in residential care. She was recently an expert member of the Samson Committee, which investigated the sexual abuse of children in foster and residential care in the Netherlands between 1945 and

2010. Lorraine is author of *Understanding the Life Course: Sociological and Psychological Perspectives* (Polity, 2010) and co-editor of *'Practical Social Work Ethics: Complex Dilemmas in Applied Social Care* (Ashgate, 2013).

Stephen Hicks is a lecturer in the School of Nursing, Midwifery and Social Work at the University of Manchester (UK). He is the author of *Lesbian, Gay and Queer Parenting: Families, Intimacies, Genealogies* (2011, Palgrave Macmillan), and co-editor of *Lesbian and Gay Fostering and Adoption: Extraordinary Yet Ordinary* (1999, Jessica Kingsley Publishers), a new, revised edition of which will appear in 2016. With Dharman Jeyasingham, Steve is working on a new book, *Social Work Sexualities: Practice, Research, Theory*, to be published by Palgrave Macmillan in 2016.

Dharman Jeyasingham is a lecturer in social work at the University of Lancaster. He delivers teaching about understandings of power, difference and oppression in social work generally and children's social work in particular. He has written about issues of power and the construction of difference in social work, geographies of sexuality and geographical approaches to understanding children's social work practice.

Fiona Kumari Campbell was Convenor of Disability Studies, Reader and Deputy Head of School at the Law School, Griffith University. Campbell is an Adjunct Professor in Disability Studies at the Faculty of Medicine, University of Kelaniya in Sri Lanka. Fiona is a person with disability and is associated with several minority groups. She has written extensively on issues related to disability – philosophy, ableism, desire, law and technology – and is recognised as a world leader in scholarship around studies in ableism. The successful publication of her first book, *Contours of Ableism* with Palgrave in 2009, has led to two further publications: *The Unveiling of (Dis)ability: Essays on Silence, Voice and Imprints* and *Crippin' the Law: Jurisprudential Narratives of Impairment*.

Siobhan Laird studied English and Philosophy at Queen's University, Belfast. Starting her career as a property surveyor she changed career and qualified as a social worker in 1994, following which, she worked for several years in community care and as a qualified counsellor in the voluntary sector. Siobhan was a social work academic in West Africa at the University of Ghana, where she was consultant to the Danish Embassy on welfare provision for street children. Her PhD examined welfare policy, social work and community development practices in Ghana. In the UK, Siobhan teaches at Nottingham University. She has been a member of the International Relations Advisory Panel of the British Association of Social Workers and Director of the World Development Movement.

Litea Meo-Sewabu is an Assistant Lecturer and PhD candidate at the School of Health and Social Services at Massey University in New Zealand. She is an Indigenous Fijian and her research looks at the lay understanding of health and well-being amongst Indigenous Fijian women in Fiji and New Zealand. Her teaching focuses on Pacific peoples well-being, community development and indigenous frameworks of health and well-being. She has published and presented internationally on her research and is towards the end of her PhD thesis.

Gurnam Singh is Principal Lecturer in Social Work at Coventry University and Co-Director of the Applied Research Group in Social Inclusion in Social Care. An academic activist, researcher and teacher, Gurnam established a (inter)national reputation in the field of social justice, anti-racism, anti-oppressive practice and critical pedagogy and has published widely on this area. His PhD, from Warwick University in 2004, focused on the history and development of anti-racist social work. In 2009, in recognition of his contribution to social justice education, he was awarded a National Teaching Fellowship by the Higher Education Academy.

Shamser Sinha is a researcher of sociology with research interests in the areas of post colonialism, racism, multiculturalism, youth culture and identity, and young refugees, asylum seekers and migrants. He is also a playwright, having been a recipient of the Angle Theatre New Writers Award (www.angletheatre.co.uk/whatson.htm) and a part-time youth worker at Dost, Trinity Centre, East Ham. Shamser is convenor of the British Sociological Association Race and Ethnicity Study Group and on the Editorial Board of Sociological Research Online.

Alex Sutton is Deputy Chief Executive of Praxis Community Projects and has led Community Projects at Praxis since 2009, having worked previously in community development, international development and youth work. At Praxis, Alex currently co-ordinates a range of community development projects that give vulnerable migrants a platform to have their voice heard in public policy and service development.

Danielle Turney is a Senior Lecturer in Social Work at Bristol University and Director of the Post Qualifying Specialist Award in Social Work with Children and Young People. Danielle has many years experience in local authority children and families social work. After undertaking PhD research exploring anti-racist practice, she has worked at Goldsmiths College, University of London and the Open University. Her research interests are in child welfare and protection, with particular reference to child neglect; relationship-based practice; critical approaches to social work theory and practice, including postmodern perspectives; the use of child observation in social work; and theorising anti-oppressive and anti-racist practice in social work.

Stephen A. Webb is Professor of Social Work at Glasgow Caledonian University in Scotland. Previous to this he was Director of the Institute for Social Inclusion and Well-Being, University of Newcastle, New South Wales, Australia and Professorial Research Fellow at University of Sussex. He is author of several books, including *Social Work in a Risk Society* (Palgrave, 2006) and *Evidence-based Social Work: A Critical Stance* (with Gray and Plath, Routledge, 2009). He is co-editor (with Gray) of *Social Work Theories and Methods* (Sage, 2008), the four-volume international reference work *International Social Work* (Sage, 2010), *Ethics and Value Perspectives in Social Work* (Palgrave, 2010), and the *Sage Handbook of Social Work* (for Sage, with Gray and Midgley, 2012). Webb's critical analysis 'Considerations on the validity of evidence-based practice in social work' (2001) is the world's most cited article in the field, and the most influential publication in social work over the last ten years (Hodge et al., 2011). He has recently completed *The New Politics of Critical Social Work* for Palgrave and the second edition of *Social Work Theories and Methods* for Sage, London, which has been translated into Korean and Polish.

Introduction: Rethinking Anti-Discriminatory and Anti-Oppressive Practice in Social Work; Time for New Paradigms?

Christine Cocker and Trish Hafford-Letchfield

Why 'Rethinking'?

The concepts of anti-discriminatory practice (ADP) and anti-oppressive practice (AOP) have been part of the social work landscape since the late 1970s. Learning how to be effective in promoting ADP and AOP are essential and fundamental areas within social work education, practice and research. These terms are embedded within the language used to describe the values underpinning social work practice, but, whilst once they may have offered an alternative critique of individual and societal relationships, they have now become part of 'status-quo' thinking, and have long since lost their political edge. Substantial structural changes, various cultural shifts, new social movements and contemporary contests from within the critical tradition of social work continue to challenge the core assumptions of social work theory and practice to develop new thinking (Healy, 2000; Powell, 2001). These evolutions have given rise to a relatively small, yet consistent and developing voice in academia, arguing for social work to think beyond the mainstream and to critique existing approaches (e.g. McLaughlin, 2005; Ferguson, 2007a; Millar, 2008; Ferguson and Woodward, 2009; Hicks, 2009, 2011; Brown and Cocker, 2011; Featherstone and Green, 2010). It is timely to look again at how social work understands the complexity of human experience and to explore different theoretical discourses to challenge assumptions and values. This book aims to kick-start this long-overdue debate and provides a vehicle for offering some fresh perspectives and opportunities for educators, students, practitioners and managers, which

1

re-focus on ADP and AOP, but remain underpinned by the relationship of these concepts to social work practice. As a core, essential text for any social work education or training programme, such concepts and issues have been reframed, challenged and reconceptualised – thus our suggested description of 'rethinking' these. This is certainly not about erasing the past but taking stock of new questions that have been posed. It is essential to remember the historical, as well as thinking about the present and the future. We hope that this book will appeal to a broad international audience as it includes contributions from a range of countries and from a range of social work theorists. The ideas within this book are intended to be transferable as well as providing a range of specific case studies which are both context- and/or service user-specific.

One of the most significant features of this particular book is that we have adopted a framework drawing heavily on the work of the French philosopher and social theorist, Michel Foucault, who offers a particularly relevant means and sound resource for reviewing and revisiting the concepts previously associated with ADP and AOP. Foucault provides valuable tools that help us to understand the contemporary world and the discourse of social work in its broader context in ways that are quite different from other kinds of analysis. Foucault and those critical theorists who have since developed his ideas, we suggest, are helpful in promoting a critical appraisal of ADP and AOP in current social work by showing how there has been and will always be other 'truths' and ways of acting upon others and ourselves, thus pointing to the possibility of alternatives for governing and constructing subjectivities (Nicoll and Fejes, 2008). As a social work student, practitioner or manager, you may not be very familiar with Foucault nor had the opportunity to reflect upon how his ideas can be applied to this area of social work practice. You may, on the other hand, already be familiar but want to find out more or achieve further depth in your understanding. Both types of audience should enjoy the journey made in this book.

In this introductory chapter we will begin with a brief review of the key debates in relation to ADP and AOP and the key contributions and collaborative exchanges that have influenced our thinking, including those from critical social work and postmodern and poststructuralist analyses. Healy in particular (1998, 2000) has highlighted how 'post' theorists have informed social work activists as to how such theories can enhance reflexivity about the constraining effects of earlier endeavours, particularly around the issue or phenomenon of power, where it is possible to exercise this humanely and justly within specific sites of practice. Foucault's methods of understanding social phenomena through his use of historical inquiry is useful here, by going back and using the past as a way of diagnosing the present and reviewing current social arrangements. This is what Foucault termed 'archaeology' and 'genealogy'. The 'archive' is a technical term used by Foucault to designate the collection of all material traces left behind by a particular historical period and culture. In examining these traces, one can deduce the 'historical a priori' of the period or its 'episteme'. None of these concepts have predictive value but are all descriptions of limited historical orders (Foucault, 1997). A brief overview of the history of ADP and AOP, whose definitions provide a starting point to gauge the meaning of the concepts historically, will therefore be useful as a basis from which to critically reflect on what might have evolved and changed, particularly given our constant need to adapt to rapid and paradigm-shifting economic, sociocultural and environmental circumstances. This introductory chapter will then go on to explore specifically how we might use a Foucauldian approach to look at discrimination, oppression, equality and diversity in social work. We will explain his key overarching ideas and the potential they hold for social work, illustrated with some concrete examples.

The book is structured into four parts that unpick and explore further some of Foucault's key concepts and themes with reference to contemporary social work practice. The deployment of key ideas from Foucault has provided a broader framework within which the chapter contributors enable us to extend the canvas and ask larger questions within the context We have framed each section of the book alongside Foucault's key themes of 'Power', 'Discourse', 'Subjectivity' and 'Deconstruction'. You will appreciate as you read on, that there is substantial convergence and divergence between these key themes and that the debates within are shaped by complexities and contradictions, sometimes highlighted by the different contributors themselves. At the beginning of each of these sections, a short editorial from us introduces the key concept underlining that theme in the book, its relevance to AOP and ADP and we also draw out the key issues illustrated in the chapters that follow. Every chapter includes a 'key ideas for practice' section. The contributions are not only from social work scholars, chosen for their expertise in different specialisms, but we have included contributions from relevant disciplines in the social sciences such as disability and sociology so as to offer a more diverse cross-disciplinary understanding, which enriches the potential for social work knowledge and practice.

The Development of ADP and AOP in Social Work

Constant change in an increasingly globalised and technological world requires a conscious capacity to adapt to rapid and new paradigms, which we alluded to earlier. This book is a deliberate attempt to grapple with the consequent perspectives on inequality and assert a re-focus on concepts of social justice with the inevitable challenges that these throw at us. Making sense of the politics of social work in its current context is a challenging task where very strong ideological positions have been taken up in many cases, in relation to the emergence of quasi-markets in the public sector, where issues such as access to and direct privatisation of services now occurs (Hafford-Letchfield, 2013). Despite globalisation and technological advances, the major factors influencing the human condition and circumstance across the world remain grounded in poverty and breaches of human rights (Wilkinson and Pickett, 2009). As the gap between rich and poor widens in many democratic Western societies, there is increasing evidence that such inequality impacts on everyone, including the rich. Whilst the social work profession may seek to alleviate many of the causes of poverty through its political action and direct support of those impacted, the way in which this is manifest in practice differs dramatically in global terms. As key concepts, both ADP and AOP are the mode for many social workers in which this commitment to social justice is actualised. The commitment to social justice is one of the key tenets of the social work profession that sets it apart from other professions. The definition from the International Association of Schools of Social Work (IASSW) and the International Federation of Social Work (IFSW) states that:

> The social work profession promotes social change, problem solving in human relationships and the empowerment and liberation of people to enhance well-being. Utilising theories of human behaviour and social systems, social work intervenes at the points where people interact with their environments. Principles of human rights and social justice are fundamental to social work. (IASSW/IFSW, 2001)

A number of publications provide comprehensive definitions of ADP and AOP, and other terms used to discuss equalities within society (Thomas and Pierson, 1995; Bagilhole, 2009; Clifford and Burke, 2009; Brown and Cocker, 2011 (see Chapter 3)). ADP and AOP now tend to be used interchangeably, although their differences have been articulated. The glossary will help you with definitions with some key terms and concepts used in this book. However, this is not to suggest we wish to adopt an essentialist use of language, as this is inconsistent with Foucauldian thinking. What these terms mean depends in part on how they are used and interpreted, and this will change over time for many different reasons. We will start by looking at the definitions and explanations of these terms written by the authors most associated with them. Neil Thompson is most associated with the term 'anti-discriminatory practice', and has published widely in relation to explaining its meaning and application to practice in his widely adopted 'Personal, Cultural and Structural' (PCS) model (e.g. Thompson, 1993, 2001, 2003, 2006, 2008, 2012). Thompson offers a number of key points relating to analysis of ADP as permeated in his writing:

- The development of sensitivity to the existence all around us of discrimination and oppression.

- The recognition that there is no comfortable middle ground – we are either part of the solution or part of the problem.

- The need to address the three key imperatives of justice, equality and participation.

- The need to revisit traditional forms of practice and amend them accordingly.

- The idea that non-discriminatory and anti-oppressive assessment is a first step towards the achievement of anti-discriminatory practice. (Thompson, 2008, p. 109)

Thompson (2012) promotes a holistic approach to discrimination and critiques what he calls the 'managing diversity' approach whilst acknowledging the importance of affirming and valuing the significance of diversity so that differences can be seen as assets to be appreciated rather than problems to be solved. ADP clearly recognises structural disadvantage and the effect this has on people's lives. It is also associated with the role of legislation and the positive actions that can be taken to prevent or curb any form of discrimination against individuals, groups and communities derived from statute in the form of powers and duties, as well as by recognising the inherent power when enacting legislation in social work. But there are limitations to this concept. These include the use of 'identity' to create a hierarchy of oppression; limitations on how far it is possible to 'learn' about someone's oppression and to counteract this oppression solely with learnt knowledge; the challenges for someone from an oppressed category to be seen as the 'expert' on the life and experiences of that category of people; and finally the institutionalisation of attributing problems to categories such as culture/gender/class etc. (Brown and Cocker, 2011, p. 40). Great strides have simultaneously been made in the service user movement, where use of the term 'co-production' is increasingly being applied to reflect the importance of securing active input by the people who use services contrasts with approaches that treat people as passive recipients of services designed and delivered by someone else (Needham and Carr, 2009). This reciprocal relationship that builds on trust, peer support and social activism within communities is yet to be theoretically refined and evaluated in practice before we can be sure of its transformative potential embodiment within practice. Recognition of this gap and documented examples of continuing exclusion of some service user groups point to the need for more sophisticated theoretical approaches that are capable of acknowledging and dealing with greater complexity and which do not overly simplify multifaceted phenomena not always embedded within ADP. For example, writings on critical multiculturalism (McLaren, 1997b; Sundar and Ly, 2013) have emphasised the need to acknowledge the ways in which race, class, gender, nationality and sexuality have been constructed within a particular socio-historical and capitalist context, which requires an interrogation of 'otherness' to address the ways in which hegemonic norms continue to marginalise and oppress people with diverse identities (Sundar and Ly, 2013).

Lena Dominelli's significant contribution to this area of social work practice has also been valuable in developing the complexities in situation and argument about inequalities, particularly from a global perspective (e.g., Dominelli, 1988; 2002a; 2009). Dominelli's critique of Thompson's PCS model highlights 'a focus on discrimination which emphasises only one element in the web of social relations' (2002a, p. 4) and says that 'additive approaches rank oppressions in a hierarchy that prioritises one form over another' (2002a, p. 5). Instead, Dominelli prefers the term 'anti-oppressive practice' (AOP), which emerges from 'Promoting social justice and human development in an unequal world provides the raison d'etre of social work practice, and is a key way of discharging society's contract in assisting vulnerable people in its midst' (Dominelli, 2002a, p. 4). In subsequent publications, Thompson argues that Dominelli has misrepresented his work (Thompson, 2012).

A major concern often heard about social work is that, over time, it has relinquished its social justice origins and moved away from social reform and its role in redressing inequalities. Dominelli, for example, referred to the preoccupation of anti-oppressive practice with the implementation of social justice as central to improving the quality of life or well-being with individuals, groups and communities. She calls for a holistic form of social work practice which engages with social divisions and structural inequalities. This approach needs to encompass all aspects of social life, including culture, institutions, legal framework, political systems, socio-economic infrastructure and interpersonal relationships (Dominelli, 2002a), as well as be able to work in a way that does not endorse any hierarchy of oppressions but is able to respond to multiple dimensions of reality which embrace teamwork and working collectively. Similarly, Dalrymple and Burke (1995) have articulated the importance of AOP and anti-racist attitudes in the development of critical approaches to social work, which have since been challenged, particularly for those working in mainstream welfare organisations undertaking the 'control' functions of social work. Some of the values expressed from within critical practice ideas have led to criticism where insufficient attention is given to the negative outcomes, such as for those who might be disconnected from networks of care and support and where expressions of mutuality, for example, have not had a chance of being realised (Healy, 2005).

Coming from a poststructuralist perspective, Healy (2005) has high-lighted the substantial structural changes over the past four decades that have threatened the continuation of critical practice traditions in social work, relegating these almost to some halcyon era. She called for the re-invention of critical practice theory which seeks a more collaborative and open-ended approach to activism in social work relevant to the twenty-first century. Given that the core mission of critical social work is to promote social justice through its practice and theories, Healy suggests that it needs to be much more adept at responding to challenges, for example, from the proponents of conservatism, economic rationalism and managerialism and their consequent authoritarian practice relations.

These developments in theory, as we shall see within the contributions of this book, have been essential in lending themselves to further analysis. For example, many of the contributors refer to the rhetoric and over exposure of terms such as 'empowerment' and 'discrimination' within social work theory and practice. As the different authors unpick some of the current debates, we will see that, by looking through the lens of different critical theorists, hith-erto the search for social work 'truths' has had the tendency to close down discussions rather than creating opportunities for on-going discourse and development within the profession. Healy accurately analysed the difficulties that social workers and social work academics confront when attempting to critique the ADP/AOP frameworks, as illustrated in her comment that:

> by characterising all those who oppose anti-oppressive practice 'insights' as self-interested or conservative, anti-oppressive theorists insulate their approach from the critical practice reflection required to understand the uses and the limits of the model for promoting critical practice in the diverse institutional contexts of social work activity. (2005, p. 190)

In other words, continuing structural injustices need opportunities for collaborative approaches that bring together the academic and practical dimensions of social work that embraces its rich tradition of working with service users and fosters dialogue from which insights from each perspective help to build knowledge and truths.

Debating Theory and Practice Relationships in ADP and AOP

Given the potential limitation of debates around equality in social work in relation to everyday ADP and AOP discourses, our aims for this book are to expand this arena by drawing on interesting ideas and theoretical discussions about diversity and difference from other social science disciplines. Social work remains in a reactionary position with regard to some of these debates, and the impact on social work practice can be seen in concerning scenarios, for example that of Tyra Henry, a 21 month old girl who was killed by her stepfather in the UK in 1984. An inquiry into her death concluded that the white social workers were too trusting of the family and were hindered by assumptions about extended family members in relation to their race and culture. Similarly, with the death of Victoria Climbié in 1999, some 15 years later, Ratna Dutt, the Director of the Race Equality Unit in the UK, commented at the public inquiry into the death:

> There is some evidence to suggest that one of the consequences of an exclusive focus on 'culture' in work with black children and families, is [that] it leaves black and ethnic minority children in potentially dangerous situations, because the assessment has failed to address a child's fundamental care and protection needs'. (Dutt, 2003)

Whilst both of these examples occurred some time ago now, these problematic dynamics were again seen in the Wakefield Inquiry (an investigation into the sexual abuse of looked-after children by two homosexual male foster carers), where the inquiry report noted that social workers involved with the case had demonstrated anxiety about being perceived as discriminatory.

> alongside anxieties on their part about being or being seen as prejudiced against gay people. The fear of being discriminatory led them to fail to discriminate between the appropriate and the abusive. Discrimination based on prejudice is not acceptable, especially not in social work or any public service. Discrimination founded on a professional judgement on a presenting issue, based on knowledge, assessed evidence and interpretation, is at the heart of good social work practice. These anxieties about discrimination have deep roots, we argue – in social work training, professional identity and organisational cultures. (Parrott et al., 2007, p. 164)

These re-occurring scenarios within the history of social work failures illustrate how social workers are far from immune from behaving in ways that privilege some forms of oppression over others, and of the consequences of creating a hierarchy of oppression that 'validates' these and which is deeply divisive. For example, in terms of lesbian and gay issues, Brown and Cocker (2011) assert that the academic social work community continues to remain largely silent, and where comment on these issues does exist, it is seen as niche and marginal. Reports that four out of every ten social workers think that homophobia is a problem within the profession (*Community Care*,

2012) and the repression of sexual identity issues for social work students (Lovell, 2013) continue to shock. This is in the context of a profession supposedly committed to social justice and during enormous legal changes within the UK and many other Western countries over the past 10 years, which espouse equal rights for lesbians and gay men in relation to the age of consent, partnerships and marriage, housing, jobs, families, and provision of goods and services (Cocker and Hafford-Letchfield, 2010).

In its 2012 annual review, Human Rights Watch (2014) documented the dangers of some countries evoking tradition and traditional values to undermine human rights, especially for women and members of the lesbian, gay, bisexual and transgender community. Far from being benign, as its language suggests, a recently passed United Nations Human Rights Council resolution 'promoting human rights and fundamental freedoms' via 'a better understanding of traditional values of humankind' tramples over diversity, and fails to acknowledge just how fluid traditional practice and customary law can be. The HRW also criticised the failure of governments, international agencies and nongovernmental organisations to see environmental issues through the prism of human rights and address them together in laws or institutions. They also focus on experiences of a range of very different groups: migrants and asylum seekers; people with disabilities in Russia; and children and adults living in, and working around, mines in Africa, all of whom suffer from lack of legal protections and a range of abuses that impact their health, their ability to fully participate in society and other human rights. Social workers must be ever alert to significant human rights issues in their own backyard. The significance of social work advocacy and its role in implementing government policy developments that seek to curb abuses and promote human rights, as this enabling role of social work is not always benign. For example, there has beeen a rise in the negative public, political and policy attitudes toward asylum-seeking families in many Westernised countries. A marked increase in legislation in England and Wales over the past 30 years has curtailed asylum seeking families' eligibility for public resources (Wade et al., 2013), where social work assessments are explicitly vehicles for establishing the rights of asylum seekers and whether human rights violations might occur if support is not given. In discussing these points, Humphries issued a wake-up call for the profession:

> social work needs to stop pretending that what it calls 'anti-oppressive practice' is anything but a gloss to help it feel better about what it is required to do, a gloss that is reinforced by a raft of books and articles that are superficial and void of a political context for practice. It needs to inform itself of theories of power that go beyond individualistic models, and to struggle with the challenges that come from engaging with debates within the social sciences. (2004, p. 105)

Similarly, Hafford-Letchfield (2013), writing about class in later life, suggests that relatively little is known about the effect of socioeconomic status on the take up of social care services by older people, as, unlike other equality and diversity characteristics, 'class' is not routinely conceptualised or evaluated and so remains relatively unexplored in relation to social care. Conceptualising and analysing class in social care has been explored to some extent through research that explores associations between the use of formal and informal help and socio-economic status (Broese et al., 2006). Given that health status appears to be a strong predictor of the potential for older people using social care, examination of health inequalities and other proxies, such as education and home ownership in relation to age alongside other demographic factors, have provided further sources of evidence. Research by Stoller and Gibson (2000), for example, has illustrated discernible patterns in the different experiences of older service users from diverse backgrounds that reflect social structural arrangements and cultural blueprints in relation to the use of care services. Debates about the future of social welfare, such as universalism versus targeting, the concept of fairness and particularly intergenerational fairness, have questioned the role and stance that social workers are expected to take up in the administration of policy around class (Hafford-Letchfield, 2013). Tracing the historical significance of personalisation, for example, has revealed an uncritical acceptance of the move towards a more individualised agenda such as through the wholesale introduction of individualised budgets, which may neglect issues of poverty and inequality. Both Ferguson (2007a) and Lymberry (2010) have asserted a flawed conception of the people who use social work services, leading particularly to the de-professionalisation of social work in the taking up of the roles of brokers, personal advisors or support workers and subsequent fragmentation of provision. To complicate matters, the cautiousness and alleged insensitivity of social workers towards poverty and class has also been associated with its own middle-class values creating class conflict between service users and themselves – a further pillar of social oppression (Strier, 2009). Fenge (2012) has highlighted the distinct lack of understanding amongst social workers of the actual experiences of older people during times of financial crisis and recession to make better use of their economic resources, and the paucity of research in this area. What we do know is that the expressed humiliation of older people in applying for and accepting care becomes emphasised through the nature of its bureaucratised exchange with social work (Hafford-Letchfield, 2011).

The few examples given here provide just a flavour of some of the complex debates intended for a 'rethink' via the contributions to this book. It is important to recognise, too, that discussions about equalities issues are not the sole prerogative of social work. Many other terms, such as diversity, equality and intersectionality, have more recently been included within the language broadly used to describe the complexity of human relationships, situations and interactions. Calls to 'check your privilege' (Freeman, 2013) have become reasonably common, but to what end? Are these really new concepts or similar ideas with new labels?

> 'intersectionality', the new buzzword ... means we must understand our own privilege: the multiple oppressions of race, class, culture and sexuality. ... Intersectionality is good in theory, though in practice, it means that no one can speak for anyone else. It is the dead-end where much queer politics, feminist politics and identity politics ends up. In its own rectum. It refuses to engage with many other political discourses and becomes the old hierarchy of oppression. (Moore, 2013)

Similarly, Featherstone and Green comment that 'dogma has often ruled in relation to anti-oppressive practice' (2009, p. 61). There is no place for dogma in social work. Whilst some aspects of ADP could be considered as potentially blaming, abstracted, insufficiently related to practice and overly simplistic for tackling highly complex human, social and political issues (Cocker and Brown, 2010), how can social work build on its historical commitment to working with marginalised and disenfranchised groups and move forward with its theorising and practice in this area? This is where we account for our choice to take up the theoretical resources from the work of French philosopher, historian, social theorist and literary critic, Michel Foucault, in order to develop a response to such questions. We haven't presented the contents in a way that systematically covers issues for different groups of service users, rather we have presented the material so as to encourage reading in breadth and depth through the use of four key concepts used by Foucault, which also furthers our understanding of ADP and AOP.

Drawing on the Work of Michel Foucault (1926–1984)

At the beginning of this chapter, we remarked on the benefits of taking a Foucauldian stance in order to try and understand the contemporary world and discourse of social work in its broader context in ways that are quite different from other kinds of analysis. Foucault and those critical theorists who have since developed his ideas are helpful in promoting a critical attitude towards current social work by showing how there has been and will always be other 'truths' and ways of acting upon others and ourselves. Much of Foucault's work called for the questioning of how knowledge is created through the vehicle of discourse and the need for transgressive counter-discourses, which involve endless questioning of the systems of thought in which we are actually located (Irving, 1999). Foucault asserted that dominant discourse provides a means of controlling the social practices and institutions in a society. Managing or governing the knowledge of society in this way led Foucault to argue that history should not be viewed as a continuous source of knowledge, but that we must also look deeper into its everyday documents to see how the discourse ruptures and where and when it changes. Such documents may be seen in social policy or everyday speech. These ideas illustrate the concept of genealogy and archives explained at the beginning of this chapter. Looking closely at these ruptures will help to identify fragments of history left behind by social and political powers and points of discontinuity between broadly defined modes of knowledge, which inevitably fail to do justice to the complexities of discourse. Foucault argues that discourses emerge and transform, not according to a developing series of unarticulated, common worldviews, but according to a vast and complex set of discursive and institutional relationships, which are defined as much by breaks and ruptures as by unified themes. Foucault's ideas are certainly transferable if we think about the archive on ADP and AOP in social work and on the question of what we should keep and what should get thrown out. Within an environment of extensive social reform intent on shrinking the welfare state, how can we find commonalities across different disciplines for research and evaluation in relation to equality and diversity? By drawing on the arts and humanities as alternative sources, the authors in this book encourage deeper questioning about what kinds of knowledge will deepen our understanding of ourselves and how we come to know other selves. This increases our potential to achieve better understanding of equality issues, however provisional. Further, one of the key benefits of social work is that it enables social workers to create connections with communities through direct contact and thus produce a larger picture of the impact of its governing and social practices to community services, and this is a theme that you will find frequently reflected upon within the chapters.

Foucault's ideas about theories of power and discourse form the first two sections of this book and we have explained them in more detail in those sections, particularly in relation to the relevance of the chapters that follow. For Foucault, our generally accepted or dominant idea of power is something that does not exist (Foucault, 1980; 1983). He suggests that the notion of power that is located or emanating from a given point is based on analysis that does not account for a number of very real social phenomena, for example, that of the organisation of people into groups. Second, a theory of power is constructed with various prior assumptions, for example, that people are equal. Starting with these assumptions is always going to require identifying a point where that started, its reality. Gerontologists, such as Powell (2000), for example, used Foucault's ideas to look at taken for granted notions such as ageing and elder abuse. Powell takes a novel way of interpreting and problematising knowledge systems about older people to generate fresh or new questions and to examine how the dynamics of power and knowledge are embedded within and (re)produced by social policy and the programmes in which social work takes an active role. Powell (2012: 6) asks 'what constitutes "old age"?' and asserts that those labelled 'old' are in the grip of power, including that operated by professional social workers through their institutions and face-to-face interactions. A Foucauldian approach, therefore, shifts attention away from a sole analysis of the state, the logic of capital or patterns of material inequality such as those associated with pensions and welfare dependency, and draws into interrogation the categories and assumptions standing at the heart of social work with older people. The mechanisms used to extend the reach of centres of power will also vary depending upon the ground on which they are required to operate. In relation to elder abuse, Powell (2012) suggests that their function is to evoke and sustain moral interpretations of particular social behaviours throughout intermittent observation, to the extent that their objects come to internalise their own surveillance. The technologies associated with elder abuse through its procedures and surveillance culture helps to stabilise policies in care at a time of considerable underlying uncertainty and serves to align assessment decisions with discourse on abuse rather than service users needs. Foucault referred consistently to the issue of surveillance, which is often presented in official policy in different social institutions including psychiatry and the prison system.

For Foucault (1997) power is, therefore, a concept fundamental to the relationship between professionals and the society in which they operate and is important in several ways. Power refers to more or less organised, hierarchical, co-ordinated clusters of relations, Foucault suggests, which tries to get at the means by which power is exercised and over what. If power is relational and does not exist except through action, it is the way in which actions modify other actions within relationships between individuals and groups that demands closer examination. Again, central to Foucault's analysis is the concept of discourse, which is the inseparable combination of knowledge and power that, along with their respective technologies, specific techniques and associated practices (e.g., assessment and care planning), operates to subjugate individuals, and which, within a regime, begins to make differentiations between groups of people, between individuals and, finally, produces components of individual subjectivity (Powell, 2012). It is not difficult, therefore, to see how Foucault can help us understand issues of equality and diversity in social work and its applicability to virtually any area we might be working in.

The Application of Foucault to Social Work

Foucault is best known for his critiques of social institutions, including psychiatry, the prison system and the social anthropology of medicine, as well as his work on the human sciences and the history of human sexuality. His writings on power, knowledge, discourse and governmentality are prominent in all academic humanity and social science subjects and also in activist circles (Powell, 2011). By defining government and control as diffuse and taking up a multiplicity of forms, his notion of 'governmentality' opened up a broad field of studies that examines the range of shaping and regulating practices. At a micro level, he used the word 'discipline' to describe the different means and diverse technologies that guide behaviour. Discipline is a type of power, a mode in which it is exercised, comprising a set of instruments, techniques, procedures, level of application, targets, virtually a 'physics or anatomy of power' (Foucault cited in Prado, 1995, p. 215). Given that social work is a political activity which has been subject to extreme forms of bureaucracy and rationalisation, which cause tensions for social workers in relation to AOP and ADP, Foucault's ideas speak directly to these tensions and the issues that can arise.

Foucault pointed out that although people can be quite clear about what they are doing at a local level, what happens in terms of the wider consequences of these local actions is not co-ordinated; 'People know what they do; they frequently know why they do what they do; but what they don't know is what they do does' (Foucault, 1982). It is these wider means and effects of ADP and AOP practice as it is embroiled with and intrinsic to relations of power that we are interested in exploring further. For example, the ambition to be inclusive through AOP may have exclusionary practices as one of its effects. People who are engaged in ADP may seem to act knowingly and have strategic purposes. In his work *The Birth of the Clinic* (1975), Foucault argued that the development of medicine did not limit itself to knowledge of illness and disease but extended its influence to everyday behaviours and defining normality. From these, emerge what he termed 'dividing practices' which constitute polarities between the self and other, good and bad; normal and pathological. Foucault has illustrated these within the history of sexuality and mental illness, where the making of specific or local systems of difference and objectivising of the 'subject' of these dividing practices result in elaborate classification systems and hierarchies of deviance. They establish multiple processes of affirmation and reward, surveillance and exclusion. Chambon et al. (1999) use the example of risk where discourses guide the judgement of professionals in assessing individuals and serves to define policy and practice priorities. Bodies and populations, for example, are made subjects and become the central focus of scientific knowledge, cultural images, political rationalities and professional expertise. The examination of subjectivities and their deconstruction provides the themes for the second two sections of this book. This structure asserts the possibility for those who are involved to see the wider consequences of a multiplicity of actions that take place locally, they may also see that there are unintended consequences which can be disturbed and reconstructed. Through a Foucauldian approach, it is possible to ask questions other than those offered by positivism or by alternative interpretive perspectives.

So, we can see that Foucault placed emphasis on texts, or language. In the context of social work, language is taken as denotative of objects; the term ADP and AOP is a real issue out there in society and when we talk about it we expect it to correspond with some equivalent reality, namely experience. Language is also connotative where we make up forms of social and human experience through our language and social practices. If, through the scholarship and practice of ADP and AOP we constitute these as something that is taken by others as real, then we are reinforcing it and seeking to make it more widely accepted as a phenomenon. As we saw earlier, critiques of current models warn against offering definitive or complicit, generalisable assertions. Poststructuralist analysis draws upon Foucault's work to allow for the production of alternative meanings, not replacements, just different meanings which may act as counter relations of power within and between policy and more dominant approaches to social work practice with equality and diversity. So, our starting point is to explore these different approaches to analysis and their possible relationship in how social work constitutes its work in ADP and AOP.

This book is not a first in comprehensively utilising the work of Foucault for analysing social work. We refer to the extensive work of Chambon and her colleagues (Chambon et al., 1999) who used Foucault as a relevant entry point for revisiting social work's mission, activities and objectives and to provide a critical re-examination of the profession's institutional arrangements and knowledge to help envision alternative practices and strategies for social change. Similarly, Howarth has written about end of life care (2000) and, as mentioned earlier, Powell has applied Foucault in critical gerontology. These are just some of the many examples that have led the way for the contributors herein.

Getting the Most Out of the Book

It is impossible to convey the nature of richness and diversity of contributions in this book here, or comment meticulously about the extensive work of Foucault. His is by no means a complete and exhausted theory, and as we will see it is enriched through development of other critical theorists and practice contributions – somewhat of a project – and we therefore invite you to become engaged in constructing a more unified theory as you read on. The specific relevance to AOP and ADP pertains to Foucault's belief that there is no fixed and definitive structuring of either social (or personal) identity or practices, as there is in a socially determined view in which the subject is completely socialised. Rather, both the formation of identities and practices are related to, or are a function of, historically specific discourses. The book aims to explore these discourses and how these are constructed in a way that encourages the student or reader to form an understanding of how these may open the way for change and contestation. We do not intend that you read the book as a body of work that can somehow be synthesised to create a singular picture that will tell the truth of what equality and diversity really is. Rather, we hope that within the structure of this book, around our four selected key Foucauldian concepts, you will be able to explore alternative narratives which actively critique and undermine dominant notions of ADP and AOP. Each part and chapter transgresses themes that may relate to different service user groups or issues and provides an opportunity for you to see how theories can manifest within different practice contexts and gives some pointers for social work practice. These are all key concepts students should be studying on qualifying and post-qualifying social work programmes and which come up in a number of areas in the social work and post-qualifying social work curriculum. We hope that you read on and enjoy!

PART I

Power

In our introduction, we explored the work of Michel Foucault and described how the framework underpinning this book mainly draws on his work. Foucault's ideas provide a particular relevant means and sound resource for reviewing and revisiting the concepts previously associated with anti-discriminatory practice (ADP) and anti-oppressive practice (AOP). As a modern critical social theorist, Foucault explicitly articulated what he termed 'disciplinary rules', which can be useful for enabling social work to question and revisit the way in which it practises in the everyday and at different levels. Foucault offers a series of poststructuralist lenses from which social work might situate a critical approach with regards to the analysis and the positioning of professional practice. Central to this positioning is the concept of power and power relations. Foucault was concerned to explore *relations* of power, in particular the changing relationship between the state and its citizens. Within Part I, each of the four chapters not only capitalises on Foucault's work but also considers the contribution of other social theorists such as George Herbert Mead and Judith Butler to analysing power in order to make sense of it within social work. The authors help us to discover different means of interrogating power relationships between ourselves as a profession; within and between the institutions of the state; and between ourselves and service users. All of these have become imbued with a growing reliance on consumerist, institutional and managerialist power, and this is where ideas developed from Foucault's authentic 'conceptual toolkit' become useful.

The authors in this Part enable us to delve further within the realms of everyday social work practice. For example, at the micro level, Dunk-West encourages us to engage with our social work self by exploring what she calls 'theories of selfhood', core to developing our social work identity. Considered alongside a Foucauldian appreciation of power, Dunk-West refers specifically to 'doing' social work in the personal domain and accessing the social-work-self through a process of deliberate reflexivity. She draws on the work of Mead to explain the significance of social interaction in social work. However, these carry risks which we need to confront when achieving a deeper understanding of how we might further use our developing awareness of complexities within social work in order to become an effective instrument of change. Dunk-West argues that it is only when we are able to truly engage with our social self that we can then think outside of the individual and more broadly about society and oneself in all of our professional, personal and everyday contexts. This essential reflexive engagement with the self, she concludes, opens up new possibilities to debate and engage in a more effective analysis of power and with the role of social work in this analysis.

The second chapter in this part finds Green and Featherstone probing much broader mechanisms or diffused processes through which power might be exercised and used to makes a difference in social work. Through the work of Judith Butler, they raise profound questions about the norms that regulate practice and attempt to move us towards what they tentatively call a more 'humble and humane project' for social work, which invites the explicit use of compassion and ethical communication. This 'project' challenges previous forms of ADP and AOP, which they suggest have become de-contextualised and are sometimes hidden behind forms of political correctness. In the study of diversity and equality, social work has inadvertently constructed hierarchies of discrimination or adopted a universalist approach which is not helpful and can even lead to ambiguity and paradox in the social work role in which power becomes completely instrumentalised. Judith Butler's themes and ideas, however, can be helpful through the way they intersect Foucault's notion of power with psychoanalytic theories to understand complex power relationships between children and adults. Further, they explain Butler's notion of performativity, where one brings an identity to life by enacting or 'doing' gender or sexuality until it becomes the norm and unquestionable. Green and Featherstone are inviting us, therefore, to find less certain but divisive and more empathic ways of engaging with difference that permit subversion and contesting of unfair or dehumanising practices or policies by social workers by refocusing their attention on these very important issues.

Further on in this section on power, Laird helps us to tackle the challenge of how the concept of power is operationalised within social work practice and steered by government through its extensive legislative, policy and procedural guidance, which are often insufficient. The nature of 'power' or 'empowerment' in social work inevitably raises fundamental questions about the very purpose of social work itself and what it aims to achieve. However, guidance is often insufficient in this endeavour and requires the use of more active professional authority. Laird's chapter explores problematic aspects of mainstream anti-oppressive theory through detailed investigation into real examples of court judgements, public inquiries and serious case reviews and the consequences of these examples. Questions have been raised about whether social workers can be truly anti-oppressive in their practice where they inevitably bring more power to their interactions with service users than vice versa (Sakamoto and Pitner, 2005), and this is nowhere clearer than in the arena of case law. Foucault used the term 'governmentality' to conceptualise those such as the social work profession's role as agents who reproduce dominant state discourses. This displacement of our normal notion of 'government' forces us to examine power in a way that emphasises its relational and discursive aspects, and to observe the complexity of the conduct of government (Foucault, 1991). Governmentality involves creating institutions that provide structure and influence to shape society and legal institutions and social work practice in those institutions resonates with these ideas as we become embroiled within it. Governmentality is explicit about the importance of little things in the operation of power and Foucault used this term to encourage us to reflect on the discourses within the layers of policy operationalisation and decisions that emerge. The analysis and commentary offered by Laird highlights the importance of ways in which microcosms of power act to marginalise some groups and exclude others. She suggests that we need to incorporate a more sophisticated analysis of the power dynamics between social workers and service users and to be confident in acting in situations where conditions of oppression are being evoked to use professional authority and persist in challenges. Her messages for practice should engage us in taking greater responsibility for knowing and interrogating the legislative environment and our professional obligations and responsibilities, alongside critical knowledge of assumptions and how these are communicated and acted upon in practice. Laird argues that thinking and learning about the way in which power, negotiation and influence occur in casework is useful. Foucault understood that power is not just negative, coercive or repressive, but is also be a necessary, productive and positive force in society (Foucault, 1991).

The final chapter in this part explicitly illustrates how a discordant relationship of social work with power is played out in direct practice with young asylum seekers. Many commentators on equality and diversity have documented a developing sense of helplessness in the face of increasing managerialism, where professional expertise has been usurped by increasing actuarial activities and a surveillance culture (Bar-On, 2002; Harris, 2003; Humphries, 2004). Despite a plethora of policy directives which seek to promote the rights, citizenship and empowerment of marginalised communities, some of the assumptions underpinning these policies have directly contributed to tensions for social workers in their everyday practice, leading to the direct abuse of power in some situations (Gilroy, 2004). In their chapter, Sinha, Burr and Sutton draw on their own research findings to illustrate the increasing importance of collaboration, training and a human rights ethos which is essential to genuinely seek to achieve improved outcomes for young asylum seekers and refugees. Bifurcated demands about how to effectively share and distribute power necessitate social workers to develop insight and a better understanding of discourses about power in order to engage with it effectively, as well as well-honed practice skills that facilitate trusting relationships combined with advocacy. Accurate assessment of need, the appropriate use of language, maintaining empathy and availability are asserted by Sinha, Burr and Sutton as essential aspects of social work practice which may become lost where social workers do not pay attention to the social interactions promoted by Dunk-West at the beginning of this part.

1

Social Work Identity, Power and Selfhood: A Re-Imagining

Priscilla Dunk-West

Introduction

Power, in social work, has been conceptualised through the application of particular narratives about selfhood. For example, the concept of anti-discriminatory social work practice relates to areas of difference in the individual (Thompson, 1993). In this area of scholarship, differences such as those brought about by gender, sexual identity, culture and race, disability, class, age and other aspects of identity are manifest in the exchange between social workers and their clients (Thompson, 1993). This chapter focuses on power, social work identity and selfhood. It is in understanding selfhood and identity as it relates to power and inequality in social work that new theoretical positions can emerge which help to critically frame and account for structural and individual oppression. As it stands, a critical and robust notion of selfhood is missing from existing social work literature (Dunk-West, 2013b). In this chapter, I propose that the Foucauldian appreciation of power, alongside the generative self offered by George Herbert Mead, have much to offer in developing a social work understanding of selfhood. In combining these theoretical traditions, we can re-imagine the social work role in relation to inequality and oppression. Despite the historical and geographical divide between Foucault and Mead, as we shall see, there are many synergies between what we might term the poststructural self and the Meadian perspective which is often aligned with symbolic interactionism. In understanding the self used in social work, this chapter commences by critically evaluating the current assumptions of self, including what is meant by the term. I then move on to examine power in the context of the interactionist depiction of self, highlighting how Foucauldian notions compliment this perspective. The chapter concludes with considering how theories of selfhood are vital to social work theory and practice which seeks to address oppression and inequality in contemporary life. The application of the generative notion of self, alongside a Foucauldian appreciation of power, is argued as central to the future of social work practice.

The Self and Social Work: A Case for Greater Engagement

If we think about the individual as distinct and separate from society then invariably we are thinking about identity. Though there are differences between the theoretical orientations from which each term is derived, the self refers to the concept of what might be thought about as 'identity', 'subjectivity' or 'the individual'. There are many different theoretical orientations associated with theorising the self, and these range from philosophy to the arts to sociology. All of these scholarly areas have been absorbed within applied disciplines such as psychology, psychiatry and social work. However, by far, the dominating idea about selfhood in social work is the notion that there is a mind that is 'inside' a person and is a complex thing to adequately understand. It is no accident that this idea persists: the historical period we are in has seen a growth in therapeutic culture (Reiff, 1966; Lasch, 1979; Furedi, 2004) and a fascination with self-improvement which gears individuals towards seeing themselves as a 'project' (Giddens, 1991, 1993). Seeing the self in this way suggests that individuals have enough agency to bring about change in themselves, however, the reality of limitations external to the self highlights the inequalities manifest in everyday life (Skeggs, 1997). Yet, what brings about such limitations and how can we describe these?

Concepts such as sexual identity, race and culture, gender, disability, age and class are ways of describing aspects of selfhood. Although these are attributable to individuals, they have particular meanings for the ways in which individuals relate and behave in social life. This is explained through thinking about the power differences between particular groups. For example, globally, women continue to have poorer employment opportunities, be at greater risk of violence and suffer a myriad of other inequalities throughout their lifespan (World Health Organisation, 2009). Similarly, particular groups – such as those from higher socio-economic backgrounds, who are white, male and educated, for example, hold powerful positions in particular societies. This means that those who fall into other categories, are less educated, come from cultural minorities and so on, are less likely to have opportunities to hold powerful positions in society. In social work it is important to remember that inequalities can be sociologically explained: this sensibility is helpful in our work with clients (Dunk-West and Verity, 2014).

The focus on addressing inequalities in social work has, to date, taken two forms. More broadly, a structural practice approach is underpinned by a radical tradition in which the social worker actively works to reduce oppression in organisational and institutional settings (Mullaly, 1997). Secondly, interpersonally, social workers have been encouraged to reflect upon and actively engage in understanding oppression for individuals, families and groups and to account for this through their practice with people and engagement with one's own self (Thompson, 1993). Notwithstanding the utility of such theoretical positions, there is room for further understanding of power inequalities in social work. Just as with research which is 'child-led', in social work we often work with such tenets, which may quickly fall down if tested: imagine a child rejecting the power of the social worker and undermining her or his role, process or intervention (Ansell, 2001, cited in Gallagher, 2008, p. 143).

The other issue stems from the concept of power itself. In traditional social work contexts, power relates to the disparity between particular groups based on identity markers or ways of describing the self. Research into everyday selfhood reveals a less than clear picture of the categories which we use to describe selves (Dunk-West, 2011). Contemporary life is characterised by rapid change: we have, in recent decades, experienced unprecedented technological change which has transformed the way we communicate, experience time (Lash, 2001), relate within globalised space (Urry, 2005), as well as relate to one another (Giddens, 1992; Bauman, 2003). A thesis of complexity has attempted to explain such shifts: this warrants further theory-building about identity and identity categories within social work. Finding new ways to understand the shifts and emerging inequalities in everyday life is crucial to addressing the changing ways in which we relate to one another in a professional context. The dogged determination with which we implement tools to understand individuals – such as through the utilisation of forms which categorise selfhood, for example, assessment formats – are out of step with the late-modern self (Dunk-West, 2011).

Since social work is interested in the 'social' aspect of identity, it is somewhat curious that there is reliance upon individualised models of selfhood rather than social models, as we shall see in this chapter. We now move on to consider in greater detail how the self has been theorised in social work and what this means in understanding power and inequality in contemporary life.

In understanding the self, we are interested in everyday life, interactions and perceptions of both ourselves and others. This 'micro' world is where the self moves and operates. In social work we have thought about ourselves in relation to what we bring to our professional role and how much of our private lives come into our work with others in a professional setting. Though there is a great deal of literature which considers this dilemma – how much of myself should I 'show' in my work with clients/should I disclose personal information to clients/is my giggling appropriate in my interactions with clients? – such deliberations relating to the self are grounded in clinical or therapeutic discourses (Reupert, 2007).

At the minimum, there is an expectation that in 'doing' the work, social workers will be required to use a part of the self which sits within a personal domain (Cournoyer, 2010). Students are encouraged to learn how to do this through their study in university and placement settings, though there is a psychoanalytic 'self' upon which this idea is modelled. Consider the following, for example:

> Engaging in activities that increase self-awareness also entails risks … Discovering aspects of oneself that were previously unknown is usually both exciting and disquieting. Students risk self-understanding that may not be as they wish to be known … [however] the benefits of becoming an instrument of change with increased self-understanding and a solid ability to consciously use oneself for the betterment of others becomes apparent. (Heydt and Sherman, 2005, p. 38)

It is clear from this excerpt that there is a self that is 'unknown' and potentially dangerous if 'discovered'. Clearly, such ideas draw from the notion that there are aspects of identity which are hidden from actors and only accessed through a deliberate, reflexive process of engagement. The impact this model of thinking about selfhood has in social work has been neglected in the literature. Firstly, it is important to note that there is implied *doubt* in this self. There is a reluctance to trust in selfhood; for the unknown terrain of the mind is powerful. Secondly, the conceptualisation of selfhood in this way has a broader impact on the profession itself. Namely, social work itself has carried somewhat of an identity crisis about what constitutes social work and whether social work ought to have professional status (Hugman, 2009). This struggle continues today. Though it is beyond the focus of this chapter to examine in greater detail social work's struggles with its own identity, it is important to note that understanding of the self occurs not only in an individual and personal context, but that it is also present in social work literature which reflects upon itself. Let us now consider the conceptual terrain upon which selfhood is placed and how this placement alters power relations and relationships.

In social work, the relationship between social worker and client ought to be realised through an alternative model of selfhood which is free from psychoanalytic assumptions (Miehls and Moffatt, 2000). Moving away from what is firmly embedded within the popular and scholarly spheres involves a somewhat radical shift (Reiff, 1966; Furedi, 2004) and the adoption of a new sensibility in which George Herbert Mead's notion of self is applied to social work (Dunk-West, 2013b). Mead's self is a departure from seeing individuals as isolated from society and, instead, selves are 'generated' through social interaction (Dasilva, 2011). Mead's ideas have been of increasing interest to the social sciences in recent decades due to a momentum powered by the social constructionist 'turn' (Burkitt, 1994).

Meadian Selfhood and Everyday Life

Mead argues that there is no such thing as a mind except for the concept which is inextricably linked to others in social life. That is, there is no mind that is internal or inside the individual, instead, the attitudes of others are reflected in self-perception:

> This is just what we imply in 'self-consciousness'. We appear as selves in our conduct in so far as we ourselves take the attitude that others take toward us, in these correlative activities ... We take the role of what may be called the 'generalized other'. And in doing this we appear as social objects, as selves. (Mead, 1925, p. 80).

For Mead, the generalised other represents society's values, rules and social mores, which help the individual to anticipate how others might view her or him. These values are learned from birth onwards, through a socialisation process in which children participate in play and games until they become so embedded that they underpin routine interaction (Mead, 1922, p. 67). The individual carries with her or him the generalised other in the form of an abstraction, this, alongside social interaction, forms a three way mirror upon which the self may understand its self:

> In the process of communication the individual is an other before he [sic] is a self. It is in addressing himself [sic] in the role of an other that his [sic] self arises in experience. (Mead, 1926, p. 199)

Although Meadian selfhood is more socially oriented than psychological or physiological depictions of identity, Mead says that one's social conduct can perplex the individual who can 'be taken by surprise by his or her instinctual impulses for better or worse' (Joas, 1998, p. 12). The sociality of self is, therefore, far from a simple process: it is characterised by idiosyncratic interaction, complexity and shared and individual meanings.

Mead's social self – a self which emerges only through social interaction – ought to be of greater interest to social work. This is because, firstly, it emphasises the foundational role of the social in selfhood and, secondly, it highlights the reliance of the individual on social interaction (Dunk-West, 2013a, b): an implicit assumption in social work. Specifically, Meadian sociality is a conceptual tool which can help social workers think outside the individual, and more broadly about society and one's self in its professional, personal and everyday context. A social focus can help social workers move away from individual pathologising and contribute to a more sophisticated grasp on client issues and experiences (Mills, 1959; Schwartz, 1974). In using Mead's socially generated self, the individual and social are examined in relation to one another, since they are interdependent. Understanding the role of society in selfhood and everyday life helps social workers flesh out how society – and its citizens – function. This bears out some attention to the consideration of individual agency and societal power.

For example, if we are socialised to obtain social competence, why do inequalities persist? Is the social more powerful than the individual? Mead's model of self formation does not explicitly examine inequality and oppression, however, it is reasonable to understand the presence of violence or social isolation as counter to the genesis of selfhood (Joas, 1998, p. 15). Here, Foucault's project of selfhood compliments Mead's.

Foucauldian Selfhood and Power

Mead's self is generated through social interaction (Mead, 1925). This is a theory which resonates with social constructionism, which followed his work some decades later (Berger and Luckmann, 1967). Foucault's self relates to its construction through social institutions and practices (Foucault, 1988a). These two traditions represent the two forces which have come together to spark a movement away from seeing the individual as removed from society:

> First, the philosophical image of the self-contained individual ... has been challenged by the focus on the social construction of self; and second, the notion of the possessive individual, so central to capitalism, has been critiqued by the idea that the self is a cultural and historical creation. (Burkitt, 1994, p. 7)

These ideas suggest, therefore, that inequality can only be understood through an analysis of broader structures, institutions and practices than at the individual level. This is because the self is created through social exchange:

> Rather than existing outside of relations of power and knowledge, the self can be conceptualized as a third dimension to power and knowledge ... This concept of

the self is not based exclusively on the notion of a personal identity but, rather, as an identity constituted through social relations (Deluze, 1990; McLaren, 1997a). The self is the relationship of the human as subject to his or herself and to others, rather than an essence of the substance of each human. According to Foucault, the self is a relationship of reflexivity which is integral to its power and freedom. (Miehls and Moffatt, 2000, p. 342)

Foucault's analysis of power occurs through the unravelling of the structures which surround the individual, including social institutions, practices and contexts, and this is achieved through a careful historical archaeology (Foucault, 1972 [1969]; Macey, 2009). For example, in Foucault's work on sexuality (Foucault, 1981a; 1986a, b) he argues that 'sexuality is an effect of the deployment of the discourses of psychiatry, sexology and the law, all governed by a will to know' (Macey, 2009, p. 188). Thus, the role that these institutions have had upon the invention and control of this thing labelled sexuality can be historically traced. The effect of power is related to the complex interactions between individuals and institutions and power is, therefore, conceptualised as multidirectional in Foucault's work. For example, the desire for 'liberation' relating to sexuality is a recurring meme which is critiqued through his analysis of the repressive hypothesis. Foucault argues that although people claim that sexuality is not discussed or is hidden, in fact, this very notion – that sexuality is repressed – is itself a product of discourse (Foucault, 1981a). As Macey notes, Foucault demonstrates that 'liberation would thus appear to mean liberation *from* sexuality and not the liberation *of* sexuality' (Macey, 2009, p. 188, author's italics).

Using his theories about governmentality and power, and the subsequent exploration of race, Foucault argues that 'the population that is regulated and controlled by biopower is divided into human groups known as "races"' (Macey, 2009, p. 189). Thus, racial categories are created through the 'biopower system' (Foucault, 2003) and these categories reinforce otherness. This perspective can serve to disrupt the inbuilt assumptions in social work's anti-discriminatory framework (Thompson, 1993) around race. Subsequent work in the area of race has articulated a 'post race' perspective in which race dichotomies are disrupted and theorised (Ali, 2003). Although theoretical positions such as post-race perspectives can appear removed from day-to-day life, there are clear applications to everyday life. Here the importance of Meadian sociality is realised through the focus on social interaction. For example, studies about 'passing' – where people are assumed to fit dominant cultural groups in social exchange – underline the centrality of the social to racial categorisation, oppression and otherness (Ahmed, 2000; Ali, 2003).

Uniting Meadian and Foucauldian Theories with Social Work

In social work theories which have explored power and difference, power has been conceptualised as dichotomous and unidirectional. Thus, we speak of the oppressor and the oppressed, those with power and those without (Foucault, 1977). Although such models can be useful in practice, they appear somewhat rudimentary and under theorised in comparison with the richness offered through Foucauldian analysis. Foucault argues that the notion of empowerment is embedded within particular socio-cultural and historical forces and social work must respond to these types of analysis (Pease, 2002).

> If we argue that power is widely diffused through networks of social relations, does it dissolve the critical theorist's claim that dominant groups possess power over subordinate groups? I do not believe it does. To acknowledge that power is diffused does not mean that people's powers are equal. Although Foucault's analysis of power undermines earlier critical analyses of society as a monolithic power structure, his theory is compatible with many critical perspectives... He is concerned with the ways in which these global manifestations of power are influenced by decentralized and localized forms of power. (Pease, 2002, p. 139)

Here Mead's placement of social interaction as central to selfhood is paramount. Foucault's concept of power moves through and is localised in social exchange. These types of interactions and locations are often the experiences and encounters social workers hear about through their clients' narratives, but they are also played out in the social work exchange itself. These ideas have been explored in social work literature in varying ways. For example, Pease suggests that social workers must 'reconstruct' their role and interactions with self and others in new ways to accommodate this new appreciation of power (Pease, 2002).

Such a nuanced understanding must draw from the theoretical work of Foucault and Mead. In adopting Mead's self-making through social inter-action, the social worker understands their interaction as generative of their own social work self (Dunk-West, 2013b) as well as the client's self. Having an understanding of Foucauldian power involves noticing what is evident within localised exchanges as well as what is missing. For exam-ple, a recent study sought to understand to what extent social work students were engaged in conversations about religious or spiritual belief in their work in practice settings (Furness and Gilligan, 2012). The researchers found that the organisational context within which students engaged with colleagues and clients influenced the degree to which religious belief was addressed in practice. This demonstrates the localised and specific ways in which power influences selfhood for both social worker and client.

Thus, work which examines the social work relationship – as a localised example of interaction in which issues of identity and power are manifest – ought to be crucial in future empirical and theoretical work in social work. Despite the complexities involved in the application of Foucauldian ideas to social work (Garrity, 2010), the benefits of turning more towards social exchange include a richer and more accountable social work which is able to respond to new and emerging forms of inequality and oppression in a critical and considered manner. This helps to draw out what is required of social work in addressing, anticipating and tackling oppression and inequality.

For Foucault, the self is always in motion, and is 'never finished' (Foucault, 1988a; Miehls and Moffatt, 2000). For Mead, the self is in an on-going genesis, fuelled by social interaction (Mead, 1913, 1925, 1934). The social work self that is critically engaged with capturing meaning at micro, everyday levels requires theoretical guidance and practical ways to engage in these cognitive and reflexive practices which occur by the self and with others. I have argued elsewhere (Dunk-West, 2013b) that Mead's version of what we might term reflexivity has relevance to social work because it locates the concept within social interaction. This model differs from the conscious engagement with the self that the role of reflexivity takes in theories of late capitalism/late modernity (Giddens, 1991).

Using Mead and Foucault in Social Work

One of the strengths of our profession is its utility in relation to theory. Yet, this is also an area of divisiveness, with social work scholarship often seen as removed from the everyday world of practice. 'How can I incorporate my understanding of governmentality in my child protection work?' asks the social work student. There is no easy answer to this question, since it relates to the ways in which social work is framed to control the practices of others (as well as ourselves/our selves). However, since so much of social work is about responding to and working towards change, the shifting geographies of practice are equipped to handle more complex ideas with which to frame our work with others. It is, therefore, crucial that social work students learn about social theory in a comprehensive and unapologetic way. Incorporating theory into practice ought to involve understanding the emerging social work self as drawing from the on-going self constituted through social interaction. As C. Wright Mills says, our intellectual work ought not be separate from our everyday practices (Mills,

1959). The following key ideas for practice are, therefore, just a few sugges-tions that are designed to prompt thinking and action about the ways in which power is exercised and conceptualised in our everyday practices. Without such intellectual work, the social work self is ill equipped to crit-ically engage with its own profession, the inequalities and oppression and the localised and institutionalised practices which limit a just and equi-table world. The generative nature of social interactions in everyday prac-tices in social work, altered because of the application of critical theory of selfhood and power, therefore change the nature of the social work self as well as social work itself.

Key Ideas for Practice

1. Reflect upon a particular client interaction. How has your idea of selfhood influ-enced your intervention? Think, in particular, about the ways in which your own theories of the self are manifest in your interactions. Do you, for example, consider that people construct their own identities or are they 'hard-wired'? If you believe there is a combination between the two, or that selfhood is socially derived, what are the theoretical ideas which underpin your approach? What are the gaps in research or scholarship?

2. When undertaking assessments, consider the ways in which particular ideas about identity are portrayed in the format within which you describe or capture one's identity. Are these categories influencing the conversations you have with clients? Do you structure your interactions according to the categories or are you allowing identity and selfhood to be more fluid and subjective?

3. How do I, through my gestures, language, organisational context and language, create my 'self' and the 'other' in my work with clients?

4. How do I make sense of inequality? How can I develop a 'sensibility' to account for this in my practice and use of theory?

The purpose of these reflexive prompts is twofold. Firstly, in beginning with the notion of the self, social workers are invited to better understand the ways in which we think about identity, difference and broader aspects of society and the power inequities which are expressed in everyday inter-action and professional exchanges. Secondly, a focus on the self – and gaining a reflexive understanding of it while also drawing from a clearly articulated theoretical framework – goes further than traditional anti-oppressive discourses in social work. Whereas anti-oppressive approaches highlight both structural and micro divisions and inequalities in power distribution, without a core concept which anchors selfhood in a theoret-ical, ethical and personal framework, social work is unable to deal with the increasing levels of complexity which contemporary society displays.

Without the reflexive engagement of the self, social workers continue to focus only upon their behaviours and thoughts. In developing a robust theoretical notion of the self – attendant with the analysis of power, inequality and oppression at interpersonal and social levels – social work becomes better accountable, a richer profession and open to new possibilities, debates and engagement in the analysis of power and the role of social work in such an analysis.

2

Judith Butler, Power and Social Work

Lorraine Green and Brid Featherstone

Introduction

This chapter explores some of the key ideas from Judith Butler's work. The aim is not to present a template for how to practise, as Butler would balk at this. She rejects totalising categories such as those embraced in social movements rooted in identity politics (for example, women in early feminist activism), seeing such movements as unable to capture/represent the experience of all within them or to respond adequately to changing situations. Were Butler writing for a social work audience, she would seek to deconstruct categories such as 'black', 'woman', 'self' and 'Other' and challenge us to question routinely accepted beliefs that may do unseen and unacknowledged harm. She is not an easily accessible writer, but she is thought-provoking.

Butler's work is a synthesis of ethics and anti-discriminatory practice, areas often considered separately in social work. She focuses on the subtle forms of *normative violence* which occur routinely but rarely register as violence or effects of power, such as not allowing particular voices to be heard because they are not considered legitimate (for example, men who are violent to women or asylum seekers). Normative violence refers to the processes whereby certain people's lives are rendered unintelligible and less valuable than others or abject, un-liveable and un-grievable for. Her early work focused on the often silenced voices of those outside hetero-normative gender typologies, including gay people, transvestites and transsexuals, but later work addresses broader political and human rights questions. Here, she illuminates how certain people's lives are depicted as less valuable or even as 'acceptable' collateral damage in the 'War Against Terror' and how this is achieved through dichotomies (for example, Western/non-Western, evil/good).

To remain in tune with her entire ethos, we need to caution against definitive understandings of what power and oppression might mean and how to counteract wrongdoing. Butler's is a tentative and interrogatory perspective. It challenges us to question and destabilise our own and others' identities and, through recognising our shared humanity and vulnerability, see the 'Other' in and through us. This is a much more precarious, dynamic and personally-involving project than one that assumes some groups have been more oppressed than others with the role of the social worker simply to understand and either treat the whole group the same in relation to equal rights or differently in accordance with assumed cultural differences or to compensate for previous oppression.

Butler focuses on the *technologies* or mechanisms through which power is exercised and makes a difference. Her writings, therefore, can support social workers to understand wider and more diffused technologies of power, not only in relation to work with clients, but in relation to themselves, the organisations they work within and the laws they are asked to implement. Her work on sex, gender and sexuality offers social workers a different lens through which to view these phenomena, themselves and clients, particularly those who reject or live uneasily with normative conceptions of gender or harm themselves or others because of failed attempts to fit into normative categories. Butler's work in recent decades also takes on profound questions about the norms that regulate who is seen as human and who it is possible to grieve for, and contributes to the debates that have emerged in social work on recognition (see Webb, 2010). While she is most famous for *Gender Trouble* (1990) and her pioneering work on sex, gender and sexuality, her emphasis on our shared vulnerability as human beings and advocacy of recognition for the unnoticed, unloved, feared and demonised is the key thread throughout her work.

Anti-Oppressive and Anti-Discriminatory Practice: A Curious Project Rooted in a Belief in Innocence and Rationality

It is problematic to offer definitive statements on the meaning of anti-oppressive and anti-discriminatory practice, although many have expressed certainty about what should be done, how and by whom. We suggest that the writings that have become most widely promoted, certainly on social work training courses (e.g., Dominelli, 2002; Thompson, 2006), bear the mark of a project that believes in its own innocence and construct social workers as disembodied carriers of a 'pure' project. This project has often been presented as one in which those who 'use' services can be located within varying categories of oppression and, therefore, fully understood. It has rested on a premise of transparency in language and thought and a highly rational and voluntaristic understanding of communication.

Although anti-oppressive practice emerged from a wider activist project in relation to class and gender in the 1970s, it came to occupy a disembodied position, neither located in any wider activism nor empirical research, with a rather abstract version of people as one dimensional ciphers and a subsequent difficulty in grasping complex relationships to power. The rejection of an older project in social work that rested on Biestekian and Kantian notions of respect and non-judgementalism was also important in encouraging tendencies towards hierarchies of who was judged worthy of being heard and respected (Featherstone and Lancaster, 1997).

We explore some of the key insights from Judith Butler's work in order to offer some thoughts for what we are tentatively calling a humble and humane project for social work. It is a project that recognises the perniciousness of power, as well as its productivity, and obliges attention to be paid to what or who is being unrecognised, unheard, ungrieved for. It refuses dichotomising notions of victim or villain and stresses the inevitability of engaging with plurality.

Trying to Pin Down Jelly? Power, Subjection and Butler

Judith Butler is a feminist, a poststructuralist philosopher and a queer theorist, but what is meant by these terms? Philosophy is concerned with questions relating to knowledge, reason, mind and language. A queer theorist refers not to someone who is necessarily gay or who writes specifically about gay and lesbian sexualities but someone who subverts the normative order around permutations of sex, gender and sexuality. Butler is a queer theorist par excellence, who seeks to destabilise and unsettle some of our most deeply held beliefs.

Queer theory is rooted in poststructuralism. Poststructuralism repudiates grand theories such as Marxism, which homogenise one category of persons and gloss over interconnected oppressions (for example, the experience of someone who is female, black, disabled *and* economically disadvantaged), historical and cultural differences, and variations within categories. Grand theories tend to locate power and oppression hierarchically. For Marxists, power resides with the ruling class, *the bourgeoisie*, who oppress the working class, *the proletariat*, the solution being for the proletariat to recognise this and overthrow their oppressors in order to create a more just, socialist society. Poststructuralism focuses on uncertainty, flux and the interrogation of truth claims and regimes of power. These operate within and across states and reside in institutions, politics and law. They are also played out at a micro level within everyday social practices and language. Butler's praxis involves questioning common-sense normalised values and deconstructing them. She is opposed to foreclosing (censoring or refusing questioning of) categories, subject positions or truth claims. Despite this, she would, somewhat contradictorily, still call herself a feminist and a lesbian and support contingent struggles in relation to specific political issues. She recognises, for example, that many women globally are disadvantaged and that masculinist epistemologies and ontologies instigate much violence (McCarry, 2007).

There has been considerable debate about power in recent decades. Is it a possession located in one place and or one group imposed hierarchically via the threat or hand of physical violence or is it everywhere and both negative and productive? Foucault, who Butler is indebted to, argues that power is infinite, immeasurable and omnipresent – pervading our every thought and move. Modes of power are channelled through technologies: *ideology* through knowledge, culture and language; *discipline* via hierarchy and surveillance; *force* through individual corporeal violence, the military and criminal sanctions; and *resources* through legal rights, time and wealth (Cooper, 1995, p. 23). Poststructuralists contest the common-sense view of power as being at its strongest when physically applied and instead see it at its weakest when brute force needs to be resorted to. Power, therefore, may, paradoxically, disadvantage and be productive in that people may gain pleasure or benefits from some aspects of the very power that negates them in other ways. One example might be women who dress in a 'provocative' way and gain pleasure from feeling sexy and men's attention and desire for them but, in so doing, they inadvertently reinforce perceptions of women primarily as sex objects.

Butler sees power as rarely top-down but as circulatory, embedded in discourse and never monolithic or irreversible. Discourses in a Foucauldian and Butlerian sense are regimes of truth. They operate through naturalised norms and practices which become sedimented in people's bodies and psychically internalised. Although power is decentred for poststructuralists and replaced with socially constructed subjectivity, the subject is never totally entrapped within discourse. They can always resist or subvert power, even though this will invariably be within the same frame of understanding, (even if it is rejected), because they have recourse to no other. Poststructuralists, therefore, reject the notion of power as a possession and view it as an amalgamation of discourses which perpetually form and re-form people who occupy different positions as subjects. In contrast to Foucault, who places great emphasis on how subjects are shaped rather than formed through institutional practices and discourses (Foucault, 1977,

1980), Butler intersects Foucault's notions of power with psychoanalytic theories to show how power/knowledge pre-exists and makes viable the formation and re-formation of the individual as a subject. Butler (1997b) illustrates this is by showing not only how a newly born baby is subjectified through its immediate gendering as 'boy' or 'girl', but how its subjectivity is borne out of subjection. A child's first attachments are, therefore, formed within unchosen and dependent power relationships involving submission and subordination. A child will 'attach to pain rather than not attach at all' (Butler, 1997b, p. 61) because attachments are the way we gain social existence and are interpolated – hailed or brought into being. No matter how gently a young infant is handled this touch 'is always to some extent unwilled, since what we might call a "will" has not been formed ... the infant is delivered over to a touch that he/she could never have chosen' (Bell, 2010, p. 136–137). Even when choice is later expressed, such as resisting being lifted out of the bath, 'forcible contact' is necessary for the infant's survival, so from the very start the power relationship between adults and infants is a complex and ambivalent one.

This section looking at Butler's theoretical allegiances and contradictions with particular regard to power may seem abstract, but it will become clearer as her ideas are explored throughout the chapter. The key messages are that power is not always measurable and tangible; it is more often than not fluid, residing everywhere and assuming many indeterminate and fluctuating forms. Power is not something we can stand back from and observe and analyse. We as active subjects inhabiting many discourses (as workers, as welfare professionals, as men or women, as British born white citizens or 'displaced' asylum seekers and so on) are both constituted within power and discourses but also continue to shape, form and re-form these discourses.

Disciplining Bodies: Making Gender Trouble

Gender Trouble was published in 1990 in the context of Butler's dissatisfaction with what she perceived as the uncritical heterosexism dominating feminist writings at the time. For much of the twentieth century, biological sex, gender and sexuality were understood as linked biological imperatives, one's biological sex creating one's gender as masculine or feminine and a corresponding heterosexuality imbued with those gendered characteristics. Between the 1970s and the early 1990s social scientists started to challenge such determinism. Sex was accepted as our designation as male or female, linked to differential sex organs and reproductive functioning. However, gender was presented as a socially and culturally constructed phenomenon that we were socialised into and which could vary considerably across societies. *Gender Trouble* was, however, to take the argument further. It argued that it was impossible to separate biological sex from gender because our understanding of sex, by necessity, emerged from our formative experiences of being gendered.

> If the immutable character of sex is contested, perhaps this construct called 'sex' is as culturally constructed as gender, perhaps it already was gender, with the consequences that the distinction between sex and gender turns out be no difference at all. (Butler, 1990, p. 7)

Gender Trouble weaves together ideas from philosophy, psychoanalysis and history to understand how certain gendered configurations become inscribed upon and naturalised in our bodies and minds. Sex, gender and sexuality are presented as being simultaneously co-constructed within a heterosexual matrix, where 'sex', gender and sexuality must all co-cohere in a particular way to be regarded as intelligible, legitimate and normal.

> [The] truth of 'sex' ... is produced precisely through the regulatory practices that generate coherent identities through the matrix of coherent gender norms. The heterosexualisation of desire requires and institutes the production of discrete and asymmetrical oppositions between 'masculine' and 'feminine', where these are understood as expressive attributes of 'male' and 'female'. The cultural matrix through which gender identity has become intelligible requires that certain kinds of 'identities' cannot exist ... those in which gender does not follow from sex and those in which the practices of desire do not follow from sex or gender. (Butler, 1990, p. 17)

But how do such coherent and seemingly natural identities and ways of being come to life? Butler's answer is *performativity*. She argues that repeated enactments of gender (speech – pitch, tone, volume and differential use of language – walking, dressing, gesticulations and all bodily movements), create that which is assumed as natural. People do not possess a gender but they 'do' gender, over and over until it becomes second nature – their *habitus* or ontological core as a person, as a bona fide man or woman. But not everyone is successful, or wants to be, and repetition may be difficult and painful. Unintelligible or only partially coherent subject positions of different constellations, therefore, exist and are inhabited where gender does not follow from sex, or sexuality does not link to sex and/or to gender: the macho heterosexual man who believes he is in the body of the wrong sex; the lipstick lesbian; the transvestite; the hermaphrodite; the gay muscle-bound leather man who looks intimidating until he adopts an accentuated camp way of walking swinging his hips whilst talking in a low, smooth honey coated tone; the butch lesbian who has a double mastectomy because she feels it makes her feel more herself; and so on. In *Gender Trouble*, Butler's subversive solution to destabilising, deprivileging and displacing the problem of binary sex and the oppressive and rigid heterosexual matrix is through parodic enactments such as 'drag', whereby the 'naturality' of hegemonic sex, gender and sexuality is exposed as farcical and as 'copy to copy' rather than 'copy to original', and the weakness in the norm is revealed.

In *Bodies That Matter* (*BTM*) (1993) Butler differentiated between performance and performativity in order to address critics of *Gender Trouble*. Butler dispelled notions of gender voluntarism through drawing on Derrida's notion of *iterability* to explain the sedimentation of gender through ritualistic and often painful repetitions. She argued such iterability could both stabilise or destabilise and undermine gender, particularly if the subject felt ill at ease with such iterations and their significance, although destabilisation and resistance inevitably carried danger. Although Butler continued to argue for a radical politics of subversive re-signification in *BTM*, she also extended her analysis out from gender to all bodies that she saw as 'violently excluded'.

However, questions about how much parodied re-enactments can actually change society persisted (e.g., Coles, 2007) and are, we suggest, still very valid. Indeed, subversive acts would have to be done publically and by many people to have any possibility of success, as intention and reception may diverge. Aldred (2004) uses the late musician, Kurt Cobain, from Nirvana, as an example of the limits of artistic parody. Cobain identified as a feminist who empathised with victimised women. He appeared on stage in a wedding dress in a wheelchair to try and prevent fans from misconstruing songs like 'Polly' and 'Rape Me', but most fans did not receive such songs as a challenge to homophobia and misogyny but the converse. Even a Rape Crisis centre, prioritising interpretation over intent, refused to accept the profits from 'Rape Me', although the lyrics clearly challenged violence against women.

In both *BTM* and *The Psychic Life of Power* (*PLP*) (1997b) Butler reworks Freud's incest taboo, arguing that a taboo on homosexuality foregrounds it, which generates melancholia – asserting that 'the "truest" lesbian melancholic is the strictly straight woman and the "truest" gay male melancholic is the strictly straight man' (1993, p. 236). This is the price Butler claims is paid for a paradoxically stable heterosexual identity which prohibits even the possibility of the slightest desire for anyone of the same sex. That foreclosure, however, lingers as a form of melancholy – a faintly flickering, unresolved, unconscious, unacknowledged state of loss. Its most visible manifestations may be extreme anger and aggression directed towards gay people, the panic and fear caused by the acceptance of gay marriages and refusal to acknowledge and mourn the lives lost through homophobic violence or 'gay plagues' such as AIDS (Allen, 2006). In *PLP*, *Antigone's Claim* and various articles (1997b, 2000, 2002) Butler further analyses kinship and lesbian and gay marriages, noting how their subversive potential is diluted by the state's acceptance of them but only if they mimic heterosexual relationships and even then there is a price to pay. Gay civil solidarity pacts in France and Germany, for example, were only given state backing if adopting children and accessing reproductive technology were proscribed, highlighting how the children of non heterosexual parents become associated with fears about pollution and cultural contamination.

Butler's *Undoing Gender* (2004b) continued the theme of kinship and gender, focusing more on transgender, intersex and gender diagnostic categories such as gender identity dysphoria (GID), and showed how transgendered and intersex people experience great violence by being forcibly re-encapsulated within the heterosexual, binary sex matrix. As Lopez's (1996) research on intransigent clients at gender identity clinics showed, these clients were constituted as 'boundary objects' and any uncertainties or ambiguities about binary gender positions were silenced by 'the medical experts', ostensibly to facilitate their social adjustment into their new gender role. Butler (2001) also analyses the tragic case of Brenda/John Reimer, who eventually committed suicide as a young adult. John was born a boy but his penis was inadvertently amputated in a botched circumcision. Butler displays sensitivity and empathy as she relates the coercion and never-ending painful surgical and other interventions John endured throughout his childhood and teenage years, simply because the experts were unprepared to let a boy with no penis exist. Similarly, adult intersexuals are becoming increasingly vocal with regard to the violence meted out to them throughout their childhood if they are fashioned to look more like one sex than the other and categorised as male or female in order to facilitate better social adjustment (and of course make society feel less uneasy). In a recent Argentinean film *XXY* (2007), Alex is an intersex teenager with male and female sexual organs who voluntarily stops taking the hormones which feminise him/her. Despite being pressurised by his/her parents to choose one sex or another and being taunted and, at one point, almost raped by a group of teenage boys, she/he defiantly says she will not hide or pretend she/he is something she is not and throws the parents' questions back at them by saying 'what if I choose not to choose?'

So what are we as social workers to make of Butler's writings around sex, gender and sexuality, and how might they contribute to less oppressive social work? Certainly when teaching Butler to social work students, even students who have an understanding and acceptance of the argument that gender is socially constructed are often confused and destabilised. For those who had not previously studied and/or barely thought about these issues, the initial response is often fear, anger and rejection. The case of Brenda/John Reimer is almost inevitably held up triumphantly by at least one student as evidence of the biological origins of gender. Following this there is normally much class-based reluctance to view this tragic scenario in ways that might lead to alternative readings and understandings. This is because such revelations require not only an understanding of what Butler is saying but essentially a 'reworking' of one's self identity which can involve a challenge to one's worldview.

However, if students are prepared to take on this challenge and emerge with a more fluid acceptance of gender alongside an awareness of the damage gender normative violence causes, then they may be more likely to practise a humane and more self- as well as other-informed form of social work.

From Gender and Language to Hate Speech and Other Vulnerable and Violated Bodies

Butler's pioneering work on sex, gender and sexuality extends in later work to other forms of violently excluded and abject bodies. In *Excitable Speech* (1997a), she shows how 'hate speech', such as 'faggot' and 'spastic', can name, subordinate and wound individuals in bodily and psychic ways, thus refusing recognition to persons. She also argues that political strategies can be employed to make subordinated or, hitherto unlistened-to, persons 'heard'.

Butler is against state censorship or regulation of speech, asserting that social context and the variable, and often dissonant, ways language is intended, received and responded to, are more important than the actual words. Criticising feminists for conflating pornographic speech with violent pornography and assuming censorship would solve the problem, Butler gives one example where 'abortion' was seen to constitute an obscene word and censored from a radio broadcast. This is an example of the need for caution about censorship, who it might benefit and how hate speech might be read or misread.

Such understandings should make social workers wary of hiding behind language games of 'political correctness' and being 'right on', or the purported necessity of using or avoiding certain terminology because it is categorically oppressive or liberating. One author had the unexpected experience of being reprimanded by a white social work colleague for asking for 'black coffee' because her colleague perceived the term to be a racist one! Butler's writings here should alert us to the importance of context and shifting projections and receptions of actions and speech in the widest possible sense. Anti-oppressive practice then becomes not just dogma or reiterating the latest acceptable terminology. It needs to focus on thinking through what one says and does and on understanding our and our service users' language and actions in the most nuanced and power-sensitive ways, where attention is always paid to both the micro and wider contexts. For example, the relatively recent use of the term 'consumer' or 'service user' to refer to social worker's 'clients' could be understood as clever, insidious use of terminology in the context of neo-liberalism (Jung, 2010). It obscures power differentials, suggests unfettered choice and draws unfair parallels between someone shopping for the best value or quality TV to buy and the mostly mandated or involuntary 'clients' social workers work with. Canvin et al.'s (2007) study of adults in deprived areas, for example, revealed their great distrust of community and health services, which might include social work services, and an associated reluctance to approach them for fear they would be negatively judged and have their children removed. These individuals did not identify as service users or consumers who had choices, their key question pivoted around whether or not they could afford to risk approaching services for 'help'. Butler, however, would argue that it is important to interrogate when and how the term might be used in very disruptive ways.

Butler (1997a), drawing on Austin's concept of speech acts, distinguishes between perlocutionary speech – that performing an actual act, such as a judge sentencing someone or a priest marrying a couple – and illocutionary speech whose effects are less predictable. She suggests that insurrectionary counter speech (insubordinate use of a derogatory or authoritarian term) should be used to defuse, subvert and challenge illocutionary speech. The attempted but contested reclamation of terms such as 'queer' by gay activists or 'nigger' by black rappers is an example of partially successful re-signification. However, sometimes there is no 'room' for apparent positive re-signification, as Anita Hill found in the famous US case which dealt with her claims of sexual harassment by Clarence Thomas (Mendoza-Denton, 1995). By recounting assertively his sexualised words and intimations in court, she was seen to be a woman standing outside the conventions of femininity and, therefore, not deserving of belief or protection. But had Anita Hill taken on the montage of passive victimised femininity, she would have been unable to articulate Thomas's offensive actions and words and would, therefore, have been equally ineffectual in gaining justice. However, it is important to note that Shulman (2011) argues that Butler needs to spend more time examining what makes insurrectionary speech more felicitous, and contests her assumption that the power of the state is always negative in relation to minorities and hate speech and illustrates how some of the greatest examples of excitable speech 'do not so much refuse the ordinary meaning of words, as transfigure them in the fire of ... "scorching irony"' (2011, p. 234).

In Butler's more recent writings she takes on broader questions of violence and identity, but her central thread remains vulnerability and recognition. In *Precarious Life: The Powers of Mourning and Violence* (PL)

(2004a) she discusses whose is a life worth living and grieving over in the context of the destruction of the World Trade Centre in New York in 2001. Documenting the atrocities and torture committed by US military in Iraq, at Guantanamo Bay and in Afghanistan as well as United States support for Israel's policies in relation to the Palestinians, Butler shows how Western consciousness glosses over or renders invisible many brutalised and lost lives whilst glorifying other lives. Butler, in *PL* and other work (2005, 2009), illustrates how discussion about and criticism of US military might and state policies is closed down through linguistic strategies and overt and covert threats. Butler, herself a Jew, has been castigated numerous times and called anti-semitic because she has publically spoken out against Israeli governmental policies and US collusion (Butler, 2003). She has charted how one can be an oppressor at one moment in time and the oppressed at another, or both simultaneously.

Such examples caution against subdividing service users into simplistic categories of deserving victims or undeserving villains, and it is not unusual, for example, to work with someone who has been racially harassed yet perpetrates sexual or homophobic violence on others. Although links between Butler's formulations of speech acts, insurrectionary speech and anti-oppressive practice may be tentative, they do draw our attention to the power of words to label both positively and negatively, to stigmatise, hide or exaggerate power differentials or to have much wider effects than one might assume. They also alert social workers to the fact that some of their speech acts are perlocutionary – they perform an act and endow a label. An approved mental health social worker or allied health professional (AMPH) who is involved in sectioning a service user, through signing those papers, causes that person to assume the unequivocal status of an involuntary mental patient and all the deprivations of liberty associated with that status. Butler's work on language, therefore, gives workers the tools to understand how language can be used in symbolic, divisive ways or to demonstrate unity or alliance and, therefore, cautions us not to accept language as a neutral or apolitical conveyor of meaning.

Butler, Recognition, Power and Social Work

Debates on recognition have emerged in recent decades with substantial contributions from a range of thinkers. The most well-known involve Fraser and Honneth (2003) and concern the extent to which conflicts about recognition of difference can be linked with conflicts about economic redistribution. Honneth argues material inequality is indicative of a much more profound disrespect and lack of recognition than mere refusal to recognise and acknowledge difference. By contrast, for Fraser, lack of recognition springs from damaging cultural representations of particular groups, such as women, whereas lack of material resources springs from power inequalities in relation to the distribution of resources (Fowler, 2009). Butler, however, takes a more deconstructive approach.

> The terms by which we are recognised as human are socially articulated and changeable. And sometimes the very terms that confer 'humanness' on some individuals are those that deprive certain other individuals of the possibility of achieving that status, producing a differential between the human and the less-than-human. (Butler, 2004a, p. 2).

Butler draws on the work of Lévinas, who asserts representations of persons are always inadequate – something always overflows, escapes our knowledge, comprehension, conceptions – the other person can never be fully known through our representation of him/her. For Lévinas the presence of the face and its demand for a response are the start of ethics itself – because we are *not* free to *not* respond, even if this response is turning away. Drawing from the work of Lévinas, Butler writes:

> I cannot disavow my relation to the Other regardless of what the Other does, regardless of what I might will. Indeed, responsibility is not a matter of cultivating a will, but of making use of an unwilled susceptibility as a resource for becoming responsive to the Other. Whatever the Other has done, the Other still makes an ethical demand upon me, has a 'face' to which I am obliged to respond – meaning that I am, as it were, precluded from revenge by virtue of a relation I never chose (Butler, 2005, p. 91).

Butler, in obliging us to embrace the stranger or the 'Other', draws attention to inclusion and exclusion in the very notion of who is considered human. Butler, therefore, opens up possibilities for rigorous painful conversations and questions. Who can be heard, whose suffering can be grieved for? Who is left out in the narratives that predominate? She obliges us to think about all those we work with, not just to pick out a legitimate 'victim'. As Frost and Hoggett point out, many people subject to abuse, humiliation and hardship subsequently turn those experiences back on themselves to further harm themselves and vulnerable others, and this 'double suffering' is often the subject of professional practice in welfare work (2008, p. 455).

Frost and Hoggett argue that some experiences exceed our capacity to digest them because we lack the resources to symbolise and accord meaning to them. These are more likely to be forced upon us rather than freely chosen, but if that experience and suffering cannot be thought through then we will have an unreflexive relation to it, which will result in it being somatised and embodied, internalised, acted out or projected. It will culminate in low self-esteem, low status, lack of social capital and lack of power to direct one's own life, which are written on the body and manifest in health inequalities and also self-destructive behaviours as well as behaviours harming those more vulnerable:

> Subjects of social suffering may not draw easily upon our compassion if they do not present themselves as innocent victims, but as aggressive, resentful or suspicious people whose hurt and loss is directed at others rather than at themselves. (Frost and Hoggett, 2008, p. 453)

Frost and Hogget, therefore, articulate the ethical challenges encountered when engaging with those who are profoundly marginalised and are harming others. This can lead to taking seductive short cuts such as those often encapsulated in contemporary child protection practice retorts such as 'I'm only here for the child' (Featherstone, White and Morris, 2014). Such short cuts can herald adverse consequences; with research evidence suggesting current practices with family members in child protection systems are riven by exclusions and lack of communication. Concrete initiatives have emerged to counter such processes such as 'family group conferences'. These facilitate listening to multiple voices and open up possibilities for dialogue in 'protected spaces' (Featherstone, 2004), but these are not mainstream resources and there is evidence that disrespect and stigma are reinforced and reproduced in everyday encounters between social workers and their clients (Pithouse, 1987; Ferguson and Hogan, 2004; McLaughlin, 2008). Butler's work offers us less certain but less divisive and more empathic ways of engaging with the suffering of the often abusive and abused clients we routinely work with. However, these new perspectives place a dual responsibility on us. They suggest that, alongside working with service users and challenging as well as supporting them, we need to work upon ourselves and our own deficits and misunderstandings and to always be open to new and ever changing challenges and understandings.

Key Ideas for Practice

1. Butler urges a more fluid acceptance of gender alongside an awareness of the damage gender normative violence causes.

2. She urges the interrogation of language to understand how it can be used in symbolic, divisive ways or to demonstrate unity or alliance and cautions us not to accept language as a neutral or apolitical conveyor of meaning.

3. Butler, in obliging us to embrace the stranger or the 'Other', draws attention to inclusion and exclusion in the very notion of who is considered human. While this has clear

implications in her earlier analyses for engaging with gender and sexuality, she extends her analysis in her later work to consider other unrecognised bodies.

4. Butler, therefore, opens up possibilities for rigorous painful conversations and questions. Who can be heard, whose suffering can be grieved for? Who is left out in the narratives that predominate? She obliges us to think about all those we work with, not just to pick out a legitimate 'victim'.

5. In so doing she furthers understandings of social work as an ethical project. Hers is a project that refuses dichotomising notions of victim or villain and stresses the inevitability of engaging with plurality.

Conclusion

Butler's work offers much to social workers looking for more humane and less oppressive ways to practise their often invisible but much maligned trade. Anti-oppressive practice has long been caught between a de-contextualised form of moral certitude and confusion about universalism versus difference. Indeed, slippery debates and definitive dictates have confused some social workers so much that in their attempts not to appear ethnocentric or racist, they have condoned violence against women and children, conflated forced and consensual arranged marriages or wrongly assumed that minority ethnic elderly people will automatically be cared for by their extended families. Others have privileged one aspect of identity matching, 'race', for example, when placing children in foster care or for adoption, with some children consequently languishing in temporary placements for long periods of time.

Butler's radical democratic constructionism, phenomenological orientation and political activism offers social workers tools with which they can critique and challenge oppressive practices, her work on gender being a prime example. Her ethics of interdependence, recognition and non-violence encourage social workers to re-focus their work with invalidated people such as asylum seekers and sex offenders. Butler's attention to the slippery, contestable and re-significatory elements of language, divergences between intentions and receptions, its ability to interpellate and also its slippages and gaps offer important opportunities to a profession that is concerned, above all, with language and talk. Butler's call to 'work' the weaknesses in the norm of hegemonic practices may be of interest to social workers who may be able to re-signify or subvert intended meanings and through this contest unfair or dehumanising practices or policies.

3

The Law, Professional Ethics and Anti-Oppressive Social Work

Siobhan E. Laird

Introduction

This chapter explores problematic aspects of mainstream anti-oppressive theory and practice in Britain. It focuses on the dilemmas and challenges for social workers as they endeavour to abide by the law and standards of professional competence in order to protect and empower members of disadvantaged minorities. Court judgements, public inquires and serious case reviews (which constitute detailed investigations into the circumstances surrounding maltreatment of adults and children) are examined to interrogate the limitations and contradictions posed for social workers by current anti-oppressive models of practice. Commencing with an outline of key statutes in force in the United Kingdom, this chapter presents a précis of each case followed by critical commentary identifying the issues raised for established anti-oppressive approaches. New departures from conventional anti-oppressive theory and practice are proposed.

Legislation and Professional Ethics

The European Convention on Human Rights, which is entrenched in British domestic law through the Human Rights Act 1998, guarantees citizens a set of universal rights. These are only enforceable against the State or emanations of the State. The eleven distinct human rights which comprise the convention are, under art. 14, to be enjoyed regardless of a person's 'sex, race, colour, language, religion, political or other opinion, national or social origin, association with a national minority, property, birth or other status'. The right to respect for private and family life and to freedom of religious belief, under articles 8 and 9 of the convention respectively, touch most closely upon social work as borne out in the cases considered below. These illustrate the potential for direct clashes between human rights, respect for diversity and some cultural or religious beliefs. In doing so, they constitute a set of tensions for anti-oppressive practice.

The Equality Act 2010 consolidated and replaced previous legislation in England, Wales and Scotland prohibiting discrimination, which was hitherto contained in a raft of individual statutes. The Equality Act 2010 concerns discrimination against anyone with a 'protected characteristic'. It creates a civil wrong if anyone who by reason of their 'age, disability, gender re-assignment, marriage or civil partnership, pregnancy or maternity, race (defined as colour, nationality, ethnic or national origins), religion or belief, sex and sexual orientation' suffers 'less favourable treatment' than another person without that characteristic. In addition to barring such direct forms of discrimination, the Act also prohibits indirect discrimination described in the accompanying statutory Code of Practice as occurring 'when a service provider applies an apparently neutral provision, criterion or practice which puts persons sharing a protected characteristic at a particular disadvantage' (Equality and Human Rights Commission, 2011, para. 5.4). In addition, the Equality Act 2010 makes it a civil wrong to harass, segregate or victimise people because of their protected characteristic or because of their association with someone with a protected characteristic. Public bodies or independent sector agencies carrying out public functions are subject to an additional duty referred to as 'the equality duty', which, according to the European and Human Rights Commission (EHRC) (2012, para. 4), requires them to:

- Eliminate unlawful discrimination, harassment and victimisation and other conduct prohibited by the Act.

- Advance equality of opportunity between people who share a protected characteristic and those who do not.

- Foster good relations between people who share a protected characteristic and those who do not.

The EHRC (2012, para. 4) emphasise that equality of opportunity includes the obligation of public bodies to: minimise disadvantage; promote participation; and meet the needs of people with a protected characteristic where these needs are different from those who do not share that characteristic. Besides the requirements of the Equality Act 2010 and the Human Rights Act 1998, social workers must also meet those set out by their regulatory bodies.

In England, the profession is regulated by the Health and Care Professions Council (HCPC), which sets mandatory standards for practice. These are detailed in *Standards of Proficiency: Social Workers in England* (Health and Care Professions Council, 2012b). They are similar in content to codes of practice for social workers elsewhere in the United Kingdom, which are regulated by comparable, but separate bodies. In essence, these standards or codes specify that qualified social workers must respect the rights, values and autonomy of service users and carers while acknowledging the impact of disadvantage and discrimination upon them and to challenge these. Taken altogether, human rights, the legal prohibition on discrimination, the equality duty, and professional standards set exacting criteria for social workers in their day-to-day engagement with people who possess protected characteristics. They can also create paradoxes for practitioners endeavouring to be anti-oppressive in their practice. This demands an intimate understanding of the realities which confront social workers when safeguarding adults and children. The following case studies, derived from public inquiries, court hearings and serious case reviews, offer insights into the challenges of being anti-oppressive in real-world practice situations.

KC, NNC v City of Westminster Social and Community Services Department [2008]

IC was born in the United Kingdom with severe learning difficulties to parents who had settled in Britain after migrating from Bangladesh. IC's parents, who were both practicing Muslims, arranged a marriage for their son, then aged 26, to a young woman living in Bangladesh, with the intention that she should emigrate to live in the United Kingdom. In a telephone call between Britain and Bangladesh in September 2006 a Muslim marriage took place involving the parents of the couple and an officiating Khazi. During the ceremony IC was heard to say 'yes' and to consent to the marriage. Under Sharia law, as IC's marriage guardian, his father had the authority to arrange his marriage as a means of protecting him and securing his future welfare. But, IC barely possessed the abilities of a three year old and lacked the mental capacity to consent to a marriage, which is a condition for a valid marriage under the Matrimonial Causes Act 1973. Moreover, under ss. 30–33 of the Sexual Offences Act 2003, it is unlawful for anyone to engage in sexual activity with a person who, due to lack of capacity, is unable to refuse to participate in that activity. In effect, IC's wife would have been committing a criminal offence if she engaged in sexual relations with her mentally incapacitated husband. When Adult Social Services, which had a long involvement with IC and his family, became aware that his parents had arranged a marriage for him, it applied to the court to have the marriage declared void in order to safeguard IC. The parents sought to argue that Adult Social Services was interfering with their right to a private family life under art. 8 and IC's right to marry and found a family under art. 12 of the European Convention on Human Rights. However, the Court of Appeal ruled that IC's marriage was void because he did not have the mental capacity to consent to it. The court also determined that a marital relationship was not in his *best interests* and was likely to cause him confusion and distress.

How might anti-oppressive theory inform an analysis of this case? It might posit that South Asian families are the victims of discriminatory practices which disadvantage them in terms of access to social care provision in a predominantly majority-white society. An assertion certainly supported by multiple studies (Ahmad et al., 2000; Bhakta et al., 2000; Mir et al., 2001; Fazil et al., 2002; Hatton et al., 2004; Hammerton, 2006). Hence, the parents' only recourse is an arranged marriage for their son in order to secure his future care. Anti-oppressive theory would also focus attention on the intellectual disability of IC and how this results in others making paternalistic decisions on his behalf. Decisions underpinned by negative stereotypes concerning disability, which ascribe global disabilities to those with a specific impairment and which construe people with disabilities as asexual. The HCPC (2012b, paras. 2.7, 5.1) requires social workers 'to respect and uphold the rights, dignity, values and autonomy of every service user and carer' while being able 'to take account of the impact of inequality, disadvantage and discrimination'. But what is an anti-oppressive stance in this situation and what constitutes 'respect' for the 'values and autonomy' of parents and son?

As this case illustrates, the law sets boundaries on the observance of religious beliefs, some of which are informed by cultural heritage. The Matrimonial Causes Act 1973, s. 12 is designed to protect individuals from non-consensual unions by requiring that a contracting man and woman both have mental capacity and give their consent to the marriage. At one level it would be difficult to argue that this is an oppressive, rather than protective, legal provision. Yet, nevertheless it reflects the Anglo-centric values of autonomy and individualism – the same values embedded in codes of professional social work practice. These values clash with spiritual and cultural influences among many families of South Asian heritage, which not only give primacy to marriage as a state desirous for everyone, but also bind together family members in relationships of interdependence and reciprocity, rather than ones of independence and autonomy (Hussain, 2005; Ashencaen et al., 2008; Laird, 2008, pp. 75–87).

Conflicting values between parents and social workers are also implicated in the interpretation of IC's *best interests*. The Mental Capacity Act 2005

Code of Practice directs informal carers and professionals to make choices on behalf of incapacitated individuals which: reflect their wishes; are the outcome of their participation; impose the least restrictions on their rights; and weigh up the benefits and dis-benefits to them. However, what constitutes the 'good life' is culture bound and determined by beliefs concerning morality, the meaning of life and valuable goals. Moreover, social workers have been known to make risk-averse *best interest* decisions, which serve professional ends concerning risk management rather than the needs, goals and desires of the incapacitated individual. Likewise, parents who manage, in often very difficult circumstances, the care of an adult child can sometimes make *best interest* decisions surreptitiously in the interests of the carer rather than the person cared for (Laird, 2010). The Mental Capacity Act 2005 does not define what constitutes a person's *best interests*, leaving it open to interpretation by the parties making the decision on behalf of the incapacitated adult.

The Convention rights to a private family life and to marriage are both qualified rights, permitting the State to interfere in the family when an individual's health is at risk and to void a marriage when this is contracted contrary to national laws. On the one hand, IC's mental health appeared to be put at risk by entering into a sexual relationship which he could not comprehend and might distress him. Equally, he might have lifelong care from a wife within the context of an extended supportive family and be granted the opportunity to experience sexual pleasure. Without marriage, IC was likely to be moved into institutional care once his parents became too exhausted to look after him. Ultimately, which one of these imagined futures is in IC's *best interests* constitutes a professional dilemma that sits outside the parameters of orthodox anti-oppressive practice and calls for a wider frame of reference: one devoted to a much more thorough consideration of culture-bound values and spiritual beliefs in tandem with a rigorous examination of the interface between cultural relativity, human rights and the professional value-base of social work.

Wakefield Metropolitan District Council *Independent Inquiry Report into the Circumstances of Child Sexual Abuse by two Foster Carers in Wakefield*

Craig Faunch and Ian Wathy, of white British descent, were in a same sex relationship and employed by Wakefield Council, in England, as short-term foster carers. Eighteen children aged between 11 and 15 years of age were placed with the couple between August 2003 and January 2005. During June

2004 a family support worker drove two children from their foster placement at the home of Craig and Ian to their mother's home for a contact
visit. During the car journey the children revealed that Craig had taken a
number of photographs of them urinating, defecating and washing in the
bathroom. The incident was reported to the children's social worker and,
although the foster carers were challenged over their behaviour, no further
action was taken against them. In October 2004, the mother of the two children reported that she had seen Craig and Ian near her home and her children's school on a number of occasions. Again, no action was taken
regarding the couple's suspicious presence in the locality. Indeed, despite a
number of social workers finding Craig and Ian un-cooperative and preoccupied by financial payments for fostering rather than the children placed
with them, practitioners consistently failed to tackle them about their objectionable behaviour. On 31 January 2005 a youth ran away from his foster
placement and informed his brother's girlfriend that Craig and Ian had sexually abused him. The police and Children's Services were alerted. The couple
were later convicted of multiple sexual offences against children in their
care.

The independent inquiry investigated why no substantive action was
taken against Craig and Ian until the police became directly involved at the
end of January 2005. In evidence to the inquiry one social worker admitted
that there was a general reluctance among practitioners to confront the
couple over their behaviour towards children in their care because 'you
didn't want to be seen discriminating against a same sex couple and to be
challenged that "you were only saying that because we are a gay couple"'
(para. 9.527). Two considerations are implicit in this social worker's account.
Firstly, she was worried about being labelled homophobic by colleagues and,
secondly, she was fearful of being accused of homophobia by the foster
carers, potentially culminating in a formal complaint of discrimination
against the practitioner. According to the independent inquiry, 'the sexual
orientation of [Craig and Ian] was a significant cause of people not "thinking the unthinkable" ... It was clear that a number of staff were afraid of
being thought homophobic' (para. 9.530). In other words, social workers, in
their anxiety to ensure that their practice was anti-oppressive, either over-
looked or excused the couple's behaviour. Yet, if this behaviour had been
exhibited by heterosexual foster carers it would have drawn the attention of
professionals and been challenged.

The HCPC (2012b, para. 5.2) enjoins social workers to 'understand the
need to adapt practice to respond appropriately to different groups and individuals'. Pervasive negative stereotypes of homosexual men link homosexuality to paedophilia in British society, as elsewhere in the world. It was this
stereotype that social workers were desperately endeavouring to avoid, but
in doing so they over-compensated and as a consequence foster children

were not protected from sexual abuse. Discrimination on the grounds of sexual orientation by local government in the provision of services or the performance of public functions is prohibited under the Equality Act 2010. Therefore, social workers employed by local government agencies, as in this case, were bound both by their professional code and by law to offer an equivalent quality of service to gay foster carers as to heterosexual fosterers. The Equality Duty requires social workers to go even further than this and to actively promote good relationships with people who are gay and lesbian alongside ensuring that they obtain equality of opportunity.

Textbooks and studies detailing discrimination against gay men and lesbians in the context of health and social care in the United Kingdom have become supplemental and occasionally core reading for social work students. Works such as Brown (1998), Fish (2006) and Fannin et al. (2008) comprehensively describe discrimination against homosexuals in British society and suggest anti-oppressive strategies to combat their disadvantage and empower lesbians and gay men. But such texts neglect to consider how individuals oppressed in relation to their sexuality might nevertheless exercise power. Anti-oppressive theory, with its emphasis upon inequalities and discrimination against subordinated social groups in society, tends to ignore the capacity of unscrupulous individuals to abuse their minority status in order to deflect criticism and scrutiny by social workers. This is where Foucault's understanding of power is helpful to social workers, as it acknowledges the complexity of power dynamics between a social worker and other professionals and service users, as well as how these play out within organisational, legal, societal and political contexts. Power is not linear, hierarchical or static. It is a constant interplay within and between micro- and macrocosms, and this interchange affects the work undertaken by social workers, particularly in terms of how social workers articulate suspicion, deal with conflict, investigate and assess. More sophisticated analysis of the power dynamics between social workers and service users and greater confidence in acting in cases where situations of oppression are being evoked to use professional authority and persist in challenges are useful skills to develop. Craig Faunch and Ian Wathy were attuned to the hesitancy of social workers to follow through on challenges concerning conduct which implicated their sexuality for fear of being labelled homophobic by others or discovering themselves to be intolerant. There is some evidence that the two men played upon the anxieties of the social workers who came into contact with them, subtly intimating that suspicions around their behaviour towards foster children emanated from homophobic sentiment.

In the light of this case study, anti-oppressive training and practice has to succeed in more than assisting students and qualified practitioners to recognise societal inequalities and identify their own prejudices. It has to instil in them confidence regarding their self-perceptions. Conventional training in

anti-oppressive practice emphasises unconscious as well as conscious prejudices. It seeks to enable students and practitioners to bring unconscious
biases into awareness and to acknowledge, explore and counteract them.
This is a crucial aspect of effective anti-oppressive training. But it needs to
be balanced by the recognition that people from oppressed groups in society can misuse their status to evoke sympathy or provoke anxiety in social
workers, inhibiting them from acting on their own professional judgement
that something is amiss. Without permitting social workers to explore the
implications of this kind of scenario for their practice, conventional anti-
oppressive models are likely to ultimately undermine professional self-confidence.

If throughout their training practitioners have been given to understand
that they harbour unconscious prejudices, it is inevitable that many of
them, when faced with the prospect of an accusation of homophobia,
quickly back-off from pursuing investigations, following through on challenges or setting boundaries on the conduct of carers or service users. In this
connection the HCPC (2012b, para. 2.9) requires social workers to 'recognise
the power dynamics in relationships with service users and carers and be
able to manage these dynamics appropriately'. But the implication of this
phrasing is that power dynamics between worker and user are not unidirectional. Individuals from disadvantaged groups can and do exercise power
within the social work relationship. Often such power is exercised covertly,
as illustrated by the behaviour of Craig Faunch and Ian Wathy. Therefore,
anti-oppressive models need to incorporate a more nuanced understanding
of the power dynamics between social worker and service user in practice
situations.

Laming (2003) *The Victoria Climbié Inquiry*

Victoria was a black African child born in 1991 in Ivory Coast and, aged
seven years, taken to live in London by her great aunt Ms Kouao. Victoria
died the following year from the physical abuse inflicted by Ms Kouao and
her partner, Mr Manning. During the course of Victoria's contact with medical and social care professionals, a number of assumptions were made about
her. Several majority-white medical practitioners who treated her in hospital assumed that a child growing up in Africa would have a rougher life and
therefore more old injuries than a child of European descent. This was
despite the fact that many of Victoria's injuries were actually to her neck,
back and buttocks, which could not be accounted for as the result of falling
or common domestic accidents. The allocated social worker for Victoria
stated in evidence to the subsequent public inquiry that during observation
of Victoria and Ms Kouao together, she noticed that Victoria was quiet in the

presence of adults. But the social worker assumed this was 'because respect and obedience are very important features of the Afro-Caribbean family script' (Laming, 2003, para. 6.300). Victoria's parents made it clear to the public inquiry that there was no expectation that she should stand to attention before them or behave in a formal manner towards adults (Laming, 2003, para. 16.4). Moreover, Nzira's research on social care within African families in the United Kingdom tackles the issue of children's discipline (2011, pp. 98–100). She describes its genesis in notions of obedience to elders, but illustrates cultural adaptation in the wake of migration and settlement in Britain, leading to a multiplicity of child-rearing practices. The inquiry concluded that 'the focus may have shifted from Victoria's fundamental needs because of misplaced assumptions about her cultural circumstances' (Laming, 2003, para. 16.6). This happened despite the fact that the social worker, her supervisor and a number of other professionals who came into contact with Victoria were themselves of black African heritage.

The HCPC (2012b, para. 5.3) requires social workers to 'be aware of the impact of their own values on practice with different groups of service users and carers'. The findings of Laming (2003) suggest that effective anti-racist practice has to build upon, but extend beyond, the paradigm of white-on-black discrimination, which remains at the core of structural accounts of racism (Dominelli, 1997). Being from a black or minority ethnic background does not inoculate practitioners against making assumptions based on cultural stereotypes about a child or adult. The Department of Health noted that black and ethnic minority social care workers 'are often subject to considerable pressure to advise and support white colleagues in dealing with black and minority ethnic users and carers without themselves seeking similar assistance in reverse' (2001, pp. 54–55). Lewis attacks this 'black staff model' predicated on essentialised notions about culture, describing how

> Black staff were thought to ensure equality of service provision, free from racist and cultural misunderstandings, because they would be like, indeed replicate, their clients regardless of divisions of class, gender, age, locality or indeed even the professional/client relation. No learning process would be required because in the social worker/client encounter like will meet like. (2000, p. 129)

At the same time, practitioners from the white majority, already anxious about working with people from black and minority ethnic (BME) communities, often over-rely on their black colleagues and withdraw from opportunities to work cross-culturally (O'Neale, 2000, p. 3; Goldstein, 2002, pp. 771–772). What this suggests is that shared experiences of racism are not sufficient to secure anti-oppressive and culturally appropriate assessment or care planning. The multiplicity of backgrounds from which white, black and Asian social workers and those they seek to assist or safeguard are now drawn, necessitates that, regardless of heritage, practitioners need to reflect upon their own racial and cultural background in conjunction with the assumptions emanating from it concerning the values, beliefs and behaviours of others. Williams (2010), in her survey of qualifying social work programmes in universities, found that the vast majority of courses lacked attention to race equality, ethnic diversity and cultural competency. Neither was proficiency in any of these areas effectively measured or assessed.

The General Social Care Council (GSCC) (2010) reported that 19 per cent of students registering for social work in 2008–2009 were from a non-white ethnic background. This accords with Eborall and Griffiths finding in their examination of the workforce that 20 per cent of registered social workers in 2007 had a non-white ethnic background (2008, pp. 47–49). It is also notable that the chronic problems of recruitment and retention of social workers in child protection teams in London, the South East and a number of other regions in England has culminated in an 'international response' by local authorities, resulting in qualified practitioners being recruited from overseas (Hill, 2007). This is partly reflected in figures from the Annual Population Survey for 2006 which show that 19 per cent of social workers, or 22,000 practitioners, were not born in the United Kingdom. However, this percentage differs between regions, ranging from a high of 48 per cent of social workers in London who were born abroad, down to just 21 per cent in the West Midlands, and virtually no social workers born abroad practising in the North East (Office of National Statistics, 2006). Of those joining the workforce from overseas, 18 per cent were from other European countries (predominantly Ireland), 19 per cent from Australia and New Zealand, while 33 per cent were from sub-Saharan African countries. The increasing diversity of the social work labour force makes it imperative that cultural diversity receives much more attention within anti-oppressive practice models.

The public inquiry into Victoria Climbié's death also revealed that Ms Kouao regularly attended church and on consulting a local pastor came to believe that Victoria's incontinence (doubtless caused by her ill-treatment) was due to her possession by an evil spirit. The pastor advised Ms Kouao that prayer would resolve Victoria's incontinence. Her incontinence did not abate and at this point Victoria was moved to sleep in the bath. Later she was tied up in a black plastic sack, and at one point Mr Manning refers to Victoria as releasing 'satan from her bag'. Later, another pastor, noticing Victoria's poor state of health, advised Ms Kouao to take her to both hospital and church. Ms Kouao did not take Victoria to hospital, but did visit another church where the pastor also articulated the view that the incontinence was attributable to possession by an evil spirit. He agreed to fast on Victoria's behalf and asked for her to be brought back to the church for special prayers. At no point does it appear that social workers enquired into the religious beliefs of Ms Kouao or Mr Manning. Yet, as documented in the United Kingdom, some children are beaten, starved, isolated or exposed to frightening rituals due to a belief by their carers that they are witches or are possessed (Stobart, 2006; National Working Group for Child Abuse Linked to Faith or Belief, 2012).

Some comprehension by practitioners of evangelical Christianity, and how Ms Kouao and Mr Manning interpreted it, could have provided greater insight into the grave situation developing within their household. It might also have led social workers to consult or involve local pastors more actively in the unfolding situation. This could have assisted to identify the sinister and idiosyncratic turn that Ms Kouao's and Mr Manning's spiritual beliefs had taken. Such actions might have contributed to a more accurate assessment of the risk of harm posed to Victoria. Ashencaen, et al. (2008), Furness and Gilligan (2010) and Holloway and Moss (2010) all cite the lack of attention to personal spirituality and faith communities in social work training and practice as a major deficit in professional knowledge and skills. Article 9 of the European Convention on Human Rights guarantees the citizens of signatory countries 'the right to freedom of thought, conscience and religion'. Dominant models of anti-oppressive approaches promote respect for religious diversity consonant with article 9 of the Convention. But religious belief, while a positive authority or influence in many people's lives, can also be a source of abusive behaviour, towards children in particular. The promotion of respect for the religious beliefs of service users and carers has to be tempered by a comprehensive exploration of the limits of that respect and the abusive behaviours which some seek to justify on the basis of their faith. Once again, these aspects of religion and belief transcend current anti-oppressive models of practice and call for new developments which engage much more intimately with ethnicity, culture and faith and their interrelated aspects.

American scholars have made considerable headway in developing working models of cultural competence. Purnell and Paulanka's (1998) model based on twelve domains; Carballeira's (1996) LIVE and LEARN model; Leininger's (2002a) sunrise model; and Campinha-Bacote's (2003) ASKED model each developed by health care professionals, together with Sue's (2001) multidimensional model of cultural competence, designed specifically for social workers, all incorporate self-examination and awareness in relation to race and culture. This intersects with a dynamic, fluid and non-essentialising understanding of culture, ethnicity and spirituality which emphasises *within* group differences. Such advocates of cultural competence are explicit in rejecting monolithic versions of culture and ethnicity which reify culture and faith, making them timeless, changeless and generalised characteristics of all members of a particular minority ethnic community.

Leininger (2002b, pp. 33–34) exemplifies this approach when she chastises professionals for seeking lists of cultural and spiritual attributes for different minority communities, a tendency she refers to as 'cookbook recipes'. Cultural competence as a new model for social work learning and practice in the United Kingdom demands self-awareness and reflection alongside a dedication to acquiring knowledge about a diversity of cultures and faiths. It also means comprehending how individuals and families translate their particular cultural and spiritual heritages into unique patterns of living. For those safeguarding adults and children understanding these unique patterns is crucial to protecting the vulnerable from harm.

Barking and Dagenham Safeguarding Children Board (2011) *Serious Case Review: Services Provided for Child T and Child R*

Satpal Kaur-Singh was born in the United Kingdom of Indian heritage and was Sikh. Her husband, who was born in India, was also Sikh. He first came to Britain in 1995 and married Satpal a year later. However, he drank heavily and the couple's relationship was characterised by domestic abuse. Ajit, their first son, was born in 1997 ten weeks premature resulting in severe learning difficulties. Both he and his younger brother were later placed on the Child Protection Register. The couple declined all offers of support and Mrs Singh refused to co-operate with Children's Services, despite the fact that both children were subject to Child Protection Plans. This became a pervasive dynamic, with social workers unable to progress assessments due to Mrs Singh's refusal to permit access to her children, bolstered by her numerous complaints against professionals. These included accusations of 'racism, lack of cultural sensitivity and unnecessary interference in family life' (Barking and Dagenham Safeguarding Children Board (hereafter BDSCB), 2011, para. 41).

Managers responded to Mrs Singh's complaint about the social worker by reallocating the family to a different social worker. The serious case review concluded that 'these complaints and comments were not valid or justified but professionals and agencies frequently failed to question or challenge Mrs Singh's views. Overall professionals attributed too much weight to the mother's ethnicity and religion in explaining her behaviour and insufficient attention to her individual psychology and personal history. They lacked confidence in dealing with a service user from a minority ethnic group' (BDSCB, 2011, para. 157). When, owing to the increasing risk of significant harm to her sons and Mrs Singh's trenchant non-cooperation with the Child Protection Plans, Children's Services informed Mrs Singh that they were applying for interim care orders to remove her children into public care, she forced Ajit to drink bleach, from which he died. In the subsequent criminal trial, evidence presented by a psychiatrist suggested that Mrs Singh had a paranoid personality disorder, making her deeply distrustful of others and impeding her ability to form relationships.

The HCPC requires social workers to 'be able to use practice to challenge and address the impact of discrimination, disadvantage and oppression' (2012b, para. 6.2). This is highly consonant with the Equality Act 2010, which not only prohibits discrimination against people with protected characteristics, but additionally obliges those carrying out public functions to 'eliminate unlawful discrimination', 'advance equality of opportunity' and 'foster good relations' in respect of those with protected characteristics. Social workers engaged in child protection are bound by the equality duty regardless of their agency. But practitioners can be so focused on being anti-racist that they fail to challenge minority ethnic carers or service-users when appropriate. Research reveals a range of responses indicative of professional anxiety around service provision and safeguarding when working with people from minority ethnic backgrounds. Burman et al. (2004) found that professionals were reluctant to challenge domestic violence in African-Caribbean and Asian minority ethnic communities for fear of offending community leaders. Justifying their position, service providers relied on notions of 'cultural privacy' and respect. However, they also admitted to reluctance to become involved 'out of a fear of being labelled as racist' (Burman et al., 2004, p. 347). This approach meant that patriarchal cultural norms were permitted to trump anti-oppressive practice in relation to gender. *Community Care* (2006, p. 29) suggests that some social workers retreat from intervention in abusive family situations where culture is implicated in order to avoid accusations of racism or disrespect towards another culture. Studies also evidence hesitancy on the part of social workers to intervene in cases of suspected child abuse where these appear to be sanctioned by cultural norms (Barn et al., 1997).

The Department of Health, which cites a series of previous inquiries revealing inhibitions among social workers to intervene to protect children for fear of being labelled racist, indicates that this is an entrenched and long-standing problem (2000, p. 40). For many social workers, the virtually exclusive emphasis during their qualifying training on avoiding being oppressive and challenging racism (defined predominantly in terms of colour and national origins) can make it difficult to discern the boundary between cultural relativism, by virtue of which the attribution of 'culture' justifies or mitigates abusive behaviour, and universal human rights, which prohibit such behaviours. Moreover, it makes practitioners vulnerable to retreating from necessary challenges and the appropriate use of authority when unscrupulous parents or carers exploit their minority status to make unfounded allegations of racism. Without greater familiarity of cultural diversity within and between ethnic communities, social workers are liable, as in the case of Mrs Singh, to over rely on culture to explain behaviour. Mrs Singh had a personality disorder which overlaid her cultural heritage. Her tirade of complaints against professionals relating to cultural insensitivity and racism should have been a matter for interrogation, not automatic credence.

Key Ideas for Practice

Each of the cases described in this chapter has been analysed using court judgements, public inquiries and serious case reviews. An anti-discriminatory lens has helped to identify some of the limitations and contradictions experienced by social workers in using current anti-oppressive models of practice. Suggestions for countering some of these limitations are as follows

1. Social workers should be fully aware of the legislative environment in which they are working, including knowing what their professional obligations and responsibilities are.

2. Assumptions should not be made about people, including what their religion, cultural practices, sexual orientation or gender may say about them or their behaviour.

3. Social workers need to move beyond being able to identify discrimination and inequality, and begin to understand their own prejudices. This is important, but is only part of what is required in practice, as social workers will be faced with people who may try to deflect scrutiny, mislead them and lie about their situations and circumstances, for whatever reason. Social workers need to be confident in responding appropriately to such cases, and this includes being persistent in assessment and investigation where challenges of discrimination or oppression potentially exist.

4. Learning about someone else's culture or experience of oppression will not stop social workers making a bad decision or taking inappropriate action with a client or service user who has had a different life experience and whose personal characteristics are different from the social worker's. Neither will the social worker having shared personal characteristics with the service user stop mistakes being made.

5. Thinking and learning about the way in which power, negotiation and influence occur in casework will be useful. Foucault understood that power is multifarious, and is used positively and negatively within society.

Conclusion

The greater protections afforded by law to disadvantaged social groups and the positive statutory duties on government employed social workers in the United Kingdom to promote good relations and eliminate discrimination against such groups tend to buttress conventional anti-oppressive approaches. However, close examination of a range of dilemmas relating to practice suggests a set of challenges beyond the scope of current anti-oppressive models of social work. Multiculturalism, together with a much more ethnically diverse workforce, has increased the complexity of professional interactions in relation to race, culture and faith. At the same time, some individuals from oppressed social groups are deploying their minority status to obstruct social work scrutiny in situations where children or vulnerable adults are at risk. Many practitioners appear reluctant to use their professional authority to pursue investigations, persist in challenges or follow through on interventions in situations where race, culture, faith or disadvantage are invoked (Laird, 2013). Contemporary models of anti-oppressive practice focus predominantly on oppressive structures in society and the potential for social workers to play into the power dynamics these create when engaging with service users or carers. But, as illustrated in the case studies above, this basis provides insufficient guidance to social workers intervening to prevent abuse. Anti-oppressive models need to incorporate a more sophisticated analysis of the power dynamics between social workers and service users. This must sit alongside training, which not only awakens practitioners to their prejudices, but also familiarises them with their apprehensions and reluctance to act in situations where issues of oppression are evoked.

4
Working with Young Separated Asylum Seekers

Shamser Sinha, Rachel Burr and Alex Sutton

Introduction

This chapter draws on our research findings with separated young people seeking asylum, and outlines the ways in which separated young people and social work practitioners might resist convention and dominant immigration rhetoric to go the 'extra mile' to support young people as new arrivals to the UK. Evidence shows that separated children and young people seeking asylum experience acute feelings of vulnerability (Hek, Hughes and Ozman, 2012), confusion and disorientation. There is great significance for their well-being in establishing a trusting relationship with at least one supporting adult (Hendry, 2012). As loco-parentis, social workers are in a powerful position to be able to provide such support, but the quality of support provided to this group of young people remains varied (Kohli, 2013). This chapter draws attention to the different rationalities that influence these practices and draws on Foucault's ideas (1988) about structural factors and ideological presuppositions to explore how social workers might avert their gaze from the technical aspects of decision making in health and welfare matters in order to contribute to genuine empowerment of separated children. Placing emphasis on building humanistic rather than task orientated relationships (Rogers, 1951), we also assert that without such a foundation, young people seeking asylum face being dehumanised in their engagement with social workers, allowing discriminatory practice to flourish. It ignores the potential capabilities of young people to support themselves and each other, which are essential to conceptually reframe anti-discriminatory practice in social work.

We draw upon two key projects. One was by the group Brighter Futures, in which young people in the asylum process nominated individual social work practitioners, with whom they perceived had engaged well, for a series of awards. Brighter Futures is a self-advocacy group of active young asylum seekers and refugees who have migrated to the UK from a variety of countries and continents; including West, Central and East Africa – from Togo to the Democratic Republic of Congo and Somalia – and countries in South Central Asia, such as Kurdistan and Afghanistan. Members of Brighter Futures become leaders through peer to peer support. They are united by a commitment to improve the quality of life for other young asylum seekers and refugees. They meet weekly at Praxis, a non-profit third sector organisation providing advice and advocacy to vulnerable migrants, which supports the Brighter Futures project. Research methods using action learning provide the framework for young people to use the group's individual experiences for their campaigns, including desk research, interviews with professionals and young people as well as focus group discussions, to research the experiences of their peers when accessing support from Social Services.

The second draws on local findings from a European Union (EU) research study 'On the Margins of the European Community', which focused on the inclusion and exclusion of young migrants in seven different EU states. The London team of the EU study assembled 30 case studies over a two-year period with young migrants from different parts of the world, including Central America, South America, Africa, Asia and Europe. Many of the young people came from countries implicated in the 'War on Terror' that have experienced or are experiencing internal violent conflict and war, and may be undergoing processes of marketisation and economic development. The findings illustrate how these economic and political forces prompted an increased drive to secure the EU and UK border, police migrants and regulate the support they receive with a commensurate anti-migrant discourse in media and politics. In common with other research (see, for example, Sinha, 2008), this has infused the provision of services to young migrants, including the support and role of social services provision to separated young people (Back and Sinha, 2010).

Key themes arising from both projects highlighted the need for a humanistic and caring relationship with a social worker (Brighter Futures London, 2011, p. 11). Recognising this need makes it particularly important for social workers to build trusting and empathetic relationships with each unaccompanied child and young person with whom they work. This chapter starts with a brief discussion of a case study from our research and then goes on to discuss issues in relation to social workers working in loco parentis with separated children. We argue that regulation of asylum seekers is not simply imposed from above in the form of direct constraint, but in supporting individuals to exercise their freedoms and choices, which has been a challenge to social workers working with immigration and where government has a more distant role. In this chapter we have used the term 'separated' rather than 'unaccompanied' when describing those under 18 years old and not cared for by parents or their usual carer, as suggested by The United Nations High Commission on Refugees (2004, p. 2). The government prefers the term 'unaccompanied', this covers asylum seekers under 18 not cared for by parents or their usual carer and looked after by social services. It also includes those separated from their usual carers or parents who are either seen by social services as part of extended families and not requiring their support as 'unaccompanied' or whose care arrangements are unknown to state authorities.

Yvette's Experience of Social Workers

Yvette, a young person involved in both research projects, talked about her first experience of social workers, which from her perspective demonstrated how very task-centred and bureaucratic their approach can be. This involved an 'age assessment' to clarify the direction that her support would take. She was accompanied by a voluntary worker. Yvette recalled that the social worker's opening words, 'are *you the young person?*', were said in an unfriendly way. There was also some dispute about the validity of her volunteer being present. Changes of social worker highlighted inconsistencies in Yvette's experience, which extended to variations within the same Social Service department, where social workers made different arrangements with different young people. This is illustrated in the quote by Yvette:

> I was living in a semi-independent house with others and we had three different social workers all of whom had three different managers. One of us had everything she wanted and all the guidance she needed because her social worker had a good manager. Even when she changed worker it was okay because it was inside the same team.

These variations included the inconsistent provision of resources such as a gym card, all of which contributed to Yvette's disengagement with the service.

Yvette also recounted a situation of a 17-year-old woman she lived with who was pregnant and amidst complications was unable to reach her social worker or key worker during the early hours when she had to go to hospital.

> 1am we started to call the key worker 'cos that's the job of the key worker, she's the key person, but she didn't get back to us. Ok we thought, maybe she's sleeping, so 6 o'clock we start to call her but she turned up at 10am and the social worker turned up at 12pm.

Yvette also recalled being told that: 'it's not the role of the social worker to cuddle you or hug you'.

> What I understand about the role of the social worker is that they are responsible for taking care of the young person. You don't have your parents here so this is especially important for us, and even young people born here who are separated from their family as well.
>
> You expect to get comfort because you really, really feel alone. They should say this is the way we are going to work with you, we're not going to be close to you. The way I understand the definition of the key worker for example is that they will be your key person, so you think this person is going to be, in a way, a substitution of your parents.

Social Workers in Role of Loco Parentis – Confused Expectations

Young asylum seekers who attend Brighter Futures, such as Yvette, experience real trauma and mental health as a result of separation from their families (Burnett and Fassil, 2002; British Medical Association, 2002; Thomas et al., 2004). Whilst the literature relating to asylum and trauma focuses on their experiences as patients, less has been written about the expectations of social workers and the institutional context of social working that affects their well-being. Yvette's observation is that separated young people often expect social workers to go beyond the role of provider, administrator and advocate to a more emotionally based caring and supporting role and to fill the emotional vacuum left by the absent family. This, of course, is complicated and raises questions about expectations and the boundaries and extent of relationships within that role. The lack of clarity and arguably unrealistic expectations highlighted by Yvette about social workers being substitute parents, we think, is both important to express and worth unpacking. However, it is an expectation that goes beyond the scope of formalised processes and professional boundaries which practitioners work to establish. Establishing relationships which mirror those of a parent and child is unsustainable and problematic for a social worker because of the number of children a social worker is responsible for and because it blurs professional and personal boundaries. This risks creeping into unregulated territories.

This case study highlights the need for a clear understanding of boundaries and the exploration of expectations that a young person may (incorrectly) hold. This will allow an honest and enabling relationship to be formed which does not risk a young person feeling let down by a social worker falling short of delivering what should be, in their eyes, parental care rather than social care. The practical and, crucially, emotional needs of these young people require consideration in how social workers and other professionals might respond. Clearly there is a gap in expectation and it is this gap which often goes unrecognised or is not properly addressed, partly because some young people find it difficult to express their needs but mainly because many social workers do not have sufficient training or support to enable them to properly understand the vulnerabilities of separated children seeking asylum. Within new immigration strategies, audit and control become key mechanisms for responding to the plurality of expertise and the inherent impossibility of deciding among the various truth claims expected by government from the social work role. Procedures and mechanisms for assessment and providing support change the role of professionals with looked after separated children, who become governed at a distance. They face the prospect of legal or organisational sanctions if they fail to follow the designated steps to ensure that all the risks are investigated and accounted for. Good communication is essential and it should also be standard practice for a social worker to clearly explain what their role is at the outset of any working relationship with a new person who is a recipient of their care. Evidence also suggests that individuals are more responsive to their social worker when clear boundaries are established, even under circumstances where the service on offer is limited (Trevithick, 2004). As the work at Brighter Futures shows, the details of what is said and then done by professionals when working with young people is hugely significant.

The emotive power of this parental expectation cannot be ignored, given how Yvette and the young people of Brighter Futures mentioned this repeatedly, and it has led to the impetus behind the Brighter Futures award for the most supportive social worker to be subsequently established. The gulf in expectations and understanding, particularly for young people who do not share the same language and have experienced the trauma, confusion and emotional stresses of leaving surviving family in unknown situations, or who have experienced the death of family members, means that this 'duty of care' is received and understood within a particular context. The differentiation of roles between social worker, key worker and foster parent may also be lost to a young person, and only compound the absence of compassion and guidance a parent or close family member might offer.

What Can We Learn From Brighter Futures?

Going the extra mile involves professionals directing their practice beyond the parameters of the centralised political State that shapes this environment. Here is one of the examples of the nomination statements given for the Brighter Futures awards that bear this out:

A social worker with Luton Social Services provided a level of individual attention beyond treating these young people merely as having an index of needs requiring a bureaucratic response. She acknowledged the young person on an emotional level and her care contrasts with the coldness and danger associated with immigration processes. In the statement a young person said:

'When I was ill she visited the hospital and worked hard to make sure that everything was in place for me. I was in hospital for 8 months and she would visit me every 2 to 3 days with an interpreter. She would make sure I had things to do, to make sure I would keep happy. When I came out of hospital after breaking my back she registered me in a specialist hospital and introduced me to skiing. Because of her I am now in the British Paralympics team.'

Such an example illustrates what separated young people can achieve if they are properly supported, and the testimonial brings into focus the way some young people can feel dehumanised by their treatment in statutory and immigration processes. The giving of time and attentive practice has been at least partly responsible in these statements for the building of a trusting relationship where the young person feels connected to their social workers.

Our findings also highlight the inherent tensions that exist for social workers. Payne categorises these into three key discourses: transformational, which focuses on social justice; therapeutic, which emphasises supporting an individual's personal growth; and social order, which largely offers support while also maintaining the status quo (Payne, 2006, p. 12). In addition, whether working within statutory or third sector services, social workers' ability to engage with particular groups is influenced by central government policy and its political, economic and social mandates. There are a number of competing discourses impinging on and penetrating different agencies who are working with separated young people. Within this, social work has inherited a diffuse mandate that leaves it in an ambiguous position. Most crucially, this is illustrated in the tensions between duties and principles laid down in the Children Act (1989, 2004) and the United Nations Convention on the Rights of the Child (1989) with changing immigration legislation. This illustrates how the exercise of power takes place in the context of a shifting set of alliances of political and non-political authorities, within which professionals are crucial to its operation. Such governmentality means that day-to-day policies and practices are not necessarily unified or integrated (Parton, 1999).

Further findings from our research uncovered presumptions described by social workers in relation to the material gains professionals believe young people wished to benefit from through their engagement – a situation exacerbated by infrequent contact. In common with other work (see Sinha and Uppal, 2009), members of Brighter Futures expressed the difficulty of arranging face-to-face time with their social worker. Whilst they lamented the large caseloads those responsible for their care had to contend with, the implication for their relationship was not lost upon them. Members reported that getting to know their social worker on a personal basis was inhibited by the amount of time spent with them, and that when appointments were finally secured they were often rushed and to the point. As such, one member stated that they would only approach their social worker when they needed something material – a computer for college or funds for an item of furniture. This in turn skewed the nature of the relationship from a human relationship to that which is task orientated and built upon material gains – neither emotionally rewarding for the professional nor the young person. As a result, social work practice may respond in a task-orientated approach rather than with therapeutic focused interventions.

These dividing practices, which inhibit the development of an intimate relationship between young person and professional, are deepened by the mismatch between the hopes held by young people seeking asylum of being able to lay down permanent roots in the UK, and the scepticism that professionals may have concerning whether those arriving in their care have legitimate claims of asylum. These issues were chronicled in various case studies on the EU Margins project. Young people with hopes of establishing a new life in safety had this aspiration undermined by challenges to the authenticity of their experiences. For some this resulted in a failed residence application, thus limiting their time in the UK and carrying with it implications on the period that the local authority had a duty of care towards them. Our experience of working alongside advocacy organisations suggests that when a negative decision is perceived as the most likely outcome of a young person's asylum claim, a social worker may be inclined to only consider short-term support plans. This contradicts statutory guidance about a young person's long-term education, career and transition support when acting in loco parentis. Social work potentially fulfils a mediating role between those who are excluded, not only between state agencies but crucially between other diverse state agencies and discourses particular those that inform and construct them. Parton (1999) reminds us that as the goal of much child welfare social work is to go beyond dividing practices, unless it works to reveal the 'essential good, the authentic and the alienated', then there is a danger that its concern with care shifts towards that of regulation with unintended poor outcomes, as illustrated in our research.

Structural Power and Work with Separated Young People

Structural influencing factors, such as the impact of global recession and austerity, and the scrutiny of the media coupled with decreasing availability of specialised training relevant to the particular circumstances of young people navigating the asylum process, all potentially inhibit an individual's ability to empathise – a critical function for any in a caring industry. Current immigration policy and austere budget cuts have contributed towards a political and economic climate hostile to migrants, which is reflected in social work practice by creating institutional frameworks that remove care and resources and thereby produce the legal ambiguity, residence insecurity and ultimately isolation which is often blamed upon self-segregating new arrivals. Rationalisation of local dedicated specialist social work teams for unaccompanied asylum seeking children have increased the work load for practitioners while diminishing the resources and specialised training they have at their disposal. These measures in such an environment carry tensions with social work professionals' mission of putting the child first. It is when times are toughest that principles of equality and diversity become most tested.

Much of Yvette's reflections and unmet expectations are traceable to weak communication, a facet made all the more challenging as established processes institutionalise language, which does little to advance a relationship based on mutuality. The process of distinguishing between those entitled to different provisions of care has led to the normalisation of language which embeds an asymmetric power dynamic – that of passive recipient of services and the all-powerful holder of resources. The term service user is discussed in detail in Chapters 6, 9 and 11, and can be used by professionals as a means of separating and making their own identity different and distinct. In the long term, they also tend to dehumanise the very people we seek to support. Young asylum seekers in care in London referred to the use of the word 'indigenous' and 'non-indigenous' within social-work practice, which were used to justify different plans for support. This resonated with other research highlighting proclamations of universal standards for young people, such as Every Child Matters, with the realities of different treatment (Pollard and Savulescu, 2004; Kelly and Stevenson, 2006; Sinha and Uppal, 2009). More widely, such discrimination is seen by some to connect with wider forms of discrimination and racism increasingly establishing a difference between those who are migrants and those who are not. For example, the 18+ team caters for those looked after young people who were in the process of leaving care. The quality and level of service provision is divided between what social workers referred to as the 'indigenous' and 'non-indigenous group'. The former were entitled to forms of income support and access to the job centre, whereas the latter 'non-indigenous' were not. In this context, the 'indigenous' included those new migrants granted permanent residence as well as UK citizens, but excluded those still seeking asylum who were categorised as 'non-indigenous'. Day-to-day use of language such as 'indigenous' and 'non-indigenous' separates young people in the asylum process from other children in care and reinforces ideas of not belonging, and, therefore, not being entitled to services, and finds expression in practices where long term plans are forsaken. It requires us to ask what underlying assumptions of citizenship and entitlement are reinforced by such language.

Social Workers and State Surveillance

Forms of state surveillance introduced by an earlier Labour administration have continued for separated young people and other young migrants. They report healthcare officials checking the immigration status of those would be patients, lecturers surveying students for signs of religious extremism or immigration fraud, and immigration officials invasively investigating the legitimacy of those who come before them (Sinha and Back, 2013). The culture of surveillance and suspicion has both laid the ground for and reflected the questioning of the validity of refugees' presence in the UK. The significance of such developments has implications for how social workers might establish a supportive relationship if a young person's first experience of children's services, as in the case of Yvette's age assessment, involves a process of establishing their credibility. This is particularly acute when such individual and institutional practice is prefaced by other immigration professionals also surveying individual asylum applicants in an invasive fashion. The construction of asylum seekers as criminal, welfare scroungers and terrorists lowers their human worth and provides a spurious justification for their coercive treatment. It is in this sense that Bauman (2004) refers to asylum seekers' cheapened lives as 'waste'. This is deeply interpolated with concepts of 'race' and 'racialisation', where biological and cultural differences are assumed to exist and are seen to be 'natural' and to explain why 'outsiders' welfare scrounge, commit crime and pose a threat, whether that is through the discourse of UK racism applied to black and minority ethnic groups in the 1970s and 1980s or to those seeking sanctuary today (Centre for Contemporary Cultural Studies, 1982; Gilroy, 2004). Gilroy (2004) argues that the construction of 'others' as different and threatening dehumanises sanctuary seekers to such an extent that they are socially positioned as lesser humans or 'infrahumans' as he terms them. This is used to justify the exceptional forms of government and bureaucracy those wanting sanctuary face. Their lower status means that humane standards, which apply to other citizens, do not apply to them because their lives are somehow worth less.

Government rhetoric of migrant and minority groups as self-segregating is far removed from the cold and inhuman reality of immigration practice and elements of social work practice that themselves segregate standards of care between those deemed to be entitled to public services and those who are not. Social workers and professionals are in a tough position because if they do not challenge this context they acquiesce with it. That is the politicised environment for contemporary social work with separated asylum seekers, whether it is conducted by social service employed social and key workers or advocates in the Third Sector hit by decreases in government funding.

Social work in this environment is not and cannot be neutral, and going the 'extra mile' or not is then a political decision with ramifications. Within social work practice, given increasing workloads and other constraints, to go the 'extra mile' in such tough circumstances really tests authentic commitments to equality and diversity. Lefebvre's (2000) work *Critique of Everyday Life* locates small individual acts as forms of resistance. Sinha (2008) has also chronicled this amongst young people and support workers who worked together across institutional boundaries to support separated young people. This ranged from youth workers to nurses and to social workers. Often, this involved them going outside their remit and institutional constraints. Amongst healthcare workers, for example, this meant refusing to withhold non-emergency treatment from undocumented migrants and/or refusing to issue a charge for emergency treatment to these people post-care. The institutional pressures on social work are clear, with social work, like education and healthcare, being drawn into the nexus of immigration control. This is either passively, through cutting back care due to austerity measures, larger caseloads and so forth, or through the active implementation of age assessments. The struggle is to make alliances both formal and informal with like-minded professionals that go the extra mile.

Moving Towards Good Practice in Equality

We suggest a number of areas in which more holistic practice will serve to enhance relationship-based practice.

Firstly, expertise in assessing the needs of young asylum seekers and refugees is critical to providing an appropriate service. Munro (2011) set out the requirements for enhanced knowledge and training in order to improve practice within children's services. Whilst this coincides with the abolition of specialist social work teams for refugee and asylum seekers there is also argument for child protection social workers to specialise in generic teams so as to provide an expert resource for other members. Strategies which promote peer learning and team work can be cost effective ways for practitioners to discuss good practice, the asylum process and country specific knowledge to facilitate increased insight into a young person's background and their reason for claiming asylum. Similarly, this curriculum is essential to professional pre- and post-qualifying education and CPD. A survey by Voice (Brighter Futures, 2011) of UK universities revealed a stark lack of dedicated teaching in the social work curriculum and lack of expertise and knowledge within its learning and teaching strategy to effectively and comprehensively address the theory and practice needs of social work in this area.

Secondly, confusion among social workers relating to immigration status of a child and their eligibility for services (Rigby, 2011) reflects why there is such inconsistent service delivery and planning. Lack of ownership and failure to take responsibility for developing knowledge on national and local legislation and guidelines often coincides with regional differences in where separated children arrive. However, current resettlement makes it likely that during their careers most social workers will knowingly or unknowingly come into contact with a child who entered the country as an unaccompanied minor.

Thirdly, as the Brighter Futures findings and Yvette's case example show, there is a dissonance between what young people feel they need and the perception and understanding of the social work role. Munro (2011) has commented on the need for active, structured and organised collaboration between social workers and other professionals who are also caring for a child, where young people are being supported in multi-agency partnerships. Social workers could be more active in instigating collaborative meetings to ensure fluent advocacy. These would include the child and other professionals, such as the key worker, a teacher (if the child is in school) and foster parents or members of the care home where they are placed, to actively advocate for services on their behalf.

Finally, in the present climate of austerity, an active and engaged social worker can be creative and work more proactively with third sector organisations who have experts working in support of asylum seekers and providing up to date information about typical experiences of asylum seeking children. With proper and respectful collaboration, partnerships such as these will create more open, engaged and realistic working relationships in which a blame culture is less likely to develop. However, some caution has been expressed in a report by ECPAT UK (2011) which points towards statutory professionals being overly reliant on third sector organisations. Likewise, Westwood (2012) found that police and social workers who were collaborating on supporting migrant children often distrusted each other's judgement.

Communication

Subject positions or identities of asylum seekers often involve the construction of binaries (Foucault, 1980). Foucault's idea of governmentality is based on the notion of people as subjects, actively involved in different processes of the exercise in power. Nowhere is this more exemplified than in the use of the term 'indigenous' as a form of institutionalised language. Relations of power can be confirmed and consolidated to ensure compliance, and so, whilst this term may be useful for social workers to distinguish between young people born in the UK and those that arrive in the care system by seeking asylum, it is important to examine the underlying discourse and why this distinction is deemed necessary. Brighter Futures, alongside numerous other organisations supporting young asylum seekers, have highlighted the predominance of the rights of the child above and beyond immigration status. Distinguishing between young people born in the UK and those seeking asylum and coupling this language with implications for services – to differentiate 'the one that has benefit and the one that does not' as Yvette puts it – can be both damaging to young people and their formation of a new identity in UK society, whilst embedding within professionals assumptions about the entitlements of young asylum seekers. While a child is considered an asylum seeker his or her circumstances are at best precarious. They are likely to feel insecure about their future and the transient nature of their circumstances has an impact upon how professionals view them. General assumptions may become embedded and pathway planning (a tool for planning a young person's future education, training and employment) may be considered redundant until permanent residence is established.

Reflecting upon how a professional engages with young people can also lead to a dynamic which is based upon mutuality rather than the binary discourse embedded in service provider and (passive) service users. In earlier chapters, we saw how gaining a reflexive understanding of the self can enhance how social workers understand the ways in which we ascribe identity, difference and broader aspects of society and the power inequities which are expressed in everyday interaction and professional exchanges. The power of Brighter Futures is the levelling of the playing field which allows young people to engage with service providers as equals, finding basis through their common humanity, rather than being based upon the job title of the state actor or upon the immigration status of the young people involved. This includes therapeutic and empathetic social work being placed at the core of the work with unaccompanied young people. Rogers (1951) referred to the need for practice to embrace 'unconditional positive regard', in other words accepting the young person where they are. Kohli found that helping young people and children understand their emotions and talk about their past experiences in order to 'deconstruct and reconstruct' their stories is an important part of the social work role (2006, p. 4).

Having Proper Training in Belief Systems and Cultural Practices

The development of culturally competent practice, according to Laird, 'demands a sustained, consistent and enduring commitment to learning about and respecting the cultural influences affecting the lives of people from different ethnic backgrounds' (2008, p. 41). Foucault (1990[1976]) referred to resistance as an aspect of relations of power, and like power it takes on local forms. Resistance is often a reverse form of power, and social workers might wish to think about how they might develop this in their everyday practice with young people seeking asylum. Given the potential ethnocentricity of social work education, which tends to be informed by a Western understanding of self-hood, a deconstructive approach to how we view the life-course of separated young people is crucial. The individually based understanding of the self is integral to psychology and child development. It is a given that a child is born at the age zero and becomes an adult when he or she is 18 years of age. Children who enter the UK are measured against these ideas about self-hood from traditional life-course theory. Yet, year zero is not universally recognised across the globe. In countries such as China, Vietnam and Laos a child is already understood to be aging from the point of conception. This means that a child is one year old when born (Burr, 2006). Different cultures approach and measure age differently. That, in turn, has an impact on the measurement of a child's age when they enter the UK, particularly because our immigration system does not recognise this cultural mismatch. A child who is 16 years of age is far less likely to enter the family-based foster care system than a child who is 15. In this sense, then, we have a significant human rights problem, because in the UK context all entitlements are age linked. As Garrett discusses in Chapter 12, concern about ethnicity and multiculturalism has become a 'screen discourse', where the whole notion of 'multiculturalism' is a good deal more complex than what is commonly acknowledged. Neither is multiculturalism simply a 'top-down government-driven policy' because, on occasions, it is also a response to grassroots demand for change, the product of local or national activism and constitutes true equality. True equality needs to go beyond celebrating cultural holidays and deconstruct how assumptions and prejudices, institutional practice and language impact upon service delivery. Within social services in England and elsewhere, the promotion of 'multiculturalism' has, at least in part, been the product of the struggles of marginalised minority groups of workers and users of services and it is important for managers to recognise that having staff from a particular country may not give insight into a young person's experience, as contexts may vary across time and regions.

Dominelli (2009) points out that those anti-oppressive values are core to social work. To be anti-oppressive, social workers need to question the status quo and their on-going practice. They should be mindful of the language that they use and also question what their professional role requires of them. In the context of this chapter's findings some social workers might wish to explore the extent to which they should be involved in assessing a person's age alongside immigration officers? Others might like to question why Yvette did not understand that she could contact the out of hour's social work team to get support when her own social worker was not at work. Evidence suggests that separated young people are not being treated as of equal worth to other young people because of the marginalisation and inequality they face. This particular observation highlights a need for systematic changes that expand well beyond the social work role. On 11 September 2012, the Joint Committee on Human Rights launched an inquiry into the human rights of unaccompanied migrant children asking if the relationship between immigration legislation and child welfare legislation is compatible with the UK's obligations under international human rights legislation.

The struggle is for diversity, equality and a multicultural future in which separated young people in London can become young Londoners, and in which all can benefit from their energy and talent. So, when we also factor in the outcomes of the type of good social work practice which is discussed in this chapter we can see that assimilation into the wider community is possible and that, contrary to government rhetoric, it is the thing that most young refugees who took part in this research desire.

Key Ideas for Practice

1. The institutional pressures on social work are clear, with social work, like education and healthcare, being drawn into the nexus of immigration control. Social workers should seek to make alliances, both formal and informal, with like-minded professionals that go the extra mile.

2. Good communication is essential, and it should also be standard practice for a social worker to clearly explain what their role is at the outset of any working relationship with a new person who is a recipient of their care. This will allow an honest and enabling relationship to be formed, which does not risk a young person feeling let down by how a social worker falls short of delivering, what might be in their eyes, parental care rather than social care.

3. The differentiation of roles between social worker, key worker and foster parent should be clear to separated young people.

4. Social workers should not allow their perception of whether it is likely a young person will be allowed to stay in the country or not to prevent them from making medium

and long term support plans, alongside the short term support plans they should continue to make.

5. The use of discriminatory language in practice should be addressed. The use of terms such as 'indigenous' and 'non-indigenous' separates young people in the asylum process from other children in care and reinforces ideas of not belonging, and, therefore, not being entitled to services, and finds expression in practices where long term plans are forsaken.

6. Training should inform social workers about the legal rights of separated young people as well as specific cultural and religious information to provide a context for social workers in their work with young people. However, assumptions should not be made about the meaning of culture and religious beliefs for young people.

Conclusion

This chapter has attempted to focus the debate about separated children and young people seeking asylum toward addressing the extreme marginalisation faced and the importance of strong relationships between social workers and those in loco parentis. Yvette's narrative provides a vehicle for recognising what it means to young people when social workers go the extra mile and avert their gaze from the technical aspects of decision-making in order to contribute to the genuine empowerment of separated children. We have shared some of our research findings which confirmed that, whilst young people appreciated the heavy caseload of social workers, their confidence in the response of a social worker to a crisis reflects an unacceptable variance. Developing relationships with young people within the current socioeconomic climate can be challenging. Yet, trust and confidence can make a significant difference to whether a young person turns to their social worker when in need or turns elsewhere and keeps vital information from their worker's attention. In practical terms this may involve taking time to develop an authentic, informal relationship outside of a crisis, as it can signal a more positive dynamic between a professional and the young person. This commitment to humanism rather than task oriented social work can change lives further down the line.

PART II

Discourse

In simplistic terms, discourse can be described as a body of statements organised in a regular and systematic way which claim to represent the 'truth' or promote dominant narratives in order to provide the rationale and justification for following subsequent rules. Parton describes discourse as 'structures of knowledge, claims and practices through which we understand, explain and decide things ... they are frameworks or grids of social organisation that make some social actions possible while precluding others' (1994, p. 13). Foucault wrote that 'there is no reality outside discourse' (1981b, p. 67). At a macro level, discourses that impact on social work, such as the common causes of social problems and their proposed solutions, primarily emanate from government policy rhetoric and its implementation. At a micro-level, an example of the effects of discourse can be seen in the way social workers manage individual situations and how they balance assessment, choice and provision within the often contradictory imperatives of the market now driving social care. These imperatives also embed unquestionable ideologies of individual and collective obligations. Critical theorists utilise discourse theory for political analysis, as the content of a phenomenon can often be best grasped by looking at its boundaries. Likewise, borders of a discourse provide a clear indication of how it connects to power and the cultural, contextual and political dimensions of that discourse. These grapplings were highlighted in Part I, where the authors critiqued social work institutions as well as the institution of social work itself. Developing our capability and capacity for discourse analysis and positioning ourselves to consider alternatives are essential skills within critical reflection and reflexivity. Engaging consciously in this process should enable us to deconstruct and challenge knowledge claims which perpetuate and institutionalise inequalities.

The authors in this part of the book seek to expose discourses in relation to disablist, euro-centric, heterosexist and neo-liberalist assumptions, and offer an analysis which might facilitate liberation and reconnection with a more authentic discourse of human rights and entitlements. One might argue that social work itself is a discursive practice, particularly if we consider the relentless debates about its purpose, methods of training and regulation. As we saw from earlier chapters on power, social work often comes from a position of uncertainty, which can threaten its sense of professional identity. Learning to accept and tolerate contingency and to assume a position of openness is essential to create spaces in which new discourses can be created. As we will see in Chapter 5, these need to be constructed in conjunction with those we are working with and who themselves may be subject to uncritical acceptance.

Social work is dependent in many ways on truth declarations, through the manner in which its subjects are 'diagnosed' or 'categorised', thus creating a need for knowledge focused on ranking, ordering and other forms of othering. In this way, truth-seeking comes to dominate the aforementioned discursive exclusionary practices. Chapter 5 offers a radical perspective on disability politics by challenging us to reconsider the way in which disabled people are commonly problematised through an ingrained network of beliefs processes and practices, which she calls 'ableism'. Campbell extends our theorisation of disability and provides a platform for reconsidering the way we think about all bodies and mentalities within the parameters of the nature/culture debate. The discourse of ableism focuses more on how the able, able-bodied and non-disabled identity is maintained, and how this presumption of ability sets the normative standard or benchmark against which everyone else is measured. Using examples from legal case studies in the UK and a fascinating study of war injured soldiers in Sri Lanka, she offers a rich excavation of the contradictory juxtaposition of discourses about disability, for example, through the masculinist and militarist lens of the war hero which serves to maintain ableness and perpetuate dividing practices. Through the study of ableism, we are invited to enrich our understanding of the production of difference, by inverting traditional approaches and fostering more critical insights into what Campbell calls 'vacuous categories' of non-disability and ability. We hope that you will find these concepts transferable to some of relational dynamics that we may have with our service users within social work assessment and interventions. They are useful for radically stimulating a rethink about marginality.

According to Foucault (1993), there are three factors characterising the boundaries of discourse. In the first place, there is the question of who and/or which agents are allowed to speak about any given situation. Within social work, these often take the form of guidance and procedures which filter and assert the hierarchy of main speakers or actors and excludes others from the discourse altogether. Secondly, there exist exclusionary mechanisms in the form of *rules, prohibitions* and *dichotomies*. And thirdly, there exist oppositions between that which is *true* and that which is *false*. Rules can be clearly expressed, but can also assume more indirect forms of discourse in relation to existing power structures. In Chapter 6, Cowden and Singh examine the discourse of service user involvement and provide the context for developing a critical understanding of the contemporary rhetoric of choice and user involvement. Using an historical lens, they chart the development of power and emancipatory movements in professional and service user relationships and review the contemporary landscape. As a mobilised and stabilised administrative category, Cowden and Singh note the slippery nature of discourse, language and paradigms around user involvement. They closely examine the substantive process of user involvement and suggest an uneasy tension for social work. Working within an ideological project of powerful consumerist neo-liberal logic, social workers can easily become disconnected from authentic voices, leading to fragmentation and reductions in service provision. Here we have a good example of a pathologising discourse, for example, in the way in which older people are perceived as reluctant to manage their own care. They conclude that service user involvement is in danger of becoming a fetish, which, whilst held up as representative of authenticity and truth in reality, has no real influence over decision making. The challenge given by these authors is to construct a new critical dialogue about the language we use in relation to user involvement and to take up the moral imperative through reconstructing a discourse of universal human rights and entitlement.

One might argue that social work has its own discourse, for example, with its clear rules and ideas on how to advance the discipline through research and the academy. Exclusion can also occur through what Foucault described as dividing practices involving oppositions and dichotomies exemplified in his example of the division made between madness and reason by Western science (Foucault, 1993). This example can be related to social work's main concern with socially excluded or marginalised populations, often the subject of social work research. Social work gains its legitimacy through the evidence gathering process whereby it claims that it is working from a normal domain, since those being researched are defined as different and worthy of further exploration. Seeking to establish 'truth' within the research process also depends on the status and authority of the person/s researching and its institutions. Research regimes identify and limit the objects, concerns and subject positions of key participants within academic practice, albeit this is slowly changing as we develop more inclusive research designs. This issue is tackled in Chapter 7. Meo-Sewabu analyses discursive practices within research from an Indigenous Fijian perspective. She questions Western paradigms associated with expert knowledge and the subjugated lay knowledge of an Indigenous population group whose 'ways of knowing' offers valuable lessons for social work and community development practices Meo-Sewabu asserts that if these are misappropriated or misunderstood, more damage and harm can be created and neo-colonisation unknowingly perpetuated within the research process. She calls for new forms of ethical practice exemplified in her description of 'Vanua' methodology. This ensures that respect; humility and traditional Fijian cultural protocols are adhered to and encompass support and affirmation for existing relationships, ceremony and knowledge acquisition through existing laws of governance. Her analysis grapples with challenging issues around reciprocity, the meaning of informed consent and the interface between the research setting and the academy.

Again, all of the authors in these chapters provide a rich source of theory for ADP and AOP and valuable pointers for social work practice to help you marry the two.

5

Ableism as Transformative Practice

Fiona Kumari Campbell

Introduction

There has been an assortment of ways to think about and designate disability and corporeal difference. We are familiar with the biomedical approach and more recent concept of the social model of disability which links the designation 'disability' to capitalist economy and social organisation. In the past decade, these approaches have been revised and developed into a relational–cultural model which sees disability and abledness in terms of an evolution; an interaction between the impairment and the environment, the person and others, the individual and their current and remembered selves (Goodley, 2013). Much of the research in Western countries has taken as its focus disability as a *problem* and has studied the disabled person in individualised modes instead of uncovering the processes of abledness that sustain the existence of disability as an operational difference (Campbell, 2011).

Thinking about Difference *Differently*

This chapter turns in another direction. Its horizon and imagination is not so much about disability but the study of abledness. Ableist practices not only shape and form discursive practices but are integral to the formation of subjectivity and associated processes of disavowal (Campbell, 2009). Today there is a close nexus, a co-dependent relation, between abledness and disability, which in the past extended to other groups. The monstrosity of the female sexed body was considered as early as Aristotle as a natural 'anomalia', meaning unevenness, anomaly; not as an aberration: a different class of ability. The tentacles of abledness (McClintock, 1995; Painter, 2010) and the marking of bodies contributed to the distinction within Western philosophy between perfected and imperfect bodies. Since the late 1300s, ability has signified a quality in a person that makes an action possible and, in turn, abledness *designates* an actionable (potentially worthy) life. Without a rugged and buoyant concept of abledness it would not be possible to maintain a view that certain bodies, intelligences and emotions are disabled or deviant. Extending the theorisation of disability, studies in ableism can enrich our understanding of the production of difference.

This chapter introduces and examines ableism as a mechanism to rethink the notion of difference, specifically commenting on how ableism entitles certain kinds of bodies to neo-liberal resources and simultaneously empties and marginalises the life trajectories of others whose differences are designated as abject. I write this chapter as a Sri Lankan Australian woman with a physical disability employed in a senior position in a university law school. I have undertaken an analysis of abledness with reference to cultural, gender and disability considerations in the form of case studies exploring (1) the trivialisation of (dis)abled difference in law and (2) cripping masculinity: injury, war and disabled soldiers in Sri Lanka to demonstrate the utility of this conceptual approach within broad ranging contexts.

Introducing the Concept of Ableism

What is meant by the concept of 'ableism'? The term is often used fluidly with limited definitional or conceptual specificity (Iwasaki and Mactavish, 2005). One perspective sees ableism as a form of prejudice that indicates a preferential treatment that devalues and differentiates disability through the valuation of able-bodiedness equated to normalcy (Ho, 2008). One early definition was developed by Rauscher and McClintock (1997) and is commonly cited in American educational literature (Kress-White, 2009; Koppelman and Goodhardt, 2011). Here ableism means:

> A pervasive system of discrimination and exclusion that oppresses people who have mental, emotional, and physical disabilities ... Deeply rooted beliefs about health, productivity, beauty and the value of human life, perpetuated by the public and private media, combine to create an environment that that is often hostile. (Rauscher and McClintock, 1997, p. 198).

More recently this kind of understanding of ableism has, at times, been known as 'ability favouritism' (Wolbring, 2012b). For some, the term 'ableism' is used interchangeably with the term 'disablism', a shorthand way of designating disability prejudice rather like 'sexism' for discrimination against women, and 'racism' to foreground racial subordination. In my book *Contours of Ableism* (Campbell, 2009), I note that disablism focuses on the negative treatment towards disabled people and social policy and argue that whilst this approach is commendable it still distorts the epistemological foundations of research and policy responses. Ableism is deeply seeded at the level of knowledge about personhood and liveability. Ableism is *not just* a matter of ignorance or negative attitudes towards disabled people; it is a trajectory of perfection, a deep way of thinking about bodies and wholeness. As such, integrating ableism into social work represents a significant challenge to practice as ableism moves beyond the more familiar territory of social inclusion and usual indices of exclusion. Bringing together ontology and episteme, ableism is difficult to pin down, it is a set of processes and practices that arise and decline through sequences of causal convergences influenced by the elements of time, space, bodily changes and circumstance. My approach to a theory of ableism builds on and adapts the work of Foucault and Latour concerning biopolitics, relational networks, governmentality and power (Foucault, 1988b; 1991; Latour, 1993). Ability and the corresponding notion of ableism are intertwined. *Compulsory ablebodiedness* is implicated in the very foundations of social theory, medicine and law; be it in terms of a jurisprudence of deliberative capacity or the foundational notion of the reasonable 'man' of law or in mappings of human anatomy. Summarised by Campbell 'ableism' refers to:

> A network of beliefs processes and practices that produces a particular kind of self and body (the corporeal standard) that is projected as the perfect, species-typical and therefore essential and fully human. Disability then is cast as a diminished state of being human. (Campbell, 2001, p. 44)

Whilst there is little consensus as to what practices constitute ableism, a critical feature of an ableist orientation is a belief that impairment or disability is *inherently* negative and at its essence is a form of harm in need of amelioration or cure. A feature of modernity is its focus on the regulation of bodies, resulting in a 'somatic society' (Turner, 1992), wherein the body has become a central site of consumption and contestation. As a referential category to differentiate the normal from the pathological, the concept of 'abledness' is predicated on some pre-existing notion about the normative nature of species *typical functioning* that is transcultural and transhistorical. This creates bodily Otherness – sometimes referred to as 'disabled', 'perverted' or 'abnormal body'.

Ableism does not just stop at producing the species typical. An ableist imaginary tells us what a healthy body means – a normal mind, the pace and tenor of thinking and the kinds of emotions and affect that are suitable to express. These characteristics then are promoted as an ideal. This imaginary relies upon the existence of an unacknowledged imagined shared community of able-bodied/minded people held together by a common ableist world view that asserts the preferability and compulsoriness of the norms of ableism. Such ableist perspectives erase differences in the ways we as humans express our emotions, use our thinking and bodies in different cultures and in different situations. Certain theories that have influenced social work practice, such as 'social role valorisation theory' and its predecessor 'normalisation', are at their essence about the minimisation of so-called deviancies and passing, which in turn shapes disability identity for disabled as well as abled-bodied people (Brune and Wilson, 2013). There is pressure in modern societies, particularly in developing economies, for all of us to be productive and contributing. Ableist belief values certain things as useful and particular *kinds* of contributions. Disabled people are often seen as a burden and a drain on the system. Hence 'disability' refers to people who do not make the grade, are unfit in some way – and, therefore, are not properly human.

The notion of ableism is not just useful for thinking about disability but also other forms of difference. Theory, far from being abstract, can help each of us make sense of our lived experiences and provide the tools for considering what is 'going on', to help us ask the critical and vital questions of contemporary life. Compulsory abledness, and its association with sameness as the basis to equality claims, result in the nullification of non-normative lives as valid ways of being human. Difference can result in an association with heightened devaluation. What remain unspeakable are imaginations of impairment as an animating, affirmative modality of subjectivity. To speak about disability in this different, unfamiliar way constitutes a *disability offence* as disability *in and of itself* is offensive. Two elements encompass ableism: the notion of the *normative* (and normal individual) and the *enforcement* of a *divide* between perfect humanity (how humans are supposedly meant to be) and the aberrant, the unthinkable, and therefore the not really-human. The effects of ableism result in a) the distancing of disabled people (and other minorities) from each other and b) the emulation of a symbolic norm (Overboe, 2007; Campbell, 2009; Loja et al., 2013). Interrogating equality practice in social work and how, despite our good intentions, *ableist effects* are produced is vital. Practitioners are challenged to negotiate integration imperatives (especially for people who have been socially 'excluded'), the *terms* of engagement as well as opportunities to develop mentoring relationships with others living marginal lives.

Themes of Research into Ableism

The term 'ableism' appeared in the literature before 2001 (Ayim, 1997; Chouinard, 1997; Clear, 1999) and the Oxford English Dictionary suggests that ableism originated in the USA in 1981. With the exception of the work of Chouinard, Carlson (2001) (who focuses on feeblemindedness and women) and Campbell (2001), this represented a turning point in bringing attention to this new site of subordination, not just in terms of disablement but also ableism's application to other devalued groups. This theoretical approach has close linkages to Foucault's formulation of governmentality and biopolitics (Foucault, 1988a; Mbembe, 2008). The instance of ableism which was written about extensively in 2011 and 2012 as an explanatory framework has been applied to: interrogations of counselling strategies (Smith et al., 2008; Morgan, 2012); curriculum exclusion (Hehir, 2002; Eisenhauer, 2007; Storey, 2007; Kress-White, 2009; Gent, 2011; Koppelman and Goodhardt, 2011; Ellman, 2012; La Com, 2012); intersections of whiteness and racism (Campbell, 2008a, b; Stubblefield, 2009; El-Lahib and Wehbi, 2011; Grant and Zwier, 2011; Schalk, 2011; St Guillaume, 2011; Kumar et al., 2012; La Com, 2012); political theory (Kafer, 2003; Campbell, 2008a, b; 2009; 2011; Kress-White, 2009; Stubblefield, 2009; Auterman, 2011; Wolbring, 2012a); gender (Kafer, 2003; Paludi, 2011; Schalk, 2011; Stevens, 2011; Chen, 2012); violence (Stevens, 2011); ableism and queer (Sandahl, 2003; Thompson, 2004; McRuer, 2006; Chen, 2012; Campbell, 2013); nanotechnologies and transhumanism (Wolbring, 2007; O'Connell, 2011); the area of sport (Wickman, 2007; Wolbring, 2007); law and jurisprudence (Campbell, 2001; 2005; 2012; 2013; 2014; Baker and Campbell, 2006; Harpur, 2009; 2012; O'Connell, 2011; El-Lahib and Wehbi, 2011; Wolbring, 2012a); and children, youth and parenting (Neely-Barnes et al., 2010; Runswick-Cole, 2011; Slater, 2012; Hodge and Runswick-Cole, 2013).

Studies in Ableism as Anti-Discrimination Practice

Studies in ableism (SiA) inverts traditional approaches by shifting the gaze and concentration to what the study of disability tells us about the production, operation and maintenance of ableism and the processes and effects of notions of normalcy and anomaly (disability). SiA offers more than a contribution to rethinking disability. These studies provide a platform for reconsidering the way we think about *all* bodies and mentalities within the parameters of nature/culture. Instead of looking solely at disability, SiA focuses more on how the able, able-bodied, non-disabled identity is maintained. *Disability does not even need to be in the picture.* SiA's interest in abledness means that the theoretical foundations are readily applicable to the study of difference and the *dividing practices* of race, gender, location and sexual orientation. Abledness, on the presumption of ability has as its normative standard the benchmark or reasonable man, where the equal standards of ordinariness and normalcy are applied. Pointing to difference can be quite dangerous on a number of grounds. Differences can be reduced to the *lowest common denominator*, with attributable and immutable characteristics that can become signs of deviancy or delight.

It would be easy to construe SiA as merely the study of non-disabled identity, given its shift in focus on non-disability (Carlson, 2001; Loja et al., 2013). However, to stop analysis at 'non-disability' would be to miss the *critical insights* of ableist relations, namely that the concept of ableism examines the production of binary mutually constitutive categories of disability and abledness (Hughes, 2008; Campbell, 2009; Runswick-Cole, 2011; Williams and Mavin, 2012). SiA is about contestations over *abledness* and not the rather vacuous categories of non-disability or ability. In exploring the nuances of abledness we need to continually ask: What does the non disabled, the *par excellent* unencumbered body 'stand for'? What kinds of sentiency are privileged and what other kinds are demoted? What effect do these understandings have on social work interventions, especially the interpretation of notions of 'risk' and 'vulnerability'? Is vulnerability exceptional or normative to the human condition? Indeed, does the state of 'non-disability' exist and if so what exactly does it denote? Non-disabled identity is not the same as abledness.

Reframing our study from disability to ableism prompts different preoccupations. SiA examines the ways that concepts of well-beingness and deficiency circulate throughout society and impact upon economic, social, legal and ethical choices. Abledness is generative of new fields of corporeal optimism; hence, where there are new forms of idealised beingness, this in turn produces instabilities and extensions in abnormalcy. More particularly, SiA foregrounds the limits of tolerance and hence the creation of objectionable lives that reside outside the bounds of society.

A call to 'sameness' appears to be easier, as these requests galvanise and re-articulate the normative, even if such a norm is somewhat vacuous and elusive. It is fruitful to look at how abledness and ability is produced and foreclosed. Are certain abilities privileged? Elusive, leaky, provisional, today's 'normals' may end up being tomorrow's abnormals! The impermanence of the body (in its changing and declining) is ramped up by the various enhancement projects promoting cosmetic surgery and now cosmetic neurology, as pathways to increased freedom and valuation. I now continue my discussion of abledness with reference to cultural, gender and disability considerations through case studies.

The Trivialisation of (Dis)abled Difference: The Whining Minority!

Employers, corporations, town planners and environmentalists already engage in the unacknowledged process of accommodating the needs of their employees, citizens and visitors (without disability). Governments and other entities spend money and energy accommodating users 'without denominating it as such' and this is the hidden aspect of hidden ableist relations (Burgdorf, 1997, p. 529). However, these accommodations are based on a narrow construction of abled characteristics and the benchmark needs of employees, customers and citizenry. In response to the perception that employers, governments and the economy are financially disadvantaged by a perceived financial burden inherent in reasonable adjustment measures for the Other (often majority-aged persons, migrants, women and disabled people), we can argue that the Othered multitude simply seek the *same* type of accommodation reserved to other 'abled' citizenry.

Inhospitable environments produce instances of exile and strangeness to one's self through reflection on being physically and psychologically 'locked out'. Social exclusion by way of geographical 'lock-outs' has a rippling effect with hostile and humiliating inaccessible environments communally impacted in that citizens, strangers and friends observe someone else's humiliation and exclusion (Klein, 1999). The subaltern in their exclusion are typically corralled into 'special' spaces (economic zones, homelands, special parking and red light districts), so called *anomalous zones* that, although permissible, are tightly regulated and policed (Razak, 1998). In William Ryan's provocative book, *Blaming the Victim* (1971), the formulation of many 'social problem' populations was based on the process of deflecting attention from any complicity that privileged populations had in maintaining asymmetrical power relations that produced poverty, suffering and injustice. This 'blame game' is postulated in the language of 'ungrateful groups, whingers, selfish and hedonistic populations', who are troubled by a 'behavioural poverty'. Ableism as a mentality and practice is *inherently* narcissist. As a practice, ableism demands an unbridled form of individualism, which is pre-occupied with self-improvement and corporeal enhancement, and struggles with the reality of illness, disability and misfortune.

In law, such narcissism plays out as the disabled litigant who is portrayed as opportunist, faker or malingerer. In the 1986 US case of *Forrisi* v. *Bowen* (794 F.2d 931–934, 4th circular) statutory protections were described as being manipulated by 'chameleonic litigants' who debase laws that are designed to protect those 'truly handicapped'. In the 1995 *Vande Zande* v. *State of Wisconsin Department of Administration* (F.3d 538, 542, 7th circular) Posner J. argued that courts had 'bent over backwards' in insuring *reasonable* accommodations, akin to *favours*, towards disabled people. This case involved Vande Zande seeking modification of the office kitchen sink by lowering it by 2 inches at the cost of USD$150 so that she might reach it in a wheelchair. In denying the request the plaintiff was told she could use the bathroom, yet, as Ms Vande Zande argued:

> Forcing her to use the bathroom sink for activities (such as washing out her coffee cup) for which other employees could use the kitchen sink stigmatized her as different and inferior. (Vande Zande [16–18] at 546)

The Seventh Circuit Court of Appeals spent an inordinate amount of time railing against spending enormous sums of money that 'would merely bring about "trivial improvements" in the life of a disabled employee' (Vande Zande, [3,4] at 542–543). Hence, when an employer was released from a duty it led to the conclusion that industrial rights via workplace disability accommodations are truncated as *special* rights (Oakes, 2005). This *de minimis* view exposes the ableist reasoning of the court judgment that discounts the *onto-effects of inaccessibility* as an instance of debasement; furthermore, the judgment is riddled with Posner's continued rhetoric of the 'complaining' (female) plaintiff, describing Zande's claim that a failed duty 'to achieve identical conditions "stigmatizing" [as] merely an epithet' (Vande Zande, [16–18], at 546). This dimension of disability narcissism is heightened by Zande's female sexed body, a body that is supposedly prone to 'rash' judgements (Nosek et al., 2003) and, together with the case of *Price* (discussed below), points to the intersection of ableism and gender.

In *Price* v. *United Kingdom* (2001), a case brought under Article 3 of the European Convention on Human Rights (Price 34, EHRR, 1285 para. 30), Adele Price was subjected to inhuman and degrading treatment which left her with physical and psychological scars. The case notes of the agency nurse brought in to assist Price in jail read: 'There is a need for us to separate Adele's little whims from her genuine problems' (para. 16). The European Court of Human Rights (ECtHR) found that Price's Article 3 rights had been violated despite the absence of 'any positive evidence of an intention to humiliate or debase'. Due to an inaccessible environment, which induced impairment effects, the ECtHR concluded that the conditions of the detainment constituted degrading treatment as the actions of the authorities were an attack on Price's bodily integrity. The judgment based its decision on the exclusionary effects of an inaccessible and hence hostile environment.

> the court considers that to detain a severely disabled person in conditions where she is dangerously cold, risks developing sores because her bed is too hard or unreachable, and is unable to go to the toilet or keep clean without the greatest of difficulty, constitutes degrading treatment contrary to Article 3. (para. 30).

The manifestation of intentionality within the context of unrealised and normalised relations is complex and needs further scrutiny. Microaggression toward disabled people is a daily unconscious affair as its presence in the assumptions that are made about disability difference are erased through non-recognition. How do you prove intentionality where the norms around debasing disability are insidious, commonplace and do not arise as a conscious form of negative intentionality? Legal reasoning itself is complicit in demeaning the experiences of disabled people under ableist relations, pitching testimony as whining and characterlogically difficult, as the agency nurse records illustrate. Lawrence's (1987) work on race relations in the courtroom suggests stereotypes are confirmed rather than unsettled by such judicial narratives. These lawyering stories rely on symbols of translation to produce common sense normalised meaning with reference to varying standpoints. The case of *Price* also points to the usage of allied health worker testimony which, when inflected by ableist readings of behaviour, can colour the outcomes of not just the trial but also the agency and motivation of the disabled person.

In the US and ECtHR cases cited above, the tensions on the limits of reasonable adjustment as an intervention are revealed when the accommodation is pitched against an alleged narcissism. Disability claims around access are inevitably framed as special measures or favours (here governments even have practices of dividing populations with similar needs into partitioned groups with different entitlements). These measures are meant to elicit *deserving gratitude* rather than entitlements about accommodations around difference. Social differentiation produces difference: the abled and disabled, which in turn are products of our ways of looking and sensing. People are made different by a process of being seen and treated as disabled (Lawson, 2008, p. 517). Furthermore, *Price* is significant because the judgment acknowledged the place of micro-aggression in the lives of disabled people, which destabilises well-being and quality of life. Seeing micro-aggression as a form of ableist relations and factoring that awareness into social work interventions in such areas as access and anti-bullying can result in the development of robust strategies aimed at storing up resilience.

Crippling Masculinity: Injury, War and Disabled Soldiers in Sri Lanka

On the island of Sri Lanka, which has an area of 1,340 km and is located off the far southern edge of the Indian sub-continent, a thirty-year terrorist insurgency, resulting in high levels of physical, cognitive and psychological disablement, has recently ended. It is estimated that 70 per cent of the multi-religious society is Theravada Buddhist (Central Intelligence Agency, 2008). Elsewhere I have argued that Theravada Buddhism has shaped the ableist body. Within Buddhism there is the convergence of two conflicting strands of disability, the first related to Karma and fate and the second to a normative acceptance of the imperfection and unsatisfactoriness of all life (Campbell, 2004). Some Sri Lankan Buddhists have argued that Sinhalese people on the island have a special claim as 'sons of the soil' (*bhumi putra*) to 'land' and 'space' as guardians of Theravada Buddhism. It is in this context that *rana viru* (war heroes) takes on a different meaning beyond mere jingoistic nationalism.

Disability in Sri Lanka is mainly produced through war, natural disasters, ageing populations and large numbers of people undertaking high-risk work. It is estimated that there are at least 700,000 landmines still in the ground, which pose a risk mostly to men aged 18–45, children and displaced persons. According to the Sri Lankan army, the civil conflict has resulted in 14,342 soldiers with disabilities (Jayasuriya, 2010), although the Association of Disabled Ex-service Personnel put the figure at nearer 15,000–20,000 for those individuals who require artificial prosthetic limbs. The impairment effects of war paint a horrifying picture (de Mel, 2007). With an increased ageing population, the prevalence of depression, cognitive and visual impairment has also increased (Weerasuriya and Jayasinghe, 2005; Jayasekara, 2007). Additionally, the suicide rate ranks seventh in global statistics, with a ratio of 31:100,000 deaths, twice the number of deaths due to war. Thalagala (2000) estimates that 40 per cent of these suicides are due primarily to depression. Correspondingly, there has also been a destabilisation of gender relations (de Mel, 2007; De Alwis, 2008). A specific form of ableist relations will be teased out in this section to consider the militarised virtuous body (Jeganathan, 2001) and the complex relationship to the disabled (*rana viru*) war hero soldier.

This chapter draws on a much larger unpublished study on rethinking disability and ableism, in which we need to think of the production of disability through the lens of the making of nations. Therefore, the bigger picture for disability is the health context of the figuring of the ideal productive citizen, a construct ultimately tied to macro-nationalist preoccupations of compliance and outsiders. *Bhumi putra* in this context evokes the war hero (*rana viru*) who becomes a trans/temporal figure, a permanent guardian of the land. Contested attributes of the contributory citizen are changeable and shaped by relations with Empire and the post-colonial. In colonial Ceylon (Sri Lanka), official records viewed huge segments of the Indigenous population (the non-whites) as pathological (Guha, 1989).

Whilst there would be considerable apprehension to articulate this flavour of rhetoric today, there are other less obvious ways that ableist renderings of the health or not-health of a nation's body politic can occur.

In development and human rights circles, the discourse of 'civil society' is commonly deployed, not just in the global north but also increasingly by activists in the global south. Yet, despite the elusive delineation of the population, a normative usage conflates civil society with 'civility'. Such civility is still based upon assumptions of deficiency appended to a (cultural and gendered) developmental benchmark which Orjuela argues is 'a continuation of a post-colonial western civilising mission' (2005, p. 122). According to Gunawardena (2010), acquiring a disability results in the creation of a new hegemonic masculinity among disabled veterans. I argue additionally that disability is recuperated by the hyperextension of a *disabled abledness*, which wedges an increasing divide between disabled soldiers and others with disabilities, affecting rehabilitation opportunities and outcomes.

Ableist norms of the exemplary Sri Lankan citizen (male) have been and are quite different from norms of the modernist West and those grounded in qualities of an assertive self-contained individualism (Jeganathan, 2001). Ceylon under British occupation construed the cultural gendering of sex as pathological, almost invoking a sense of women and feminisation as a type of disability, a mutilated male. Racism and ableism converge and conspire to represent the masculinity of Sinhalese men as inept and arrested, as profoundly feminised. The practice of *konde* (men tying their hair into a bun) caused a great deal of anxiety for the British and in 1906 a restricted regulation was introduced to cut off the *konde* (Wickramasinghe, 2006, p. 65). The British associated the practice of wearing a comb by Sinhalese men with becoming women.

> The deficiencies of so-called feminised men meant that they were circumscribed as passive, fragile and emotional. This contrasted with the exemplary abled-body of the British, graced with masculine virtues. He was a man in self control and disciplined. (Wickramasinghe, 2006, p. 67)

This association demonstrates the processes of *purification* and *translation* between masculine/feminine, weak/strong and abled/disabled. The notion of psychological and bodily *lajja-bhaya* (shame-fear) to avoid instances of public shaming are expressed in the sense of filial duty and deference to elders and authority figures (Obeyesekere, 1981). De Silva (2009, p. 88) contrasts the vigorous and athletic English body of the gentleman of the Victorian era with what she refers to as the 'composed body and sedate bearing' of Sinhala masculinity (see Roberts, 1994). Thus, dependency becomes a transfigured concept when applied to disability, and ableist relations induce a *disablisation of race*. Perera (2007) notes some caution with prescriptions around masculinity and points to multiple modes of risking the body as well as the interplay between public constructions and personality.

The image of the perfect citizen in a modern militarised Sri Lanka is encapsulated in the figure of the über-male; a virile, healthy, masculine figure of the male soldier whose purpose as a supreme protector (of the motherland) is to participate in warfare that is 'ugly, unglamorous and dirty' (Thompson, 2002, p. 109). The abled low caste peasant from the rural village finds in military service a mechanism for the evacuation of his lowly status. A relational cultural model insists that notions of abledness and disabledness are produced within such cultural dynamics. As a militarised society of 30 years, this militarism prompts a different kind of masculinity from the past, one where 'hardness, violence and contempt for women reach previously unscaled heights' (Fernando, 2009) and where there is an emergent ethos instilled in early childhood of 'risking the body' (de Silva, 2005). This kind of image of the 'hardened modern', de Mel argued (2007; 2009), plays a central role in the national imagination. Rugged masculinity is deployed with reference to warrior tradition which places decisiveness and strength as key qualities of the modern soldier. Such images sit uncomfortably alongside a representation of the street dwelling disabled person, who is also 'ugly, unglamorous and dirty' and perhaps in his not-health, de-masculinised and, by inference, unfit for military duty. The Seva Vanitha (2009) video, *Brave Hearts*, recalls ancient times of victory before moving to images of troops protecting the lands, including assisting poor villagers with disability, helped in their hour of need by a meritorious military hero surrounded by the skirmish of the battlefield. It is this military hero who, in the 'blink of an eye', is cut down and becomes disabled through his valiant service. Dangerous circumstance brings with it social and economic capital, a rare chance of the good life, especially for a boy from a rural poor farming community.

This ableist ethos of the male (soldier) that is presented in the ideal of *rana viru* (war hero) was, according to Perera (2007), stepped up in the 1980s as the military combat with guerrillas increased. Any incongruence can be reconciled through ableist processes of translation. Perera points to the bizarre circumstance of a Rambo styled, bandana clad billboard character that adopted the name *Diyasena*, reminiscent of an ancient military hero. Yet, on the street this ableist image bears no resemblance to 'real' males – the soldier appears in neat uniform and is often of a lean and (feminised) small stature. The framing of the healthy masculine ideal is set in contrast with other forms of marginality based on difference – women, minority races, gays and, of course, disabled people. The existence of the disabled soldier, and there are many of them, represents a radical confrontation with the archetypes of the ideal loyal, gendered citizen; the soldier hero. Theoretically and in public policy we should be looking for any points of transgression or recuperation of the trope of hero and its intersection with the imaginary of disability and notions of culpability, deserving and non-deserving sources of causation.

With respect to war-related disablement there has been limited planning dealing with social determinants of health (access to medicine,
health care, livelihood schemes, etc.) (Landmine and Cluster Munitions
Monitor, 2009). Retaining the ethos of *rana viru* images of burden
normally associated with disability means the rendering of soldier(ly)
disablement is transfigured to a kind of *crippled hyperabledness*, whilst the
masculine (sexual) self remains contained or elusive. Unlike Cambodia,
where there is also a high incidence of soldiers acquiring disability, the Sri
Lankan soldier is still party to a salaried arrangement post-injury and not
necessarily discharged from the military. Disability does not cancel the
'good life', as the soldier receives a high salary which is maintained until
he reaches 55 years of age (de Mel, 2009, p. 41). Various representations of
the disabled soldier reveal a degree of tension between traditional notions
of charity and the necessity to let the hero maintain deliberative capacity.
The posters of the Ranaviru Fund in spruiking about rehabilitation and
medical aid for disabled soldiers, has the slogan within its own rhythm of
'going, telling and saying': 'when you go home tell them of us and say we
gave our today for your tomorrow', playing to that tradition of the
prophetic story. Social workers providing assistance in this kind of context
(and there are many theatres of war around the globe) need to be vigilant
about the effects of nationalism, masculinity and the ways these features
are written on the disabled male body in the context of negotiations
around social welfare provision and access to services.

The Sri Lankan Army, on 3 October 2009, announced its plans to build
a 'wellness resort' dedicated for soldiers who acquired impairment when
undertaking military duties. With the slogan 'Care for the Brave', the army
states its mission:

> To provide lifelong care for totally disabled war heroes. Most of these war heroes
> are in their prime youth with a full life span ahead of them, but with permanent
> disabilities ... This is a very 'special community' in our country that has taken
> over a magnanimous burden in the name of the country and are now burdened
> with traumatic experiences. (Seva Vanitha Branch, 2009)

The women's league of the Sri Lankan army, the Seva Vanitha Branch,
initiated a highly polished fundraising campaign to construct a 'wellness
resort' (*Abimansala*), as a centre 'for rest and recreation of [52] totally
dependent war heroes ... who sacrificed their legs and limbs for the sake
of the country' (Seva Vanitha Branch, 2009). The focus of this facility is on
creating a place where 'disable [sic] and totally dependent war veterans
can seek mental and physical solace, rest and recreation for the rest of
their lives' (Seva Vanitha Branch, 2009). Here, tragic images of pity and
suffering are not deployed to elicit donations. Earlier I referred to the *Brave*

Hearts video, which focuses on bravery and reciprocity and the inter-linkage between independence and dependence. The pitching of the rehabilitation hospital where there is no direction or indeed hope, contrasted to the risking body of the disabled soldier who is uplifted through work and sport, all made possible through the founding of the wellness resort. This 'resort', we need to remind ourselves, is not really a holiday camp but rather a place of containment. The cultivation of anti-discriminatory practice within this setting by professional staff such as social workers presents mindboggling challenges. Another Seva Vanitha video, *For our War Heroes*, choreographs dance previews of a larger event '*Tharu Dilena Reyak*' (Starry Nights) and was considered quite an edgy video in the Sri Lankan context. The dancing is graphically tactile and resplendent with portrayals of aesthetic beauty and eroticism amongst the male soldiers themselves and female performers. The hyperextension of abledness is achieved through the foregrounding of the nobility, camaraderie and dynamic movement of the disabled soldiers, who are proud and victorious. Such fabrications do not square with reality, soldiers with disability rarely have a public (normative) presence in street life in Sri Lanka and their access to public Buddhist Temples (the hub of communal life) is extremely difficult (Campbell, 2012).

What interests me is the way that abled-disabled soldiers are presented and called upon to be authoritative knowers; through their sacrifice they become authentic symbols and oracles – witnesses and truth tellers. How are these seemingly contradictory images of the disabled soldier to be interpreted? Using a lens of ableist enquiry, in these examples a hyper-able body is extended (at least rhetorically), made possible through the utilisation of the masculinist norms of *rana viru*. Invoking the trope of the hero enables the masculine disabled body of the soldier, through a past bodily form, to become re-materialised and risked in the contemporary (almost moving through time). It is not difficult to imagine, as a non-lineal temporality is ensconced in communal life – a notion of time where the past–present–future mutually intercede and enfold each other. Without solace in the masculinist lens of the war hero, disabled soldiers would otherwise be rendered as belonging to that more familiar category of the deficient citizen, alongside other more mundane populations of disabled people, impaired by poverty, illness, violence and circumstance. Abledness is extended by being coupled with *rana viru* and appended to disability under limited spatialised circumstances, ensuring that militarised virtuous masculinity remains intact. This deployment ensures that the notion of abledness remains and ableism as a process is robust.

Key Ideas for Practice

1. When connecting with people with disabilities in your day to day work, move away from thinking about the situations as problematic from your own team or organisations and focus more on uncovering those structures, attitudes and processes which sustain problematic thinking about people with disabilities. This reframing might involve negotiating the terms on how you as a practitioner engage with the opportunities that come from developing relationships with those living marginal lives that do not focus on their impairments from a negative perspective.

2. Given that assessment and support planning processes themselves can be harmful in the way they focus on normative assumptions about how a person ought to be living their life, use the process to focus more on what is really going on and the purpose of 'assessment' when disabled individuals and groups raise issues that confront them in their contemporary lives. This may involve challenging divisions that services perpetuate through their 'special arrangements' for disabled people and distributing resources, and to consider what measures or assumptions are used to assess the way the person lives their life and for whose benefit these are being prioritised.

Where to Next?

Studies in ableism as a theoretical and methodological tool reaches beyond intersectionality theories which still operate on the basis of an interpenetration between self-evident distinctions in difference. Conceptualising difference and problematising the norms of the human through an ableist lens enables the study of dividing practices, constitutional binarisms that rank bodies on the basis of linear continuum modelling (from the optimal to debased subjectivities). In contrast, SiA (Campbell, 2009; 2011; 2013) suggests that ableist relations are a *thoroughly relational* dynamic which arises and declines, and simultaneously operates through the interfusion and interactivity of translation and purification in specific conditions and causes. For social work practice this is good news, as the kinds of relationships and professional practices we may have with disabled people have the potential to short circuit, if not refuse ableist relations. It is hoped that this chapter stimulates re-thinking of marginality through the re-calibration of difference, generating new insights and a broader spectrum of research.

6

A Critical Analysis of Service User Struggles

Stephen Cowden and Gurnam Singh

Introduction

This chapter seeks to offer a critical analysis of issues of power and oppression in relation to what in the UK has become known as 'service user involvement'. Over the past 25 years, a series of major policy changes has significantly raised the profile of service user involvement in the delivery of public services. Beginning with the National Health Service and Community Care Act (1990), which placed statutory duties to consult service users, to more recent developments such as *Putting People First* (Department of Health, 2007), service providers have been mandated to ensure full user involvement in the planning, commissioning and delivery of services. However, if institutional responses are relatively recent, the struggles of service users and citizens over health and welfare provision are not. Therefore, in this regard, any discussion that seeks to uncover the challenges and possibilities in ensuring effective participation of service users needs to be situated in a broader examination of the history of service user movements.

Whilst charity organisations seeking to care for vulnerable citizens (mostly children, families and disabled people) have existed since the Victorian period, self-advocating, user-led, anti-oppressive movements began to emerge in the late 1960s and early 1970s. In the US, we saw the emergence of Disabled in Action, whose motto 'nothing about us, without us' (www.disabledinaction.org) clearly signifies the demand of disability activists that no policy or service can be decided without the full participation of those impacted on most by that policy. One of the first organisations to challenge the power of professionals in the UK in the early 1970s was the Mental Patients Union (MPU). Emerging out of counter-culture movements, the organisation was strongly rooted in Marxist analysis of psychiatry as an instrument of social control of working class people. Quite simply, the MPU sought to confront the dominant medical model in psychiatry that they felt resulted in the accentuation of distress through the medicalisation of problems. The movement, as Andrew Roberts recalls, was political in nature and, in the same way that workers formed trade unions, it argued that mental patients also needed a union to fight for their rights against political oppression and social control (Roberts, 2008). Similarly, the disability rights movements inspired by the workers struggles and new social movements, particularly black civil rights and feminist movements, emerged in the 1960s across many developed countries to both question the prevailing medical models of disability and the dehumanising practices of isolation, institutionalisation and silencing of disabled service users (Campbell and Oliver, 1996). But, as we will argue in this chapter, discourses of choice and control emanating from an understanding of the structures of oppression and the processes of dehumanisation, marginalisation, inequality and both real and symbolic violence (Young, 1990; Bourdieu and Wacquant, 1992), have a totally different beginning to those driven by contemporary neo-liberal managerial reforms of welfare services.

This history gives us a valuable context for developing both a critical understanding of the contemporary rhetoric of 'choice' and 'service user involvement' and an appreciation of the service user movement as a social movement fighting for social justice and human rights. Whilst each country will have its own set of policy developments, by contrasting the dominant policy discourse with the everyday realities and struggles of service users and carers, it is possible to gain a much clearer insight into the relevance of ideology and politics. As we have argued elsewhere, developing a critical and historical perspective enables one to see what appear as local concerns over welfare through a universal lens, thereby enabling one to make connections with similar struggles in other countries (Singh and Cowden, 2013). And so, although the precise discourse of 'service user' involvement tends to reflect policy developments in the UK, in terms of the underlying critiques of power in professional and client relationships, public welfare and the impact of neo-liberalism, these will have a resonance beyond the UK. Neo-liberalism, as Harvey suggests, represents a policy approach which suggests that the only way 'human well-being can best be advanced [is] by liberating individual entrepreneurial freedoms and skills within an institutional framework characterized by strong private property rights, free markets and free trade' (2007, p. 2).

Thus, against the backdrop of a history of conflicting imperatives, this chapter poses some questions about what 'user involvement' actually means and why it has become such an important issue. In doing so we argue that, as Foucault highlights, there is a need to be alert to the contested nature of discourse (1980). Whilst the language of 'user involvement' pervades much of social policy and social work, the available evidence on the effectiveness of these policy initiatives remains sketchy (Branfield, 2009). Despite the rhetoric, it has become unclear what the substantive processes of user involvement actually represent and this reflects one of the key problems we see in social work today, which is a crisis of meaning around the language of user involvement as embodying one of the core principles of anti-oppressive practice, that being to give voice to and validate the insights and experiences of oppressed people (Dalrymple and Burke, 2006) or enabling subjugated discourses to be registered (Foucault, 1980). Moreover, despite the clear emancipatory impulse behind demands for user involvement, which clearly resonates with a wider discourse of anti-oppressive practice, citizenship and human rights (Beresford, 2003; McLaughlin, 2009), often these discourses are trumped with a counter and more powerful consumerist neo-liberal logic that tends to lead to fragmentation and reductions in service provision.

The language around 'personalisation' and 'personal budgets' in adult social care is a good example of this. This whole project is driven by rhetoric of personal choice and even 'liberation', but far from extending service provision, the implementation of these policies is leading to an acute danger of valuable services being closed down. There is also a growing evidence base that shows there are many service users, particularly older people, who do not want personal budgets, but would rather have professionals organise services for them (Woolham et al., 2013) or simply that the shift from a centralised provision to a fragmentised service may introduce both inefficiency and instability (Spiker, 2013).

How is this apparently 'backward' demand by older people understood within the rhetoric of choice and involvement, which is meant to empower service users? Is it that older people are just too old fashioned and set in their ways to accept change? Or might it be that these people are worried about the complexity of having to employ their own carers, as well as work out things like National Insurance contributions and make holiday arrangements for the carers they now are employing? Might they also be genuinely concerned that the new system could well be accompanied by closures of services that they valued? What does 'personal choice' mean in this scenario? It is in this regard that one can see the discursive shift surrounding the idea of 'empowerment' in social work. As Pullen-Sansfacon and Cowden (2012) note, once a term that denoted a demand for rights and recognition in the face of social marginalisation, it has now shifted to denote an individualised process of accepting 'personal responsibility' in one's life.

We conclude the chapter by setting out the key challenge facing practitioners, activists and academics who are concerned with addressing the needs and concerns of service users in the context of the economic crisis of 2008 and a resulting intensification of liberal social policy that is characterised by the dismantling and mass privatisation of welfare, creating a new discourse of 'deserving' and 'undeserving'.

Who is a 'Service User'?

The differential impact of current attacks on the welfare state on service users offers a useful starting point for posing a simple but apposite question: who is a service user? The difficulty of answering this illustrates the complexity of different meanings and uses the term has. At what point does one become a service user? Is this simply an administrative category, or is it a political category? What about service users' families – are they service users? At one level it is like asking 'what is a human being', but the key question in all of this is having the critical understanding that allows us to unpack the different ways in which service user subjectivity has been mobilised politically. Much of the literature on service user involvement has tended to treat the category of 'service user' as undifferentiated, relatively stable and unproblematic (Beresford, 2003). Whilst this notion of service user appeals to administrators and managers in terms of managerial mechanisms of audit and regulation, for service user 'activists', their self-definition has different antecedents and aspirations; which are primarily about 'voice' and recognition of the nature and range of their experiences. There has always been an inherent tension concerning the different ways in which the term is mobilised between the stabilised administrative category and the more organic and experiential use of the term. In this sense, the term 'service user', like all other categories mobilised around difference, needs to be understood as inherently political, meaning that the question of who is responsible for defining who is and who is not a service user is crucial. As McLaughlin notes, labels really do matter as they identify 'a power dimension and hierarchy of control' and, therefore, act as 'signifier and an external social control' (2009, p. 1114).

Another key issue within this is the question of which 'service users' we are talking about? In other words, we need to acknowledge that service users are themselves differentiated in many different ways, hence the importance to incorporate a diversity perspective into the analysis. The tendency to essentialise or attribute natural characteristics to what is a wholly socially determined category runs the danger of setting-up 'service user' as a binary other to 'service provider'. This fails to recognise the fluidity that exists between these categories. Indeed, it is difficult to imagine any professional who is not also a user of public services.

Service user involvement has become one of the central concepts in the strategy of 'reform' and 'modernisation' of public services initiated by the then New Labour government and subsequently intensified by the incoming Conservative–Liberal Democrat alliance in the shape of the Health and Social Care Act 2012. Whether one is talking about 'parent power' in education, the new 'patient-led' National Health Service (NHS), or the requirement that social care services to place 'service users' at the centre of service provision, subsequent governments appear to be committed to the slogan *user* (or in more recent times *customer*) *knows best!* The key point to note here is the way that questions of power and powerlessness, of social justice and social inclusion have become reduced to the issue of 'choice', and it is a reductionism which has been effortlessly maintained by the subsequent Conservative–Liberal Democrat coalition.

Whilst New Labour did at least attempt to fund their rhetorical claims, what makes these new claims incredible is the impact on actual and pending cuts in expenditure on services. For example, a joint Age UK–College of Social Work survey of 300 adult care social workers reported that 90 per cent were worried that life would 'become more difficult for older people who need social care as frontline cuts start to bite' (Brooks, 2013). Likewise, at a time in which demand for mental health services has actually increased, a government commissioned report notes proposed reductions in mental health services expenditure by £150m in 2012 (Department of Health, 2012). In other proposals, as reported by the BBC (2012), the government suggested that NHS Trust Hospitals be invited to expand by setting up hospitals in other countries, thus further characterising the general policy direction towards marketisation.

In circumstances such as this, where systemic decisions about public services are made on ideological grounds, often against the demands of citizens, patient and user groups, it is essential to ask practically and theoretically, what 'user involvement' actually means? We have already noted the way successive government ministers have reduced the issue of 'power' to one of 'choice', and rather than being accidental, this is an essential part of the strategy which seeks to reframe service-user involvement not as a political demand based on a concept of entitlement, but as a consumerist demand for a 'good service'. This is entirely consistent with the ideological project of neo-liberal reforms whose impetus is to undermine health and welfare services as socially based entitlements, thereby facilitating their commodification and privatisation.

Where did Service User Involvement Come From?

We began this chapter by discussing the crisis of meaning that surrounds the language of service user involvement, and in the face of this it is important to revisit the basis on which the service user movement itself evolved. This was a movement that developed as a consequence of the assumptions of social welfare in the post-war period and it was constructed on the basis that professionals 'knew best'. Service users, referred to as 'clients' at this time, were seen as having an entirely passive role, often being silenced and in the worst instances reduced to a Foucauldian 'docile body' (Foucault, 1977). The positivist medical model, which was the basis of this approach, came under sustained critique in the 1960s and 1970s, and influential writers like Thomas Szass (1961; 1970) and R.D. Laing (1960) challenged the efficacy of professional and scientific knowledge. This questioning was part of a broader *Zeitgeist*, as manifested in the new social movements and a realisation that 'knowledge from below' is at least as valid as dominant 'authorised' knowledge. These movements in effect gave birth to new forms of theorising, which sought to deconstruct dominant concepts of 'good/bad', 'functional/dysfunctional', 'sick/healthy', 'normal/abnormal' and also to develop a greater appreciation of the relationship between society, human oppression and wider social divisions (i.e., race, class, gender, sexuality and disability). Configured around the 'politics of difference', built on existing Marxist understandings of capitalism and imperialism, it was in this process that new ideological formations emerged as influential paradigms for the theorisation of human difference, power and oppression (Collins, 1986; Young, 1990).

During the late 1970s and throughout the 1980s a series of struggles took place around welfare in Britain, and we see this period as crucial in setting the context for what took place in relation to the form and direction of the welfare state and the emergence of user discourses. Gail Lewis has importantly noted that historically the welfare state was never 'a single homogenous entity' but rather 'a series of overlapping and negotiated positions through which relations between a number of actors were articulated' (1998, p. 40). These positions developed essentially from 'the context of a particular set of international and political and economic relations, which followed on from the Second World War' (Lewis, 1988, p. 40). The most significant implication of this is the idea that the post-war welfare state was based essentially on a series of assumptions about entitlements. These assumptions need to be understood structurally as expressions of relations between genders, classes and 'racial'/ethnic groups. For example, the assumption that the male wage was a 'family wage' was crucially an assumption about the nature of the political relationship between men and women in society. It was this assumption that was being challenged when women in the trade union movement fought a political battle to obtain the same pay for the same work as men. Similarly, some of the early political campaigns waged by the black community in Britain concerned the disproportionate number of children from African-Caribbean backgrounds who were classified as 'educationally subnormal' and placed in separate educational institutions, known popularly as 'sin-bins' (Centre for Contemporary Cultural Studies, 1982, Bryan et al., 1985) The struggle against these was central to contesting the idea that people from these communities had no right to make demands about what education was meant to be about. Alongside this, the welfare state was also a key site for the articulation of the power of professional groups. For example, it was the power of the medical professions which determined the decision to place groups, such as the learning disabled people and those with mental health problems, in institutionalised care.

Throughout the 1970s, a disjuncture emerged between professionals and non-professionals and the assumptions that had underpinned the post-war world (Lewis, 1998, p. 45–48). Despite the slow demise of old class-based collectives, we saw the emergence of new social movements – black and anti-racist, feminist, lesbian and gay liberation, mental health survivors, disability rights and service user groups – for whom questions of welfare provision and entitlement were central to their demands for social justice. Indeed, concerns surrounding welfare frequently acted as the focal point for political mobilisation. For example, this was true of West Indian parents concerned about their children's education and labelling, feminist campaigns about reproductive rights and disability activist struggles against stigmatised and marginal provision of services. These campaigns typically challenged professional authority in determining how these entitlements should be enacted, making this a period in which the power of professionals was questioned and challenged.

As mentioned earlier, R.D. Laing's work, which argued for a radically new understanding of mental illness (1960), is a good example of this and it is one that illustrates the relationship between new understandings, which challenged the dominant form of provision, traditional psychiatry, and the development of political movements, such as the mental health 'survivors' movement. Collier (1977) points out how Laing's thinking, and that of the survivor movements more generally, was influenced by the existential Marxism of Sartre. In essence, health and social care professionals, by prescribing and enforcing certain conceptions of what it is to be 'normal', become complicit in acting against human will and, therefore, individual freedom. Rejecting the idea of mental illness outright, Laing's therapeutic methods were based on a presumption that people were generally healthy and that their so-called mental illness was simply a manifestation of their own attempt to achieve a balance.

Alongside this sense of the assumptions of the welfare state no longer having the 'fit' with those of the wider society, which they had previously had, a crisis emerged amongst the ruling classes concerning the long-term decline of Britain's economic competitiveness. This was one of the most important themes in the regrouping of the New Right, which in Britain during the 1970s specifically became allied to this anxiety about 'national decline'; the idea that Britain, the country that once ruled half the world, was no longer a world power, no longer 'Great'. Lewis (1998) argues that during this period, critiques of welfare can be understood as having emerged from two sources: the centre and the margins. The critique from the centre is that developed by the New Right, at that stage grouped around the Conservative Party and various right-wing think tanks. A central concern within this grouping was the fear of the decline of the long-term profitability of the British economy, and the desire to re-establish Britain's international competitiveness through welfare retrenchment and dramatic curtailing of trade union influence.

The critique from the margins came from the user groups, campaign groups and community groups, the 'new social movements'. These groups were very critical of existing state provision, but the context of this criticism was not the undermining of welfare as such, but making it more accountable to the people who used it, and less dominated by professionals who decided what was best for the service user. The book *In and Against the State* can be seen as a classic statement of this position. In the introduction the authors argued that: 'It is not just that state provision is under-resourced, inadequate, and on the cheap. The way it is resourced and administered to us doesn't seem to reflect our real needs' (Conference of Socialist Economists, 1980, p. 9). It is in this sense of being assailed by critiques from both the 'centre' and 'margins' that Lewis describes the welfare state in the 1970s as 'coming apart at the seams' (1998, p. 62–72). One may well ask what the point is of going back to these debates. But the central value in developing such a historical perspective is that so many of the initiatives that form the context of how we understand and work in the sphere of social care is a consequence of the way those earlier debates were resolved.

In order to gain support for the radical changes they were introducing, the Thatcher led Conservative government shrewdly appropriated certain of the criticisms and language of those political movements. However, their intention was not to reconstruct welfare on a more democratic basis, as the social movements were demanding, but rather significantly to reduce the scope of welfare entitlements as part of their restructuring of the British economy. The language of choice and consumerism was essential for the achievement of this hegemony, as it gave the appearance of being on the side of 'the people' rather than 'the bureaucracy', which of course meant the welfare state. Rather than being challenged by the subsequent New Labour administration, this language and approach were hugely expanded (Clarke et al., 2000). In the context of the banking collapse of 2008, the coalition government in power at the time of writing continued the very same rhetoric. The key point here is that any attempt to understand the issue of 'user involvement' must develop beyond seeing this simply as a self-evident good thing. It needs to be situated within a broader attempt to define a public policy agenda designed to reduce the role of the state through a strategy of commodification and privatisation (Clarke, 2004).

User Involvement in Practice

If we look at the question of user involvement in practical terms, one of the problems noted in much of the literature is that, rhetoric aside, there is very little clear sense about what its context was supposed to be. As Simon Heyes notes: is it simply about involving users as 'consumers' in their treatment, or in planning or evaluating services? Or is it something more than that? Is there a real transfer of power to the service user? Does it include them running services themselves? (1993, para. 6).

Heyes goes on to argue that the notion of user involvement really starts to unravel when it is looked at in relation to the concrete example of mental health services. Should users be able to decide whether or not they are to have electroconvulsive therapy (ECT)? The point is that the notion of 'consumer' becomes increasingly meaningless in the areas of mental health, where the treatment is forced upon the user. As a former patient of one mental hospital acerbically put it, 'I consume mental health services like cockroaches consume Rentokil' (Barker and Peck, 1996, p. 6). The off-the-shelf high street conception of consumer choice privileges high visibility and high take-up without any serious consideration of the underlying social relations involved, which are much more difficult to audit and measure.

The related policies of 'direct payments' and 'personalisation' (HM Government, 2007) in adult social care services, which have in different guises been 'established across Europe, Canada, the USA and Australia' (McLaughlin, 2009, p. 1109) provide a clear example of the chasm between rhetoric and reality. The ideological shift reflected in these policy frameworks is around service user 'choice' and 'control'. The first point to note here is that the original impetus for choice has not come from a social justice imperative, but directly as a consequence of a neo-liberal marketisation agenda that is in some sense the antithesis of many of the underpinning values of social work and anti-oppressive practice.

It is also significant to note that, as in the earlier discussion around 'community', progressive rhetoric about the value of the service user's perspective sits uncomfortably alongside the expectation that social workers will impose their own professional understandings when the time is right to do so. This is not to suggest that they should not do this, but rather to note the incoherence of the importation of a business/consumer model into a complex profession like social work. The Department of Health has for some time required all social work students to be assessed by users as part of the process of meeting competencies, but remains unclear about which users and what are the desired outcomes. Will the parents of the children whom Social Services recommend to be placed in Local Authority care be asked to do this? There are many who would welcome a much greater and more genuine dialogue being opened up with social workers and parents whose children have been placed in care, yet, the legal framework and lack of resources have pushed the whole agenda in child protection toward risk management.

The crucial question here is the issue of power, yet, without understanding the context in which this disconnect with the rhetoric and reality of practice, the voice of the user – which in the case of child protection work becomes something of an absurdity – becomes, as we have previously suggested (Cowden and Singh, 2007), a fetish – something which can be held up as a representative of authenticity and truth, but which at the same time has no real influence over decision making. In the absence of the kind of democratisation that has been historically demanded by community based users' groups, it has largely become service managers who have decided on those instances in which users are to be consulted, and what weight is put on their views when this takes place (see Carr, 2007). Within his work on user involvement in research, Peter Beresford has noted that, within the dominant 'managerialist/consumerist' model, user involvement has been presented essentially as 'a non-political neutral technique for information gathering from service users' rather than a basis for 'altering the distribution of power or who makes the decisions' (Beresford, 2003, para. 16).

We would argue that the conception of 'user involvement' through this managerial lens raises further issues of concern. Our own experience has been that service users, in the guise of professional consultants and trainers, are often employed by Social Services Departments and NHS Trusts to provide the 'service user input'; and in their role as paid consultants one may cynically suggest that they run the danger of becoming incorporated into a system that they are seeking to fundamentally challenge – one can see parallels with this and what became somewhat disparagingly referred to as the 'race relations industry' during the 1980s and 1990s. This is not to say that this process is not potentially valuable; but it also points to the way in which it is easy for institutions to define 'user involvement' through an essentially collusive arrangement between themselves and groups of 'professional users'. Having established this contractual basis on which to interact with users, those institutions again continue to be in control of the process of which users they listen to and which they decide to be 'too difficult' to incorporate. In this sense, while it is perceived as 'non-political', managerially driven user involvement is actually highly political. In effect, strata of articulate service users are being incorporated into the institutional framework. The danger of this is that it can easily become fetishistic – where the imprimatur of particular service users is being used by agencies to legitimise their work, but without service users in general having any substantive influence in how the service is organised or run.

Similarly, the primacy given to 'service user perspectives' within the context of a consumerist model obscures the important insights around the impact of alienation and oppression provided by theorists such as Paulo Freire (2007) and Franz Fanon (1986). The reality is that life on the margins can result in the internalisation of oppression, resulting in confusion, denial and fatalism on one hand, through to self-harming behaviour on the other. Their work points to the way in which sustained conditions of subjugation can make it difficult for the subaltern or oppressed individual to identify both the reasons for their oppression and what they should do about it. It has always been those with the greatest amount of what Pierre Bourdieu (Bourdieu and Wacquant, 1992) has called 'cultural capital' (meaning the knowledge which individuals from more educated and privileged backgrounds have of how 'the system' works and how to get what they want most effectively from that), who have historically obtained the best quality services from the welfare state. This will become even more so as services are cut and professionals are increasingly forced to decide who they can 'afford not to see'. People with complex needs and people who lead complex and often unstable lives are amongst the groups who will lose out most in this situation. We noted earlier that we live in an era when 'empowerment' essentially means we all have to accept 'personal responsibility' for making the best choices for our and our families health, welfare and education, and where, as Baistow notes 'not being in control of your everyday living arrangements ... suggests that there is something seriously wrong with your ethical constitution' (1994, p. 37).

In a situation where many professionals increasingly and uncritically internalise these expectations of themselves and service users, it is the poorest and the most 'difficult' of service users who drop through the cracks, which are themselves getting wider all the time. A survey of 4,500 disabled people entitled 'The Tipping Point' carried out in 2012 by The Hardest Hit, a group fighting against cuts to disability benefits in the UK, reported that 85 per cent claim that losing their Disability Living Allowance (DLA) would drive them into isolation, and would leave them struggling to manage their condition (84 per cent) whilst 95 per cent fear that losing DLA would be detrimental to their health (Hardest Hit, 2012).

'User Involvement' and Ideology

We have argued so far that that the rhetoric of service user involvement is being deployed as part of an on-going process where the language of progressive social movements has been emptied of its historical meaning and become a passenger on the vehicle of neo-liberal social policy. In this sense we can understand the idea of 'user involvement' through Louis Althusser's conceptualisation of the notion of ideology. Althusser was a Marxist, but he broke away from what he saw as simplistic Marxist under-standings of ideology as 'false ideas'. He argued that ideologies are not passive – they work by telling a story of how things are. He presented two theses about ideology. The first thesis was that ideology was not just false ideas; rather it was 'a "representation" of the imaginary relationship of indi-viduals to their real conditions of existence' (Althusser, 1971, p. 241). In other words, ideology does not represent the real world as such, but rather a relationship to that real world which is *constructed*, in the sense that it emphasises some things while excluding others. Partially this is because it is really hard to understand the sheer complexity of the real world, and hence representations of that world are how we make sense of this. Althusser understood ideology, then, as the imaginary or represented version and the stories we tell ourselves about our relation to the real world.

In relation to user involvement as ideology, the key point here is that rhetoric associated with this, and the related notion of 'customer', of a story we are being told, which is that whereas in the past users would simply be told what do by professionals, now there are all sorts of opportunities for users to shape the services they receive. This story is in fact imaginary because the decisions about resources for funding welfare services, as well as how users can and should be involved, are all still controlled by government and welfare bureaucracy, with professionals often complaining that their role has been reduced to one of a broker carrying out financial assessments. So, under these new arrangements, the promise of choice and freedom seen from a critical perspective operates at best as a mirage and at worst as a divi-sive force that shifts the focus away from the issue of social justice and equality to a pervasive notion of self-empowerment. For professionals, projected into the role of 'commissioner' rather than 'provider' of services, often frustratingly so, they find that underpinning moral imperatives asso-ciated with anti-oppressive practice becomes compromised by a new logic of financial prudence. In this sense, the professional–user relationship becomes even more problematic than the previous one based on paternalism that service user activists were so critical of.

This brings us to the second point that Althusser (1971, p. 155) makes about ideology: that 'Ideology has a material existence'. It isn't just about things people think, but about the actions, both individual and institu-tional, which result from that way of thinking. Hence, for Althusser to say that 'ideology is material' is to say that ideology always exists in two places – in an apparatus or practice (such as forms of behaviour dictated by the specific ideology) and in a subject, in a person, who is, by definition, material. In the 1970s and 1980s recipients of social services were referred to as 'clients'. This term, we were told, was patronising and stigmatising (Jones, 1983). With the ascendancy of the 'New Right' and the subsequent privatisation and commodification of public services, 'customer' and 'consumer' is a way of shifting the story in such a way that valorises seeing these services as businesses, rather than as not-for-profit public services as they were once thought of. In his book *Capitalist Realism* Mark Fisher has pointed out that in effect what has been 'successfully installed [is] a "business ontology" in which it is *simply obvious* that everything in society, from healthcare to education, should be run as a business' (2009, p. 17).

Indeed, as Malcolm Carey has noted, now that 'key areas of social care are ... dominated by business interests which, in principle, seek to gain profits' (2008, p. 919), the only space left for the service user voice is as a consumer whose role is to endorse various forms of social care management. User involvement becomes very important to managers because the 'user' acts as a voice that can validate the contracts of private providers and thus ensure their renewal. However, the users of these services very rarely have any actual influence over how these services are organised, resourced or managed. The result, as we have previously argued, is that the voice of the service user is nothing more than a fetish aimed at legitimising the idea that this or that private care group really *does* care (Cowden and Singh, 2007). And so, whilst no doubt some service users may feel that the availability of choice brings an improved care experience, for many others, as demonstrated in the scandals such as Castlebeck, the private care home provider that was exposed for neglect and systematic abuse of service users (Care Quality Commission, 2011), and other similar serious enquiries, the future is likely to be uncertain at best.

Key Ideas for Practice

1. In the context of neo-liberal reforms to welfare provision it is easy for service user concerns to be incorporated into an agenda dominated by performance management, contract compliance, audit and evaluation. Under this scenario, service users groups are constructed as consultants and consumers of services and the consensual approach employed here elides and obscures issues of power relations. Whilst this approach may benefit the few, it is likely that a growing number of service users will not access services for a range of reasons, such as lack of knowledge, fear about financial implications, fear of loss of dignity or simply that they no longer exist.

2. The nature of modern social work is that ethical and practical dilemmas are ever present. However, in the context of neo-liberal reforms of public services, those dilemmas and disconnects are, if anything, intensifying. Perhaps the most enduring dilemma of all is the one between the imperative to defend and expand welfare

services as a cornerstone of a democratic society. This will require social workers to seek out and consolidate collective ways of working with new social (including user) movements. Membership of and effective involvement in professional bodies will further enhance social workers' capabilities to resist compromising their professional ethics.

3. The task of social work is essentially a practical one of supporting vulnerable individuals to live lives with dignity and comfort. However, one should not equate practicality with simplicity, for enabling people to live with dignity requires deep levels of thought about the kinds of actions, processes and conditions that diminish dignity. For this reason, professionals must remain committed to developing critical reflective practice, to on-going learning about the shifting discourses of oppression, which become increasingly camouflaged within managerial rhetoric. Hence, in a climate where we see a combination of diminishing resources and unstable organisations, social work professionals – in ways that, for example, medical professionals have done – will need to develop a much greater degree of professional autonomy and self-confidence to stand their ground, both as individuals and citizens.

Conclusion

In this chapter we have sought to develop a critical analysis of the notion of 'user involvement' and in doing so we have suggested that the establishment of this discourse represents two opposing stories. There is an important story to be told about the user movement, particularly in the arenas of disability and mental health, and its success in giving service users a voice in decision-making spaces and places that would have been unimaginable in the 1970s. Moreover, one cannot ignore the impact that service users' perspectives have had on research and education, by, for example, drawing on their lived experience to take on roles as researchers, educators and consultants (Beresford and Holden, 2000).

The other story is one where we are seeing the construction of a settlement in which progressive critiques have been incorporated into a system driven by financial and managerial imperatives. Moreover, we have seen the democratising and human rights agenda, which service user struggles historically represented, being marginalised and displaced with choice and consumer rights. Whilst there will always be services available to people that are capable of leveraging financial resources or those protected under statute, driven by the austerity agenda, attacks on service users and citizens more generally are likely to be intensified. And worryingly, health and social care professionals will increasingly find themselves in a pincer movement, between frustrated and angry service users and carers on one hand and employers demanding increased productivity on the other. However, rather than respond with cynicism to this state of affairs, we would argue that it is a mistake to dismiss service user involvement as simple rhetoric.

Instead, we argue that service users' needs and perspectives need to be given real substance. But that this can only happen if front-line staff (ie) connect with the historical struggles of service users as citizens for dignity, care and protection within a framework of welfare as a basic human right and not a commodity.

7

Research Ethics: An Indigenous Fijian Perspective

Litea Meo-Sewabu

Introduction

This chapter focuses on discourse in the research ethics process and practice from an Indigenous Fijian perspective. It aims to illustrate how Indigenous epistemological frameworks may be adopted in both traditional and non-traditional research settings. Indigenous ways of knowing offer valuable lessons for social work and community development practice, as exploring the underlying values and norms of Indigenous population groups enables practitioners to work more effectively within these communities. Examples from original research relating to relational networks, forms of collaboration and communal resilience will be used to explore governance processes within Indigenous community groups, and the associated values that embrace localised forms of social and cultural capital.

Human ethics processes, as organised within the academy, may be viewed as technologies for the calculation and management of risk. While there are risks within any research project with regard to ethics processes and the conduct of research, this chapter will illustrate how Western paradigms associated with expert knowledge and the lay knowledge of an Indigenous population group give rise to competing understandings about ethical practice. It is argued that expert knowledge, as used within dominant Western notions of research, often subjugates Indigenous frameworks of knowledge construction. When Indigenous ways of knowing are appropriated or misunderstood, more damage and harm can be created and neo-colonisation unknowingly perpetuated. The chapter will focus on how Indigenous epistemologies may be used to disrupt dominant Western research practices. A poststructural analysis of discursive practices within research suggests that when working within Indigenous population groups new forms of ethical practice are required.

I begin with a story relayed to me by participants in my research that illustrates the themes at work within this chapter. While I was in the research site, the Fijian village, participants informed me that they had recently participated in a discussion with researchers from a university in the northern hemisphere who had arrived to conduct research on the island. They told me that the researchers gave them a dollar each for participating in an interview. Participants told me that they often joked about the gift as money for lollies for their *kava* drinking sessions. Kava is a plant, *Piper methysticum*, and a drink is made from the plant. Due to its bitter after taste many will take sweets after drinking to soften the bitter taste. This practice of taking lollies after each bowl of kava is also referred to as 'chasers' and is mostly done in informal kava drinking sessions. I asked them how they felt about getting the money; the response was that they felt belittled, but with a big smile they just told the researchers what they wanted to hear and nodded to their questions. Because of the Fijian value of respect and humility, the participants did not question authority, nor did they feel it was necessary to discuss their complaints as the researchers had already done the formal protocol of entering the village. So, to maintain harmony, they instead just went along with the research. This story is one that Indigenous participants would only disclose to a researcher with whom they felt it was safe to do so.

As an Indigenous researcher, I was at first infuriated by what the participants were sharing with me because, despite the push to decolonise research methods (Tuhiwai-Smith, 1999) and introduce Indigenous frameworks and literature on working with cultural difference (Thaman, 2003; Baba et al., 2004; Gegeo, 2008; Nabobo-Baba, 2008), here was an instance in the twenty-first century of 'colonial science' (Connell, 2007) in action. Indigenous knowledge was devalued, with a monetary value of a dollar securing its appropriation by Western scientists who seemed incapable of reflecting on the ethics of their practice. Kenney (2011) suggests that one reading of such practice illustrates the way in which Western researchers colonise the discursive spaces of Indigenous people, preventing them from becoming experts in their own lives and experiences.

Locating Myself

I am an Indigenous Fijian woman and also an academic. I locate myself in Oceania, the home of my ancestors, which, according to Hau'ofa (1994), is often perceived as islands in the far sea, but which should be seen as a sea of islands that encompasses the vast Pacific Ocean that surrounds them. Hau'ofa states that:

if we look at the [our] myths, legends, and oral traditions, and the cosmologies of the peoples of Oceania, it becomes evident that [our] world is not conceived in such microscopic proportions. Their [Oceania's] universe is comprised not only of land surfaces, but the surrounding ocean ... the underworld ... and the heavens above ... our Oceania is anything but tiny. (1994, p. 152)

Hau'ofa (2000) reiterates the point of being defined by the 'experts', or, as Foucault states, those with the power define the knowledge (Fillingham, 1993; Gutting, 1994; Danaher et al., 2000). However, people from Oceania clearly define Oceania as their grand universe rather than islands in the far sea – which are often romanticised as exotic and tiny – knowledge that often belittles Oceania. The story told in the introduction is an example of the questions Foucault would ask – how did this practice of placing a monetary value on knowledge come to be? Power in this instance is located with the researcher dictating how much the knowledge is worth, a value that is derived from preconceived ideas about how Indigenous knowledge is viewed in the Western world. These preconceived ideas have come from years of researching Oceania and Indigenous cultures, in which researchers from other cultures have the 'power' to determine what knowledge is valued, meaning that the subject positions of Indigenous people are not respected and are in fact undermined.

In rethinking anti-discriminatory practices, I have chosen to write about the ethical processes of conducting research in an Indigenous community. Lessons learnt from personal experience have challenged my practice as a community worker and researcher in so many instances. These lessons may help us to critically think about our process when we work with cultural difference.

There are now many Indigenous scholars who have written on research practices and Indigenous epistemologies. For example, Tuhiwai-Smith (1999) wrote extensively on decolonising methodologies, Nabobo-Baba (2006, 2008) similarly discusses an Indigenous Fijian framework on knowledge. In addition, Gegeo (2008; Gegeo and Watson-Gegeo, 2001) has written on Solomon Island epistemology, Thaman (2003) on decolonising education in Oceania and Kenney (2009) on midwifery. Other Indigenous authors, such as Bishop (1996), Durie (2004), Cram (2001), Thaman (2007) and Mila-Schaaf (2009), provide further examples of literature from Oceania on research practice and Indigenous epistemology.

These authors amplify the voices of Oceania in the need to rethink discriminatory practices, emphasising that theories are not necessarily universal, as often they are not applicable for Indigenous population groups. In telling our stories, we ask that social scientists critically think about our Indigenous frameworks, our processes and our ways of being, with the aim of shifting schools of thoughts and publicising what is considered ethical in our Indigenous world. Another important factor to highlight in relation to Western interpretations of Indigenous ways of knowing was expressed by Tuhiwai Smith, writing about Indigenous research, when she stated that, 'much of what I have read has said that we do not exist, that if we do exist it is in terms which I cannot recognize, that we are no good and that what we think is not valid' (Tuhiwai-Smith, 1999, p. 35). The statement reflects experiences of many Indigenous population groups when 'judgements are based on the cultural standpoint of the researcher rather than the lived reality of the Indigenous population' (Cram, 2001, p. 37).

In *Southern Theory*, Connell argues that the universal theories or expert knowledge that have become the basis of social science are driven 'by men, capitalists, educated and the affluent' (2007, p. vii). The discourse is that Indigenous epistemology is often considered periphery or lay knowledge that is outside of what is regarded by experts as social theory. The phrase 'southern theory' encapsulates Connell's challenge to social theories that have been generated in the northern hemisphere, which embed 'the viewpoints, perspectives and problems of metropolitan society' while presenting themselves as geographically dislocated 'universal knowledge' (2007, pp. vi–viii). Connell advocates for a re-evaluation of the periphery episteme through the acknowledgement of theories from Indigenous population groups; this includes our association with the land, our social structures and dynamics of kinships, our cosmology and spirituality, and ways of knowing that are our daily realities. The fact that lay knowledge from Indigenous populations is often not written about in the Western context does not make that knowledge any less important or its appropriation any less disturbing. The Foucauldian perspective allows us to explore how this knowledge has come to be. Foucault shows us that there are competing discourses of colonisation, Western knowledge and Indigenous knowledge. Western knowledge has subjugated Indigenous knowledge. Years of colonisation and bias towards Western knowledge have resulted in such discourse. This chapter aims to encourage practitioners to acknowledge and foreground lay knowledge within Indigenous communities as a way of interpreting experience and daily life.

The ethnographic research discussed in this chapter explores the cultural constructs of health and well-being amongst Fijian women living in Fiji, and considers how these understandings have evolved amongst Fijian women who have migrated to Aotearoa/New Zealand. The study used a 'combination of observation, participation and unstructured interviewing' (Sissons, 2007, p. 276) in which individual narratives about health and well-being were collected, employing photo-voice and focus group discussions using *Talanoa*; defined in Fijian, Tongan and Samoan as sharing a conversation and knowledge (Otsuka, 2005; Nabobo-Baba, 2006; Vaioleti, 2006). Exploring Fijian epistemology in the context of health and well-being is an integral part of this research. This chapter, however, focuses on the ethical processes and the intricate weaving of what is academically sound in the Western world and what is culturally appropriate as an Indigenous researcher.

In this process the praxis of research is viewed through an Indigenous lens and an insider perspective. In addition, lessons learnt offer valuable insight into what is considered ethical practice within an Indigenous population group that may have wider applicability to research that is conducted across other forms of structural difference. To explore structural differences, I will discuss the governance process within our land and explain the different forms of collaboration that occur. As explained previously, our connection to the land is paramount and, therefore, I will incorporate discussions on my role as an insider and outsider as a researcher/academic and the interface, specifically focusing on what is ethical from the Fijian worldview context.

The interface in research can be likened to a weaving process described by George:

> Weaving or plaiting is used from within a *Kaupapa* Maori context to denote the action of bringing people, or threads, together in meaningful relationships or patterns. Using those metaphors in relation to research is significant because research as a human endeavour is fundamentally created around relationships. By consciously weaving the threads together in ways that honour the contribution and participation of all those who weave the piece, it is possible to work more harmoniously, to create a more beautiful pattern, to plait a stronger rope. (2010, p. 15)

The statement discusses the importance of building relationships and trust when working alongside Indigenous populations. Working together, in partnership, creates a stronger bond. First, we need to understand how Indigenous epistemology is constructed.

Governance Process and the Vanua (land)

Indigenous peoples epistemologies are derived from: their immediate ecology, such as land; people's experiences, perceptions, thoughts and memory, including experiences shared with others; and from the spiritual world discovered in dreams, visions, inspirations and signs interpreted with guidance of healers and elders (Battiste, 2008, p. 499).

Vanua literally translates as 'the land' but has a deeper philosophical context that is defined 'as a people, their chief, their defined territory, their waterways or fishing grounds, their environment, their spirituality, their history, their epistemology and culture' (Nabobo-Baba, 2006, p. 155). In the context of research, Vanua methodology ensures that respect, humility and traditional Fijian cultural protocols are adhered to, encompassing what Nabobo-Baba defines as:

> Vanua research supports and affirms existing protocols of relationships, ceremony, and knowledge acquisition. It ensures that the research benefits the vanua and that love, support and resources given by the people are appropriately recipro-cated. The vanua researcher ensures that no harm is done to the vanua, which means that all information is carefully checked to ensure that that [sic] might be unsettling or have the potential to damage relationships is not made public. (2006, p. 25)

Both Western and Indigenous researchers aim to minimise harm amongst participants. Reducing harm within Indigenous frameworks means acknowl-edging kinship and relationships with participants. Creswell notes that 'researchers need to respect research sites so that they are left undisturbed after a research study ...' that interviewers need 'to be cognizant of their impact and minimize their disruption of the physical setting' (2009, p. 90). Creswell may have meant 'relatively undisturbed', as research of any kind disturbs a research site to some extent. A Foucauldian perspective encour-ages researchers to disrupt universal perspectives on research, that is, to disrupt the universal standards for conducting research that give no regard to Indigenous protocols and processes. Indigenous approaches provide an alternative perspective and require researchers to show respect in a research site, which means addressing the existing layers of governance within the research setting. Addressing the different structures means acknowledging kinship within the village and amongst the participants; this will often disrupt the village norm but is an ethical part of what is culturally appropri-ate when entering the research setting.

Insider Position and the Vanua

Tuhiwai-Smith argues that:

> at a general level both insider and outsider researchers have to have ways of critically thinking of their processes, their relationships and the quality and richness of data and analysis. However, the main difference is that insiders have to live with the consequences of the processes on a day-to-day basis forever more. (1999, p. 137)

In the Fijian context, the first protocol involves addressing governance of the Vanua or the land. As an Indigenous researcher, I am never an individual but always part of a collective. Even though in the academy the study is considered my own, studying within my own cultural setting means there are cultural obligations and protocols that must be adhered to as part of a collective culture, but, more importantly, as an ethical part of acknowledging the Vanua. Therefore, doing anything that goes against my cultural values marks me and my family for a lifetime, as the study within an Indigenous worldview becomes part of the collective and reflects on the family as a whole.

From an Indigenous context, Silverman's (2006) term 'ethical safeguards' means carrying cultural protocols and obligations in accordance to the Vanua. Adhering to the cultural protocols of the land safeguards my cultural position as an Indigenous researcher. To go alone into my own cultural setting would be an insult not only to my immediate relatives, but also to those receiving me at the village. Therefore, I had a group of relatives who I refer to as the 'cultural discernment' group. Their role was to ensure that I conducted the research in a way that was culturally ethical and culturally appropriate. The university ethics committee questioned the role of this advisory group, and by attempting to respond to their question I had to explain the concept of 'cultural discernment' to the committee. Cultural discernment can be defined as a process in which a community or a group of people collaborate to ensure that the research process is ethical within the cultural context of the research setting (Meo-Sewabu, 2012). The process means understanding the complex cultural systems of Fijian knowledge or the Indigenous setting being studied. There was no doubt in my mind that taking the group of relatives to the research site was ethical within the cultural setting, but within the academy I had to substantiate my arguments with existing literature. The concept of communal discernment devised by Gula (1998) and cited by Angrosino and May de Perez (2003) assisted in explaining the necessity for this process. Ethical safeguards were discerned by the cultural discernment group throughout the research process, some of which are expressed in this chapter.

Within the Western research tenet, Silverman (2006, p. 323) discusses ethical safeguards, stating that researchers should ensure that people participate voluntarily, make peoples' comments and behaviour confidential, protect people from harm and ensure that there is mutual trust between researcher and people studied. Within the Indigenous framework, it is critical that trust is established through respecting and adhering to the cultural protocols within the Indigenous community. Adhering to these cultural norms is the first step towards ethical research practices within that community. In the next few examples, I will draw on these ethical safeguards, as explained by Silverman (2006), and discuss the interface in the ethics process within the academy and experiences in the field, primarily focusing on structural difference, ethical requirements within an

Indigenous framework and the discourse of power within the field of research. The interface of the Vanua protocols and the academy involved finding common ground on what is ethical from both ideologies, while at the same time not compromising what is culturally appropriate.

Cultural Protocols and Links to the Vanua

Creswell (2009) notes that in the data collection process, research should ensure that participants are not put at risk and that vulnerable populations are respected. Once again, the universal standard has been set and practised globally. However, within the Fijian context, minimising risk to participants involved giving up academic power and control through letting go of the research process and trusting that participant directed research would yield productive results. Minimising harm from the Fijian knowledge context relates to understanding cultural protocols and links to the Vanua.

Knowledge of the empirical world and knowing the relationships and social-order and our links to the Vanua can also be illustrated as I prepared for the research in the main city. My relatives came together because they had a sense of responsibility in ensuring that everything was done in a culturally appropriate manner.

The first ceremony that has to be conducted by every visitor to address the village governance or any traditional Fijian setting is the *sevusevu*. The *sevusevu* acknowledges entering the land. To accomplish this a *tabua* (a polished tooth of a sperm whale, considered the most valuable item of Fijian property and used in exchange and ceremony) and/or *yaqona* (another name for the kava plant discussed earlier) is presented to the village elders or leaders of the setting.

Relatives valued the relationship regardless of the value of the item being given. This idea of giving also reflects the notion of reciprocity and maintaining relationships in the village. Knowing what to do and what to take is knowledge based on the norms of the village and what will be expected. The cultural discernment group ensured that these cultural protocols were done appropriately.

When the actual cultural protocols took place, everyone in the village knew what their tasks were. The roles and responsibilities within each clan are allocated by inheritance, and when born into these roles, one is equipped or deemed to have the traits of the assigned roles. Our clan's heraldsman came to the house we were residing in moments before the ceremony, where I met him for the first time. I was quite nervous as another uncle 'rattled off' the details of the study to him, a brief summary of what was written in the information sheet, to which the heraldsman nodded his head, agreeing that he understood. I was so sure he had missed the whole thing and that it would all be wrong. To my surprise and amazement he presented our protocols with such eloquence using metaphors and figures of speech that could only be perfectly stated by an orator. This experience definitely made me appreciate and acknowledge what Subramani (2001) refers to as the 'Oceania library', defined as metaphors, sayings and analogies derived from a world of vocabularies and knowledge that can only be appreciated by an insider.

In response to our cultural protocols, the village elders gave us 'blanket' permission to conduct the study and move around the village freely. The cultural process acknowledged the importance of their Indigenous knowledge and how they valued the thought of contributing to the research. What amazed me in this whole process was the eloquence of vocabularies and the manner in which they were delivered. The rhetorical exchanges which took place reflected the philosophical understanding displayed through the eloquent rhetoric, which I believe was an exchange of philosophies from the Indigenous world – an example of what Connell (2007) would refer to as 'southern theory'. Historical accounts were relayed to me in metaphors and poetry, everything in the village had a purpose and a relational meaning to village members; this, I believe, was the philosophical glimpse of the knowledge of the Vanua and philosophies discussed by Indigenous Fijian writers (Ravuvu, 1987; Tuwere, 2002; Nabobo-Baba, 2006; Ratuva, 2007). This would have been missed by a Western researcher who was not connected to the village or one whose way of thinking was heavily dictated by Western philosophies, hence, placing a different meaning and interpretation on the information gleaned in research, likely to be superficial. This is important in anti-discriminatory practice because not only is difference acknowledged, but meaning systems of the populations who are being worked with or studied are foregrounded.

Selection of Participants and Participation

'Indigenous research approaches problematise the insider model in different ways because there are multiple ways of both being an insider and an outsider in the Indigenous contexts. The critical issue with insider research is the constant need for reflexivity' (Tuhiwai-Smith, 1999, p. 137). One such instance was in the selection of participants. The women in the village selected the participants for me after I briefed them on the details of the research. The women ensured that the participants included an equal distribution amongst the three clans within the village. In addition, they made changes when they realised that one of the clans did not have equal distribution from one of the *'tokatoka'* (sub clans, consisting of groups of families). What was ethical as an Indigenous researcher was to ensure that the villagers agreed on the process and that I did not disregard their knowledge of what is appropriate.

Once selected, and before the research began, information about the research was once again explained to participants to ensure that details of the study were clear. Each participant was then asked if they still wanted to be part of the study. Many responded: 'why not?' They felt elated to be part of the study. Others responded that they wanted the world or New Zealand to get a glimpse of their lifestyle; these words were uttered with a sense of pride. None of the participants refused to participate; however, participants were also assured that not participating in the research had no negative implications and that it was a choice they must make and their decision would be respected. It is also important to note that most Indigenous cultures are hierarchical and someone coming from outside with an academic title or considered to be of a certain status is always regarded with the utmost respect. It is, therefore, important that one takes off their 'professional hat' and seeks to establish trust by first respecting the cultural protocols and humanising oneself or making oneself more 'down to earth', so to speak. It is only when these humanising qualities come into play that participants find it easy to discuss their concerns. The danger is that if these qualities are not reflected by the researchers, participants are more likely to tell you what they think you want to hear and will mostly probably just nod for all the questions without any real explanation.

Another aspect of being an insider researcher was to ensure that there was no backlash from clan members for anyone selected who did not wish to participate in the study. Fortunately all participants willingly gave up their time to participate, and discussions that occurred took place freely and with ease. Women who were present at the meeting but were not selected as participants were part of the training programmes organised by my mother, ensuring that they did not feel left out of the whole process. Learning to let go of controlling the research process allowed for and operationalised a number of things that contributed significantly to the success of the study. The sampling process gave the women control to choose participants and decide activities that I was to be involved in. Participants felt empowered by the process, as most felt that whenever a foreigner comes they are there to educate them. When the tables were 'turned', so to speak, they were elated by the idea of teaching me, they wanted to teach me everything traditional that still existed, and they wanted to show me everything and explain why this is so. I often found myself moving around the village, as villagers would send their children to come and get me to see how food was being prepared or how pots were being washed or to show me the catch of the day from the sea.

Fieldwork and Ethics

Informed consent: 'Blanket' permission

When explaining their individual rights as participants, I found that a lot of the participants looked puzzled and could not understand why there is such a thing as 'individual rights'. The collective consent to participate in the research was given during the *sevusevu*. In this cultural process the approval is given by the village elder, which implied 'blanket' consent for us to be in the village and for all villagers to participate and support our work, whether for research or anything else of that sort, therefore it seemed redundant to request individual consent. From the academy's perspective, I had to state their individual rights as research participants, but from the cultural perspective this was perhaps an insult to the blanket permission already given by the village elders.

I was surprised that all participants wanted to sign the focus group consent form as they felt it made things official for them. Even women who could not write properly wanted me to sign on their behalf – there was an overall feeling of belonging after the signing. I felt that this partly had to do with how I explained to them that in the Western world we have to ask for the consent of each individual and that what I was asking was in no way disrespecting the blanket permission endorsed at the village level. I explained that they, however, needed to consider the option, but are not in any way obligated to sign the forms. Some of them stated that signing is similar to getting money out of the post office, they have to sign to make it official, and another likened the process to the election, all Western notions of individual identification processes. I will note, however, that most research within Indigenous cultures indicates otherwise; 'consent forms' are often frowned upon and viewed as suspicious (Tuhiwai-Smith, 1999; Cram, 2001; Riessman, 2004; Nabobo-Baba, 2006).

Photo consent in the village

An additional area of consent was the photo consent in the village. One of the participants wanted me to come to her house to show me *masi* (traditional Fijian bark cloth made from Mulberry tree or *Broussonetia papyrifera* and used in weddings and other Fijian ceremonies) and mats that she made for her daughter's 21st birthday. When I came to her house, everything was laid out as if the person being honoured was there. It was a beautiful array of masi and mats that she had tirelessly worked on for the past year, and I marvelled at it. She wanted me to take pictures of it to show the world, as she was so proud of her work. She then wanted to show me how she made the dye for the masi. I just listened and recorded her story and took pictures of all that she had displayed. She would pause every now and then to ask me: 'Did you get that?' She felt that I had to capture every second of the process in order to fulfil her role as teacher.

This is one example of the many times I was constantly asked to record stories or take pictures. The story is explained to demonstrate that the whole village was in control of what should be included in the photos, therefore, the process of photo consent became redundant and almost an insult to the villagers. Participants and villagers wanted me to take pictures of everything. There was an initial hesitation on my part, as I felt that this was far from what the academy had rigorously wanted me to reassure them of. It became a contest for participant clan members as they found out that two other clans had their songs recorded and were dressed up for the work that we conducted together. I could soon see a buzz of participant clan members asking me to retake their pictures in their best attire, with make-up and necklaces included. They felt that every picture taken should be shown to the world. They wanted the world to catch a glimpse of who they are; villagers wanted to teach me everything. Not taking their picture or not wanting to be part of this would make them feel that it was not important enough to be included in the study. I therefore took pictures of everything, as instructed by the villagers.

An ethics committee may find the taking of photographs to be problematic and insist on individualised consent for each photograph. The story, however, illustrates how this worked out differently and that if I did not take photographs their feeling was that the activity (and by implication the person) was not important enough for me to notice. Having their voices heard empowered the women in the sense that 'truth' about their lives was being told by one of their own. More importantly, it was being interpreted in a manner that respected who they are rather than as part of the discourse that has shaped how they have been portrayed historically.

Reciprocity and Gift Giving

Reciprocity and gift giving is an integral part of Fijian culture and collective cultures. A story was once relayed to me about a man who for years had continuously given to his community. His daughter was to be married and he was on his way to the bank to get a loan for his daughter's wedding when members of the community came for a visit. They had an envelope that contained the community's collection to assist with the wedding. There was no need for him to get a loan as the collection was well over what he needed. All over Oceania, reciprocity is the essence of our communal and collective value that capitalises on social capital and is not time specific. We do this for weddings, for funerals, for birthdays and for births, in the village and wherever we live globally. Social, cultural and capital exchanges occur globally to maintain our collective culture. This flow of exchanges has been likened to that of 'transnational co-operations' also referred to as transnationalism (Spoonley, 2001; Mafile'o, 2008; Vertovec, 2009). Within Oceanic cultures, despite living in diaspora, these exchanges allow us to maintain our sense of belonging to the Vanua.

Reciprocity and Status

Discourses in reciprocity and gift giving have for years been questioned by research ethics globally. Reciprocity in a Fijian worldview can also relate to status. Riessman (2004 as cited by Silverman, 2006) noted that ethical universalism that has been constructed in one cultural context and exported to another without modification poses practical risks in research. Hence, the notion of reciprocity and giving money or receiving gifts may be viewed in the Western research context as a 'dubious bargain'. In discussing a study conducted by Marvasti (2004), Silverman (2006) notes that such a dilemma is common for researchers in 'third world' countries. Once again, the assumption is that participants from 'third world countries', who are defined as poor according to Western definitions, are desperate for the money. Therefore, Silverman suggests that a possible solution is to solicit interviews without any rewards; the situation is likened to that of giving a starving person a plate of food in exchange for an interview (2006, p. 322). I agree with Riessman (2004) in stating that ethical universalism is dangerous in this context as it informs researchers of what to expect in the third world. This may be true for some countries, but researchers should not assume it is true for all third world countries.

Reading texts on 'ethics and research' with, no doubt, good intentions from the northern hemisphere, answered the question in the story I told at the beginning of this chapter. Why did the researchers from the northern hemisphere university who conducted their research in the village give participants a dollar in exchange for the interview? The critique, perhaps, was based on the fact that we are part of the third world and perceived as poor, so the dollar is more than enough for our troubles. What is missing is the understanding of the cultural context on the significance of giving and reciprocity within the so-called 'third world' cultures. The perception of us as 'poor' is a definition constructed by capitalists because of the perceived lack of economic capital, but we are 'rich' within our Oceanic cultural worldview because of our connections to our families, to our Vanua. Our cultures thrive on social capital, allowing us to work collectively to source our livelihood from the ocean and land that surrounds us, with very little need for economic capital. Reciprocity in terms of gift giving and status are explained as follows, when once again I had to substantiate the need for reciprocity within my cultural context.

Reciprocity also implies that not only gifts are given, but also that the knowledge and skills of visitors or researchers are shared with the village during the visit. In this context, it was appropriate that my mother conducted some training in Christian education (her field of expertise) as it was expected by the villagers and provided an avenue for maintaining relationships with participants and the Vanua. As an academic, I clearly understood the concerns of the University's ethics committee concerning what may be viewed as an overlap in the aims of the research and the training that my mother was going to do, but at the same time I knew that I had to be true to my culture as I am accountable to my people for the rest of my life.

Key Ideas for Practice

1. In order to work successfully with Indigenous communities, social and community workers need to build relationships and display respect for their communities. You will not be able to get the 'jewels' of your research if your relationship with them is superficial. This is primarily the reason most Indigenous communities do not like being researched. It is because researchers or workers treat them as subjects rather than as people who have a story to share. Therefore, it is important that you build relationship with your Indigenous communities, be genuine in your approach to get to know them and their cultural processes and protocols. These processes have to be adhered to in order that respect is gained. In addition, be prepared to disrupt your own notions of how research should be conducted, including working differently with the Western ethics committees. These processes may take some time but you will be thankful at the end as the rewards will be immense.

2. Reciprocity and gift giving are prevalent in most Indigenous cultures. It is important that you find out what it is appropriate to provide for your community group as a sign of appreciation for their time and effort. In terms of ethical requirements, most countries with Indigenous population groups will also have their own research ethics requirements within their government agencies. Find out what these are before leaving for that country. Be prepared to 'go with the flow', on paper everything is set in stone but in practice things do not always go as expected and you have to be prepared to disrupt your own worldview, be patient and go along rather than get frustrated when not meeting timelines. As discussed earlier letting go of your academic power is often difficult, but if you know the aims of the research and understand the communities you will be working with you will gain so much more when working alongside Indigenous communities.

Conclusion

In conclusion, I would like to reiterate that research ethics are never univer-sal; what is considered ethical in one culture is not always considered ethi-cal in another. The research setting should be considered unique, with its own set of values. We all agree that the aim of any ethics process is to ensure that harm is minimised. 'Harm' however has different cultural meanings within different cultural groups. The discourses explained in the examples and stories told here are an illustration of the ethical process for 'minimis-ing harm' within my own culture. Expert knowledge as part of a collective culture was conceded by the 'cultural discernment group', ensuring that the research process was ethical within the village setting. Tuhiwai -Smith states that the 'one thing she consistently teaches her students and researchers is that Indigenous research is a humble and humbling activity' (1999, p. 5). In rethinking anti-discriminatory practices, social and community workers need to critically consider ethical practices within the Indigenous groups they work with. Doing so is a humbling process for workers, as Indigenous knowledge, social systems, relationships and meanings of systems are fore-grounded and acknowledged as 'expert knowledge' rather than that of Western paradigms. Within Indigenous communities, foregrounding Indigenous lay knowledge is a step into the right spaces of resistance and hope, in which self-determination, decolonisation and social injustices are addressed (Tuhiwai Smith, 1999). The Vanua research framework (Nabobo-Baba, 2006) and the practices used in this study are examples of decolonis-ing research methods that are grounded in the realities of the Fijian village. Nabobo-Baba (2006) reiterates that when research and practice are framed within the Indigenous culture being studied, trust is established and the information and data collected will more than likely be accurate. The over-all theme within the research process explained in this chapter accentuates the need for new forms of ethical practice when working within Indigenous groups.

I acknowledge Professor Robyn Munford, Dr Suzanne Phibbs and Dr Lilly George for their feedback on drafts of this article, and the editors for their invaluable comments. Vinaka vakalevu Dr Apolonia Tamata and Dr Api Talemaitoga for your support.

PART III

Subjectivity

By now, you will appreciate the essential interdependent relationship between the ideas emerging from within different sections of this book. This section builds further on poststructuralist ideas, which is an umbrella term embracing a number of theories concerning society and the individual. A major theme of poststructuralist writers is the instability in the human sciences due to the complexity of humans themselves and the impossibility of fully escaping structures in order to study them. These ideas are also concerned with language as the main medium of construction. We saw in the previous section on discourse how an understanding of discourse helps us think through different linguistic explanations of the psychosocial order or 'the self', and which were illustrated through the examples of 'ableism' and 'user involvement'.

As governing attempts to shape, foster and maximise the capacities of our communities and then each individual, the target of governing practices becomes the 'thing' to be governed – its subjects (Fejes and Nicholls, 2008). Subjects are not assumed to have specific characteristics and agency. Subjects are shaped through different historical practices and by those discourses produced by and producing certain practices, and the different subject positions which in turn are constituted through them. If that is hard to grasp, then this section starts with a background to the concept of subjectivity. Chapter 8, by Webb, explicitly asks what is the 'subject' of social work? Subsequent chapters develop this theme, to build on your understanding of subjectivity. Chapter 9, for example, explores the concept of intersectionality by drawing on the author's own experience as a lesbian woman living with mental health issues, and Chapter 10 involves two co-authors who come from different backgrounds and share their personal encounters with sectarianism and critical race theory. These accounts will hopefully challenge your ideas around identity and help you to recognise, at a deeper level, the various tensions arising in the different categories commonly applied to service users and groups. Following on from Cowden and Singh's discussion on the impact of labelling in Part II, Carr brings a service user perspective to the discussion. All the authors draw attention to some of the conceptual tools that social workers can use in their practice to think differently about individuals and communities using social care by focusing more on the 'how' and 'what' of power. This type of critical questioning increases the visibility of how power operates and its effects in order to understand experiences and act more appropriately.

Discourses themselves are the bearers of various subject-positions: that is, the positioning of agency and identity in relation to particular forms of knowledge and practice. One way of understanding this is to think firstly about the subject that is produced *within* discourse, as well as *subjected to* discourse. As we take up a *subject position*, in which we become the subject of a particular discourse, we are the bearers of its power/knowledge. Here, we tend to locate ourselves in the position from which the discourse makes most sense. We thus become its 'subjects' by subjecting ourselves to its meanings, power and regulation. This can be more easily understood if you think about the nature of social work professionals and their practices and the different subject positions we take up as a profession. Subjectivity is constituted through discourses and the power being exercised, in which the person is being positioned at any one point in time, both through their own actions and the acts of others. The idea of multiple and contradictory processes constructed through the discourses in which we participate, therefore, enable us to ask important questions about the relationship between subjectivity and social work.

In essence, unlike objectivity, in which the object under consideration is scrutinised based on observable facts that are perceived in the same way by everyone, subjectivity is based on an individual's own experience of life and their own ideations. Subjectivity comes from an analysis of an individual's opinions, which, in turn, are based on past experiences and what the individual knows from their history. An example might be their background and upbringing, the environment and its influences as well as interactions. The writings of Foucault have had tremendous impact on contemporary thinking about subjectivity, and notions of the subject have a considerable history. These underpin the chapters in this section which provide a comprehensive history of, and treatise on, the evolution of subjectivity, particularly in relation to social work, and how it has capitalised on ideas of subject and self that have developed throughout Western thought. The authors document moments that are important both to Western thought about the subject and to what we bring as subjects at the present time. In summary, the chapters in this section bring literature, literary theory, history and philosophy into close relation with the notion of subjectivity in social work and seek to open up a new phase of debate, which will, we hope, prove stimulating reading.

In Chapter 8, Webb gives a clear and coherent explanation of subjectivity, which needs no introduction from us. He charts the historical influences on subjectivity and how these came to impact on social work, for example, the impact of Cartesian and Kantian philosophy on reflective practice giving way in social work to critical studies and postmodernism. Webb addresses the problem-solving aspects of subjectivity in conventional social work that is based on accounting and auditing practices and technicised subjectivities. Whilst this has been important for fulfilling the function of identifying and intervening to achieve change at the practical level, there are limitations in generating possibilities for understanding the complexity of the social context. Webb introduces the idea of material subjectivities, where a new breed of thinking about subjectivities is based on a foregrounding of materiality or material culture and the dramatic effect on how social work practice is undertaken in relation to discrimination. This helps us focus on the particularities of material culture rather than some 'discursive ether'. As an example of this, Webb discusses the intricacies of networking and the embodiment of material environments such as religious artefacts in social work micro-practice. Such a perspective allows social workers to ask what subjectivity is performed when we talk about a discriminated subjectivity or a subjected body. How do social workers calibrate subjectivity when thinking about discrimination and oppression as a network of embodied relations? Webb suggests a politics of the subject that concentrates on the materiality of issues. This is not about discourses but rather avenues of connectability, around which discourses and subjectivity come to be woven.

In Chapter 9, Carr, writing from a user perspective, explores the metaphor of intersectionality to describe and explain ways in which mental health, disability, heterosexism and racial and gender discrimination compound each other. Intersectionality discourse is political or postmodernist, and Carr explores the role of identity, categorisation, structural and social division and how it can be used as an analytical tool for sociopolitical change. Carr uses intersectionality as a primary analytic tool for theorising identity and oppression grounded in lived experience. She stresses the importance of unpacking experiences and rethinking power, which includes challenging the ways that both social workers and clients keep oppressive stories alive either through not unpacking experiences or being neutral. She suggests that this enables them to retain the power to determine what is anti-oppression. Biographical approaches are suggested as ways of resisting or overcoming the limitations of artificial and reductive categorisations in social work and social care procedures. Chapter 9, therefore, asserts the development of thinking and the interaction of diversity, categorisation and oppression with individual biography. Carr draws on work by academics working with lesbian, gay, bisexual and transgender (LGBT) populations, where theories of intersectionality grounded in lived experiences are used as a framework for reflecting on anti-oppressive practice long assumed into a wider oppressive system.

In Chapter 10, Bernard and Campbell note the shift in discourse from critical race theory to ADP and AOP. They chart the disagreement in the history of knowledge about equality and diversity in terms of how social work has worked through what is considered to be the best methods of how to address racism in social work. These can be emotionally charged debates and have caused unease. Bernard and Campbell incorporate a pedagogic perspective which seeks to acknowledge multi-layered subjectivities and identities. Campbell refers to popularised notions about the conflict in Northern Ireland and draws parallels with Bernard's discussion on critical race theory given that sectarians were/are forged and fashioned by phases of colonialism. Parallels about awareness of the complexity of this conflict and its impact on all levels of society create a number of challenges for social work practice and education. The issue of how identity is perceived by the self and by others is crucial in the way we understand experiences of sectarianism and racism and how we as social workers can respond. This includes not being seen as the 'other' and needing respectful spaces. Bernard and Campbell argue that anti-discriminatory practice is not about simply posturing on the nature of discrimination and its causes; there is a need for social workers to deliver meaningful services and challenge structures that prevent social change.

8

The Subject of Social Work: Towards a New Perspective on Discrimination

Stephen A. Webb

Introduction

Subjectivity inevitably involves the human subject. It has been an important concept for research, and for intervening in social and political life, since the 1970s. The concern over the meaning of subjectivity has spawned debate across a range of disciplinary fields including studies of the 'political subject', 'white subjectivity', 'gendered subjectivities', 'workplace subjectivity', 'colonial subjectivities' and 'embodied subjectivity'. As we shall see, any consideration of discrimination and oppression will inevitably make either direct reference to or assumptions about the nature of subjectivity.

The subject (as a noun) of social work is keenly concerned with subjectivity in its various guises, whether this is as personhood, the self, character, individuality or identity. There are manifold ways of articulating the term 'subject' that bear upon social work. Indeed, we shall discover how social work values of anti-discrimination depend heavily on a very particular perspective of the subject. Moreover, the entire discourse of rights is based on a strong notion of subjectivity as self-ownership. Human rights arguments inevitably appeal to some form of reflective self-direction and personal freedom. To have such autonomy is to be capable of pursuing one's own projects or values in a suitably unconstrained manner.

What is surprising, given subjectivity's indispensability in discussions ranging from social work interventions to ethics of social work, is the scant conceptual analysis specifically devoted to the term. Subjectivity, broadly referred to as 'the subject' and her or his feelings, desires, interpretations and perceptions, sits centre stage in social work. Indeed, one may go so far as to suggest that social work would be subjectless without a subject (as a verb). It needs a theory of the subject to stay afloat. Resting on contemporary notions of individual autonomy, the preoccupation with subjectivity in social work often bypasses other concerns such as its contrast with objectivity. Let us look briefly at the way these historical influences on subjectivity came to impact on social work.

The Cartesian Subject in Social Work

'It goes without saying', writes Vincent Descombes, 'that philosophy as such, or at least modern philosophy, was on the side of an affirmation of man as "subject"' (2004, p. 9). After God and king, humankind was the natural successor for the status of subject, at the centre of all things. The modern distinction between subjectivity and objectivity was historically formed through a philosophical focus enshrined in Rene Descartes' *cogito*, Enlightenment rationalism, and, later, Kantian free-will philosophy. This is commonly referred to as the Cartesian theory of subjectivity. The psychological sister concept of the 'self' entered English language usage along with the rise of rationalism and the Enlightenment. The important thing to underscore here is that the formation of the subject is a historical process. It was Marx who keenly observed that: 'man is only individualised through the process of history. He originally appears as a generic being, a tribal being, a herd animal – though by no means as a "political animal" in the political sense' (1964, p. 96).

Descartes believed that subjectivity was the essence and storage house of the mind, that the self is guarantor of its own continuing existence and the basis of all reality. The result of this Cartesian influence was an asymmetrical dichotomy: separated from the external world of 'matter' (or nature), the cogito of the subject assumed the role of reasoning task master or self determining overseer in the world – a role fuelling the enterprise of disciplines like psychotherapy, counselling and social work (Dallmayr, 2009). Similarly, the Kantian subject has the self-assurance of its 'knowledge of truth, and is understood by Kant as capable of apprehending itself as a self through an act of reflexive apperception' (Weber, 2006, p. 327). This aspect of Kant's theory can be traced back to Descartes' theory of the cogito, and remains influential in social work's account of reflective practice. Reflective practitioners are Kantian in the sense that they regard individual processes as based on autonomous persons who are able to achieve a transparency of understanding about what is right and wrong as well as of critical insights into social work processes (D'Cruz et al., 2007). This view endorses a certainty of self, based on verification of personal experience and through the process of rationally guided introspection and reflection (Webb and McBeath, 1989).

Historically, a certain construction of the Cartesian subject came to dominate contemporary discourses about personhood. Moreover, the Cartesian view of subjectivity found a home in a range of psychological discourses as they emerged in the professions that developed in the post World War I period, such as social work. One of the most significant contributions of Descartes to the field of modern psychology is his view that a person is more certain about her own thought processes than about any other phenomenon. The leitmotif 'know thyself' is indicative of this preoccupation with the search for truth of an inner self. Subjectivity is to be found inside the person. It is a benchmark of rationality. Indeed, person-centred models in social work are based on the positive view that a person who is fully in touch with their inner-self would be pro-social in their attitudes and reasoning. For social workers you are never responsible enough.

In psychology, it is assumed that there is a natural human impulse within everyone to affirm, perpetuate and increase the self to its complete totality. In psychoanalysis, each self undergoes a process of individuation on its journey of completion. As Sampson (1983) has argued, psychology itself, which emerges within this historical context, is also responsible for the perpetuation of this imagined human subjectivity. 'The problem', he writes, 'is that psychology has uncritically adopted the atomistic individual as the world creator and has ignored the social forms that are essential in shaping the concept of the actual life of that individual' (Sampson, 1983, p. 97). Models of psychosocial intervention transferred to social work view subjectivity as a private mental state and disembodied cognitions which are not contingent on culture or ideology. The theories of motivation and perception which underpin the psychosocial models of intervention are profoundly Cartesian. The model regards subjectivity as one whereby human beings are actively constructing themselves or else negotiating their immediate environment. Cartesianism is the paradigm case of a model of subjectivity which explains purposeful action exclusively in terms of a person's intentions and inner will. From the post World War I period to the early 1980s Cartesian theories of subjectivity dominated social work and permeated its models of intervention.

Presently, the fate of subjectivity or subject-centeredness, however, hangs in the balance. This is no small matter. Ever since its historical foundations, subjectivity and the psychology of the individual has been the central focus and point of privilege of Western modernity and social work. One of the most sophisticated accounts of the emergence of modern forms of subjectivity is presented by Charles Taylor's (1989) *Sources of the Self*, where he insists that the view of the human individual as an autonomous agent, endowed with inwardness, individuality and freedom is an invention of the modern West. Non-Western cultures operate with very different understandings of subjectivity.

The Death of the Subject

The Western versions of subjectivity discussed above are regarded as under threat. Today, authors increasingly talk about the 'death of the subject', the 'demise of the self' or the 'end of subjectivity'. Within social work, this intellectual development figures most prominently in what is referred to as postmodern or critical social work.

Fredric Jameson was the first to coin the phrase the death of the subject in his book *Postmodernism, or, the Cultural Logic of Late Capitalism*. He talked about 'The death of the subject itself – the end of the autonomous bourgeois monad or ego or individual – and the accompanying stress, whether as some new moral ideal or as empirical description, on the decentering of that formerly cantered subject or psyche' (1991, pp. 15–16). Similarly, in *The Order of Things*, Foucault (1986) wrote about 'the Death of Man' which refers to an end to a theory of subjectivity that arose (or at least reached its fruition) in Europe under humanism, a subjectivity that came to influence much of social work thought. By this he meant that subjectivity understood as human consciousness and free will had been discredited. He remarked that:

> As the archaeology of our thought easily shows, man is an invention of a recent date. And one perhaps nearing to its end. ... one can certainly wager that man would be erased, like a face drawn in the sand at the edge of the sea. (Foucault, 1986, p. 387)

For Foucault, notions of individual freedom and responsibility and the philosophies that support them are mistaken, claiming that the priority given to any self determining individual cogito is a fallacy of modern Western rationalist thought. He made the further point that the human sciences did not discover subjectivity as an empirical fact, waiting to be investigated. Rather, he argues, these very scientific discourses themselves brought subjectivity into being. Foucault's critique is expressly aimed at the modern construction of an ahistorical, autonomous subject as sovereign originator of meaning. He draws attention to the way subjectivity is thoroughly enmeshed with and constructed by particular historical, discursive and political contexts. His work conceived of subjectivity as formed within the apparatuses of power, the discursive practices and technologies of the social through which subjectification occurred. For Foucault, subjectivity, or, better still, 'subject positions', is historically contingent and produced through the formations of discourse and power. Here the Cartesian mind is shrunk to self-consciousness that is mere awareness of the body and an effect of discourse. Typical of the 'discursive turn' as the determinant of subjectivity is Adlam et al.'s observation:

No region or level of the social formation is contemplated which stands outside the discursive practices in which the material activities of concrete subjects consist; the social formation is equivalent to the non-unified totality of these practices. The human subject is not seen as occupying a given 'place' within a 'social structure', but as constituted in the intersections of a determinate set of discursive practices which take their particularity from the totality of practices in which they are articulated. (Adlam et al., 1976, p. 46)

With the discursive turn we can recognise a crucial distinction between subjects as produced in power/discourse and subjectivity, which we could call the effect of being subjected (Balibar, 1994). According to Davies: 'The experience of being a person is captured in the notion of subjectivity. Subjectivity is constituted through those discourses in which the person is being positioned at any one point in time, both through their own and others' acts of speaking/writing' (2000, p. 57). The idea of multiple and contradictory processes constructed through the discourses in which we participate enables important questions about the relationship between subjectivity and social work to be asked.

The feminist writer Judith Butler is also a subject-killer. In *The Psychic Life of Power: Theories in Subjection*, she discusses the subject as an effect of power, rather than as the initiator of power relations. Butler sees gender not as an expression of what one is, but rather as something that one does. In decentring the subject she radically reverses the relation between subjectivity and power in developing what is called the 'paradoxical' account of 'subjection'. 'If, following Foucault, we understand power as forming the subject', she writes, 'power imposes itself on us, and weakened by its force, we come to internalise or accept its terms' (1997b, pp. 2–3). 'Power, that first appears as external, pressed upon the subject, pressing the subject into subordination, assumes a psychic form that constitutes the subject's self-identity' (p. 5). It is the internalisation of the 'discourse' of power that creates the subject. With Butler's formulation, subjectivity is an effect of power and discourse, rather than its cause, and is often associated with the postmodernism discussed below. 'Subjection consists precisely in this fundamental dependency on a discourse', leading Foucault to talk of the 'discursive production of the subject' (p. 5). For postmodern writers like Jameson, not only is individualism dead, but it never existed – it is a myth of modern bourgeois capitalism. Postmodernism prefers situations to subjects.

One of the most important books on subjectivity was the jointly authored book *Changing the Subject* (Henriques et al., 1984), which had an enormous influence on social work, education and nursing. This book attempted to link together a Foucauldian approach to subjectification with an attempt to use psychoanalysis to understand how positions were held together for any one subject. The authors of *Changing the Subject* crafted subjectivity as 'more than the sum total of positions in discourse since birth', (Henriques et al., 1984, p.5) and so in using psychoanalysis in conjunction with Foucault sought to understand the complexities of the experience of being a subject.

As will be seen, the 'death of the subject' has dramatic implications for social work. What happens when the centre is suddenly found to be absent? What consequence does the postmodern challenge to the view of human subjectivity have for social work? Can we continue to make sense of concepts central to social work – such as rights, autonomy, well-being and feelings – if we no longer retain a strong conception of subjectivity? Postmodern formulations are devastating for social work because they deny the very possibility of a self-determining client who acts reasonably. It makes even less sense to talk about clients exploring inner feelings to make sense of their relationships. Group sessions focusing on jealousy or violence as potential for subjectivities to be opened up and closed down would be misconceived. Subjective feelings of separation and loss would be regarded with suspicion. The commonly held social work assumption that feelings of attachment enhance subjective well-being would be dismissed by the likes of Foucault and Butler, who deny any ontological status to subjective feelings as inner states. Rather, feelings and emotions are regarded as interpretive acts and influenced by discursive representations. A subject that intends something is perfectly acceptable for writers such as Foucault and Butler provided that they are seen from the perspective of forces, powers and contexts. However, with the postmodern critique, the supposed accessible kernel of subjectivity promoted by the reflective mediation of the social worker becomes a fiction. Instead, reflection is reduced to the operations of narrative, story or language. The entire panoply of psycho-therapeutic intervention, which remains within horizon of Cartesian subjectivity and on which social work has traditionally rested, becomes suspect. This is because psychological material is thought to be essentially subjective. The process of social work intervention provides the means for self-reflection and a focus on the main 'problems' of the client. For Butler, self-reflection is nothing more than a temporal moment of textual performance.

The death of the subject thesis gained significant momentum in social work in the 1990s with the publication of poststructuralist, deconstructionist and postmodern literature. As Philip Mendes summarises:

> Over the last decade or so, critical social work approaches have integrated older modernist forms of structural analysis and newer postmodern ideas which emphasise more diverse sources of power and emancipation. These perspectives ... target social change at both the individual and societal levels. (Mendes, 2009, p. 26) (e.g., Ife 1997; Pease and Fook, 1999)

At an experiential level, the fallacy of Cartesian subjectivity becomes easy to appreciate. Indeed, many of you will have experienced a killer blow against the rules of subjectivity at some time or another in your lives. I am thinking here of incidences where subjectivity literally ceases up and comes to an abrupt halt. When the sheer force of circumstance throws you completely out of kilter. These are times when you can't believe what is happening to you. Intense moments such as these subtract from preconceived routines and everyday habits. You can't fathom why this is happening to you. The functioning rules of cognition simply stop working during this dazed state of intense existential anxiety. This is exactly how it might be when someone is unexpectedly told by a doctor that they have cancer or they receive a phone call informing them that their partner has died without warning. Indeed, terminal illness, the death of a loved one, divorce after years of marriage, love at first sight and loss of trust in a friend or colleague are all shocking instances that are likely to invoke this falling away of the self. The evacuated site of Cartesian subjectivity is experienced in a stupor. Language and reason fail you. Self-direction, autonomy and freedom go out of the window. The Cartesian subject is lacerated and the ego, built up to withstand the responsibilities of reality, shudders to a stuttering halt.

The Subject Divide in Social Work

Despite being the target of strong and sustained critique by postmodern and critical social work, the Cartesian subject continues to have a significant role in social work practice. The subject is probably less likely to have been killed off than severely wounded. Primarily, it is because of its applied psychologistic base that it remains a powerful intellectual tradition and is still considered essential to fields of conventional practice in social work, counselling and teacher education. The utility of the Cartesian subject remains practical, functional and self-evident for conventional social work. In part, the continuing appeal of this normative version of subjectivity rests on the centrality of assessment requirements that hinge on notions of measurement, value and certainty. For Law (2004) subjective reality is ephemeral, elusive, complex, messy and heterogeneous. The fact that our conscious 'inside' is not homogenous is so obvious. Empirically orientated professions such as social work tend to exclude and repress such heterogeneity in favour of neatness, order and the search for certainty. And this is the case because the dominant methods of social work tend towards standardisation, individualisation and regularisation.

Those psychosocial approaches, such as task-centred, crisis intervention, solution-based or cognitive-behavioural interventions, are best described as conventional and based on a problem-solving approach to subjectivity. Bob

Mullaly (2007) argues that there exists a continuing division between what he calls the conventional view of social work and a progressive or critical view. The former view, which is arguably dominant in the profession, recognises that social problems exist, but constructs social work practice around the specific needs of the individual. It is assumed that social work interventions can empower service users without requiring any fundamental change to existing social structures. In contrast, the minority critical social work perspective holds that service users can only be empowered by eliminating oppression and inequality.

The classical psychosocial definition by Helen Perlman captures this conventional empirical approach to social work:

> Social casework is a process used by certain human welfare agencies to help individuals cope more effectively with their problems in social functioning. (1957, p. 4)

Similarly, Doel and Marsh (1992) suggest that problem identification is a key stage in task-centred practice. They suggest that intervention should begin with compilation of a list that includes all the client's problems. From this instrumentalist vantage point, subjectivity is regarded as a set of individual responses to a series of problem-solving interventions carried out by the social worker. The social worker needs to get the measure of the person who she/he is dealing with. It is predicated on the view that each individual treatment will improve the functioning of the client (for example, reduce anti-social behaviour or family dysfunctions) and that interventions will lead to marked, pervasive and durable changes in behaviour (for example, parent functioning or reducing depressive symptoms). In this sense the problem-solving view of subjectivity in conventional social work is based on accounting and auditing in enterprise. Here, subjectivity is to be dealt with as a technical problem that is calculated and measured as the basis for a successful outcome.

Although the Cartesian view of subjectivity implicit in problem-solving social work interventions fulfils an important function by identifying how change occurs within individuals or families, and proposes practical advice to service users, it also has limited breadth and range of scope for social workers in understanding the complexity of social context (see Law and Moser, 2011). By failing to question the ideological nature of subjectivity of service users, for instance, problem-solving models of social work are unable to evaluate the extent to which interventions (for example, crisis or task-centred) may actually help reproduce the social structures that cause the individual or family problems in the first place. Such instrumental approaches to subjectivity are predicated on normative assumptions that are often left unexplored. These tend to be: social work is a moral and necessary good in itself; individual or family problems represent a 'breakdown' in normal subjective relations; there is a direct causal relation between norma-tive subjectivity and the maintenance of social order.

We have seen how mainstream social work not only defines the self as primarily rational and emotional; it also defines the self as autonomous and profoundly alone. However, recent European social theory tends to approach the subject not as essentially separate from other human beings, but rather as inextricably intertwined with these beings. It tends to speak not of subjectivity, with its overtones of independent, autonomous action, but rather of inter-subjectivity, which implies that being with others is a necessary condition to any action whatsoever. If the self is profoundly inter-subjective, if the identity and continued existence of any particular individ-ual depends upon the presence and actions of others, then to highlight autonomy as the hallmark of social work ethics is deeply misguided. Autonomy must be contextualised within a network of relationships and understood as emanating from social discourses, rather than as existing as an innate characteristic of the human being. Here, the self remains always marked by the other, always entwined by the other, always enmeshed with the other, so much so that to understand it as outside of social interactions is to misunderstand it completely. This notion of being enmeshed with other actors and things leads us to now focus on discrimination in relation to what are called 'material subjectivities' in the social sciences.

Material Subjectivities and Discrimination

In sociology, there is a new way of conceiving of subjects and subjectivity that is currently very fashionable. The new breed of thinking about subjec-tivities is based on a foregrounding of materiality or material culture. In this section, I will argue that people's subjectivity is not determined by an inte-rior set of cognitive processes or discursive representations but is derived from the coupling of substantial flows and sensory awareness in the world of material objects. The essential relation is not between substance (subject) and attributes (self), but between materials and forces. Simply put, from this perspective subjectivity is defined as that which makes a difference. It can include both human and non-human agents. If this is right, it may have a dramatic effect on how social work practice is undertaken in relation to discrimination.

To get a sense of the radical difference between an approach that focuses on materiality and one which places human subjectivity as the centre of all proceedings, let's look at how John Law and Annemarie Mol put it, 'entities ... enact each other. In this way of thinking agency becomes ubiquitous, endlessly extended through webs of materialised relations' (2008, p. 59). What matters, then, is not what these entities are, but what they do, and reciprocally, what is done to them. In the 'Cyborg Manifesto', Donna Haraway playfully declared that 'Our machines are disturbingly lively, and we ourselves frighteningly inert' (1991, p. 152). Her intention was to provoke thinkers who continued to treat the human subject as essential to think again. For Haraway, the emphasis is on matter and processes of materialisation. Attention is drawn to the way human beings are influenced by matter and how our everyday lives are surrounded by and immersed in material practices. This new paradigm privileges material objects and things over subjects and subjectivity. The life of things is allowed back into the analysis of culture and history. Most radical of all, materiality tries to unpick our constitutive relationalities with the machinic but also more than the machinic – with the non-living and the non-human. So, discussions are likely to occur about the agency of guns, land mines and cock-fights, as opposed to those who fire, plant or bet on them, in order to endorse the centrality of object-oriented agency (Geertz, 1973; Gell, 1998). From this vantage point, writers like Haraway (2003) have argued that social relationships crucially include non-humans, such as dogs or cats, or what she calls 'companion species', as well as humans as socially active partners. To flag up a few mundane examples, family therapy is renowned for thinking across the human–non-human divide. I recall when working as a trainee family therapist in a child psychiatric setting how 'systemic work' would often involve inviting the family to bring their companion dog along during the clinical assessment phase (see Walsh, 2009). Important insights were often gleaned about how the position of the dog was illustrative of family functions and roles. Similarly, it is evident that obsessive-compulsive disorders are primarily about relationships with things and between things – a towel and towelling rail or cupboard space, a soap bar and the washbasin.

With these examples, 'the social' is thus displaced from its exclusive location in human doings and subjective goings on. It is the networked relations between humans and non-humans that come to take centre stage. Incidentally, if you don't believe this ask the shepherds from the Borders region of Scotland, whose animal husbandry could easily be a leitmotif for attachment theory (Gray, 2011). Bruno Latour, Michel Callon and actor network theory (ANT) are at the forefront of this radical new approach to subjectivity. ANT researchers regard network relations as prior to and constitutive of human subjectivity. In other words, human subjects are the effect of their variable positions in a network of relations. If subjectivity emerges from associations with heterogeneity of other actors, one form of impact of non-humans tends to be on the human body (Michael, 1996). Human subjectivity is variously constituted by non-humans in ways which accord with the capacities of the human body. Here we can see in sharp relief how, for example, race and gender may come into play, with issues such as dress, diet and biological reproduction as well as with religious institutions like mosques, monuments and prayer books. When thinking about discrimination, this helps us to focus on the particularities of material culture rather than some 'discursive Other' which is somehow distilled in micro-situations. As Michael suggests, it allows us to examine concrete points where artefacts are calculated, transformed and reproduced as part of a discriminatory regime. Examining the way the body is delimited in its capacities, for example, would give social work an entirely different perspective on domestic violence, old age and disability. How does social work assume or problematise bodily capacities and their associated technological artefacts to allow this or that condition to occur? In what way are material hybrids (for example, the clothed body) reproduced in practising social work? With such a material perspective, intervention would be best conceptualised as a 'practice engagement', focusing on relational contexts of people's embodied engagement with their lived-in environments. From this materiality perspective, Ingold (2000) explains that when people from different backgrounds orient themselves in different ways, this is not because they are interpreting the same sensory experience in terms of alternative cultural models or cognitive processes, but because 'their senses are differently attuned to the environment' (2000, p. 162). Ultimately, the dwelling place of which Ingold speaks is neither an individual, nor even a collective 'project', but rather a shared experience where seeing and being seen, speaking and being heard come together. It is the bodily experience that marks our hold on the world. Translating this viewpoint into social work would mean that the category of subjectivity is not concerned with the individual human, but should be extended to some configuration of relations between humans and non-humans. Multicultural and multilingual composition is framed as a series of material practices of cohabitation with otherness in a narrow space that is configured by enmeshed objects (computers, buildings, vehicles, etc.) and people. So the social worker will be concerned with network building activities, constraints and resources entailed in technologies and the way people are embodied in institutions (Barry, 2001).

Implications for Social Work Practice

The materiality perspective described above allows social workers to ask what 'subjectivity' is performed when we talk about a discriminated 'subjectivity' or a 'subjected body'. How do social workers calibrate subjectivity when thinking about discrimination and oppression as a network of embodied material relations?

While social workers will interpret information and take decisions on the basis of heterogeneous factors that are not necessarily well defined, I think it helpful if we adopt in social work the notion of a 'calculating subject', albeit in a materialist way. Callon and Muniesa define calculation as starting 'by establishing distinctions between things or states of the world, and by imagining and estimating courses of action associated with things or with those states as well as their consequences' (2003, p. 5). From this definitional point of view the distinction between judgement and calculation is avoided (Callon et al., 2002). Focusing on the economy of qualities allows us to describe the relationship between social workers and clients as a performativity – a calculable performance. Aggregation, sorting and assessment methods are constantly at work in social work (Bowker and Star, 1999). A new way of conceiving of the relations of discrimination running through and structuring social work thus emerges, by considering that they are inscribed in relations of calculation. Calculations of wage, mobility, position, supply and demand for services and, at an individual level, the potential for change. The very shift from the term client to service user in social work not only refers to an evaluation of traded goods, but the way such goods are calculatingly allocated in a discriminatory way. Discrimination is a material device for calculating values on the basis of several interlocking social dimensions (for example, class, gender, race, age, sexuality and ability). We should take as our point of departure the transactions that occur in discriminatory relations, that is, not the macrostructure of say a racial discourse but its 'microstructure', a particularly useful concept borrowed from economics – the slave trade in women, children and ethnic groups being a particularly poignant and horrific example of such calculating markets. Moreover, such a perspective on discrimination allows us to ask which 'subjects' are exempt (or prevented, depending on the point of view) from calculation.

To give a feel for the implications of the materiality perspective on discrimination for social work practice, a 'politics of the subject' is proposed that concentrates on the materiality of issues. That is how the materiality of issues, such as zero hours contracts or confinement of asylum seekers, function to (re)produce certain forms of relations and, in this case, relations of social and economic discrimination. This is a form of realism which asserts that real things exist – these things are objects, not just amorphous 'matter', objects of all shapes from nuclear waste and poverty to birds' nests (Morton, 2011). Such an approach to politics is not about discourse, the mode of analysis that has preoccupied postmodern social work for a decade or more. Some might object that things like roads, houses and power plants are cultural in character. This is true. However, they are not discourses. Rather, they are avenues of connectability around which discourses and subjectivity come to be woven, but without being reducible to these discourses. People recently mobilised in Britain when government minister Iain Duncan Smith carelessly claimed he could live on the standard weekly welfare benefit of £53 and defended his 'bedroom tax'. They did not march through the streets. Rather, groups like Disabled People Against Cuts and UK Uncut protested outside his £2 million Tudor mansion in Buckinghamshire and served him an eviction notice in protest at the bedroom tax. In this instance, issue-based politics – the issue being class power, inequalities of property ownership and wealth – focused exclusively on the minister's house and garden. The protest group brandished banners, lit fires, danced to reggae, frolicked on Duncan Smith's lawn and enjoyed walks around the extensive grounds of his mansion. This is an object-oriented protest against economic discrimination, which attenuates the materiality of the subject, and does so in a rather creative way at that. Social work can learn much from the new materiality of practice.

9

Critical Perspectives on Intersectionality

Sarah Carr

Introduction

> Social workers ... they can get the physical disability side but they can't get the mental health side. Or they can get the mental health side but not the physical disability, so when you've got both AND you're gay as well ... it's almost too much for them to take in at any one time... (Alison Gray, quoted in Social Care TV, Social Care Institute for Excellence, 2008)

This chapter explores some of the implications of intersectionality theory for anti-oppressive practice in the English social work and social care system. Selected key theories on intersectionality, which build on Foucault's ideas about power and discourse, are introduced and used to critique some of the more procedural approaches to anti-discriminatory practice that appear to have become absorbed into local authority managerialist bureaucratic processes. The critique also draws on Finkelstein's 'administrative model of disability' (Finkelstein, 1991) and forms an argument about the historical tendency of social care services to practice a form of 'administrative reductionism' in their processes. Some of the challenges arising from such administrative approaches for achieving person-centred support and anti-oppressive practice which promote equality and diversity are examined. A particular theory of intersectionality put forward by Patricia Hill Collins (Collins, 2000) is used to identify and critique the inter-related domains of power in the social care system and the implications for oppression within that social structure and discipline. The barriers posed by the technical categorisation of people in the social care system are explored through a brief examination of viewpoints on the impact and persistence of managerialism in social work and social care. Finally, some of the challenges posed by lesbian, gay, bisexual and transgender (LGBT) people who use social care and support are examined, and the contributions of biographical approaches are explored as ways to overcome some of the reductionist effects of manageri-alism. The arguments here are informed by a service user standpoint (Tew et al., 2006) because I have had personal experience of the welfare and mental health system, and the associated effects its 'governing' discourses had on my subjectivity. This provides an additional dimension to the critique, because it is also informed by knowledge gained from lived experience (Beresford 2003), which gives particular insight into the operation of the disciplinary domain.

The context for the critique presented in this chapter is that of a supposed transition between proceduralisation and personalisation as approaches to 'doing' social care and social work. Introduced in England in 2008, the personalisation of health and social care policy reforms are aimed at increas-ing choice and control for people using care and support services through self-directed support, direct payments and personal budgets (HM Government, 2007; Needham, 2011; Carr, 2012), with the recognition that people using care and support as citizens are part of communities which require capacity building (Think Local Act Personal, 2011). However, the policy is not without its critics. Principal concerns about implementation have focused on the unintended consequences of an overinvestment in administrative procedures to address choice and control through personal budget procedures, at the expense of developing local social care markets; tightened assessment, rationing and allocation techniques; and the progress of genuine service user empowerment and control (particularly as direct payments originated with the service user movement) (Fox, 2012; Beresford, 2009). This gradual and as yet largely conceptual transition has significant potential implications for the way anti-oppressive practice has and could develop in the future. In a sense, this chapter will explore the meanings and outcomes for what could be understood as an intersectional stage in social care and social work theory and practice.

Administration and Intersectionality

Before the concept of intersectionality is explored, it is useful to briefly exam-ine the critical potential of the 'administrative model of disability' in social work and social care, as articulated by the disability activist and academic, Vic Finkelstein (1991; 1993). It is important to understand the service users' perspective, particularly as they are inevitably the people who are within the administrative system, being processed and categorised. My own experience of administration in the mental health and welfare system has been that of multiple assessment and categorisation: I have been categorised because of my sexual orientation, my psychiatric diagnosis and treatment, my behaviour and functioning, my disability and my social and financial circumstances (see, for example, Carr, 2011a). Using the 'social model of disability' (Union of the Physically Impaired Against Segregation, 1975), Finkelstein criticises social care services for being medicalised and bureaucratised in their approach, citing the 'cure or care' administrative model, which for disabled people using social care means either rehabilitation or personal care (Finkelstein, 1993). Instead of disabled people having choice and control over their preferred support and occupation (the aim of independent living and the goal of personalisation), he argues that non-disabled practitioners are administering un-negotiated, professionally-determined solutions to them: 'what is important is not *which* profession is dominant but that disabled people are marginalised in their own affairs as *others* administer to their needs on their behalf because, one way or another, disabled people are regarded as incapable of doing this comprehensively for themselves' (Finkelstein, 1996, p. 9). Finkelstein indicates that there are inherent problems with categorisation and reductionist service delivery:

> In my view the administrative model of service provision ... facilitates for disabled people constructed on the foundation of the administrative model [which] assumes services can be delivered in the separate but tightly linked, 'cure or care' areas of intervention. (Finkelstein, 1991, p. 27)

Grounded in lived experience, Finkelstein's analysis of the social care administrative system, therefore, poses a potential problem for the practical realisation of some of the theoretical ideals of anti-oppressive practice, independent living and the personalisation policy agenda. In his analysis, the disabled person's capacity and behaviour is limited and predetermined by the professional working within an oppressive system, as is their care, support and, ultimately, life.

Intersectionality has been described as:

> the interaction of dimensions of inequality – such as gender, class, race or sexuality ... instead of merely summarizing the effects of one, two or three oppressive categories, adherents to the concept of intersectionality stress the interwoven nature of these categories and how they can mutually strengthen or weaken each other. (Winker and Degele, 2011, p. 51)

Disability is also counted in these 'dimensions of inequality'. Elsewhere it is argued that intersectionality

> refutes the compartmentalization and hierarchisation of the great axes of social differentiation ... the intersectional approach goes far beyond the simple recogni-

tion of multiplicity of systems of oppression functioning out of these categories and postulates their interplay in the production and reproduction of social inequality. (Bilge, 2010, p. 58)

Here, I will use a specific theory of intersectionality to illuminate how inequality and oppression can be produced and reproduced in the social work and social care system.

The term 'intersectionality' was first used by the black feminist scholar Kimberlé Crenshaw when she 'used the metaphor of intersecting roads to describe and explain the ways in which racial and gender discrimination compound each other … and "crashes" occur at the intersections' (Dhamoon, 2011, p. 231). Much subsequent discussion among sociologists, feminists and critical and political theorists has focused on: the extent to which intersectionality discourse is political or postmodernist (Yuval-Davis, 2006); the role of identity, categorisation, structural and social division; how it can be used as an analytical tool for sociopolitical change (Verloo, 2006; Bilge, 2010; Dhamoon, 2011); and how it 'has become a primary analytic tool for theorizing identity and oppression' in global politics and public policy (Hankivsky and Cormier, 2011). The discourse around intersectionality can be complex and highly theoretical, and there is little room to undertake a detailed exploration in this chapter. However, of particular relevance to the discussion here is the foundational work of the African-American feminist theorist Patricia Hill Collins, whose perspective is grounded in lived experience and whose theories have political and practical ends. Coming from the intellectual activist tradition, Collins builds on Foucault's theory that the disciplinary domain manages oppression to create a dynamic theory of intersectionality.

Collins refocuses 'attention on the socio-structural analysis of inequality, and specifically on the organisational and institutional manifestations of power dissymetries' (Bilge, 2010, p. 61). Such a perspective is ideal for critically analysing the tendency of the system within which social work and social care operates to classify and depersonalise, because it is dominated by a proceduralist culture. The 'power dissymetries' between the disabled person and the professional in Finkelstein's administrative model of disability are an example of this. As an African-American woman, when thinking about the complexities of intersectionality, Collins' concern is with structural and social inequalities and she is very clear about the influence of 'lived reality' on her thinking. Her work in problematising essentialism and categorisation and 'reconceptualising the social relations of domination and resistance' (Collins, 2000, p. 273) has led her to conclude that: 'oppression and resistance remain intricately linked such that the shape of one influences that of the other. At the same time, this relationship is far more complex than a simple model of permanent oppressors and perpetual victims' (Collins, 2000, p. 274). Such a perspective echoes that of Finkelstein as he challenges the view that disabled people can do nothing for themselves and are 'perpetual victims' (or as he puts it, 'socially dead') in a binary administrative model with fixed role identities (Finkelstein, 1991). From the standpoint of lived experience, both argue it is more complex than that. Similar to Foucault, central to Collins' theory is the framework of four inter-related domains of power: structural, disciplinary, hegemonic and interpersonal, which operate together as a 'matrix of domination'. So, for Collins, 'viewing domination itself as encompassing intersecting oppressions of race, class, gender, sexuality and nation point to the significance of domination' (Collins, 2000, p. 275).

Of the four domains of power mentioned by Collins, oppression and intersectionality in the social work and social care system can best be anal-ysed by using her theories about the structural and disciplinary domains. For example, when considering managerialism in social work and social care, Harlow concludes that, 'technicist practice is also encouraged when social workers are required to follow detailed procedural guidelines and to adhere to checklists when carrying out assessments' (Harlow, 2003, p. 35). This can be understood through Collins' argument that 'the structural domain organ-ises the oppression, while the disciplinary domain manages it ... through its reliance on rules, the disciplinary domain manages oppression' (Collins, 2000, p. 276). By examining the way in which structures and disciplines such as bureaucracy work and are socially organised, Collins maintains that oppressive structures rely on 'multiple forms of segregation' (Collins, 2000, p. 277), echoing Harlow's (2003) observations about 'technicist' managerial social work practice resulting in the objectification, fragmentation and clas-sification of the person. Most crucial to the discussion here is Collins' critique of the structural and disciplinary domains within which it can be argued social care and social work are a part:

> As a way of ruling that relies on bureaucratic hierarchies and techniques of surveil-lance, the disciplinary domain manages power relations ... the style of organisa-tion becomes highly efficient in both reproducing intersecting oppressions and in masking their effects ... bureaucracy will function in particular ways regardless of the policy being implemented. (Collins, 2000, pp. 280–281)

Here, Collins offers an alternative way of thinking (or an 'alternative inter-pretive perspective') to that which has been posited on traditional, dualistic arguments: 'intersectionality ... constitutes an alternative paradigm to the antagonism between positivism and postmodernism which was part of the dichotomies structuring Western epistemology' (Bilge, 2010, p. 61). Like Foucault, she points to the role of social structures in creating bureaucracy which results in the type of categorisation, administrative reductionism and binary thinking, as experienced and analysed for disability by Finkelstein. In her exploration of anti-oppression, postmodernism and intersectionality in social work, Brown argues that 'anti-oppression discourse must contend with both the politics of diversity and the problems of essentialism' (Brown, 2012, p. 52). For Collins, the answer is to focus on 'intersecting oppressions', and Brown notes that social workers need to be aware that they too are caught up in Collins' 'matrix of oppression'; her illustration of the power relations in social work affirms the 'administrative model of disability':

> Normalising or regulating techniques of power infuse daily cultural practices and as they escape substantial contention, they reinforce socially constructed reality ... Rethinking power includes challenging the ways that both social workers and clients keep oppressive stories alive either through not unpacking experience and/or through the social workers attempt to be neutral ... the experiences of service users are often appropriated by social workers who 'retain the power to determine what is anti-oppression' [Wilson and Beresford, 2000, p. 564]. (Brown, 2012, p. 50)

In her paper on intersectionality and global feminist politics, Yuval-Davis further discusses the complexities and challenges of 'essentialist' strategies which create typologies and administrative lists for the 'managerial-technicist' social work practice as described by Harlow (Harlow, 2003). This type of administrative system is dependent on social construction, divisions and homogenising, reductionist or restrictive classification:

> [it] tends to treat all who belong to a particular social category as sharing equally the particular natural attributes (positive or negative) to it. Categorical attributes are often used for the construction of inclusionary/exclusionary boundaries that differentiate between the self and other, determining what is 'normal' and what is not, who is entitled to certain resources and who is not. In this way the interlinking grids of differential positionings in terms of class, race and ethnicity, gender and sexuality, ability, stage in life cycle and other social divisions, tend to create, in specific historical situations, hierarchies of differential access to a variety of resources. (Yuval-Davis, 2006, p. 199)

For anti-oppressive practice in social work, this view of the influence of 'specific historical situations' as well as personal identity produces a new paradigm of discrimination that poses a challenge to the proceduralised form it is taking as part of managerialism in social work and social care (Dominelli, 1996). As Verloo argues in the context of discussing multiple inequalities and intersectionality: 'Inequalities are dynamic problems that can be located in various distinct structures, that are experienced differently, and that can be (re)produced in different ways' (Verloo, 2006, p. 224). In their report on 'super-diversity', Fanshawe and Sriskandarajah (2010) argue that the current form of identity politics in the UK public sector has limited usefulness because the wider structural and disciplinary domains used to administer equality initiatives (as described by Collins) create oppressive, homogenising classification and bureaucratic systems. They contest that among the diverse people they interviewed there was a 'shared frustration of how the "tick box" approach to categorising people is unwieldy, because it is too generalised, and often meaningless. It has no finger on the pulse of how life is actually lived, whether it is about sexuality, ethnicity or any other form of capturing diversity' (Fanshawe and Sriskandarajah, 2010, p. 6). The practical question asked by Fanshawe and Sriskandarajah is particularly relevant here:

> Discrimination might be an everyday event, but it is no longer an all-day event ... [how can we] now go forward with an approach that more closely matches the experience of people's day-to-day lives and achievements and responds to their more complex feelings of identity as well as dealing with their experience of prejudice? (Fanshawe and Sriskandarajah, 2010, p. 7)

One way to address this situation could be to build on the intersectionality theories and lived experience critiques of Collins and others, with a particular focus on individual and community experiences and narratives, as Brown suggests when she notes the importance of understanding 'oppressive stories'. For new (or renewed) types of social work and social care practice in person-centred care planning and support, under the policy direction of personalisation and self direction, this means engaging with people where they are and with the experiences, complexities, stories and solutions they bring.

Managerialism and Anti-Oppressive Practice

As suggested in the previous section, specific systemic barriers exist within mainstream social care which can make it very difficult to incorporate biographical approaches into the type of anti-oppressive practice and flexible person-centred care which accounts for diversity and difference. These barriers will now be explored in more detail through examination of some of the critical viewpoints. Over the past forty years, managerialism and associated levels of bureaucracy in social care and health have increased (Kirkpatrick, 2006). 'New public management' was formalised in policy with the introduction of the NHS and Community Care Act in 1990:

> The expectation was that Social Services Departments (SSDs) would be transformed into 'managed services', focused on meeting needs, targeting resources and

> effectively regulating the practice of frontline professionals ... considerable emphasis was placed on investing in systems for strategic planning, financial control and management of contracts. (Kirkpatrick, 2006, p. 16)

Such systems introduced, and continue to rely on, particular types of administration and processing, which can mean that the focus is not on the individual service user (except as an object for administration) but on the processes: 'the vast majority of SSDs, it would appear, remain operational-led rather than needs driven in focus' (Kirkpatrick, 2006, p. 17). In an overview of research on the operation of managerialist approaches in SSD processes, Kirkpatrick points to findings which describe the nature of 'proceduralisation' and increasing bureaucracy: 'a marked increase in the volume of rules, procedures and tick box pro forma used to standardise decisions about care planning and needs assessment' (Kirkpatrick, 2006, p. 18). Harlow (2003) also provides a helpful critical overview of the effects of managerialism, or what she calls the 'managerial-technicist approach', on social care and social work practice. Such an approach means that a 'uniform quality, standards of service or benchmarks are set centrally and against these standards the performance of social work and social care organisations is qualitatively measured' (Harlow, 2003, p. 32). In order to operate within such a system, 'recipients of care became customers and social workers practicing with adults were re-designated as care managers' (p. 30) or 'bureau-professionals' (p. 34). Such technicism and uniformity (which has arguably become confused with equality) is challenged by the differentiation and diversity of individual service users and local communities:

> Equity, as those whom the issue affects will tell you, is not about achieving uniformity, but about ensuring equality while recognising local difference and personal diversity. Everyone having an equal opportunity for choice and control over their care and support and an equal opportunity for independent living is not the same as everyone having access to uniform care and support. (Carr, 2011b, p. 45)

It is argued that by its nature technicism cannot accommodate complexity and 'human interdependency' in social care and social work practice: 'a managerial-technicist practice that fails to place due emphasis on the non-rational component of the human condition and the process of caring' (Harlow, 2003, p. 29). Harlow concludes that 'the managerial context that emphasises rationality, fragmentation, technicism, and positivistic evaluation of performance, denies the emotional content of practice and the significance of the relationship' (p. 38). It appears that in such a rigid, technical administrative system, anti-oppressive practice is at risk of excluding human complexity because it is subsumed as another procedure requiring the categorisation of diversity.

Coming from what Harlow calls the 'socialist-collectivist approach', Dominelli also argues that managerialism is critically damaging to anti-oppressive practice and for the 'client–worker relationship'. She argues that 'the Seebohm reorganisation of previously specialised services led to ... the creation of large impersonal bureaucratic empires in the personal social services' (Dominelli, 1996, p. 155). Like Harlow, Dominelli argues that managerialist processes do not 'engage with the person as a real individual human being, but as a category of "client"', which she believes is 'incompatible with anti-oppressive social work' (p. 159) that should be critical of the system itself and the distress it can cause service users through marginalisation and oppression. Elsewhere, she contends that in her experience 'students and practitioners have consistently commented upon the difficulty of practicing equality and feeling disempowered by new managerialism that promotes techno-bureaucratic professionalism' (Dominelli, 2010, p. 165). Anti-oppressive practice, with its 'person-centred philosophy', comes into conflict with managerialism as social workers and social care practitioners are 'undermined by the adoption of proceduralism over holism that engages service users' realities, processes, inputs and outcomes' (p. 166). This situation poses a challenge not only for anti-oppressive practice but for the policy project of personalisation and the ambition to improve attitudes and approaches to equality and diversity in the public services, particularly through understanding some of the workings of intersectionality on individuals and their personal biographies.

Intersectionality, Sexual Orientation and Biography

A strong argument is emerging that inequalities cannot necessarily be solely situated with the individual but are a product of oppressive institutions which rely on managerialism and bureaucracy for power. Verloo contests that inequalities 'are reproduced through identities, behaviours, interactions, norms and symbols, organisations and institutions, including states and state-like institutions' (Verloo, 2006, p. 224). The given identity within the process of categorisation will probably not be representative of the individual as a whole person, their life history and relationships. This is a great challenge for social care and social work, as Harlow argues:

> It is suggested that new managerialism has given rise to a managerial-technicist approach to social work practice that now dominates earlier forms. The consequent lack of attention to the inner world of service users and the social work relationship is now a cause for concern. (Harlow, 2003, p. 29)

Can social care and social work achieve anti-oppressive practice where practitioners resist determining what oppression is for particular individual service users, as they can be conceived as working within Collins' 'matrix of domination'? As an example of how this could be addressed, commentators and practice-oriented academics are beginning to think about the role of biographical work with LGBT people for overcoming some of the problems associated with managerialism, where 'generalities may replace "complexities" in the assessment of, and intervention in, LGB[T] people's lives' (Cronin et al., 2011, p. 425).

One particular group emerging as experiencing oppression and multiple inequalities within the social care and mental health systems are LGBT people (or people who have same-sex relationships) who are from black and minority ethnic (BME) backgrounds. For example, building on the work of Fish (2008) and Fanshawe and Sriskandarajah (2010), I have argued that for individual LGBT people from BME communities, and/or those with refugee status or seeking asylum, access to mental health and social care support can be compromised by categorisations which fragment the individual's whole identity:

> people with multiple identities, including LGB[T] people from different ethnic and cultural backgrounds, experience inequalities and do not often have the opportunity to express their identity and consequent needs to mental health services because of exclusionary categorisations, structures and assumptions. (Carr, 2010, p. 21)

I suggest that the person-centred approaches to care and support being implemented as part of personalisation reforms in health and social care could offer a way of addressing these difficulties because they imply 'tailoring rather than targeting' and relationship-based working methods (Carr, 2010, p. 21). Fish specifically discusses how intersection theory can be used to understand and respond to the multiple inequalities that can be experienced BME LGBT people. She argues that the type of thinking developed by African-American feminists like Crenshaw (1993) and Collins 'offers possibilities for understanding multiple inequalities without abandoning the politics of social movements' (Fish, 2008, p. 1). She is also very critical of the tendency of the social work and social care system to categorise people, and points out the effect this can have on BME and other LGBT people:

> Although there has been some success in identifying LGBT people as a social category, the focus on the inter group differences (that is between LGBT people and their heterosexual counterparts), has occluded intra group differences (that is differences within the LGBT as an inequality category, for example, in terms of race, disability, age). (Fish, 2008, p. 3)

While administrative categorisation in health and social care is now expected to recognise sexual orientation (although this is very recent and inconsistently applied), the procedural system often operating in local authority equalities initiatives often requires LGBT people to be a uniform group, and cannot accommodate a diverse group of individuals who are from different ethnic and cultural backgrounds, of differing ages and disabilities (McNulty et al., 2010). Like others, Fish posits that a solution could lie in focusing on people's everyday lives:

> The continuing project ... is to build inclusive categories which acknowledge the multiplicity of sexual and gender identities. Intersectional approaches facilitate consideration of the ways that 'race', class and gender are experienced simultaneously in people's lives. (Fish, 2008, p. 8)

Biographical approaches are being explored as a way of resisting or overcoming the limitations of artificial and reductive categorisations in social care and social work procedures. In particular, practice-focused academics have developed thinking about the interaction of diversity, categorisation, oppression and individual biography for LGBT people. Their thinking reflects Collins' recognition that 'each individual biography is rooted in several overlapping cultural contexts – for example groups defined by race, social class, age, gender, religion and sexual orientation' (Collins, 2000, p. 286). Cronin and colleagues have strongly advocated incorporating biographical methods into social work and social care practice for older LGBT people (Cronin et al., 2011). They are critical of the bureaucratic approach to equality and diversity which homogenises minority groups:

> a tendency to uncritically conflate sexual minority identities in convenient groupings may have little currency for people's lived experience. When we refer to LGB[T] people as one seemingly homogenous group, we risk missing important differences that should inform practice and the formation of policy. (Cronin et al., 2011, p. 425)

Cronin and her colleagues go on to argue that 'the biographies of older LGB[T] people do not reflect one idea or image of what it is to be lesbian, gay or bisexual. Rather they suggest a multiplicity of ways of living, reflecting individual circumstances and life experiences' (Cronin et al., 2011, p. 423).

Focusing on how the adoption and fostering system works, Hicks criticises anti-discriminatory practice in social work, which assumes 'a set of sexual types or identities with specific social welfare needs ... So we might say that social work processes produce an observable set of sexual types' (Hicks, 2008b, pp. 66–67). While the recognition of different sexual orientations on this level is not necessarily a bad thing, Hicks argues that such an essentialist approach is limiting and ultimately fails to confront broader systemic problems with 'heterosexism' in social work and social care practice. Drawing on his own teaching practice for social workers involved in adoption and fostering work, Hicks argues that a better way is to 'move away from a "checklist" approach – "what are the assessment questions to ask about sexuality?" or "what should we ask lesbians and gay men?" – towards helping social workers to think through the complexities of sexualities in such assessments' (Hicks, 2008b, p. 75).

In a similar vein, the sociologist Brian Heaphy argues that older LGBT people's lives should be recognised as 'storied and complex' (Heaphy, 2009, p. 119) when thinking about choice and informal care and support networks. Again, a critique of inflexible categorisation is apparent in Heaphy's viewpoint:

> only a partial understanding of older people's relational lives is gained via a narrow focus on family supports and traditional families. This is especially the case with respect to older lesbian and gay men's relationships because, as a number of studies indicate, friendships and friendship families are often an important resource in this context. (Heaphy, 2009, p. 120)

Further, Heaphy has an important message for the types of anti-oppressive practice in social care which tend towards homogenisation and bureaucratisation (as described by Dominelli, 1996; 2010):

> However, while we may have good cause to celebrate the strong stories about lesbian and gay life that it is now possible to tell, it is also important to be attuned to those weaker stories that may be harder to hear. (Heaphy, 2009, p. 135)

Those 'weaker' stories are often ones from people whose lives and identities are at 'intersections' but who are often most in need of self-determined, anti-oppressive and person-centred support. One area of concern which exemplifies this are older LGBT people from different backgrounds who are living with dementia. As Hicks asserts, without a classificatory and generalising approach to understanding people in social work and social care, 'sexuality within a life story or profile, then, becomes a complex area to assess' (Hicks, 2008b, p. 75). However, work with older LGBT people living with dementia in Northern Ireland suggests that without this approach, which recognises personal complexity and biography, they could experience significant inequality and poorer care and support: 'In the absence of such elements of an individual's identity being ... identified, it is clear that those important aspects of identity cannot meaningfully feature as part of the care planning process' (The Rainbow Project/Age NI, 2011, p. 17). Cocker and Brown

(2010) point out the importance of 'reflexive observation' for social workers undertaking assessments for adoption and fostering. They too argue for storytelling, but as part of generic assessment which avoids homogenisation and categorisation and 'takes account of differences and possible impacts of marginalisation and the historical impacts of discrimination' (Cocker and Brown, 2010, p. 25). So, the challenge is how to identify and respond to a person's identity/ies, experiences and stories without defaulting to checklists and categories.

Key Ideas for Practice

1. This critique is from the perspective of someone with lived experience of being processed through the mental health and social welfare system. It is designed to give an insider's view of how controlling discourses in bureaucratic systems can affect the subjectivity of the service user and influence understandings of their identity, life and support needs.

2. The critique is also intended to raise awareness of how managerialism and bureaucracy in mental health and social care fails to accommodate 'intersectionality', or the facets of individual identity and the complexity of their life experience. Practitioners are, therefore, asked if it would be more appropriate to start with the person, their situation, relationships and history when assessing diversity and difference, rather than relying on a bureaucratic approach which can be reductionist and homogenising. The challenge of 'personalisation' means addressing the complexity of diversity from a person-centred standpoint. Using biographical approaches is one way this could be achieved for LGBT people.

3. Patricia Hill Collins offers practitioners a helpful framework for examining and reflecting on anti-oppressive practice in the light of service user experience. Collins builds on Foucault's theory that the disciplinary domain manages oppression and examines how this 'hides the effects of racism and sexism under the canopy of efficiency, rationality and equal treatment' (Sage Publications [no date] p. 8). Practice could be improved if practitioners had the opportunity to reflect on their positioning within this 'disciplinary domain' and examine their practice in order to reduce the negative impacts of bureaucratic oppression and 'power dissymmetries' on people who identify as LGBT or who have same-sex relationships.

Conclusion

The literature examined here leads to the conclusion that anti-oppressive practice which responds to the challenge of intersectionality and supports self-determination cannot be achieved using the managerialist administrative mechanisms that still persist in social work and social care services. It can be argued that the outcome of administrative reductionism is the bureaucratically fragmented person; and in a society that is being recognised as 'super-diverse', this is becoming unworkable and potentially meaningless for social work and social care practice. Collins' theory of intersectionality, which is grounded in her lived experience, can be used as a framework for reflecting on anti-oppressive practice that has been subsumed into a wider oppressive system, characterised by the institutional 'power dissymetries' described by both Collins and Finkelstein. Collins' analysis of inequality has led her to identify structural and disciplinary domains of power that rely on rules and dichotomies resulting in 'multiple forms of segregation' of the type reproduced in the homogenising, classificatory approaches to equality and anti-discrimination work.

To return to the words of Bilge, as quoted earlier, 'the intersectional approach goes beyond the simple recognition of multiplicity of systems of oppression functioning out of ... categories and postulates their interplay in the production and reproduction of social inequality' (Bilge, 2010, p. 58). The risk of reproducing social inequality in social work and social care practice can be demonstrated for LGBT people, particularly those who are older and living with dementia. Practice teachers and practice-oriented social work academics are exploring what intersectionality means for anti-oppressive and person-centred practice with LGBT people from all backgrounds and of all ages. One solution suggested to address the oppression of classification is to gain an understanding of intersectionality and discrimination not through bureaucracy but through personal biography. Some of the stories will be about experiencing discrimination and negotiating identity – living at intersections within oppressive systems: 'Individual biographies are situated within all domains of power and reflect their interconnections and contradictions' (Collins, 2000, p. 287).

10
Racism, Sectarianism and Social Work

Claudia Bernard and Jim Campbell

Introduction

This chapter is the product of a number of discussions we have had about our identities and experiences of teaching anti-oppressive practice to social work students over 20 years. We share a common interest in using critical lenses to explore issues of inequalities and social justice which affect the profession but these are, understandably, framed differently given the contrast in our biographies, in terms of race, gender, religion and class. The first author is a black, British woman of Caribbean descent who has taught English social work students on the subject of anti-racist practice. The second author grew up in Northern Ireland, born into a Protestant, working class unionist family, becoming a social worker, then later social work educator (Campbell, 2013c).

Teaching on discrimination, race and racism has, to a greater or lesser extent, been present in all UK social work programmes during the last two decades, but we identify a shift away from what was originally perceived as a radical position, towards narratives that are more muted and couched in terms of diversity and cultural difference. From their early conception, anti-racist and anti-oppressive perspectives in social work teaching and practice have been challenging to social work scholars (Ahmad, 1990; Ahmed, 1994; Penketh, 2000; Dominelli, 2008; Graham and Schiele, 2010; Bhatti-Sinclair, 2011). In particular, how scholars have theorised anti-racist thinking has been influential in developing black perspectives in social work and in advancing the social justice agenda in social work (Graham, 2000; 2009).

At the core of the chapter is a discussion which enables the authors to draw upon their experiences and explore how issues of discrimination and oppression can be challenged, as understood through a shared case vignette.

In this discussion, it is argued that this more critical stance to established ideas on anti-oppressive practice is crucial if we are to understand the ways in which issues of power, race-constructed otherness and the social relations produced by sectarianism become inscribed and are played out. We use some of Foucault's ideas (Healy, 2000), particularly around the concepts of power and subjectivity, to explore how relationships are produced and reproduced through a complexity of social, economic and political factors, resulting in nuanced interplay between the self and 'other' and involving agency and structural determination. How we understand the formation of our identities is in part biographical reflection, part critical awareness of the need to consider the past and deconstruct the discourses which often reinforce division and prejudice. It is asserted that, in order to engage critically with uncomfortable truths, managed risk taking is a necessary and meaningful way to transform silence into action. The chapter ends with a number of suggestions of how this analysis can be used in other social work contexts, internationally.

In the next two sections we briefly outline aspects of our backgrounds and diverse social locations to illustrate how our subjective experiences and understanding of relationships of power shape the way we view anti-racist and anti-sectarian practice.

Race, Anti-Racism and Anti-Racist Social Work

Claudia Bernard (CB) is deeply influenced by black feminist thinking and critical race theory. A number of thinkers from a range of perspectives within black feminism have greatly influenced her intellectual development and their particular insights informed her pedagogical approach (for instance, Crenshaw, 1993; Hill Collins, 1990; hooks, 1984; 1989; King, 1988). Briefly described, the term black feminism refers to a particular approach to feminism that articulates how the intersecting effects of gender, race and class contribute to the oppression of black women (Athey, 1996). Essentially, critical race theory arises from an oppositional stance and refers to black people's unique angle of vision on self, community and society. A key tenet of critical race theory concerns social justice and transformation (Yosso, 2005). According to this approach, black people's multiple social locations produce specific understandings of their racialised, gendered and classed positions in societies where these dimensions are significant markers of experience. Critical race theory's starting point is that black people's histories are situated within the legacies of slavery, colonialism, imperialism and patterns of migration, and that these elements profoundly shape the way we experience and construct our understandings of our social world. In this sense, coming from a perspective that is working at the intersection of feminism and anti-racism, black feminist thinking gives CB a language and framework for understanding multiple and intersecting forms of oppressions. CB, therefore, has a strong commitment to making visible the issues of social justice for excluded and marginalised groups.

These ideas have had a variegated impact upon social work education and training. Keating (2000) notes the importance of black perspectives for creating a discursive space for black educators and practitioners to give voice to lived experiences in the social work arena, thus influencing theory and practice. Essentially, these scholars raise important questions about discursive power and subjugated knowledge (Graham, 2000; Keating, 2001; Williams and Parrott, 2012). In so doing, they have called attention to the deficit-oriented view of black experiences and have challenged the Eurocentric assumptions underlying social work's underpinning knowledge (Aymer, 2002; Graham, 2000; Keating, 2000; Robinson, 2009). Most importantly, scholars adopting an anti-racist stance have not only been at the forefront of advancing debates about oppression experienced by marginalised groups, but have also illuminated the reification of dominant discourses that pervade much social work theory (Graham, 2007).

However, a number of scholars have argued that in recent years anti-racist perspectives have come under continuous attack, and the discourse has shifted from race to diversity and difference (Keating, 2001; Dominelli, 2008; Graham and Schiele, 2010). Graham (2000) and Williams (1999) suggest that this has the effect of obscuring critical debates about race. The discourse of racism is now shrouded in a language of difference and culture (Solomos and Back, 2000, p. 20). Williams (1999) further notes that the main criticisms levelled at anti-racist perspectives have been that it is seen as reductionist and offers formulaic approaches, and that categories such as black and black perspectives are poorly defined.

Typically, critiques of anti-racist perspectives have pointed to the necessity for a broader conceptualisation of oppression. Indeed, a variety of scholars have argued that an over-emphasis on anti-racism is limited in addressing the complexities surrounding multiple forms of oppression based on gender, class, sexual orientation and abilities (Macey, 1995; Dominelli, 1996; Macey and Moxon, 1996; Wilson and Beresford, 2000; Fook, 2002; Mullaly, 2002; McLaughlin, 2005; Baines, 2007; Adams, Dominelli and Payne, 2009). This premise asserts that broadening the conceptualisation of anti-oppressive practice will be better able to address multiple intersecting oppressions (Baines, 2007). It has to be noted here that as the ethnic and racial makeup of the population has become more diverse in Britain, a more sophisticated analysis is required for understanding the complexities and diversity of race and ethnicity. It follows from this that conventional notions of a black–white binary of race are no longer adequate when analysing race and racism (Deliovsky and Kitossa, 2013). While some scholars insist that an anti-oppressive framework is the most appropriate one for addressing new tensions created by racial and ethnic diversity, others argue that, as racism occurs in more subtle ways, the complex articulation of race is lost in anti-oppression discourse.

Despite such important contributions, disagreements over the best method for addressing racism in social work persist. It is clear that, despite many debates about anti-oppressive practice and the growth in the knowledge base, questions about race and racism in social work continue to be emotionally charged and cause unease. Clearly there is a need to utilise pedagogical strategies that can critically engage in dialogues about racism, for it is then that we can begin to accept that racism is everyone's problem.

Sectarianism and Anti-Sectarian Social Work

Jim Campbell's (JC) understanding of sectarianism is shaped by a mix of lived experiences, growing up as an adolescent during the height of the Troubles in Northern Ireland, and then formulating ideas about how his social work practice was impacted upon in later years (Campbell and Healey, 1999). This understanding is informed by the use of critical ideas about the social and psychological construction of prejudice and consequent, discriminatory behaviours. For many people who live in the rest of the UK and elsewhere in the world, the sectarianism which characterises Northern Irish society often appears as a mystery, an age-old conundrum, the origins of which appear to be lost in a past when religion defined politics and society. In particular, an essentialist 'two tribe' narrative (a religious war between Protestants and Catholics) only serves to obscure more plausible contributory factors (Brewer, 1991).

A precursory analysis of the conflict leads, therefore, to a somewhat surprising conclusion; this form of sectarianism, as in other parts of the world, is only tentatively associated with religion. If formal religious ties are not at the heart of this conflict, how then can we explain such profound, long-lasting divisions, and what implications does this have for social work policy and practice? It is at this point that we need a more sophisticated analysis which acknowledges multi-layered subjectivities and identities. At times sectarianism appears mundane, reified and incorporated into conscious and subconscious thoughts, attitudes and behaviours (Kapur and Campbell, 2005; Houston, 2008). These innumerable intra- and interpersonal interactions inform, and are informed by, cultural and institutional formations, which confirm the binary opposites of Protestant v. Catholic, Unionist v. Nationalist, British v. Irish. As with other types of oppression, we need to analyse these lived experiences using critical ideas and avoid taking for granted discourses that are often present in popularised notions about the conflict.

Here parallels can be drawn with racism; this sectarianism was forged and fashioned by phases of colonialism, most notably during the process of the plantation of the north east of Ireland by Britain in the early modern period. The complexity of class-based relationships that emerged following the industrialisation of this part of the island served to reinforce divisions between Protestants, who tended to view themselves as British, and Catholics, as Irish (McVeigh, 1997). This, in turn, was reflected in the way that power was, and continues to be, played out in everyday life, within social institutions and by the state. These divisions were underpinned by unequal social and economic opportunities that worked to the general disadvantage of Catholics and longstanding systems of direct and indirect discrimination that, until the 1980s, were not seriously addressed by a succession of governments. In addition, the impact of political decisions made outside the jurisdiction are often missing in simplistic, populist, analyses of the conflict. British, Irish and other international governments have all, to a greater or lesser extent, been complicit in the violence, through omission or commission.

One way of understanding how experiences of sectarianism become reified and habituated can be partly explained in terms of Foucault's ideas of how discourse obscure the operation of power and identity. Thus, power is often exercised through subtle practices, for example, in the way that thoughts and actions help construct representations of 'the other'. Brewer and Higgins (1999) argue that at different stages of this history anti-Catholic discourses were used as a form of 'ethnic mobilisation' to protect the interest of Protestants, often involving the generation and implementation of stereotypes (physiological, social and cultural). Another perspective, represented in the views of McVeigh and Roulston (2007), which attends more to a critical analysis of political formation, firmly asserts a close comparison between sectarianism and racism when analysing the causes of conflict in Ireland. In their analysis of society and politics they challenge the assumption that interventions by the British State since the 1980s had, and in the future can, challenge the causes and effects of sectarianism. At the core of their argument is the assertion that the Northern Irish State is not reformable, and, to support this claim, they present a more critical notion, one which seeks to deal with the 'undertheorising' of the concept of sectarianism in this context. McVeigh and Roulston argue that the history of sectarianism in Ireland strongly resembles other colonising processes and that, as a consequence, Catholics were subject to forms of structural discrimination and the type of stereotyping that occurs in other racist contexts. The fact that religion is the 'identifier', rather than skin colour, should not, they argue, detract from this analysis. A similar point is made by Garrett (2002b) in his critique of social work policies and practice applied to Irish people living in Britain. McVeigh and Roulston conclude by describing the political processes that followed the Belfast Agreement as 'post-reformist', with a reconfiguration of embedded forms of sectarianism at different levels of politics and society. Their analysis does not end here. They challenge the popular assumption that the growth of racism towards new migrant communities somehow replaces age-old forms of sectarianism that the Belfast Agreement was designed to address. In the last two decades there is considerable evidence to suggest that, alongside these new forms of racism, the society is just as sectarianised, in terms of housing, education and social attitudes, as it was in the past.

The consequences for Northern Irish society have been profound, leading to differentiated patterns of violence and social conflict. At the peak years of violence in the 1970s, young men were much more likely to die than women, although women were often left to manage traumatic after effects and deal with the needs of families when partners died, were injured or imprisoned. It is also the case that proportionately more Catholics than Protestants were killed (Fay et al., 1999). Most of the deaths that occurred were in working-class, urban areas and in specific rural communities. This is not to say that sectarian ideas and behaviours did not exist in more affluent communities, but these are expressed and mediated through more nuanced discourses and living circumstances (Kapur and Campbell, 2005). Of course, these patterns of conflict are not fixed, occasionally class politics emerged to challenge the sectarian discourses and divisions, sometimes necessarily protected and subsumed within the trade union movement. In the past decade, the voices of new, previously hidden, communities have emerged to offer new perspectives and subjectivities that challenge conventional assumptions about life in Northern Ireland (Pinkerton and Campbell, 2002). There are growing, vibrant LGBT communities and emergent green politics. Shifting patterns of inward migration has increased the numbers of BME groups living in Northern Ireland (Northern Ireland Office, 2012) with emergent alternative cultural forms that create new opportunities for social change, but also racism and xenophobia

The complexity of this conflict, and its impact at all levels of society, creates a number of challenges for social work practice and social work education. As we write this chapter, nearly 20 years after early attempts to resolve the conflict in Northern Ireland, culminating in the signing of the Belfast Agreement (The Belfast Agreement, 1988), there are few signs that the problems of sectarianism have been resolved. During the 40 years of the current 'Troubles' nearly 4,000 people were killed and tens of thousands physically and psychologically traumatised. It remains a struggle to find ways of resolving both the legacy of these years and the on-going sectarian violence, despite attempts to create space to reflect upon the past and deal with the multitude needs of victims and survivors (Ferry et al., 2008; Office of First Deputy First Minister, 2009).

Only in the last two decades have discernable policies and practices on anti-sectarian practice emerged amongst social work communities. Early attempts to introduce anti-sectarian teaching in social work programmes were undermined by fear, resistance and problems caused by on-going violence in wider society (Smyth and Campbell, 1996; Central Council for Education and Training in Social Work, 1999). In some ways, this resistance may have parallels with attempts to incorporate anti-racist and anti-discriminatory practice across the UK, described earlier in this chapter. In the case of Northern Ireland, however, the additional constant of civil and political conflict creates an inevitable sense of fear, which is hard to underestimate. It is extremely difficult, and dangerous, to expect social work students to expose their feelings to the 'other' at a time when they may have lost loved ones during the conflict. For such reasons, the subtle mechanisms that feed sectarianism have the effect of closing down opportunities and creating safe spaces for the exploration of difference and competing identities. To stand still in these circumstances, however, would dissipate opportunities to deliver anti-oppressive practices that can enable social workers to challenge systems of discrimination and find ways to transform relationships of power (Danso, 2009). As the process of conflict resolution has developed in recent years, the teaching of meaningful anti-sectarian practice has become more possible, but only if commitment, resources and mindful approaches are employed in ways that acknowledge the subjective experiences of discrimination, whilst holding on to a critical awareness of the causes of sectarianism (Coulter et al., 2013). An even greater challenge involves the creation of organisational policies and systems of support and supervision which allow dialogue and innovative practices to occur in the workplace (Central Council for Education and Training in Social Work, 1999).

Applying Theory to Practice: Dialogues Across Racial Divides

In the following section we share a case vignette from Claudia Bernard's practice to illustrate how some of the ideas discussed earlier in the chapter can be applied in a real world context.

Elizabeth is a white 17-year-old Northern Irish young woman from a Protestant background who is homeless. She was first interviewed following a duty call and was in a very distressed state: she was new to London having been sent, against her wishes, by her parents to live with a relative, after disclosing that a family friend had raped her. Elizabeth had threatened to report the rape to the police, but her parents did not want her to do so because of their concerns about the implications (the alleged rapist was someone who was well known in the community). Three months later, and after she had received support, Elizabeth arrived in the social work office in a very angry state because another duty officer had written to the benefits office, which had threatened her income. She felt that her social worker had breached confidentiality by divulging her address to the benefits office without her consent. She was screaming and shouting, calling her social worker a 'black cunt', and stormed out of the office. Her social worker wrote to Elizabeth, pointing out that her behaviour was unacceptable and setting out the conditions with which she would continue to work with her. On receipt of the letter, Elizabeth immediately met with her social worker and apologised for her behaviour. This became the turning point in the working-alliance. It led to a very difficult conversation about race and identity, and Elizabeth's encounter with anti-Irish racism, and of being seen as 'other', which challenged her understanding of her British identity. How she engaged in meaning-making when rendered as 'other' became the focus of our work together.

The issue of how identity is constructed and perceived by the self and by others is crucial in the way we understand experiences of sectarianism and racism, and how we, as social workers can respond. This encounter with Elizabeth raises important questions for us as social work educators as we strive to facilitate a meaningful dialogue about race, sectarianism and social work practice. The principles of an anti-oppressive practice, which has at its core relationship building and advocacy for social justice, informs our understanding of sometimes profound social divisions between practitioners and service users, despite impediments that are often threatening and dangerous (Sakamoto and Pitner, 2005). We have to be mindful that all social work encounters are shaped by power and unequal relationships (Strega and Carriere, 2009); this was evident in the encounters between the social workers and Elizabeth in the vignette described above. hooks' (1989) argument about the importance for members of marginalised and oppressed groups to find a voice to express their feelings is pertinent in this respect.

This enabling approach, however, must be informed by the sorts of critical ideas we have discussed in this chapter. The use of a layered analysis about the nature of sectarianism in Northern Ireland (Brewer, 1991; McVeigh and Roulston, 2007), which avoids simplistic, essentialist assumptions about race and sect, can help us explore the reasons why Elizabeth might have reacted in the way that she did. In all likelihood she was brought up in a family in which notions of Britishness were firmly embedded in everyday relationships and reinforced though educational and social institutions. This is a concept of Britishness, of Protestantism, which is, as we have suggested, characterised by notions of real and perceived social and economic advantage, as well as a sense of ethnic and cultural otherness to Catholics in Northern Ireland. This particular, some would argue peculiar, sense of Britishness does not easily translate and travel when Northern Irish Protestants live in other parts of Britain; at worst it can create a sense of dislocation and alienation. Nor would Elizabeth be prepared for the multi-cultural, socially diverse communities of London. In retrospect, Elizabeth's attitudes to race and nationality might have been different if she had more recently lived in Northern Ireland, given the incremental growth of black and ethnic minority communities in the last decade (Northern Ireland Office, 2012). On the other hand, racism remains an ever-present feature of contemporary Northern Irish society. In sum, these important contextual factors had to be borne in mind when making an assessment and intervention in such situations.

Meaning-making probably became a difficult process for Elizabeth because she was being confronted with problematic questions about her self-identity and ideas about an 'other', in these threatening sets of circumstances, for the first time in her young life. Her sense of Britishness appeared to have little currency in these circumstances. Instead, it is probable that a new, more threatening subjectivity was in the process of construction. This was an alien identity, one of an Irish person in Britain (Garrett, 2002b). Being viewed as 'other', and the realisation that this came with a devalued status, must have been a bewildering experience for Elizabeth.

One of the challenges of such encounters, which we often find in social work practice, is to create a respectful space that would enable Elizabeth to have a voice which could explain the nuances of her experiences, whilst at the same time not shying away from the need to confront her and help her to reflect upon her own racism. Engaging in a dialogue with Elizabeth enabled her to examine her experience of being 'othered' and encouraged her to examine her assumptions about race in the context of the dynamic complexities which had shaped her Northern Irish identity.

Having established this notion of 'respectful space', it is important to consider, in partnership with Elizabeth, other aspects of anti-oppressive practice which can be delivered at a variety of levels. We have argued in this chapter that anti-oppressive practice is not about simply 'posturing' about the nature of discrimination and its causes; there is a need for social workers to deliver meaningful services and challenge structures that prevent social change (Dominelli, 2008; Brown, 2012). There are many pragmatic issues to be dealt with in Elizabeth's situation, not least her housing situation and impoverished social and family relationships. There may be opportunities to help Elizabeth engage with Irish communities, Protestant or Catholic, to help her find social solidarity and support. The situation which led to the confrontation with Elizabeth was partly the result of a misperceived breach of confidentiality, but also borne of socialised representations of 'the other' which led to her racist comments to the social worker. There is evidence (Central Council for Education and Training in Social Work,

1999) that organisations and their staff are not necessarily culturally competent in dealing with outworking of racism and sectarianism in everyday
management and practice, an argument that has been more recently
rehearsed in the literature (Strier and Binyamin, 2013). More coherent,
meaningful approaches to the education and training of social workers at
qualifying and post-qualifying levels are necessary. These can equip practitioners to deal with the conflictual, sometimes contradictory, practice situations that occur in these circumstances (Coulter et al., 2013).

Key Ideas for Practice

1. Early attempts to deliver meaningful anti-oppressive education and practice in the UK
    during the 1990s have become dissipated and often replaced by alternative
    discourses on diversity and cultural difference. It is crucial that more critical narratives
    are used to explain and address all forms of discrimination.

2. Some parallels can be drawn between the analyses of racism and sectarianism in
    terms of colonial and postcolonial theories, hierarchies of social relationships and
    political formations.

3. We should avoid 'essentialist' approaches to anti-oppressive practice which view iden-
    tities as types of oppression to be fixed; we should interrogate such narratives to
    reveal the complexities of personal and political knowledge and experiences and the
    inevitable relationships of power which exist between practitioners and clients.

4. Anti-oppressive practice should be multi-layered and involve consideration of practi-
    tioner–client biographies, social positioning, interpersonal skills and political advo-
    cacy.

5. Our understanding of anti-oppressive practice remains tenuous and we need to build
    awareness of the diffuse experiences of students, practitioners and educators in a
    global context.

Conclusion

In this chapter we have described early attempts to deliver meaningful anti-
oppressive education and practice in the UK during the 1990s and have
critiqued the way that these have become dissipated and often replaced by
alternative discourses on diversity and cultural difference. It is crucial that
more critical narratives are used to explain and address racism and discrimination. These approaches must recognise the complex factors which
explain discrimination and racism across a range of domains and layers of
understanding. This chapter has explored the potential intersections
between analyses of racism and sectarianism through the use of colonial and

postcolonial theories, hierarchies of social relationships and political forma-tions. The literature implies that much of social work practice involves engagement and encounters that have roots in oppression and social inequalities. Anti-oppressive practice should, therefore, be multi-layered and involve consideration of practitioner–client subjectivities, social position-ing, interpersonal skills and political advocacy. For genuine anti-oppressive practice to take place, students and practitioners must be able to develop the skills and knowledge necessary for building trusting relationships with indi-viduals, groups and families. Thus, to achieve this goal, students must be critically reflexive (Brown, 2012), understand the nature of multiple forms of oppression and engage in dialogues that are emotionally loaded and discomforting. As Boler and Zembylas (2003) suggest, teaching and learning about uncomfortable issues such as race and other forms of oppression requires pedagogical approaches that equip students to navigate the emotional terrain of engaging with discomforting truths. This, then, provides the foundation for moving into practices which are informed by a critical awareness of the causes of discrimination and racism and the devel-opment of appropriate skills and methods of intervention.

Although this chapter has focused on our own experiences and has been largely confined to UK perspectives, we believe that some of these ideas are transferable to other contexts, which help us to understand the nuanced characteristics of racism and sectarianism in various historical, social and national contexts. As we have argued, this requires a consideration of patterns of inequality created by colonial and neo-colonial processes, as well as contemporary forms of prejudice and discrimination. This, in turn, helps us consider the possible responses from social workers and their organisa-tions in an increasingly fractured, globalised world in which social and political conflicts are commonplace (Campbell, 2007). For this reason, we are particularly mindful of the need to look beyond the UK and test such ideas in different, often more complex settings across the world (Sinclair and Albert, 2008). This entails becoming attentive to the diversity of values, meanings and power which underlie the knowledge claims that social work-ers and social work agencies draw upon in different national and cross-national contexts (Campbell and Duffy, 2008; Rush and Keenan, 2013). At the same time, we must not lose sight of the issues of social injustice which are the product of social and political structures.

PART IV

Deconstruction

As we have already seen in previous chapters, Foucault's work was clear in its analysis of resistance to power and the development and attempted suppression of subjugated knowledge, which included the productive and not just repressive aspects of power. Foucault (1990) draws attention to the potential for a reverse discourse, where the voices of those that have been so disqualified to speak on their own behalf are able to speak, and to demand legitimacy. This ability to deconstruct and reverse discourse is key to effective and authentic approaches to equality and diversity in social work. Key principles and ethical approaches that underpin our understanding of 'deconstruction' within the final four chapters in this book offer what we see as a finale for the themes already covered. Here, the authors will introduce and explain the concept of deconstruction which is commonly associated with 'reversing hierarchies' in order to displace existing systems that operate in social work contexts. Deconstruction is actually a philo-sophical or critical method which asserts that meanings, metaphysical constructs and hierarchical oppositions (for example, between key terms that are commonly adopted in social work literature, practice or research) are rendered unstable by their dependence on ultimately arbitrary signifiers. We will be encouraged by the authors to recognise and identify these signifiers to keep our thinking open and alive. As you will see through their analyses, these signifiers are subject to analytical examination in the form of common social work theo ries or practices, with a view to revealing their inadequacy. This is achieved through the method of critically analysing language or texts. Each author pays attention to the internal workings of language used to describe specific areas of social work, its assumptions and conceptual systems in order to uncover the rela-tional quality of meaning and the assumptions implicit in forms of expressions used. For example, Turney focuses on the vehicle of language, where she high-lights how as a tool of social work, in both its textual and relationship forms, deconstructive approaches can enhance AOP and ADP. Garrett provides us with a critique of current understanding of the terms 'diversity' and 'difference' in their full political context; Hicks tackles a common institution such as the family and argues how a deconstructive approach can enhance our understanding and practice with different families; and Jeyasingham helps our understanding of what constitutes knowledge about sexuality in social work and the binary cate-gories used to marginalise those with different sexual identities.

Deconstruction comes from the work of Jacques Derrida from the late 1960s, who commented on how language shapes us and how 'texts' in their different forms create hierarchical opposites which are accepted as reality. Using examples in this section such as heterosexual/homosexual, professional/service user, white/black, we will show how the second term is often seen as a corruption of the first and not as an equal opposite. Derrida asserted that all text contained a legacy of these assumptions and should be reinterpreted with an awareness of the hierarchies implicit in language. However, he also made it clear that we will not reach an end point of interpretation, a truth. This is because interpretation is multiple and meaning is diffuse, so that it becomes limitless or even impossible to establish certainty and to thus privilege certain types of interpretation and repress others. The authors in this section, through the contributions of other philosophers, literary critics and theorists who have taken up Derrida's ideas, have adapted the notion of disturbing and overturning binary oppositions and signifiers used in social work. They explore deconstruction as a way of disturbing this idea of stable, constant meaning often used in ADP and AOP literature, teaching and practice, and expose the ways in which theory and practice is inevitably provisional. Deconstruction is also particularly concerned with the borders between categories, which may be permeable. Using the interpretive turn, articulation of other subordinated voices and perspectives, such as those included in this part on families and sexuality, assert contributions from the margins of social work mainstream and value different sources of knowledge

In Chapter 11, Turney uses deconstruction as a framework and language for analysing social work theory, practice and research and to explore the tensions and challenges of ADP and its continuous complexities from an ethical perspective. Returning to earlier themes by Cowden and Singh, she examines terms used to describe service users by engaging in linguistic analysis that questions assumptions behind particular hierarchies which are fundamental to challenging AOP. Turney also invites us to think about different aspects of social work writing and recording practices, citing the importance of reflexivity as a useful bridge to the third position identified in social work discourse about language and writing as an expression of relations of power. She suggests that accounts of practice can be used to reject fixed determinate meaning and its consequences and to focus on the text as discursively produced. Therefore, by critically interrogating these sources, we can identify the knowledge, assumptions on which they depend and keep thinking alive as a means of achieving an ethical challenge.

In Chapter 12, Garrett talks about the critical importance of taking a political standpoint for the active disruption of talk which is centred on rhetorical notions of 'difference' and 'diversity' to plot a way forward. He draws on the work of Alain Badiou and Nancy Fraser to add complexity to the debate when rethinking ADP and its related themes. Garrett's definition of anti-discriminatory practice is rooted in a critical analysis of the history of economic, state and cultural processes which seek to marginalise, stigmatise or exploit different collectivities. His example in England of the discourse on 'race' and 'ethnic minorities' founded on a 'black'/'white' binary is given to demonstrate how this has rendered Irish people invisible (Garrett, 2004). For example, through the use of Fraser's recognition theory, he highlights the silence of social work on divisions evolving in the wider polity, for example, the association of multiculturalism and diversity with terrorism and the impact on multicultural communities. Further, social work's value base and awareness of factors connected to class, race, gender and oppression and its association with political correctness has been seized upon politically. Understanding competing paradigms requires a two-dimensional conception of justice, in which redistribution and regulation play equal and intertwining parts. For Garrett, this perspective dualism provides a force for change beyond mere affirmation. Complicity of social work in such processes needs to give way to evolving a form of ADP practice which also challenges these processes.

Turning specifically to an area in which social work has an intimate relationship, Chapter 13, by Hicks, asks how social work can begin to deconstruct traditional or dominant accounts of family life in order that wider forms of relationality are allowed and hierarchical notions are challenged. These are those based upon oppressive and limiting ideas about gender, sexuality or race. Hicks considers the standard, nuclear family model as a moral code or form of evaluation in which white, heteronormative and gendered forms are prioritised and he examines family diversity through various sociological analyses. By examining hierarchical relations and decontextualising families, Hicks uncovers how meanings are deployed in everyday contexts, for example, how various people, actions, places, artefacts and so on are categorised and negotiated as family. Current ADP and AOP theories tend to present monolithic accounts of understanding the 'needs' of these groups and so denigrate other forms, and Hicks draws on his own and others research with LGBT parents. He uses poststructural theories, largely found within literary and cultural studies, which play with the inherent instability with the supposed differences of families

In the final chapter in this book, Jeyasingham picks up on the underlying philosophies and contradictions in explorations of sexuality in the AOP literature. Through two case studies on the experience of sexuality, he demonstrates how the binary categories of homosexual and heterosexual are distinguished from each other and positioned as opposites, or as one deviating from the other alongside the gendering of homosexuality. He disturbs dominant constructs by uncovering the contradictions between them. The double bind of disclosing homosexuality or 'coming out' is, for example, one contradictory system which operates as a site for powerful manipulation of sexuality in society. The metaphorical closet is a societal structure that requires negotiation irrespective of people's sense of who they are, and operates in subtle powerful ways in social work, which can discriminate and oppress. Jeyasingham provides essential insights into the penetration of queer identity into the private arena of family relations, psychiatry and the challenges in communicating sexuality within practice.

11

Deconstructing the Language of Anti-Oppressive Practice in Social Work

Danielle Turney

Introduction: Social Work and the 'Linguistic Turn'

Social work is an activity that is irreducibly dependent on language, whether in the form of talking, reading or writing – so the way in which language is used matters. Since the late 1980s, different theoretical approaches have been used to develop a range of 'linguistically grounded' models of social work (Rojek et al., 1988, p. 137). For example, Rojek and colleagues (1988) turned to Foucault, while Humphries (1997) and Jack (1997) drew on the language of discourse analysis to frame their respective discussions of social work education and child protection practice. Elsewhere, hermeneutic (Whan, 1986; Turney, 1997) and deconstructive approaches (Solas, 1995; Turney, 1996) have also been explored to inform understanding of different aspects of practice.

While a strand of social work theorising has been developed that is committed to a Foucauldian view, deconstruction has, in different ways, also continued to be an influence in social work literature, providing a framework and language for analysing social work theory, practice and research (for example, Fook, 1996; 2000; Healy, 2000; Garrett, 2001; McDonald, 2006; Fook and Gardner, 2007; Ploesser and Mecheril, 2012). Fook and Gardner (2007), in particular, make links between broad poststructural ideas and forms of critical practice. They identify that postmodern (within which they include poststructural) thinking 'brings with it particular ways of thinking that to some degree transcend yet complement those associated with reflexivity' (Fook and Gardner, 2007, p. 31), a point to which we will return.

This chapter explores a deconstructive approach in more detail, with a view to understanding its potential contribution to anti-oppressive practice (AOP). It starts with a brief account of the way deconstruction has been framed by one of its main exponents, Jacques Derrida, and the particular understanding of language that he proposed. Moving on, it considers how, as a tool for social work in its textual and relational forms, deconstructive approaches contribute to an 'ethics of encounter' that can inform AOP. To some, deconstruction may appear to be an odd source to draw on to explore the tensions and challenges of AOP from an ethical perspective: as the chapter will discuss, one of the critiques of deconstruction has been that it has no ethical or political commitment, that it encourages a form of extreme moral relativism or, worse, nihilism that has no place in an ethically-informed practice. But I hope to show here that deconstruction, far from being either unethical or non-ethical, can be a valuable resource to help us to understand some of the continuing complexities of AOP and to develop strategies for action.

Deconstruction, Language and Undecideability

Deconstruction proceeds by drawing attention to the detail of texts, the language used and the rhetoric deployed to achieve particular ends. Derrida (1976) suggests that analysis of any text reveals that each is structured around a set or sets of hierarchically organised concepts (for example: white/black; male/female; professional/service user). They are hierarchical in the sense that one 'side' of the pairing is held to be superior: one term is defined as the key concept, against which the other is negatively defined, and occupies a privileged position in relation to the other. Deconstructive criticism investigates the conceptual oppositions that govern a/any text, and through this investigation shows how a particular meaning is maintained. In Derrida's analysis, this meaning is invariably maintained through the suppression of the 'inferior' term of the governing hierarchy or hierarchies.

Deconstructive practice typically involves two elements or stages: in the first place the hierarchical opposition is reversed, allowing the previously suppressed term a priority or superiority. In terms of anti-oppressive practice, we can see this move in efforts to challenge entrenched positions that depend on hierarchies of dominance and 'inferiority' in social work theory and practice. For example, in the context of anti-racist practice, this has been evidenced in the development of clearly articulated black perspectives on a range of topics (Ahmad, 1990; Graham, 2007b; Robinson, 2009), and a similar story could be told about the emergence of feminist perspectives in social work. But simply reversing a hierarchy is only half the story – a necessary half, for sure, but this is not an end in itself as the conceptual system that generated, and still contains, the opposition, remains.

Derrida (1987, p. 41), therefore, suggests that this process of reversal is followed by an attempt to subvert the distinctions on which the opposition is grounded to show that the two terms, far from being mutually exclusive, are inextricably linked and mutually dependent. The implication of this is to collapse the boundaries that have held the opposition in place, recognising instead the element of *undecideability* that is always present in language, and allowing for the emergence of a new way of thinking or concept, 'a concept that can no longer be, and never could be, included in the previous regime' (Derrida, 1987, p. 42). The force of deconstruction lies in its capacity to scrutinise minutely the concepts that we otherwise take for granted – the ones that structure our everyday thinking but remain at the un-thought level of common sense – and to unsettle them. It provokes 'a kind of internal distancing, an effort at defamiliarization which prevents those concepts from settling down into routine habits of thought' (Norris, 1987, p. 16). What this seems to be suggesting is that some of the powerful governing principles of everyday thought can be destabilised; they can be challenged and perhaps even begin to be re-thought through this double process of reversal and re-inscription.

There is a hint here of the potential for political change occasioned by deconstructive analysis: that it may be possible to think differently about some of the more constricting categories that currently dominate our discursive and other social structures. This is not to say that the distinctions maintained in these hierarchies are not 'real' or that they can just be removed with a grand rhetorical flourish. On the contrary, they exert a very real force and would provide a linguistic/conceptual straightjacket if it were not for the particular feature of the way language operates that Derrida refers to as *dissemination* (Derrida, 1981). This is not used in the same way as the English term 'dissemination', and what Derrida is suggesting through this concept is that texts are not 'watertight' and meanings cannot be fully and finally circumscribed. Loose ends remain: connections to other texts and discourses are always present, and these offer what might be called 'sites of resistance' from the dominant interpretation or message of the text. As Norris explains: 'Texts are "stratified" in the sense that they bear along with them a whole network of articulated themes and assumptions whose meaning everywhere links up with other texts, other genres or topics of discourse' (1987, pp. 25–26).

We can look at the process of *dissemination* and the way language changes through time to see the force of some of Derrida's arguments. One example might be the language that is used to identify people who use welfare services. I want to draw here on an interesting article by McLaughlin (2009) that asks the question: 'What's in a name?' and then examines the changing terminology that has been adopted to refer to those who use, or are on the receiving end of, services. McLaughlin's paper addresses the dynamics of knowledge production and considers how the status or significance of knowledge changes according to the way we perceive the provider/producer of that knowledge. He charts the shifting meanings associated with the terms 'client', 'patient', 'customer', 'consumer', 'service user' and, finally (so far), 'expert by experience' and the different understanding of power relations reflected in each form of relationship – or, in deconstructive terms, the conceptual hierarchies that are held in place within each new formulation. The interesting point to pull out here, from my point of view, is the way each term is adopted to address perceived failings in the previous one. Each one is, at least temporarily, seen to provide 'the answer' – yet is, in turn, superseded.

The idea that language could be fully transparent, providing a '"natural bond" between sound and sense' (Norris, 2002, p. 29), is seen by Derrida as part of the *logocentrism* that dominates Western thinking. Logocentrism (Derrida, 1976) works to persuade us that if we could only hit on the 'right' term or formulation, we could achieve the ideal of a 'pure' language – in this case, one that is free of all connotations of oppression. But this could only be possible if the identity between signifier (for example, a word) and signified (thing or object in the world) were fixed and complete. But, as Derrida's analysis indicates, language is in a perpetual state of flux. The signifier never 'catches up' with the signified, and the sign always remains different from itself – or, to put it more straightforwardly, the word for an object, experience, mental state and so on is not the same as the thing itself. Meaning is neither fixed nor final and cannot be 'pinned down' in a way that would allow certain meanings to be removed from our common vocabulary by the simple act of changing one word for another.

So, returning to McLaughlin's paper, an argument is made for the term 'expert by experience' on the grounds that it denotes a significant change in the relationship between professional and service user:

> The social worker working with the expert by experience is suggestive of a relationship of equals whereby one expert's expertise has been accrued through their training and practice and the other through their experience. This suggests that the social worker needs to acknowledge and affirm the expertise of the other – the expert by experience – in assessing and agreeing a way forward. (McLaughlin, 2009, p. 1111)

But, while this is an interesting and potentially important shift in terms of understanding relational dynamics, this new formulation is still not entirely unproblematic. It raises questions it cannot itself answer: Who qualifies as an 'expert by experience'? What criteria are used? Does everybody learn from experience in the same way – and what about those who do not appear to actually learn from experience at all? What do we do about situations where two 'experts by experience' have very different views of, or responses to, a service? Highlighting these questions is certainly not to dismiss the importance of respecting service users' views, knowledge and experience. Rather, it is to remind us of a deconstructive 'truth' – namely that there is no final 'right' language.

Why, then, bother about language at all? If the logic of deconstruction leads to the abandonment of the search for a 'pure' language – one that carries no traces of any form of oppression – is there any point in the process of substitution alluded to above, where terminology is modified and new terms adopted, only to be replaced in turn themselves some time later? It might be easier to simply accept the impossibility of arriving at an 'untainted' form of words and relax! A deconstructive approach would, however, counsel against that. While the idea of a once-for-all switch in meaning, in the manner of a gestalt shift, is a fantasy, the *process* of change nonetheless has significance. Indeed, I suggest that the decision to engage in the kind of linguistic analysis that questions the assumptions behind particular preferred conceptual hierarchies is a form of ethical commitment, and fundamental to an engaged form of anti-oppressive practice.

The understanding of language presented here directs attention to the notion of social work *text* and the practices of reading and writing through which we engage with it. So, in the next section, I will consider this 'encounter' in more detail.

Engaging with Social Work (as) Text

At a basic level, it is the texts of social work that define what social work is about; a library of books exists to tell social workers about the law, psychology, social policy and intervention techniques that structure and guide their practice. Research is written up for publication in academic journals, and debate about the whole enterprise of social work is carried out in the trade press and wider public news media. As we know, social workers themselves spend a considerable amount of time producing text in the form of case files, reports, letters and assessments. We can read social work writing in all its forms – and there is certainly no shortage of written materials on which to concentrate.

With the introduction of the degree in Social Work as the basic qualifying award, requirements set down by the Department of Health explicitly state that candidates for training must have achieved at least Key Skills Level 2 in English (GCSE English at grade C or above) and must satisfy training providers that they 'can understand and make use of written material and be able to communicate clearly and accurately in spoken and written

English' (Department of Health, 2002, p. 2). Similar assumptions carry forward into the reforms to social work education recommended by the Social Work Task Force. At one level, of course, it is reasonable to expect a basic level of literacy amongst training and qualified social workers. The day-to-day demands of the job require the ability to read or decode a range of documents, to complete forms correctly, to record verbal information, to prepare written records and reports, and so on. Indeed, these perhaps became even more central with the requirements of the Integrated Children's System and other electronic information recording and management structures, and the increased proceduralisation that has been identified with the rise of managerialism in practice.

But the notions of reading and writing explored here go beyond the routine activities mentioned above and involve a more detailed understanding of the processes by which texts are constructed and knowledge is produced, by both readers and writers. An awareness of the textual nature of the social work enterprise highlights the role of social workers as both producers and readers of text. While this discussion focuses on the literal written texts of social work, there is also a more metaphorical sense in which social work itself operates as a text, as a range of signifying practices that are open to analysis and criticism. This is an understanding that interpretive and poststructuralist approaches to language have fostered, and leads beyond the individual works of social work literature and towards an appreciation of a general textuality (Ricoeur, 1981, pp. 197–221; see also Solas, 1995). Prinz summarises the position that deconstruction takes in this regard; he observes that for Derrida:

> language is not a window onto an objective world; it imposes structure on the world by creating divisions that would not exist without language. We are never able to think without language, so we have no direct access to an objective world. In this sense, the world itself is a text – a set of objects, properties and events that acquire their meaning though language. (Prinz, 2009, p. 56)

So, from this perspective, any activity, including that of social work, can be textualised and hence 'read'.

The following discussion looks first at different ways of conceptualising social work text as forms of *writing* and then moves on to consider practices of *reading* and how these activities can contribute to the development of AOP.

Reading, writing and reflexivity

Attention to writing in social work has had three main points of focus – writing as recording, writing as reflection and writing as an expression of relations of power. The next section looks briefly at how each of these areas has been addressed.

Much has been written in recent years about the way social work has become locked into a complex bureaucratic structure that requires the production of substantial quantities of written data in the form of case records, assessments, court reports and so on. The reliance particularly on electronic data recording and management systems has been widely remarked, with concern expressed both at the amount of time that practitioners have to spend compiling these records (Bell et al., 2007; Broadhurst et al., 2010; Munro, 2011) and the quality of some of the outputs that are produced (Selwyn et al., 2006; Holland, 2010; Munro, 2011). The focus on recording has encouraged publication of a number of texts designed to support social workers in everyday writing tasks. Some of these texts have addressed the function and purpose of the writing tasks and problematised aspects of these different activities and outputs, but this has generally been alongside, or secondary to, an emphasis on skills development (Prince, 1996; Healy, 2007; O'Rourke, 2010).

Moving away from this form of task-focused writing, there is a longstanding tradition of reflective writing in social work; it has particularly been used as an educational tool to promote professional development both for students in training and experienced practitioners, and numerous texts outline approaches to teaching and facilitating reflective writing. Recording events and experiences in written form, it is argued, supports and develops reflective ability, as Rutter and Brown note:

> Because critical reflection relies so much on making connections and judging our thoughts and information, writing is one of the main activities that can help by starting this process of capturing and expressing basic assumptions, underlying knowledge and the memory of any experience. (2012, p. 37)

Reflection has become a cornerstone of good practice, with 'critical reflection' identified as one of the capabilities that should 'explicitly inform initial social work training, continuing professional development, performance appraisal and career structures' (Munro, 2011, p. 8; The College of Social Work, 2012). Richardson and Maltby (1995) suggest that reflection requires a range of skills, including self-awareness. Self-awareness, in turn, seems to be a key element of an anti-oppressive approach to practice.

While there is a strong case to be made for the value of reflection in and on practice, then, it is also important to acknowledge that the notion of reflection has also been subject to a range of critiques, starting with Ixer's (1999) provocative assertion that 'there's no such thing as reflection'. He challenged the status of reflection in professional (and specifically social work) education and suggested that, despite its popularity and the fact that it enjoyed 'something of a cult following amongst curriculum planners and those responsible for professional education' (1999, p. 513), little was actually known about reflection. He was particularly concerned about its use as an assessed element of students' professional qualifying training. Interestingly, this critique has not been widely taken up and, more than a dozen years later, has perhaps lost some of its force. At the least, a lot more has been written about the theory and practice of reflection since the publication of Ixer's article, to provide a clearer framework for the inclusion of reflective writing in programmes of learning (see, for example, Rai, 2006; Bolton, 2010; Knott and Scragg, 2010; Rutter and Brown, 2012).

Nonetheless, other critiques of reflection have been framed: Eby (2000, p. 54) notes that, although reflection is intended to improve practice, its use 'to promote self-development can lead to a sense of self-doubt and self-disapproval, since endlessly striving to improve leaves little room for a sense of personal wellbeing'. Taking this point further, the focus on personal monitoring can potentially become quite oppressive: A Foucauldian critique suggests that by 'making the individual practitioner visible and inciting them to reveal the truth about themselves' reflective practice operates as 'a form of surveillance that disciplines the activities of professionals' (Taylor, 2003, p. 246). So, while the self-awareness and personal learning that can be derived from reflective practice can promote emancipatory and anti-oppressive practice, in this sense it also has the potential to operate as a 'technology of the self'.

The critique of reflection based on its 'psychologism' or individualism has encouraged the development of approaches that locate the practitioner explicitly within a broader sociopolitical and cultural context. This can be seen in the move from 'reflection' to 'reflexivity' or 'critical reflection' (cf. Taylor and White, 2000; see also D'Cruz et al., 2007). Reflexivity includes the more inward-looking personal reflection discussed already, which involves reflecting on how one's values, beliefs, social identities and experiences impact on practice. But it moves beyond this to address the situated nature of practice and the wider social picture, promoting not only self-awareness but also social and political awareness. Taking into account, for example, the impact of factors such as racism, sexism and other forms of discrimination, reflexivity encourages a form of critical practice. Fook's work has been particularly important in terms of linking reflexivity and critical practice. As Fook and Askeland (2007) point out, the reflexive practitioner is able to use critical thinking skills to reflect on the sources of his/her knowledge and to examine the bases of practice. That is, reflexivity allows the practitioner to analyse what she/he knows and how she/he knows it, to maintain a questioning approach that does not take things for granted – especially social arrangements that are based on inequality or disadvantage (see also Thompson and Thompson, 2008).

The notion of reflexivity provides a useful bridge to the third position identified in social work discourse about language: writing as an expression of relations of power. Rojek and colleagues provided one of the first attempts to analyse the language of both mainstream and radical social work as 'forms of power'. As the authors state, the central argument of their book was that 'language which social workers are trained to use in order to free clients very often has the effect of imprisoning them anew' (1988, p. 1). Recognition that language is not a transparent or neutral medium has subsequently been expressed by a number of writers within the field of critical practice. Fook's observation sums up the significance of attention to language in this regard: 'Language is [...] about much more than words – it is about power' (Fook, 2002, p. 66).

As the preceding discussion indicates, quite a lot of attention has been paid to different aspects of social work writing. Reflexivity, however, draws attention to the nature of the activity involved in responding to the texts of social work; that is, the role of *reading*. This seems to me to be a significant move, and my contention is that a considered approach to both reading and writing is itself a prerequisite for engaging in reflective practice, rather than just a strategy for reporting it. I suggest that the ability to read (situations, people, written documents) critically, to be aware of different and competing interpretations, and to understand the power dynamics that hold certain interpretations of events in place and marginalise others – all elements of a deconstructive critical reading approach –underpin competent, anti-oppressive and reflexive practice.

Deconstructive reading

> From a poststructural viewpoint, the deconstruction or analysis of discourse is similar to reflexive analysis of texts, in that both involve similar processes of peeling away layers of meaning to uncover hidden assumptions and their sources.
> (Fook, 1999, p. 14)

Deconstructive approaches share an attention to *how* a text is constructed and the ways in which *how* a text does something is related to *what* it does. In all cases, attention is focused on how the text is articulated, with deconstructive reading taking particular interest in the internal contradictions that inevitably inhabit the text. The emphasis is on the interplay between various elements in the production of meaning. The reader, as a culturally and historically specific individual, brings a framework of assumptions, values and interpretive strategies to bear on the text. Also, the text itself is not seen as a neutral or finished object: both its production and its reception take place in an actual, 'real' world, 'a world that is culturally, socially and institutionally determined; that is messy, noisy, and full of disturbances, surprises, and instabilities' (Birch, 1989, p. 2). Understanding a text thus becomes a matter of interpretation. This emphasis on the element of inter-pretation and, ultimately, of *undecideability* has provoked considerable criti-cal challenge to the utility and morality of deconstruction, and it is to these challenges that I now turn.

Derrida's approach to the text is designed to expose and destabilise assumptions embedded in language, but the strategies he adopts in order to carry out this 'deconstruction' have been seen (and critiqued) as ranging from the wilfully obscure to the bizarre. Deconstructive reading of the kind demonstrated by Derrida is a challenge – both to undertake and, in some cases, to understand:

> Rather than attempting to defend his views using clear analytic arguments, he [...] uses words in novel ways, makes puns, breaks up words in unusual places, exploits ambiguities and traces inventive etymologies that reveal connections between words that were not obvious before. (Prinz, 2009, p. 56)

Furthermore, while the importance of context in the creation of meaning is widely accepted, the emphasis on interpretation, and recognition of *undecideability,* that deconstruction introduces has been seen as problem-atic. If the text does not have a fixed meaning, it is argued, we soon find ourselves in a world governed by the logic of Humpty Dumpty (Carroll, 1872, p. 100).

This leads to a more general critique – that undecideability leads unavoidably to extreme relativism or even nihilism 'which would render ethical accounts impossible' (Pupke, 2003, p. 299). Thus, the argument runs, if there is no external referent to guarantee our notions about 'truth', 'justice' and 'right' – that is, if their meaning is always context dependent – then there can be no judgement, no differentiation; in the end, we are locked into a world where 'anything goes'. This proposition is critical for any consideration of AOP, implying that deconstruction entails no political or ethical engagement.

Undecideability, Ethics and Action

Having identified some of the critiques that can be levelled against a decon-structive approach, the following section tries to respond to these chal-lenges. Acknowledging the unavoidable element of undecideability, it highlights deconstruction's radical and unsettling potential in order to illus-trate the possibilities for ethically-informed action even when the search for fixed and final meaning is set aside.

Reading from the margins

I have challenged the idea that because meaning is unstable, we have a kind of ethical opt out in terms of how we use language. Indeed, it was suggested that the of kind of linguistic analysis that questions the assumptions behind particular preferred and powerful conceptual hierarchies is itself a form of ethical engagement. In this section, I look further at what this might mean in practice.

As the previous discussion indicated, poststructuralist approaches to language reject the empiricist preoccupation with fixed, determinate meaning and, in consequence, focus on the text as discursively produced. Such approaches suggest that meaning is not 'contained' within a text like a nut in its shell, waiting to be prised loose by the reader or critic. So reading is not directed towards finding a work's single, unchanging meaning but rather acknowledges the irreducibly *interpretive* nature of understanding. The relevance of this 'interpretive turn' (Hiley et al., 1991) is that it opens up the text to analysis and critique from a range of sources – including from 'outside' the formal, establishment fold. So, for example, the possibility of political and social challenge can be seen in a variety of feminist approaches to textual criticism, which have sought to highlight the discursive frameworks and practices within which different texts and different readings of those texts are situated. Within literary criticism, feminist critics have challenged the idea of the literary canon for representing patriarchal (and commonly also white, middle/upper class, heterosexual) values as universal, thereby excluding from serious consideration the texts and reading strategies of those who 'fall short' of these 'ideals'. Such critics have argued that language does not reflect reality but creates it, and creates it in historically and politically specific forms. Thus, they have defined a task for feminist critique, which Moi describes as follows:

> speaking from their marginalised positions on the outskirts of the academic establishments, they strive to make explicit the politics of the so-called 'neutral' or 'objective' works of their colleagues, as well as to act as cultural critics in the widest sense of the word. (1985, p. 87)

Moving beyond the world of 'lit. crit.', social work too has been the site of analyses from a wide range of feminist perspectives (for example, Langan, 1992; Featherstone, 2001; Dominelli, 2002b). These, too, have taken advantage of their position on the academic or cultural margins to offer a different perspective on the dominant discourses at the centre of the profession. The relationship between centre and margins has also been reshaped or redefined by the articulation of other 'subordinated' voices and perspectives – for example, those of black writers and others from minority ethnic backgrounds: gay, lesbian and queer theorists and activists; those who use social work services; and so on. Of course, these are all themselves heterogeneous groups, and various approaches to textual analysis have proliferated, the most relevant of which, for my purposes, make use of 'the relationship between language, power and the political consequences of how "we" constitute subjects and objects and allocate value and status to them through discourse' (Hiley et al., 1991, p. 9). The links to critical reflexivity, as discussed earlier, seem clear here.

These different forms of writing are not uniform either in their choice of approach or theoretical technique or conclusions, but invite a different kind of reading and relationship to text. What they share is the challenge that they can offer firstly to our perception of 'acceptable' kinds of writing for/about social work and, beyond that, to broader social, political and cultural relations. Gates, writing some years back in relation to black literary criticism, suggests that there might be one point of agreement among its diverse productions – and the point he makes seems to me to be both current and transferable to a broader range of texts: 'one important benefit of the development of subtle and searching modes of "reading" is that these can indeed be brought to bear upon relationships that extend far beyond the confined boundaries of a text' (Gates, 1986, p. 17). Reading, then, is not a neutral activity that is carried out in social and political isolation. Reading and writing from the margins recognises, and indeed highlights, the embed-dedness of any text or act of reading in a broader discursive framework.

This kind of reading raises issue about hierarchies of knowledge and the ways certain sources of knowledge and processes of knowledge production (for example, formal research knowledge) are privileged over others (for example, service user knowledge). In the context of a study that asks how social work can benefit from the knowledge of people living in poverty, Krumer-Nevo observes.

> Too often the voices and knowledge of poor people are perceived by policy-makers and researchers as anecdotal, providing items to be used when introducing an arti-cle or lecture, but not as a source of knowledge necessary for the setting of policy or the refinement of intervention methods. [In research, policy and practice] researchers, policy practitioners and social workers tend to talk at poor people, not with them or to them. The assumption is that people in poverty are to learn from the professionals and never the other way round. (2008, p. 556)

Making space for marginal voices to be heard does not mean *replacing* research knowledge with service user knowledge at the top of a new hierarchy, but recognises that there has been a tendency to discount or under-value this kind of knowledge and to see it as less valid than what has been produced through apparently more 'objective' academic processes. A deconstructive approach would challenge the value of an 'either/or' response to these different forms of knowledge, and instead suggest that 'both/and' may be more productive. This allows us to move from a position where service users are seen as *sources* of knowledge for professional researchers to an understanding of their potential contribution as *creators* or *(co-)producers* of knowledge – in some cases, with involvement in formal processes of research as principal or co-investigators.

The above discussion has implications for the processes of knowledge production, and, furthermore, both for what social workers read and how they read it. Deconstruction challenges and broadens our understanding of what constitutes a valid text and provides strategies for engaging with the variety of texts that now become available for study. It also draws attention to the way texts are produced and received. The social worker, as reader or writer, is heavily and unavoidably implicated in the process of establishing meaning, of coming to some understanding of the text (person, action, situation) with which she is engaged. These 'readings', then, form the basis of social work assessments, care plans, intervention strategies and so on. Reading and writing in this sense are, therefore, not esoteric or narrowly academic pastimes, but are rooted in the reality of day-to-day practice and have potentially far-reaching consequences. From this perspective, reading and writing take on a more central role and can be seen as core competences for ethical and anti-oppressive practice.

Undecideability and ethical practice

As we have noted at various points, deconstruction has the capacity to destabilise established patterns of thought and conceptual hierarchies, to challenge certainties and to expose 'the paradoxes, contradictions and elisions which undermine the purported coherence of philosophical or conceptual systems' (Popke, 2003, p. 306). In this last section, I propose that, far from leading to a non-ethical stance, deconstruction, precisely through its willingness to engage with the notion of undecideability, provides a basis for an 'ethics of encounter' that speaks very directly to the concerns of anti-oppressive practice. My thinking here is influenced by a discussion of ethics found outside the social work literature, within the field of human geography. The paper I refer to (Popke, 2003) explores the challenges that the main tenets of poststructuralism pose to traditional ethical thinking. I do not have the space here to rehearse the arguments in detail, but draw from Popke's discussion some principles for social work (and particularly anti-oppressive) practice based on an understanding of the ethical imperative of responding to the Other.

Popke argues that:

From a poststructuralist perspective, universal claims to knowledge and truth can become a barrier to fostering a sensitivity to difference, and thus ethics would need to find its purchase in the radical instability of meaning and the deconstruction of universal normative claims. (2003, p. 300)

This is highly relevant as it calls into question any formulaic or automatic response to the Other, any response that is based on stereotype or standard procedure. In short, deconstruction requires a response that does not fall back on understandings of a generalised Other. Applying this to social work, a form of practice which is organised around the need to relate to specific Others: decision-making in practice takes place in a world of undecideability, uncertainty and complexity where there are no external guarantors of truth or 'rightness', where the justness of a decision cannot be ensured *a priori*. But Popke's observation on the significance of undecideability is worth repeating in full here, as it seems to be directly relevant to the concerns of anti-oppressive practice:

> to assert that the decision is ultimately undecidable does not mean that there can be no such thing as truth, right or good. It means, rather, that if we purport to know in advance the specific content of such notions, then the event of the decision is divested of its political content, it is simply 'deduced from an existing body of knowledge ... [as] by a calculating machine' (Derrida, 1999: 240). Deconstruction, then, affirms the necessity to judge, to analyse, to make decisions, in the context of an event that is conditioned by our inexhaustible responsibility to the other (Derrida, 1997: 18). (Popke, 2003, pp. 307)

So, deconstruction challenges as potentially unethical the 'if this ... then that' response of proceduralism, which fails to take account of difference or otherness, and urges a response to the Other based in a process of critical-ethical engagement and continuing unwillingness to fall back on stock responses. Thinking in this way reminds us that there are rarely, if ever, standard answers to the dilemmas of practice. Recognition of this continuing need to question and critique formulaic understandings and a commitment to respond to the uniqueness of the individual underpin ethically engaged and anti-oppressive practice.

Key Ideas for Practice

1. The focus of this chapter has been on language and I have argued that understanding language – how it is used and what is does – is key to the development of AOP. Looking at the role of reading and writing within social work, I have suggested that textual analysis has the potential for promoting reflexivity. That is to say that the critical reader will,

in the course of engaging with the otherness of the text (using 'text' in the broadest sense), have the opportunity to reflect on her own interpretive framework, values and assumptions, and those of the broader discursive structures within which she and the text are situated.

2. Reflexivity and a capacity for critical analysis are seen to be essential components of good social work practice, and by adopting an approach that foregrounds the social worker's capacities to read and write critically we can promote the development of AOP amongst practitioners at every stage of professional development. Accounts of practice can be explored and critically interrogated to identify the knowledge, assumptions, etc. on which they depend. Through critically analysing and appraising their own reading and writing, and exploring the processes through which meanings are created, practitioners will have the opportunity to develop much-needed capacities for reflection and enhanced self-knowledge.

3. Critical reading allows a broader range of texts to 'come into view' and to be treated as credible sources of knowledge for the profession. Challenging the centre/margin hierarchy enables social work to give serious consideration to texts from outside the mainstream which counter the Eurocentric (also sexist, ageist, heteronormative, etc.) perspectives that often still dominate social work theory – and even to look outside the 'academy' altogether at different forms of knowledge production and knowledge producers. It makes the boundaries around what counts as a relevant source of knowledge appear more permeable and allows for a different orientation to 'the literature'.

4. Lastly, deconstruction has something to offer social work and AOP more broadly in terms of its ethical stance, particularly the ethical commitment entailed in engaging seriously with the undecideability of language, and the consequent responsibility to challenge the tendency to fall back on ready-to-hand understandings and responses, particularly to individual service users.

Conclusion

In this chapter, I have explored the possibilities of using deconstructive approaches to inform and develop thinking about AOP. Starting from an awareness of the role of language in structuring and creating meaning, I have proposed that deconstruction offers a way of engaging with social work text that challenges established ways of thinking and supports the development of critical and reflexive practice. Furthermore, by acknowledging and working with undecideability, deconstruction helps to ensure that social work thinking and decision-making do not become routinised. AOP depends on a willingness to embrace an 'ethics of encounter', a relational approach that does not rely on stereotypical responses to a generalised Other but requires us to continue to question our (individual, organisational and procedural) taken for granted assumptions, reactions and ways of intervening, and to keep thinking alive.

12

Transcending the Politics of 'Difference' and 'Diversity'?

Paul Michael Garrett

Introduction

The chapter begins by outlining some of the key developments relating to anti-discriminatory social work practice and related themes in England and the Republic of Ireland. Both countries are currently governed by coalition administrations intent on pursing neo-liberal policies resulting in cuts to services and the undermining of social protection. Nevertheless, not surprisingly, there are certain national defining characteristics. An interest in anti-discriminatory practice appears to have been quite prominent within the discourse of social work in England, whilst there has been a relative lack of interest in the Republic of Ireland (see also Garrett, 2012). After sketching in some of the main preoccupations, mostly as they relate to questions pivoting on 'race' and ethnicity, the chapter will examine how social theorists associated with the political left have endeavoured to disrupt talk centred on notions of 'difference' and 'diversity'.

A number of chapters in this book are, as we have seen, heavily influenced by Foucault's theorisation. In contrast, my own short contribution is sensitive to Foucault's failure to adequately acknowledge and conceptualise resistance to power (Said, 2002). Unlike theorists and political activists such as Antonio Gramsci, Foucault does not 'concentrate on the mechanisms by which people could consciously mobilise to change a given "discourse" in a progressive direction ... Gramsci places much greater emphasis on agency and how collective political action can topple, or at least alter, systematic inequality and oppression and lead to more equal power relations' (Ives, 2004, pp. 142–144; see also Garrett, 2013, Ch. 6). In what follows, it will also be suggested that other social theorists, insufficiently taken account of in the academic literature on social work, may help us to plot a way forward.

Hence, the second part of the chapter will discuss the French thinker Alain Badiou and a philosopher from the United States, Nancy Fraser.

Prior to progressing the discussion, it is probably helpful to define some terms to be used. Here, the book on new 'keywords' edited by Tony Bennett and his colleagues remains a useful guide for students and other readers (Bennett et al., 2005; see also Williams, 1983). **Difference** 'emerged as a keyword in cultural politics in the late 1960s. It became a central principle in the political imagination and thinking of a wide range of so-called new social movements that have proliferated since the late 20th century ... [T]he word "difference" – literally the quality of being unlike or similar – loses its descriptive innocence and becomes a highly charged concept, to the point of being elevated as the proud emblem for a passionate political, often personal-political cause' (Ang cited in Bennett et al., 2005, p. 84). A key example of the:

> state-led recognition of difference is the policy of **multiculturalism**, which officially sanctions and enshrines ethnic linguistic and cultural differences within the encompassing framework of the state. In this bureaucratic context, difference becomes the cornerstone of diversity: **diversity** is a managerial, birds-eye view of the field of differences, which needs to be harmonized, controlled, or made to fit into a coherent (often national) whole. The celebration of cultural diversity – popularly expressed in community festivals of ethnic food, song, and dance – is an article of faith in self-declared multicultural societies. (Ang cited in Bennett et al., 2005, p. 86)

Such words are fluid, and resistance to concrete or solid definition and contestation and arguments over meanings forms a key aspect of the *politics* of social work (Gray and Webb, 2013). My own expansive and political definition of **anti-discriminatory social work** is: 'practice which is rooted in a critical analysis of the history of economic, state and cultural processes which seek to either marginalise, stigmatise or exploit different collectivities. Anti-discriminatory social work practice seeks to understand social work's complicity in such processes and tries to evolve forms of practice which challenge these processes' (Garrett, 1998, p. 200).

'Difference', 'Diversity' and Anti-Discriminatory Practice in Social Work in England and the Republic of Ireland

England

Since the 1980s, social work's professional value base has been rhetorically underpinned by a commitment to combating discrimination. Social work students in the mid 1990s, for example, were required to demonstrate that they 'respect and value uniqueness and diversity'. Furthermore, they had to 'identify, analyse and take action to counter discrimination' (Central Council for Education and Training in Social Work, 1995).

Throughout the last quarter of the twentieth century, 'race' featured as a key component in debates on adoption and child placement. In the early 1980s, for example, the Association of Black Social Workers and Allied Professionals (ABSWAP) challenged child placement policies and practices founded on a liberal and assimilationist perspective. The critique focused on the damaging consequences for black children of being placed with white adoptive and foster carers, but it also, more broadly, drew attention to the impact of racism in British society (Small, 1982; Small with Prevatt Goldstein, 2000). Partly on account of such challenges, a new attentiveness to questions of 'race' and ethnicity was gradually incorporated into practice guidelines for children in contact with social services and into the 1989 Children Act. Section 22(5) of the act, mandated that, with children in public care or 'looked after', local authorities had to give 'due consideration' to their 'religious persuasion, racial origin and cultural and linguistic background'.

However, for 18 years social work was shaped by the political project of the right wing Conservative Party, which had an antipathy for such ideas and values (see Gledhill, 1989). Social work's value base and awareness of factors connected to class, 'race', gender and oppression led to the charge of 'political correctness' (see also Bennett et al., 2005, pp. 260–262). Child adoption, or more broadly child placement, was one of the key welfare state areas where the battle against so-called 'political correctness' was waged. Frequently this focused on the issue of 'race' and placements. Developments in the United States may have played a part in terms of the 'inchoate backlash against a professional sensitivity to the "race" and ethnicity of children in need of placements' (Garrett, 2000) In the United States, following the passage of the Multiethnic Placement Act (MEPA) 1994 and the 1996 provisions on Removal of Barriers to Interethnic Adoption, it became no longer possible to use 'race' 'categorically or presumptively to delay or deny adoptive or foster care placements' (Brooks et al., 1999, p. 167). In the past couple of years, the Conservative/Liberal Democrat coalition government in England have reactivated this theme (see, for example, Gove, 2012).

During the period of New Labour administrations (1997 to 2010), there were no radical departures from the principles of the Children Act 1989 and the dominant approach which had evolved and been implemented in the 1980s and 1990s. Moreover, New Labour introduced a range of new policies to promote greater equality. Such measures included the Race Relations Amendment Act (RRAA) 2000; the Disability Discrimination Act (2005); the Equality Act (2006); and the Equality Act (2010). Running counter to such legislation, the policy ambiance was contaminated by the so-called 'War on Terror', with Western Muslims being viewed, in recent years, 'exclusively through the prism of counter-terrorism. Sensitive issues of integration and community cohesion have become entangled in the securitised discourse of the war on terror' (Hasan, 2011, p. 34; see also Craig, 2013). However, Surinder Guru (2008, p. 272) has remarked that social work has 'remained ominously silent' on how this development 'may affect their clients and their own professional practice' (see also Nickels et al., 2012).

More broadly, multiculturalism was assailed by Prime Minister David Cameron (2011) in a speech – significantly – held at an international *security* conference. In the keynote intervention, Cameron called for a 'much more active, muscular liberalism'. He went on to say:

> we have allowed the weakening of *our* collective identity. Under the doctrine of state multiculturalism, we have encouraged different cultures to live separate lives, apart from each other and apart from the mainstream ... We've even tolerated these segregated communities behaving in ways that run completely counter to *our* values. (Cameron, 2011, emphases added)

The Republic of Ireland

New patterns of migration into Ireland were prompted by the 'boom' of the so-called 'Celtic Tiger' period and between '1995 and 2005 nearly half a million people moved into Ireland' (Munck, 2011, p. 10). The Integration Centre (TIC) (2013) has usefully summarised that, according to the 2011 Census, there were 544,357 non-Irish nationals from 199 different nations living in Ireland. The non-Irish share of the population had doubled in under a decade, growing from 6 per cent in 2002 to 12 per cent in 2011. Some 708,300 persons recorded on Census night in 2011 were born outside the island of Ireland, representing 16 per cent of the usually resident population. Polish nationals were the largest non-Irish nationality grouping recorded, with its size almost doubling between 2006 and 2011 from 63,276 persons (15 per cent of the non-Irish population) to 122,585 (23 per cent of the non-Irish population). UK nationals were the second largest group, with 112,259 living in Ireland in 2011. Significantly, and complicating often overly simplistic accounts of 'race' and ethnicity within Ireland, almost 40 per cent of people of black ethnicity and 25 per cent of people with Asian ethnicity are Irish nationals (TIC, 2013).

At the level of policy rhetoric, Irish governments have endeavoured to enunciate a 'third way' in terms of responses to migration. Hence, the focus has been on 'interculturism', which can be interpreted as seeking to evolve an approach to migration, 'race' and ethnicity which is located somewhere between the 'assimilationism' of France and the 'multiculturalism' of Britain. This is detectable in Ireland's first targeted migrant integration strategy statement, *Migration Nation* (Office of the Minister for Integration, 2008). Nonetheless, in practice there has been a 'fairly unreconstructed assimilationism' (Munck, 2011, p. 4). Conceptually and politically, this discourse can also be connected to the focal and problematic conceptualisation of 'social exclusion' (Moran, 2006; see also Levitas, 1996).

Ireland has 'strong equality legislation' (Council of Europe, 2013, p. 6). Nevertheless, a number of 'austerity' related cuts have diluted the state's ability to address discrimination. Racism is encountered by Irish Travellers, with successive governments refusing to recognise them as an 'ethnic group' (McVeigh, 2007; Council of Europe, 2013). As in other European countries, Roma families are frequently scripted a paradigmatic 'undeserving' and parasitic presence within the state. Asylum seekers are compelled to remain in 'direct provision', enduring a form of quasi 'internment', and this continues to have an especially deleterious impact on children (Arnold, 2012). In Bourdieusian terms, each of these three groups, in different ways, is apt to find themselves freighted with 'negative symbolic capital' (Bourdieu et al., 2002, p. 185).

In October 2013, children from two Roma families were removed by police officers. These state interventions occurred days after the removal of a child, called Maria, from a Roma family in Larissa in Greece (Commissioner for Human Rights, 2013). In Ireland, one child – a seven-year-old girl – was removed from a family in Tallaght, west Dublin, and placed in the protective care of the Health Service Executive (HSE). The other child was a two-year-old boy, called Iancu, from Athlone in the Irish midlands. In both instances the removals were prompted by police concerns that these children were not – on account of their appearance – the biological children of their Roma parents; subsequently both children were reunited with their families. These cases dominated Irish media, political and popular discourses for a brief period (Mullally, 2013). The reasons for this centrality are complex, and a fuller exploration lies beyond the scope of this short discussion. However, it is clear that the actions of the police and initial media reporting were underpinned by stereotypical perceptions of Roma and more rooted forms of racialisation (Pavee Point Traveller and Roma Centre, 2013). This can be associated with historical myth-making pivoting on the idea that Roma are 'child stealers', but what also prompted the hasty and ill-judged removals was a rather crude form of racial profiling (Immigrant Council of Ireland, 2013). In short, these two children were subjected to excessive attention and over emphatic intervention on the part of the police and child protection services because they 'did not look like Roma were expected to look'. For example, Iancu, pictured in the media with his parents having been returned to their care, was fair-haired and blue-eyed. When interviewed by

The Irish Times, his father pointed to 'a picture of the child's fair-haired grandfather' and simply asked: 'What can I do about that?' (MacConnell, 2013).

In responding to the removal of the Roma children from their families, Pavee Point Traveller and Roma Centre (2013) argued that 'serious child protection concerns' did, in fact, jeopardise the welfare of Roma children, but such concerns were manifestly connected to structural considerations: for example, to lack of 'access to doctors, medical care and participation in education'. Concerns were 'further exacerbated in the context of recent budget cuts to education supports'. Unfortunately, there was now a 'real danger ... [that] action, undertaken on the basis of appearance [and racial profiling] would create the conditions for an increase in racism and discrimination against the Roma community living in Ireland'.

Following the state abduction of these Roma children, the website of the Irish Association of Social Workers (IASSW) did not include any press releases condemning what was occurring. More generally, there is 'little evidence' of 'practices or policies in social work' seeking to address issues arising from how the population of Ireland has changed in terms of 'race' and ethnicity (Walsh et al., 2010, p. 1984).

> the development of specific texts on working with refugees and asylum seekers and the inclusion of equality and human rights on social work courses have not translated into visible anti-racist or anti-oppressive policies or practices in social work ... The lack of attention to cultural differences in child protection guidelines and child welfare legislation is one tangible example of a continuing inertia. (Walsh et al., 2010, p. 1984)

As well as the absence of meaningful engagement with anti-racist concerns, there is a 'persistent lack of a feminist discourse within social work despite the predominance of women within the profession' (Skehill, 2000, p. 702).

The next part of the discussion, still largely centred on the dividing practices associated with racialisation, will turn to address how some theorists and commentators on the political left appear increasingly concerned about what they perceive as a social policy and cultural fixation with 'difference' and 'diversity'.

Challenging Multicultural 'Happy Talk': Disrupting 'Difference' and 'Diversity'

A decade ago it was maintained that social work, certainly in England, was perhaps being distracted from pursuing a 'just society' because of an overemphasis on 'difference' and 'diversity' (Garrett, 2002a). This critique, unlike the jibes from the political right directed at 'political correctness', emanated from the political left. Here the central charge was that social work, perhaps for a time unduly influenced in its academic literature by postmodernism in focusing on questions associated with 'identity politics', risked losing sight of the centrality of social class. This critique is also informed by an awareness of how neo-liberalised capitalism appears keen to encompass the ideas pivoting on keywords such as 'identity', 'multiculturalism', 'diversity' and 'difference'. For Zizek (2002, p. 172), the global market 'thrives on the diversification of demand' and multiculturalism 'perfectly fits the logic' of contemporary capitalism. According to Boltanski and Chiapello (2005, p. 441), capitalism has commodified 'difference', internalising 'the intense demand for differentiation and demassification that marked the end of the 1960s and the beginning of the 1970s'. This is apparent, for example, in terms of how large multinational corporations seek to present themselves and their services in adverts, 'values' and 'mission' statements. These now prefer the 'inclusive look of multiculturalism and the apparent valorization of cultural diversity' (Goldman and Papson, 2011, p. 157). Ahmed (2012, p. 10) has argued that embracing cultural diversity is now part of the 'happy talk' of organisations beyond the private sector; that is to say, a focus on 'diversity', often present in the way in which they position themselves in terms of focal symbolic imagery, is central to the way in which institutions construct a 'happy' story or narrative. A related argument posits the notion that organisations – irrespective of the deployment of the multicultural 'happy talk' – tend, in reality, to maintain *'inequality regimes,* defined as loosely interrelated practices, processes, actions and meanings that result in and actually maintain class, gender, and racial inequalities within particular organizations ... Even organizations that have explicit egalitarian goals develop inequality regimes over time' (Acker, 2006, p. 443, emphasis added). This critique, therefore, is centred on the way in which ideas associated with 'difference' and 'diversity' are deployed within a social and economic system that prioritises the accumulation of private capital over the public and collective good.

Another perspective challenging the centrality of these discourses argues that the preoccupation with 'difference' and 'diversity' is mostly a product of factors connected to US society. Prominent here has been the intervention of the French intellectuals, Bourdieu and Wacquant. In an attack on US 'cultural imperialism', they asserted that 'multiculturalism' was – along with words such as 'globalization', 'flexibility', 'governance', 'employability', 'underclass', 'exclusion', 'new economy', 'zero tolerance' and 'communitarianism' – an example of what Orwell termed a 'strange Newspeak' (Bourdieu and Wacquant, 2001, p. 2). 'North American "multiculturalism" is neither a concept nor a theory, nor a social or political movement' it is a false conversation or 'screen discourse'. Bourdieu and Wacquant criticised terms such as 'minority', 'ethnicity' and 'identity' as being simply a facet of a 'new planetary vulgate – from which the terms "capitalism", "class", "exploitation", "domination" and "inequality" are conspicuous by their absence' (Bourdieu and Wacquant, 2001, p. 2). (Vulgate refers to an ancient Latin version of the Scriptures made by St Jerome and others in the fourth century.) More recently, Wacquant (2004, p. 99) has attacked 'false critical thought' which 'under cover of apparently progressive tropes celebrating the "subject", "identity", "multiculturalism", "diversity" and "globalization", invites us to submit to the prevailing forces of the world, and in particular to market forces'.

However, to suggest that a concern about ethnicity and multicultural-ism is the staple of the gullible, conned into participating in a 'screen discourse', or that it is a symptom of 'false critical thought', is problematic. The whole notion of, for example, 'multiculturalism' is a good deal more complex than Bourdieu and Wacquant acknowledge in that debates centred on it are *not* simply a result of US dominance of international intellectual fields. Multiculturalism can be interpreted as a 'travelling theory', which 'disguises very different and fluid struggles in different countries, and even in different cities and localities. This is because multi-culturalism is always mediated by pre-existing structures and policies already in place' (Werbner, 2000, p. 154). Neither is multiculturalism simply a 'top-down government-driven policy', because it is also a 'response to grassroots demand for change, the product of local or national activism ... Critical multiculturalism – unlike corporate multicul-turalism which exists in some European countries – is a mode of *dissent* adopted by excluded or marginalized minorities to attack old paradigms and desanctify tabooed discourses and sacred cows' (Werbner, 2000, p. 154, original emphasis). Within social services in England and elsewhere, the promotion of 'multiculturalism' has, at least in part, been the product of the struggles of marginalised minority groups of workers and users of services. In the Republic of Ireland, as we have seen, there seems to be a relative absence of concerns with similar themes, despite the changed composition of the population in the recent past.

Perhaps the key point here is that keywords, such as 'difference', 'diver-sity' and 'multiculturalism', are malleable and can be *put to work* for forces which represent – in the broadest of terms – the political left or right (see also Clarke and Newman, 2012). In what follows, we will turn our attention to two theorists whose work might enable us to transcend the politics of 'difference' and 'diversity' in order to map out a route for more progressive social work theorisation and practice in times of grim austerity and, seem-ingly, renewed neo-liberalisation: Alain Badiou and Nancy Fraser.

Alain Badiou: 'There is Only One World'

Some of Alain Badiou's key ideas are contained in a short volume on the apostle St Paul (Badiou, 2003). In Badiou's reading, Paul was committed to a profoundly levelling, singular universality. Although a Roman citizen, Paul rejected 'any legal category [seeking] to identify the Christian subject. Slaves, women, people of every profession and nationality [were] therefore admitted without restriction or privilege' (Badiou, 2003, pp. 13–14). These ideas on St Paul and his promotion of a singular universalism are connected to Stephen Webb's move to inject similar thinking into social work. Webb (2009) uses Badiou to criticise what he perceives as social work's problematic engagement with 'difference': 'Social work should be "indifferent to differences" by transcending the politics of difference' (Webb, 2009, p. 309). Here, a focal concern is that this alleged centrality of 'difference' within the social work literature is a direct consequence of the 'displacement of class as *the* universal signifier of oppression' (Webb, 2009, p. 309, original emphasis). Webb avows that:

> identity politics of difference rest on *anti-essentialist* claims that there are multiple starting-points of equal status rather than one single one from which to assess the ethics of social work ... The net effect of the critique of difference and diversity discourse is to demonstrate why ideas and institutions embraced by many progressives, in fields such as social work, can in fact be conservative. (Webb, 2009, p. 309)

The risk associated with identity politics is that it gives rise to divisiveness, since a 'predilection towards highlighting difference can lead to a latent form of xenophobia in peoples, a partitioning rather than an understanding' (Webb, 2009, p. 310).

What is more, there is a 'contradiction', even duplicity, intrinsic to the 'respect for differences' talk because it shields 'an "ideal type", a unitary identity that is tucked away for the proselytisers of difference': the affluent, white, Westerner, against whom all 'differences' are defined (Webb, 2009, p. 311). When the liberal rhetoric is viewed more closely, the message being conveyed to immigrants is merely: 'Become like me and I will respect your difference' (Badiou in Webb, 2009, p. 311). Badiou, in fact, argues that 'the right to be defended today is not "the right to difference", but, on the contrary, and more than ever, the right to sameness' (Hallward in Webb, 2009, p. 311).

Within and beyond social work, a progressive politics must identify areas of commonality and solidarity, if not 'sameness', if it is to counter neo-liberalisation. As evidenced in his theorisation and political practice, Badiou is also aware that the promotion of a confining, stultifying 'sameness' is socially retrogressive. In a note sketching the new imperative for leftist activists following the presidential victory of Sarkozy in May 2007, Badiou asserted that the foundational statement the left should coalesce around should be the assumption that 'all workers labouring here belong here, and must be treated on a basis of equality, and respected accordingly – especially workers of foreign origin' (Badiou, 2008, p. 44). His commitment to 'one world' politics, however, has little in common with the shallow rhetoric of 'globalisation' dominating the discourse of so-called 'world leaders' and slides, on occasions, into the social work literature.

For Badiou, holding fast to the idea that we all inhabit the same world does not contradict a person's right to 'maintain and develop' what they may conceive as their sense of 'identity' and to 'preserve and organize those invariant properties' such as 'religion, mother tongue, forms of recreation and domesticity, and so on' (Badiou, 2008, p. 65). This would be particularly important, in fact, for migrant workers who feel compelled to refuse 'the imposition of integration' (Badiou, 2008, p. 65). If 'preconditions' are placed on migrants – if the state labels them as 'asylum seekers' and confines them to 'reception centres' – the 'same world' principle has clearly been abandoned (Badiou, 2008, p. 62). Rather than denying 'difference', Badiou alerts his reader to the 'immense differentiating unity of the world of human beings' (Badiou, 2008, p. 64).

More broadly, notions of 'difference' and 'diversity' pivot on complex and highly charged theoretical (and political) questions. This is also apparent if one looks at some of the debates generated on recognition theory that have begun to find a place within social work's academic literature. Although not framed by a Badiousian perspective, and using an entirely different vocabulary, these exchanges explore similar issues. Here, Nancy Fraser has played a key role.

Nancy Fraser: 'Recognition Theory' and Parity of Participation

Within philosophy, 'recognition designates an ideal reciprocal relation between subjects in which each sees the other as its equal ... one becomes an individual only in virtue of recognizing, and being recognized by, another subject' (Fraser, 2003, p. 10). Due 'recognition is not just a courtesy we owe people. It is a vital human need' (Taylor, 1992, p. 26). The German philosopher Hegel (1770–1831) coined the phrase the 'struggle for recognition' (*Kampf um Anerkennung*), but it was the early 1990s which marked a resurgence of academic interest in this theme. A number of writers located within the field of social work, drawing on the ethics and politics of recognition, have recently provided thoughtful contributions which have stressed the relevance of this theorisation for practitioners' day-to-day encounters with the users of social services (Froggett, 2004; Webb, 2006; Houston, 2008). A critical literature is also beginning to emerge (Garrett, 2010).

As we saw earlier in our discussion on the recent example of how Roma families were treated in Ireland, members of socially and economically marginalised groups are systematically denied dignity, self-esteem and recognition, either as persons or on account of their way of life and culture. Such processes of denial and disrespect extend into the practices of social work and into the lives of children and their families seeking help, or having interventions imposed upon them. In Ireland, we can also connect some of the ideas related to recognition theory to the findings of a number of inquiries which have examined clerical abuse in institutional settings (Murphy et al., 2005; Commission of Investigation, 2009; 2010; Commission to Inquire into Child Abuse, 2009).

Shortcomings – and abusive 'care' practices – can, in part, be attributed to a failure to accord meaningful recognition to specific groups and individuals (Wardhaugh and Wilding, 1993). In England, the dynamics of (mis)recognition, may, for example, be associated with the response of social services to Victoria Climbié and Peter Connelly (Secretary of State for Health and the Secretary of State for the Home Department, 2003; Ofsted, Healthcare Commission, HMC, 2008; see also Garrett, 2009).

Nancy Fraser's own approach to the question of recognition is grounded in the 'principle of parity of participation' and the promotion of embedded social arrangements that permit all members of society to interact with others as peers (see, for example, Fraser, 1989; 1997; 2000; 2003; Fraser and Honneth, 2003a). The aim, therefore, should be to preclude 'institutional norms that systematically depreciate some categories of people and the qualities associated with them' (Fraser, 2003, p. 36). Her formula on participatory parity is also able to 'exclude opportunistic and destructive claims', such as those of racists and xenophobes (McNay, 2008, p. 149).

However, Fraser is worried that the rise of a 'politics of recognition' has been at the expense of what she calls the 'politics of redistribution'. For her, there is the risk that the politics of 'difference' – preoccupied with questions of 'identity' and often associated with the demands of social movements representing particular 'minority groups' – might lead to the marginalisation, or displacement, of a politics of equality grounded in notions of class and focused on economic inequality and campaigns for economic justice. Fraser suggests that some reject the politics of recognition outright because of the global increase in poverty and mass inequalities. For them, claims for the recognition of 'difference' are an obstruction to the pursuit of social justice. Conversely, some of the promoters of recognition are sceptical about the politics of redistribution and disdain the failure of difference-blind economic egalitarianism to bring about the justice for women and minority ethnic groups. Thus, it can appear that we are 'effectively presented with an either/or choice: redistribution or recognition? Class politics or identity politics? Multiculturalism or social democracy?' (Fraser, 2003, p. 8). In contrast, her own carefully argued claim is that neither 'alone is sufficient' (Fraser, 2003, p. 9). Instead of endorsing either one of these paradigms to the exclusion of the other, she seeks to develop a 'two-dimensional' conception of justice. Without 'reducing either dimension to the other, it encompasses both of them within a broader overarching framework' (Fraser, 2003, p. 35).

Consequently, Fraser advocates a theory of social justice in which redistribution *and* recognition play equal and interwoven parts: injustices confronting individuals and groups are rooted in economy *and* culture. That is to say, economy and culture are intertwined and interpenetrating social spaces. No zone of society can be purely economic or purely cultural since '*every* practice' is 'simultaneously economic and cultural, albeit not necessarily in equal proportions' (Fraser, 2003, p. 63, original emphasis). She argues, therefore, that in 'all societies economic ordering and cultural ordering are mutually imbricated' (Fraser, 2003, p. 51). This understanding highlights the complexities inherent in engaging, as social workers do, with people whose lives (and life chances) are determined by their positioning within a grid of intersecting forms of domination and opposition.

According to Fraser, what is required, therefore, is a conceptualisation equipped to 'theorize the dynamic forms of status subordination characteristic of late-modern globalizing capitalism' (Fraser, 2003, p. 8). Fraser terms this 'perspectival dualism' (Fraser, 2003, p. 63). To illuminate her approach, she focuses on gender, arguing that the 'two-dimensional character of gender wreaks havoc on the idea of an either/or choice between the paradigm of redistribution and the paradigm of recognition' (Fraser, 2003, p. 22). More fundamentally, Fraser argues that a 'genuinely critical perspective … cannot take the appearance of separate spheres at face value. Rather, it must probe beneath appearances to reveal the hidden connections between distribution and recognition' (Fraser, 2003, p. 62).

'Perspectival dualist' approaches should, therefore, be founded on helping to create the conditions for 'parity of participation'. Such analyses are, for Fraser, not merely describing and interpreting the world; they are part of a political aspiration to *change* the world. Thus, she stresses the need to go beyond 'affirmative strategies' – reflected in mainstream multiculturalism – for 'redressing injustice which aim to correct inequitable outcomes of social arrangements without disturbing the underlying social structures that generate them' (Fraser, 2003, p. 74).

Key Ideas for Practice

1. Central here is the idea that all dominant ideas related to 'difference' and 'diversity' should be approached warily and even disrupted. Events, such as those in Ireland, involving the state 'kidnapping' of Roma children point to the significance of racism rooted in the practices of the state and its agents.

2. However, following Badiou, there is also a need to try to foster and promote 'one world politics', which is attentive to building alliances rooted in the commonality of experiences and notions of human solidarity. Added to this we might try to think about what a 'one world social work' might look like? How might this progressive form of practice address some of the issues raised in this chapter?

3. The work of Nancy Fraser might also serve to remind us that what she terms the 'politics of retribution' should not be diluted because of the focus on the 'politics of recognition'. This message would seem to be especially important in times of so-called 'austerity', when cuts are undermining the well-being of many of those receiving and providing services.

Conclusion

In drawing attention to the work of Badiou and Fraser, it is acknowledged that their theoretical interventions can be challenging because of the complexity of their arguments. The language they use is often rather technical. However, engaging with them and trying to *think* with them can be immensely useful in seeking to transcend the politics of 'difference' and 'diversity'. More broadly, they could aid our efforts to act in a way which could produce a transformed social work better able to resist neo-liberalism.

13
Deconstructing the Family

Stephen Hicks

Introduction

Social work has an intimate relationship with 'the family', since many aspects of practice are concerned with family life and family problems. Child protection, adoption, support for older people, interventions with young people in trouble, residential, kinship and substitute care, helping people cope with dementia or providing support to disabled people, for example, draw upon ideas and expectations about family life. This means that social workers are not only involved in negotiations with families about difficult issues, but that their interventions have powerful effects, since they rely upon and involve claims about family. So, what does this imply for social work? Isn't 'the family' obvious? Why should social workers want to 'deconstruct' it, and what does this mean?

It is important to address such questions because social work produces powerful claims about families and intervenes in similarly powerful ways (Gavriel-Fried et al., 2012). To recommend that a child be removed from its parents and placed elsewhere, perhaps with foster carers, for example, relies upon a whole series of assumptions, some of which have to be challenged by social workers, since child care law states that local authorities have a duty to promote the upbringing of children by their families. Social work is also involved in making powerful claims and decisions about families and, at times, concerns have been raised about the possibility of oppressive and damaging practice, especially in relation to black, gay, lesbian or single-parent families (Swift, 1995; Graham, 2007b; Hicks, 2011).

This chapter addresses social work's relationship to the family and asks how social workers can begin to deconstruct traditional or dominant accounts of family life. The chapter begins by considering the standard, nuclear family model and goes on to question this via discussions of family diversity and various sociological analyses. It then outlines and questions approaches to the family found in anti-discriminatory and anti-oppressive social work theories, as defined by Thompson (2012) and Dominelli (2002a), before going on to discuss two different notions of deconstruction and how these might be applied to social work with families. Finally, the chapter considers how social work practice with families can be developed and looks at the implications of a deconstructionist approach.

The Standard, Nuclear Family

Smith describes the 'standard family' as:

> a conception of The Family as a legally married couple sharing a household. The adult male is in paid employment; his earnings provide the economic basis of the family-household. The adult female may also earn an income, but her primary responsibility is to the care of husband, household, and children. The adult male and female may be parents (in whatever legal sense) of children also resident in the household. (Smith, 1999, p. 159)

This standard model, sometimes also referred to as 'the nuclear family', is often promoted through images, texts and government policy. One way in which it is upheld is via identification of other forms of family as an attack on, or the decline of, the standard family. This supposed decline is often blamed upon groups and individuals that do not fit the standard mould – feminists, single mothers, disabled people, black families, lesbians and gay men (see, for example, Phillips, 1999; Almond, 2006; Morgan, 2007; Blankenhorn, 2009). Smith argues that the standard family is upheld through the 'identification of deviant instances, such as "female-headed families"' (Smith, 1999, p. 160). In this sense, the standard family works as a moral code or form of evaluation in which the nuclear, white, heteronormative form is prioritised.

Other feminist writers have criticised the standard family model, since it reproduces traditional ideas about gender roles, expects women to perform unpaid household and caring work, rests upon prioritisation of the heterosexual couple and traps women into economic dependence. Feminists have also pointed out that the family, often designated as a place of safety and comfort, is also the primary site of violence and abuse experienced by women and children (Barrett and McIntosh, 1982; Segal, 1983; Delphy and Leonard, 1992; Stacey, 1996; Chambers, 2012).

One response to the prioritisation of the standard family is to emphasise family diversity, the whole range of forms that family life may take. This approach has included examination of: new reproductive technologies (such as medically assisted conception or surrogacy); ethnic or cultural diversity in family forms; lesbian, gay, transgender or bisexual families; step-families and other reconstituted formations; foster-care, adoption and kinship care; and residential care and other forms of community living. This family diversity perspective is important, as it recognises a range of forms and challenges the notion that the standard family ought to be prioritised. Cheal, for example, notes that cohabitation, single-parent families, extended families, polygamy, culturally contingent family models and lesbian or gay families all represent 'the open and undecided character of contemporary family life' (Cheal, 2008, p. 44).

However, there are potential problems with the family diversity perspective. Highlighting a range of family forms may, unfortunately, seem to suggest that they occupy places of equal worth or standing, when actually they are often placed in hierarchical relation. In addition, a diversity perspective does not pay much attention to the ways in which the designation 'family' is achieved in various social contexts. Rather than taking family as given and merely asking about its various incarnations, then, it is important to ask how meanings are deployed in everyday contexts; that is, how various people, actions, places, artefacts and so on achieve the categorisation 'family'.

Sociological Approaches to the Family

Sociological approaches ask critical questions about the ways that 'family' is achieved and put to work in various contexts. Morgan, for example, notes that government policy, 'even where this does not explicitly refer to family matters, draws upon common assumptions about family life and has consequences for the ways in which people understand or construct their domestic lives' (Morgan, 1996, p. 196). Education, health or social welfare policies make many assumptions about family forms, expectations of parents, housing and inheritance or who qualifies to make decisions about the vulnerable. As Wilkinson and Bell note:

> feminist and queer critiques of 'the family' are still as pertinent as ever, as policy makers have yet to grasp the diverse range of family formations that exist, and policy is still tied to a deeply normative and conservative understanding of family. (Wilkinson and Bell, 2012, p. 426)

In order to shift analysis away from the family as given and to focus, instead, upon its role as a form of meaning in social life, sociologists have analysed practices, discourses, display or enactment and, in some cases, have questioned whether 'family' is the best term to capture what might otherwise be termed contemporary forms of relationality, intimacy and personal life (see, for example, Edwards and Gillies, 2012a, b; Edwards et al., 2012; May, 2012; Wilkinson and Bell, 2012).

Smart's work has asked whether 'family' is the best model for understanding, since it tends to prioritise biological relations over others and may reinforce private/public spheres. Smart uses 'personal life,' instead, as this 'does not invoke the white, middle-class, heterosexual family in the way that, historically at least, the concept of "the family" has' (Smart, 2007, p. 30). She wishes to open up the field to forms of relationality other than those based upon traditional notions of kinship, and this is an especially important point for social work, since it often grapples with the prioritisation of blood and kin ties over other, non-standard, bonds.

Morgan's work has emphasised the need to view family as a set of practices, using:

> 'family' as an adjective rather than as a noun, using the term to refer to sets of practices which deal in some way with ideas of parenthood, kinship and marriage and the expectations and obligations which are associated with these practices. (Morgan, 1996, p. 11)

In later work, Morgan broadens this definition to include gay, lesbian or bisexual family practices, in order to challenge the 'heteronormativity implied by the emphasis on "family"' (Morgan, 2011, p. 165), but his point is to ask how some practices or persons may be recognised as family while others are not. Being a family, therefore, becomes associated with various practices to do with care, proximity, space, or gender, and family practices are 'to do with those relationships and activities that are constructed as being to do with family matters' (Morgan, 1996, p. 192). Talk about 'private life' or about 'personal matters', for example, often designates particular relationships, topics and activities as to do with family. This notion does not play down social and historical mores or constraints – as Morgan says, these are not 'just any old practices' (Morgan, 1996, p. 192) – but, at the same time, shifting focus onto how people *do* family, rather than what a family *is*, allows for analysis of how it is brought into play and used to create hierarchical distinctions, a perspective that has informed some social work research (Mitchell, 2007; Jones and Hackett, 2011; 2012; Morris, 2012; 2013; Saltiel, 2013).

Anti-Discriminatory and Anti-Oppressive Practice?

Anti-discriminatory and anti-oppressive social work theories question reliance upon the standard, nuclear family model, or 'familial/ist ideology'

(Dominelli, 2002a, p. 51; Thompson, 2012, p. 57). This model is seen to promote the expectation that women should carry out unpaid caring and domestic work, sticking to clearly defined gender roles. As Thompson notes, this 'emphasis on the nuclear family as "normal" thus defines other family forms as "deviant" and undesirable' (Thompson, 2012, p. 57). Dominelli also points out the heteronormative nature of the standard model, and both argue that this model is used to 'pathologise' black families through the operation of stereotypes (Dominelli, 2002a, p. 73; Thompson, 2012, p. 82).

Nevertheless, questions about family discourse or practice are largely absent from anti-discriminatory and anti-oppressive theories. Social workers are exhorted to challenge reliance upon the standard family, yet it could also be said that these theories offer little analysis of how family designations are achieved and put to use in everyday social work contexts. How, precisely, do 'the family' and ideas about families operate within social work, and how might social workers challenge dominant, hierarchical models?

Anti-discriminatory and anti-oppressive theories refer to family forms other than the standard model – black families, single-parent families, lesbian and gay families, unmarried couples – yet, in adopting this diversity perspective, there is a danger of reifying those categories as types. 'The black family', for example, is potentially as restrictive a category as the nuclear family, not because it is accorded similar status, but because it may suggest a singular form. In addition, references to the family within anti-discriminatory and anti-oppressive theories are usually related to questions about gender, women or race, but family discourse is also relevant to sexuality, class, age, disability, religion, culture, in fact all of social work policy, theory and practice.

In one of the few places that gay or lesbian people are discussed in Dominelli's text, she focuses on struggles for partnership recognition by some unmarried, gay or lesbian couples:

> In projecting their demands within familialist arrangements, unmarried and same sex couples are lending heterosexual institutions a new lease of life and strengthening their legitimacy. Rooting their definition of the problem and its solution within hegemonic discourses also carries with it the danger of undermining some of the struggles for equality that women within heterosexual unions have undertaken, for example the goal of disaggregating resources within the 'family' unit. (Dominelli, 2002a, p. 31)

It seems ironic that, in a text that largely treats family questions as having to do with heterosexuality, lesbians and gay men are mentioned only briefly, and largely as a target for criticism. Actually, whilst there are many who do support partnership registration or marriage rights, this is by no means the sum total of lesbian or gay argument in the field. There are others who question lesbian and gay partnership recognition or marriage as either the most pressing political issue or as models for ways of life (see, for example, Ettelbrick, 1989; Butler, 2004b; Polikoff, 2008), and whether such marriages or registration of partnerships legitimate heteronormativity is also open to debate. For example, it is possible to argue that gay marriage might actually challenge hegemonic discourses about the family, since it provokes questions about the primacy of heterosexuality. The need to ask whether standard family models might be reinforced through a focus on gay marriage is an important and welcome point, but Dominelli seems to represent all gay and lesbian couples as assimilative, and provides no detailed discussion of how heteronormativity works in the field of family discourse.

In addition, it is possible to argue that anti-discriminatory and anti-oppressive theories present monolithic accounts of social workers as always promoting the standard family. Although Thompson is keen to avoid such 'reductionist oversimplification' (Thompson, 2012, p. 82), the combination of a lack of detailed discussion of how family practices are negotiated within the social work context with an exhortation to avoid familial ideology may reinforce the idea that social workers merely repeat dominant models. Further, engagement with analyses of family practices and discourses is opposed by Dominelli, who describes some of these ideas as the 'failings of postmodernism' (Dominelli, 2002a, p. 168). Mentioning Foucault (1983; Rabinow, 1984), she suggests:

> postmodern theorists perceive power as an insidious and ubiquitous force that subsumes any form of opposition to its dictates in hegemonic discourses. Moreover, hegemonic power does not allow for the creation of alternative knowl edges which can challenge the dominant one because knowledge is conceptu-alised as an institutionalised and controlling system of thought. (Dominelli, 2002a, pp. 169–170)

Yet, Foucault's work was clear in its analysis of resistance to power; the development and attempted suppression of subjugated knowledge; the productive, not just repressive, aspects of power; and the potential for 'reverse discourse' – the voice of the 'disqualified' speaking 'in its own behalf' – to demand legitimacy (Foucault, 1990, p. 101). In addition, Foucault's work challenges dominant conceptions of family as these were used to define sexual and gender norms within psychiatry, medicine, education and even social work (Foucault, 1990; 2006). Thus, Dominelli's 'people do resist oppression' (2002a, p. 170) was a claim made consistently by Foucault. Of course, aspects of this discussion are open to debate – Dominelli is not impressed by work that focuses on language-use – yet it may also be argued that the models of power presented in anti-discriminatory and anti-oppressive theories are, themselves, rather limited. People seem to have or lack power, and there is little emphasis on power as every-day practice, or on concepts like 'family' as ways of knowing and defining the social world.

In relation to anti-discriminatory and anti-oppressive practice theories, then, these perspectives often deal in rather straightforward types or categories, such as 'the black family', 'gay people', and so on. Social work is frequently exhorted to understand the 'needs' of such groups, but there is little attention to the ways in which social work processes contribute to the construction of ways of knowing about sexuality, race, gender and so on (Hicks, 2008b). The suggestion that social workers may reinforce dominant 'familial/ist' ideology seems to fix them as mere dupes of powerful systems of thought. But in David Saltiel's study of two UK social work teams, for example, the social workers 'understood very well that the families they worked with came in a huge diversity of forms in which the conventional nuclear family ... hardly featured' (Saltiel, 2013, p. 16).

Deconstructing the Family: Deconstruction Version 1

Turning now to differing versions of deconstruction, the first usage of the term means to defamiliarise, to subject the mundane to analysis. Ribbens McCarthy, Doolittle and Day Sclater use this in their text on family meanings. They refer to 'teasing open' the question of family meanings, a process:

> sometimes described as one of 'deconstructing' what is normally taken-for-granted about families. To do this, researchers analyse 'family' as something that is socially constructed rather than a natural and concrete object, so that it is shaped and produced by social forces and contexts ... The task of analysis, then, requires the researchers to 'de-construct' these processes and make them visible. (Ribbens McCarthy et al., 2012, p. 62)

To argue that the family is socially constructed is to suggest that ideas about families are powerful meaning-givers, and that dominant or even common sense notions about family often repeat constraining and culturally specific patterns. Knowledge about the family is arrived at between people, involving complex social interaction, and this tends to produce accepted norms, as well as other, subjugated versions. A particular notion of family, like the standard model outlined earlier, has consequences, such as the denigration of other forms and ways of life. Ways of talking and doing family, therefore, set up expectations, sometimes formulated as policies, and these also designate accepted – and so unaccepted – forms. To 'deconstruct', here, implies analysis of such socially achieved notions of family, and this may be best demonstrated through two examples that question standard accounts.

Carol Stack's 1974 study of family and kin relations in 'The Flats', a poor, black (African-American), inner city community in the US, is important because it presents an account of life that is not usually highlighted, and so begs questions about standard family notions. Stack carried out detailed research based upon participant observation and interviews over a three-year period (1968–1971) in an urban area characterised by over-crowding, poverty, poor health/environment, high unemployment and in which most of the working population were in service as maids, cooks or janitors (caretakers/cleaners). Stack found this community had developed extended networks of support and exchange (helping out, lending, passing on items, recycling), in which 'socially recognized kin ties' were vital, and in which 'the "household" and its group composition was not a meaningful unit to isolate for analysis of family life' (Stack, 1997, pp. 29–31). As she notes:

> Ultimately I defined 'family' as the smallest, organized, durable network of kin and non-kin who interact daily, providing domestic needs of children and assuring their survival. The family network is diffused over several kin-based households, and fluctuations in household composition do not significantly affect co-operative familial arrangements. (Stack, 1997, p. 31)

Stack made some important observations about community life in The Flats. First, friends or family regularly fostered children, and these forms of 'acquired parenthood' (Stack, 1997, p. 47) were the norm. Second, friends were treated as kin, allowing for 'creation of mutual aid domestic networks which are not bounded by genealogical distance or genealogical criteria' (Stack, 1997, p. 61). Third, heterosexual women often described social welfare and kin support as providing them with more security than men, although the stereotype of the black, matriarchal family with the absent father was not confirmed by Stack's research. Of course, it is important to remember that Stack's findings do not represent all black families, and also that the dynamics she describes have as much to do with questions of poverty, class, gender and community context as they have to do with race. However, her research questions standard family models and the primacy of the heterosexual couple (see Chapter 7, 'Women and Men', Stack, 1997, p. 108–123). Thus, family forms relate to local circumstances and we are reminded that, in working class and poorer areas, women have always worked outside the home. This suggests that the standard family model is a middle class one, a point also made in Young and Willmott's 1957 classic study, *Family and Kinship in East London* (Young and Willmott, 2007).

My research, based upon interviews with lesbian, gay and queer parents, as well as social workers and managers in fostering or adoption services, was carried out between 1994 and 2010 (Hicks, 2011). The study raises questions about standard accounts of family, since it argues that restrictive notions of kinship, intimacy and personal relationships, as well as the involvement of the state in sanctioning particular forms of these, presents many lesbian, gay, bisexual or transgender (LGBT) families with dilemmas, since they do not wish to live according to heteronormative expectations. Treating friends as family, not prioritising blood-kin relations or challenging gendered expectations about family life are just some of the ways that LGBT families seek to break free of standard models (Hicks, 2011).

Standard notions of 'gender role', for example, hold that children require both a male and female parent at home in order properly to understand how to become a man or woman, an idea that inevitably promotes the standard, nuclear family. This kind of theory assumes distinct and natural gendered differences, and sees gender as something acquired over time, in the early years of childhood (see summary of this perspective in Kane, 2013). Any kind of resistance to standard gender or roles, or any person that does not seem to fit such roles, is described as deviant, and this kind of role theory is frequently used by those opposed to all LGBT parenting (see, for example, Wardle, 1997; Phillips, 1999; Morgan, 2002). But the notion of gender role models is not just held by right-wing commentators, it is also a fairly common sense argument, and it is often raised when considering LGBT people as parents. In my research, for example, I found that gender role was a concern of social workers and of adoption or fostering decision-making panels, even where those people were supportive of gay or lesbian carers (Hicks, 2011). That is, a concern about gender role models for children was frequently raised, with gay men, for example, being asked how many women they knew or were in contact with and how they would ensure their children came into contact with females.

Many LGBT parents talk about the constraining effects of ideas about gender role, some even referring to 'gender role strain' (Benson et al., 2005, p. 3):

> The social worker did ask us quite a lot about role models, and female role models ... It must have been difficult for her and I think she struggled with it ... But we don't define who does what ... it was almost as though she wanted us to be these stereotypical roles ... Those gender roles used to get on my nerves really. (Hicks, 2011, pp. 120–124)

Many lesbian or gay applicants are asked to provide evidence of balanced gender role models, which raises the phenomena of gay or lesbian people being seen as gender deviant in some way, and of gender being seen as some kind of thing passed on by parents. This, of course, is a very fixed and limited view of gender, one that reinforces the notion that children are overly influenced by their parents or carers, or that they are not able to think about, take up and use gender in various ways (for a very different view, see Kane, 2012 or Thorne, 1993). The notion of gender role modelling is also a way of reinforcing normative gender and sexual identities. These are challenged or opposed in various ways by LGBT parents, yet it is difficult to maintain opposition to gender norms in the face of traditional or institutional expectations. LGBT parents are aware that to question gender norms, or to expect their children to do so, is difficult, that this may simply confirm stereotypes of LGBT people as gender deviants and, in some contexts, may actually be dangerous, since gender expectations form part of the fabric of everyday life (Hicks, 2011; 2013). But this is an important point, since it highlights the social nature of those expectations and allows us to begin to deconstruct gender hierarchies.

Deconstructing the Family: Deconstruction Version 2

A second version of deconstruction is that associated with poststructural theories, largely found within literary and cultural studies (Belsey, 2002; Norris, 2002; Culler, 2008). This version of deconstruction, largely inspired by the writing of Jacques Derrida (1976), is not, as Barbara Johnson notes, 'synonymous with *destruction* ... [but] much closer to the original meaning of the word *analysis*, which etymologically means "to undo"' (Johnson, 1980, p. 5) (see also the more detailed discussion of Derrida's work in Dharman Jeyasingham's chapter in this book).

This form of undoing the family, whether in discourse (texts, images) or practice, is characterised by, first, attention to the way in which meaning is deferred or displaced. This implies that the meaning of a text may be subject to endless difference/deferral, since meaning is not fixed or inherent in a text but actually open to or haunted by other, sometimes unintended, possibilities. Indeed, the intention of an author is not of particular relevance to deconstructive criticism, since meaning emerges from interactions between author, text and reader/viewer(s).

Second, binary oppositions – the supposed polarisation of two terms, such as man/woman, white/black, family/friends, family/not-family and so on – are a focus for deconstruction, since it is important to recognise that the first term in any opposition is usually prioritised. In addition, however, deconstruction plays with the inherent instability within the supposed difference, and within individual terms themselves:

> The differences *between* entities (prose and poetry, man and woman, literature and theory, guilt and innocence) are shown to be based on a repression of differences *within* entities, ways in which an entity differs from itself. (Johnson, 1980, pp. x–xi)

For example, Johnson explains that, amongst feminists, the 'notion of woman – or feminist – is shown to have more than one meaning, to be a subject of dispute in its own right' (Johnson, 1998, p. 193). But, for deconstruction, this is the place where analysis starts, that is, with the multivalence of any term or concept. The potential instability of a term like 'family' is, therefore, of interest to deconstruction.

Third, deconstruction is interested in what is repressed, inherently contradictory or elided in any discourse. As Johnson notes, slippages and contradictions are brought to the surface in order to 'undercut the certainties [that] texts have been read as upholding' (Johnson, 1987, p. xvii). Some of Johnson's questions, then, are of interest:

> What are the political consequences of the fact that language is not a transparently expressive medium? ... How can the study of suppressed, disseminated, or marginalized messages within texts equip us to intervene against oppression and injustice in the world? (Johnson, 1987, p. 7)

Deconstructing Aspects of the Lesbian and Gay Family

Gigi Kaeser and Peggy Gillespie's US text, *Love Makes a Family: Portraits of Lesbian, Gay, Bisexual, and Transgender Parents and Their Families* (1999), employs a key argument often used to defend families perceived to be 'different'; that is, that sexuality does not matter that much and that all families are the same deep down. The work makes a number of claims about the 'love and humanity in all types of families' and about LGBT families being 'not so different after all' (Family Diversity Projects, 2004–2008). For example, Rob, a gay dad, says:

> It's very important for people to understand that love makes a family. Without love, there's no family. Gay families do the same thing straight families do – which is to love each other. Gay parents have the same power of love as anyone else. All they do is love their children and try to do their best to raise a family. (Kaeser and Gillespie, 1999, p. 76)

Perhaps this emphasis on normality is understandable in the context of heteronormative reactions to LGBT families, as it acts as a challenge to

stereotypical views. However, for a deconstructionist reading, such arguments may be subject to question, since they can never be so straightforward. As has already been noted, a family diversity approach is problematic
because there is no 'level playing field'. LGBT families are subject to discrimination and are sometimes described as abnormal, in comparison with the
standard family. That, of course, is one of the reasons for *Love Makes a
Family*'s existence, to challenge such views. But, wherever a new version of
the family is introduced, it may very well reinforce conservative views of the
LGBT family as 'just like' heterosexuals, or it may require them to be so.

A deconstructionist account would probably be much more interested in
analysing the ways in which claims to family status work within discourse,
rather than merely attempting to challenge stereotypes with positive images
(Hicks, 2011). The very notion that 'love makes a family', for example, draws
upon fairly conventional, sentimental and idealised imagery (whether
textual or visual), and it also suggests sameness, or likeness, to the standard,
heterosexual model. For social work, however, sameness needs careful
critique, since approaching practice questions, such as foster care or adoption by LGBT people, via the notion that 'sexuality doesn't matter' is
unlikely to be helpful. This is because a sameness approach – for example,
saying that all foster care or adoption applicants should be assessed in the
same way, regardless of sexuality – may actually reinforce heteronormative
practice, as it is likely to compare LGBT people with, and expect them to
emulate, heterosexual versions of family or intimate life (Cocker and Brown,
2010; Brown and Cocker, 2011; Hicks, 2011).

Sameness models may also confirm rather conservative assumptions
about forms of kinship and intimacy; for example, the notion that LGBT
families should only take the form of the long-term, registered couple with
children, or that biological ties to children are more important than others.
Riggs has argued that 'love makes a family' type explanations may explain
away questions of potential difference that being in a LGBT family raises,
and, further, that any claim promoting respectability or normality may, in
fact, produce racist ideas about who counts 'within the national imaginary',
since this is a practice that reinforces whiteness as a norm (Riggs, 2006, p.
80). Think, for example, about notions of the 'mother-/father-land' and the
racial dynamics involved in many claims about belonging (Puar, 2007;
Yuval-Davis, 2011).

Gillespie has said, in relation to *Love Makes a Family*:

We were trying to counter homophobia ... [The] rather happy feel ... is a step
towards 'normalizing' these families in the eyes of people who are unfamiliar
and prejudiced about LGBT people having children and families ... [I]f you are
expressing pride about being gay, it's fine to show all the forms of gay life ... But
in the name of getting equal rights ... it is probably 'better' to just portray the

more traditional gay/lesbian families and not focus on for example a family that is involved in a group marriage or multiple partners, etc. (Gillespie, personal communication, in Hicks, 2011, p. 80)

For some viewers/readers, the text/photographs will indeed present positive images. But a deconstructive account needs to open up these debates, so that the problems and contradictions within claims about 'the LGBT family' are addressed. Gillespie's argument highlights the need to 'normalise' LGBT families in the face of homophobia, yet this is also in danger of allowing only a very limited – or what she calls 'traditional' – version of intimate life.

Reconstructing Practice

Nigel Parton points out that, for social workers, questions of 'uncertainty … difference, complexity, and ambiguity' are important (Parton, 2012, p. 143). Not only are they central to complex areas of practice, such as child and adult protection or safeguarding, but they also remind social workers of the need to be aware of difference, and the ways in which certain claims or interpretations of events may become privileged over others. Parton also adds that deconstruction's insistence that 'phenomena are continually interrogated, evaluated, overturned, and disrupted' is important, as this opens up the possibility of change or seeing things differently (Parton, 2012, p. 144). This also relates to the recommendation, in Lord Laming's inquiry into the death of Victoria Climbié, that the 'concept of "respectful uncertainty" should lie at the heart of the relationship between the social worker and the family … social workers must keep an open mind' (Laming, 2003, p. 205).

One fairly common response to deconstruction is the notion that it becomes impossible to act, to carry out social work practice, in the face of such critique. If everything inherently contains contradictions and the possibility of multiple meanings, then how is it possible to develop 'good' practice? But, as Johnson notes, deconstruction wishes 'to intervene against oppression and injustice in the world' (Johnson, 1987, p. 7). It is not synonymous with destruction; rather its focus is on analysis of contradictions and the challenging of hierarchical relations. In relation to ideas about the family, this is vital, as social workers need to work with many family forms – a lot of them far from 'traditional' – but must also avoid reinforcing standard ideas about what kinds of relationships count or are recognised. It is not just LGBT or black families that are sidelined by standard accounts, but also many forms of residential, substitute, community, group or institutional forms of care and living.

This brief discussion of deconstruction and the family has a number of important implications for the development of social work practice. Social workers will need to remember that any practice relating to relationships, obligations, tensions, connections, parenting and so on are claims to knowledge about family; that is, they are not innocent descriptions, but rather powerful ways of constructing knowledge. This means that social workers need to maintain a reflexive practice – the subjection of 'our own knowledge claims to critical analysis' (Taylor and White, 2000, p. 35) – in relation to the kinds and forms of knowledge about families that they produce and use.

In relation to family forms, social workers need to be aware of the cultural dominance of the (white, heterosexual) standard, and open their minds up to a diversity of ways of living, including those that question traditional practices. However, this understanding needs to be situated within a critical awareness of the hierarchical claims, laws and policies that prioritise certain family forms over others. Social workers need to deconstruct binary relations – family/not family, family/friends, biological/non-biological kin, home/institution and so on – and ensure that the first term is not accorded some kind of natural and privileged status over the second. Young people in forms of residential or substitute care, for example, need to feel that their way of life is legitimate. Adopters and adoptees should not be made to feel that their bonds are artificial or second best. This means that social workers will need to ask critical questions about forms of relationality and see family as a set of *practices*, which can be changed and rethought, rather than as a fixed entity.

Key Ideas for Practice

1. Social workers need to adopt a critical stance in relation to the standard, nuclear family, and be aware of powerful hierarchies that attempt to denigrate other forms.

2. Ways of talking about families and practices that can be said to constitute family life should be given critical attention. This helps avoidance of treating family as a thing, and instead asks how it is practised and claimed.

3. Anti-discriminatory and anti-oppressive theories of families and social work may be rather limited in their scope, and social workers should be aware of a wider range of sociological writings/research in the field.

4. The production of claims or forms of knowledge about the family must be studied within their everyday context, and this will also allow for differences in understandings of relationality to emerge.

5. The contradictions and complexities within texts/narratives/images about family should be opened up, so that a range of possible meanings is allowed, and so that dominant and traditional voices are not given preference.

Conclusion

Family is constructed in and through social work practice, in claims made in assessments, recommendations about where children should live, questions put to prospective foster carers or adopters and forms of care for older people. Social work has played a key role in opening up new forms of relationality and family life, such as adoption, care homes, group living, supported lodgings and so on, and so it is important that social workers maintain a critical stance regarding the assumption that certain, dominant forms of family life are best. One of the ways that social workers can do this is to consult writings and research about family 'difference' and aspects of personal life. But deconstruction also requires us to focus on the contradictions and complexities of any family narrative. My discussion of some aspects of LGBT family life, for example, has shown that such families are 'not *completely* constituted by normalizing discourses, nor are they radical examples of resistance' (Hequembourg, 2007, p. 51), since they embody aspects of both. Sameness/difference is a key binary, here, that needs deconstructive attention. A disruption of 'the family' by social workers is, therefore, necessary to allow for other voices to be heard and to allow for other possibilities. Taken-for-granted ways of thinking about families must be overturned so that they are seen for the culturally and historically specific, and indeed dominant, forms that they are.

14

Deconstructing Sexuality in Anti-Oppressive Practice

Dharman Jeyasingham

Introduction

This chapter uses deconstruction in order to examine the underlying concepts, assumptions and contradictions in explorations of sexuality in anti-oppressive literature (AOP). Although I use the term AOP, the discussion in this chapter is just as relevant for anti-discriminatory practice (ADP) texts. While oppression and discrimination are different things, social work texts which state that they are about either AOP (for example, Dominelli, 2002a; Dalrymple and Burke, 2006) or ADP (for example, Thompson, 2012) all discuss instances of discrimination and their occurrence in wider contexts of oppression and so have the same broad focus.

The chapter begins by introducing the idea of deconstruction, some aspects of the work of Jacques Derrida (the philosopher most closely associated with deconstruction) and writing that has drawn on Derrida's work to examine the construction of sexuality. It moves on to use these ideas to consider the different ways in which sexuality is discussed in AOP literature. AOP is an important focus for deconstructive work because it is so prevalent: academic social work literature which engages with the idea of difference is, at this point in time in Britain, characterised as either AOP or a response to AOP and, while its resonance in practice is more limited (McLaughlin, 2005; White, 2006), it has some significance here too. While AOP texts can be seen as featuring disparate conceptualisations of sexuality, deconstruction can identify the existence of underlying constructs that are both pervasive and internally inconsistent. This chapter seeks to reveal some of these inconsistencies and identify how such constructs limit the ways that sexuality is understood in social work.

Deconstruction

Before we explore what deconstruction is, we need to consider how meaning is produced or constructed in the first place. We might think it is possible to understand the meaning of something by exploring its nature, its origin, its resonances in ourselves or its structure. For Derrida, these approaches all fail to consider how meaning is established *through difference*, so our starting point for understanding how meaning is produced should instead be what something is positioned as *not* being. This approach does not seek to discover essential meanings or establish the true significance of a thing. Instead, Derrida's work is committed to disturbing the idea of stable, constant meaning by considering how it is produced through fixing the world for certain purposes, in ways that are inevitably provisional.

For Derrida, difference is not a simple, absolute matter. Meaning is dependent on the pretence that this thing is different from its other, but language ties things to their supposed opposites in relations that are never complete or predictable. Take the binary 'man and woman' – two positions which are constructed as each other's opposite. A deconstruction of this dyad could start in many different places. What happens if we reverse the order? The effect is strange enough to draw attention to some problems in the opposition that were more hidden by the former version. This is not a pairing of equal opposites, but two terms which are ordered and linked in particular ways. The word 'man' occurs twice in this phrase – 'man' and wo'man' – and the initial meaning of the word 'woman' (at least in old English) is 'wife of a man'. Man is both gendered and ungendered (another meaning of man is simply hu'man'), meaning that woman is the only constantly gendered term here. The term 'woman' could be said to be defined entirely through gender and entirely through difference from 'man', but 'woman' also makes 'man' mean male: 'woman' is both gendered and gendering. We should also question the ways in which this pairing appears as natural – does it function to construct heterosexuality as a 'natural' set of relationships? And then we have to consider the differences between the two referents – are they really so clear? Are the similarities between all those defined as 'men' great enough and different enough from the similarities between all 'women' to warrant the two groups being set up in contrast? And what about other gendered and ungendered positions, between or beyond these categories? The exercise of deconstructing this opposition (and there is much more to say about it than I have done here) shows that difference is never established, never complete and always open-ended. Derrida refers to this as '*différance*' – a term which sounds the same as 'difference' but which, in French, evokes ideas of both difference and deferral of meaning. Deconstruction is the exercise of showing these deferrals – the incompletions and breaks in the structures that produce meanings, which hold the possibility for social constructs to be dismantled or deconstructed.

Some of Derrida's work, written shortly before his death in 2004, considered the construct of 'animal' (see, for example, Derrida, 2002). Derrida asks: 'What is an animal?' Is it a being that doesn't wear clothes; that doesn't know the difference between good and evil; that doesn't think, talk, write, feel scared or experience suffering? None of these distinctions stands up to scrutiny, even though they are often given as explanations (and yes, Derrida shows how non-human animals 'write' or leave their mark). Derrida is interested in the role of 'animal' – this grouping of disparate beings, which really only exists in order to produce 'human' as a supposedly discrete category. Distinctions made between humans and animals claim to be absolute and unchanging, but Derrida shows that they have a history, one which is entering a new, unprecedented phase. As he observes: 'Animal is a word that men have given themselves the right to give' (Derrida, 2002, p. 400).

This idea is useful for understanding crucial contemporary issues, such as the exploitation of natural resources and the rights of animals who are farmed or used in medical research, and these are certainly important matters for social workers to consider (Besthorn and Canda, 2002). However, it also matters in ways which are central to almost all social work practice. Deconstruction is particularly concerned with the borders between categories. An edge of one part of a binary opposition is both part of that category and part of its opposite; scrutinising this point of distinction reveals inconsistencies and contradictions. As Derrida explores, the distinction between humans and animals has never been of greater significance but the boundary between the two is also permeable. Status as 'human' is fragile for many of those who come to the attention of social work services. One may be required to present oneself as gendered in specific ways in order to be seen as a human subject and this may not be available to everyone (Butler, 1993) – think of how the word 'it' is often used in the abuse of intersex, trans and gay people and lesbians in order to dehumanise those people. Certain groups may be positioned as having sacrificed their human rights because they are said to have done 'inhuman' things (for an example see Slack, 2011). A great deal of racial talk is concerned with people's bodies – their appearances and smells, people's washing, eating and sexual practices – and this corporeal focus allows some people to be presented as less human, more animal than others. So the question 'who is being positioned at the edge of human?' is important for social workers to ask. It helps us to identify and begin to understand more critically how hierarchies of moral value operate in practice contexts (for instance, see Practice Example 1).

Practice Example 1: Humanising Trafficked Children and Young People

A lot of media reportage, everyday talk and political rhetoric in Britain has reproduced dehumanising discourses about refugees, which make reference to threats of pollution, disease and violence. In contrast, organisations working with refugee children have tried to raise awareness about the experiences of children and young people who have been trafficked into Britain in order to be sexually exploited or abused in other ways. This work appears to challenge the increasing hostility to refugees that is occurring in Britain, and we might suppose that presenting sympathetic accounts of young people's experiences could help to challenge the dehumanising discourse that is so prevalent. However, some of these accounts, while attempting to humanise trafficked young people, also feature amoral, predatory traffickers or shadowy figures who employ 'primitive' methods such as witchcraft to control young people's behaviour (for an example, see Hoskins, 2012). Rather than deconstructing dehumanising discourses, these accounts work to reposition the boundary between human and its others to include trafficked children, while continuing to reproduce a discourse of dangerous, uncivilised and animalistic others beyond them. Such accounts can be damaging for refugee children, as well as for those who help them to come to Britain. They require children to be seen as victims in order to be sympathetic and they deepen distrust of other people in the same communities, such as people who accompany children into this country for purposes other than their exploitation or adults who have in the past been refugee young people themselves. This is not to deny that children who enter this country after having been separated from their carers might be vulnerable to exploitation or abuse; some, but not all, such children are. However, this vulnerability arises because of a combination of factors, including huge social and economic inequalities globally and economies in rich countries which are reliant on migration and mobility. Belief systems (both young people's beliefs and professional accounts of the problem) are also implicated, but these develop alongside social, economic and political factors, rather than preceding them. In their work with such children, it is important that social workers attempt to deconstruct racialising discourses of children's experiences, rather than reproducing them.

Deconstructing Sexuality

In order to explore how deconstruction might be useful for social workers in practice, I now want to consider a specific area of experience – sexuality –

and examine how it is constructed in contemporary Western culture generally and in social work in particular.

What does it mean to 'have' a sexuality? This suggests that sexuality is a belonging or a feature of oneself but surely sexuality is about relations of desire and pleasure? Sexuality is certainly understood in these ways a lot of the time but it is also, perhaps more often, talked about as an aspect of identity, one which Foucault's work shows has come to be viewed as the most intimate and personal part of an individual. It has also most often been understood as a question of whether the individual is or is not a homosexual. Foucault (1990) discusses how, during the twentieth century, the homosexual came to be seen almost as a separate human species, one requiring criminalisation, corrective treatment or rights, depending on the perspective from which it is viewed. We can understand this as both a narrowing of the meaning of sexuality to one aspect alone – the gender of a person's object choice – and the intensification of meanings that can attach to that question.

I have approached this as a question of whether a person is or is not homosexual, rather than whether someone is homosexual or heterosexual, and this is deliberate because the opposition of homosexual and heterosexual only works if heterosexuality is not required to be present or available for scrutiny. To explore this further, we could imagine sexual difference through a collection of shapes, positioned in relation to each other. We could see heterosexuality and homosexuality as two spheres of equal size (they are equally valid, after all) but separate and positioned opposite each other, because attraction to the same is the opposite of attraction to difference. On reflection, we might want to question certain aspects of this representation. Perhaps homosexuality should be made much smaller than heterosexuality because, we might assume, most people are heterosexual? We could introduce a third sphere between the other two to represent bisexuality. Or we could make the spheres shrink, grow and merge into each other, to show that people move between these categories – sexuality is a fluid thing (or so we keep hearing). Each of these adaptations offers a different emphasis, and certain ones will appeal more than others, depending on our politics and where we place ourselves in this representation. However, none of them really troubles the idea that heterosexuality and homosexuality are each identifiable things which are already in existence, more or less stable and different from the other.

Let us imagine something else. Now, there is just one huge sphere and it has the word 'heterosexuality' written across its surface in enormous lettering. But, because it is a sphere, we can only see part of this word at any one time. From certain angles, we can't tell if the whole word is heterosexuality or something else. Cracks appear in the sphere and, even though heterosexuality is written on its outside, we can't be sure that there isn't something else inside. Then we look up and suddenly we realise that we and the sphere are enclosed within a much bigger sphere and the writing on that one says something altogether different.

This representation is concerned with how notions such as heterosexuality come into being. Heterosexuality seems to be self-evident but the more closely we examine it, the clearer it becomes that heterosexuality is only conceivable if there is also a possibility of homosexuality to define it against. Heterosexuality is always haunted by its others. The origin of the two terms illustrates this point well. The word 'heterosexuality' was first used in a pamphlet by Karl-Maria Benkert in 1869 which was concerned with understanding attraction between men as an inherent, unchangeable sexual identity. Homosexuality is the focus of the pamphlet, heterosexuality an inevitable consequence of this new idea. So the first use of 'heterosexuality' as a term is actually pre-dated (albeit briefly) by 'homosexuality'. In teaching about this issue, I ask students 'when was heterosexuality invented?' and someone often then makes a reference to Adam and Eve. Heterosexuality is presented here as the beginning, homosexuality presumably a later deviation. The stability of such common sense ideas relies on an obscuring of their foundations which deconstruction can start to uncover.

Queer theory tells us that the idea of heterosexuality in Western culture is always inhabited by the question of its own homosexual desire. Heterosexual identity holds a central significance for contemporary Western culture – national identities are constructed through particular forms of heterosexuality (Bhattacharyya, 2008) and social status is negotiated in relation to it (Seidman, 2010) – but it is impossible to establish unquestionably. All sorts of things come to be potential signs of male homosexuality, many of which relate to all men but are disavowed in homophobic Western culture, such as the penetrability of all male bodies and the homoerotic potential of masculine display. If we scrutinise heterosexuality in this way, we find that it is less a discrete 'thing' than the shifting locus of a set of claims made in order to achieve social status and establish moral value.

It is important to acknowledge that this discussion has switched to a focus on the question of male homosexuality rather than homosexuality generally. Many of the mechanisms of homophobia towards men are different from those towards women: a great deal of homophobic disgust is initially concerned with male homosexuality while lesbians are excluded either through association or through different processes – the casting of lesbianism as inconceivable or inconsequential (Jagose, 2002) and hatred of lesbians and other women who refuse to be objects of heterosexual desire (Wittig, 1980). This is not to say that homophobia is more often directed at men than women but that the logics of homophobia are largely gendered.

So far I have suggested that we can disturb dominant constructs by uncovering the contradictions within them, but Sedgwick (1990) questions whether things are this simple. The opposition of homosexuality to hetero-sexuality and the construction of homosexuality as a deviation from hetero-sexuality are contradictory but also highly productive systems. If we make strange this relationship between homosexual and heterosexual, we are led to countless other binaries that are infused with the question of homosex-ual difference and are highly productive of meaning. Sedgwick names the following structuring systems amongst many others: secrecy/disclosure, knowledge/ignorance, private/public, natural/artificial, domestic/foreign, health/illness, active/passive, voluntarity/addiction and wholeness/deca-dence (Sedgwick, 1990, p. 11). Such binarisms work together to shore up common sense, logical understandings of what homosexual difference must mean, which underpin ways that sexuality is known more broadly. Sedgwick identifies the closet as one such contradictory system, which operates as a site for powerful manipulation. Being gay is constructed as something which must be disclosed (not to do so would be a deception, a pretence of hetero-sexuality) but also something that must be kept covered up (because it is sexual, private and because speaking of it is an unacceptable imposition on others). So, while homosexuality is not necessarily condemned itself, either disclosing or concealing homosexuality *is* reason for condemnation, a system which Sedgwick calls the 'double bind' (1990, p. 10).

It is important to note that Sedgwick is writing about the 100 years lead-ing up to the point at which she wrote her book, a period in Europe and North America during which there were movements of sexual liberalisation and repeated attacks on sexual minorities. Others have argued that lesbian and gay identities in the West are not necessarily primarily constructed in relation to the closet anymore (see Seidman, 2003). Of course, this depends on geography – there are a lot of differences both between and within differ-ent countries in the West. It also depends on factors such as age, educational history and ethnicity. Recent research about prevalence of LGBT identity in the US provides some interesting findings in relation to these questions. Data from the largest surveys to date suggest that African-American people are 40 per cent more likely than white Americans to identify as LGBT. Adults under 30 are three times more likely to identify as LGBT than those over 65, and those without a college education are significantly more likely to iden-tify as LGBT than those who have a degree (Williams Institute, 2012). The most plausible explanation for these differences is that the closet still oper-ates, at least in relation to surveys, for many people in the US and, in partic-ular, for those who are older, white or degree educated. However, we should not assume that all LGBT people are likely to view their identity in terms of the closet or, if they do, that they experience shame or internalised homo-phobia because of it. The closet is better seen as a social structure that requires negotiation irrespective of people's sense of who they are. It is also one which is context-specific. Someone may be out to his or her family, friends or at work, while having to negotiate expectations that homosexuality be unspoken in certain of these arenas. There is evidence to show that the closet operates in such subtle but powerful ways in social work, as Practice Example 2 illustrates.

Practice Example 2: Negotiating the Closet in Children's Social Work

When I was a social worker in local authority children's services in Britain several years ago, I was involved in the removal of a child from the care of their father. In the subsequent care proceedings one of the father's written statements to the court made reference to having seen me in a nightclub having sex with another man. Even though reference to social workers' activities outside of work is highly irregular in care proceedings and, arguably in this case, not relevant, the statement still provoked some debate in legal meetings. In these discussions I explained that what was being stated had not happened, which then led to questions about how this service user knew that I was gay. When I said that I had told him as part of my work with him as a carer for a child who was subject to child protection plans, my actions came to be seen as inappropriate. Why would such private information be shared? I explained that the man had told me that he was worried that I might see his father, who was gay, as a potential risk to the child. I had said that being gay would not be seen as a risk, that I was gay myself, and that if his father wanted to take a role in childcare we would assess this in the same way as with any other relative. While legal meetings were framed in relation to the court not being homophobic, they also seemed preoccupied with my sexuality or, more specifically, with my having spoken about it. My contention that I had talked about my sexuality with a client seemed to be seen as suspect in two ways: as an inappropriate thing to do in practice and as a potential lie to counter the service user's allegation that he had seen me engaged in a sexual act in public. Saying that I was gay whilst practising as a social worker came to be conflated with a public sexual act. This all occurred alongside affirmations that a gay relative could, of course, be a suitable carer for a child who was at risk and the court would never draw any homophobic conclusions about the suitability of a gay man to practise as a social worker. I remember one legal meeting where this was explained to me as if it was all self-evident by the barrister who was representing the local authority for which I worked, who appeared to be gay himself. The case proved difficult for me to negotiate because the ways in which sexuality was being interpreted seemed so contradictory. One could be obviously gay and this was fine but – also obviously – one could not speak about it in certain situations. Gay identity was a relevant issue to discuss in relation to service users and their families but couldn't be acknowledged in relation to oneself.

Dynamics such as those identified in Practice Example 2 are difficult enough for lesbian and gay field social workers to negotiate, but can be much more hazardous for residential workers, personal assistants and service users themselves. While social care services must ensure that they do not discriminate on the grounds of sexual orientation and the legislative context in Britain is post-homophobic (in the sense that almost all of the legislation that requires differential treatment for sexual minorities has been repealed) these kinds of changes do not automatically mean that LGBT service users and social workers now experience equality, just as legislation about gender and race equality has not achieved equality in those areas. There is also a risk that increased equality regulation affirms a narrow, legalistic conception of equality alongside further expectations of normative behaviour on the part of sexual minorities if they are to be granted the right to participate in public life (Duggan, 2003; Richardson, 2004).

A deconstructive approach can help us to identify how this is sustained in practice. The following discussion considers how two binary systems in particular – public/private and sexual/non-sexual – might be operating in Practice Example 2. My discussion draws on Lauren Berlant and Michael Warner's (1998) problematisation of sex and privacy. Berlant and Warner identify how Western culture positions sex as a private matter, not by restricting the articulation of sex in public spaces but by normalising the public presence of heterosexuality. Public heterosexual relations are, therefore, constructed as unremarkable and non-sexual while heterosexuality is established as a valued identity through reference to intimate spaces such as the home and relationships such as marriage or marriage-like partnerships. Queer identities, in contrast, are positioned as overtly sexual and requiring management in public arenas. This helps to explain why my coming out to a service user was understood as unacceptable. Speaking about being gay brings homosexuality into the public arena of work but, in children's social work, it also marks the penetration of queer identity into the private arena of family relations and children's care, which are key for the maintenance of the idea of heterosexuality as productive and caring. It is useful to compare my act of saying I was gay to the ways in which other professionals might imply their own heterosexuality to colleagues and to service users in ways which are deemed appropriate. This can happen in a number of ways, through reference to family arrangements, through dress and appearance and through ways of moving and presenting bodies. For instance, another social worker who was involved in these proceedings would make reference to the role he took in caring for his own children. The kinds of division of care tasks to which he referred communicated heterosexuality even before he indicated that his partner was a woman. As I suggested in the practice example, certain kinds of performances of gay identity are also acceptable (such as the local authority's urbane, effeminate barrister), but these are performances which involve homosexuality being recognisable as a kind of aesthetic, rather than a sexual identity, and are more available to professionals whose expertise relates to a public realm such as the law than to social workers who need to present themselves as knowledgeable about family relationships and children's care. In this example, we can see how distinctions of public and private, sexual and non-sexual, function in contradictory but powerful ways in social work practice to privilege certain forms of heterosexuality.

Deconstructing Sexuality in Anti-Oppressive Practice

Sedgwick's work shows how ways of knowing sexuality are constructed in contradictory ways which are nevertheless highly resilient. Similarly, anti-oppressive practice is grounded in contradictory knowledge frameworks but also has features that have enabled it to persist as the standard way of articulating engagements with the topic of difference in social work. AOP texts often present various facts about inequality and frameworks for intervention as if they are incontrovertible but, as Charlotte Williams (1999) has explored, anti-oppressive theory also embraces many different, often competing paradigms, such as cultural relativism, materialism and social constructionism. This ideological eclecticism jars with the inflexible forms of knowledge that AOP literature often produces. Williams observes that theorisations of AOP in social work have tended to fail because of their 'ongoing tendency to try and identify formulae, specific ingredients, category and structure rather than problematics, processes, complexity and dynamic. Paradoxically, therefore, the debate suffers from being both too abstract and too concrete' (Williams, 1999, p. 225).

If anything, this tendency has increased in AOP literature since Williams' article was published. Dominelli, for example, seems to have responded to criticisms that AOP is too simplistic by developing more complicated models and frameworks rather than by engaging with uncertainties or considering the socially constructed nature of all forms of knowledge (see Dominelli, 2002a, p. 24 for an example of a particularly elaborate diagram showing the multidimensionality of oppression in context). However, AOP can also be seen as a highly flexible set of ideas and values because it has a variety of emotional and aesthetic associations which give it lasting appeal, perhaps particularly for social workers, and which enable it to be used in contradictory ways whilst appearing to be consistent. AOP is used to mean different things by different authors and, while it is not unusual for academic writers to interpret terms in differing ways, it is remarkable that AOP authors do not necessarily acknowledge these differences. This tells us something about the contradictions inherent in AOP constructs and the mechanisms which allow these positions to co-exist. Because of restrictions of space, I want to explore this in relation to just one social category, lesbians, and through a reading of three different texts: *Anti-Oppressive Social Work Theory and Practice* (2002a) and *Feminist Social Work Theory and Practice* (2002b), both textbooks by Lena Dominelli which make reference to lesbians alongside other communities that experience oppression, and 'Using an Anti-Oppressive Framework in Social Work Practice with Lesbians' (Hines, 2012), an article by Jude M. Hines which seeks to apply Dominelli's work to social work prac-tice in the US context.

Before I discuss these texts, it is worth noting a feature of social work discourse about sexuality which I have explored in more detail elsewhere (Jeyasingham, 2008). In the 1970s, a great deal of psychiatric and social work literature about homosexuality presented it as a mental disorder, but this understanding had largely disappeared by the mid 1990s. The key manuals for diagnosis of disorders (the American Psychiatric Association's Diagnostical and Statistical Manual of Mental Disorders (DSM) in the USA and the World Health Organisation's International Classification of Diseases (ICD) in most other places) no longer made reference to homosexuality as a psychiatric disorder, and discrimination against lesbians and gay men in social work practice was now being identified and critiqued. However, a great deal of more recent literature has dwelt instead on internalised homo-phobia as the primary way in which lesbians and gay men are oppressed. For psychiatrists, homosexuality is no longer a mental illness but dissatisfaction with one's sexual orientation *is* now a psychiatric disorder ('ego-dystonic sexual identity' is listed as a disorder in the current, tenth edition of ICD, although a similar diagnosis was removed from DSM with the publication of its fourth edition). For many social work writers since the 1980s, internalised homophobia has seemed to provide the most dramatic evidence of the depth of lesbians' and gay men's oppression and the impact that this had on many people's well-being (for a discussion of specific texts, see Jeyasingham, 2008). These ways of approaching lesbians' and gay men's problems hold in mind an alternative version of a healthy lesbian and gay identity, where people have come out, are connected to a community and are participating in sexual relationships which are healthy and positive. It is important to note that these two ideas of lesbians and gay men as either self-hating or healthy and proud are complementary rather than contradictory. Each holds within themselves the idea of the other – of a potentially proud future for those who currently feel shame and of a self-hating or closeted past for those who have now achieved pride. The problem for psychiatry and social work is that people are usually referred to these services because they are understood to have an emotional, mental health, social or relationship problem. It is easy, given the dominance of the model of gay shame/pride, for problems to be seen as emanating from shame and solutions to be about building pride. A model that is apparently positive about homosexuality *per se* can, therefore, be used to identify the sexual identity of all lesbian or gay service users as the likely source of problems and the appropriate focus for intervention.

One feature of Dominelli's work more generally is her refusal to engage with either medicalising discourses or negative representations of oppressed groups, and there are no references in either *AOP Theory and Practice* or *Feminist Social Work Theory and Practice* to internalised homophobia, ego-dystonic sexual identity or lesbian shame. Instead, lesbians are presented in rather different terms: they question heterosexual privilege (2002a, p. 46); celebrate lesbian sexuality (2002a, p. 48; 2002b, p. 4); engage in struggles for their identities as fully accepted members of society (2002a, p. 48); and unite in groups to take action to achieve social change (2002a, p. 110). Oppression is also named, but located as external to lesbian subjectivities: discourses about the ideal female body lead lesbian bodies to be valued least (2002a, pp. 19–20); social policy is said to foist financial dependency on lesbian partners (2002b, p. 108); courts rule against lesbian mothers in disputes about where their children should live (2002b, p. 117); and anti-feminist men attack lesbians' rights to access sperm banks (2002b, pp. 90–91). For Dominelli, lesbian difference is a positive matter; it is only when Dominelli concludes that some lesbians are seeking conformity that she becomes rather critical (as Steve Hicks discusses elsewhere in this volume).

Dominelli does offer an account of how exclusionary processes might impact on subjectivity in her discussion of accommodationist and rejectionist responses to oppression. Rejectionist responses are characterised by people rejecting their exclusion from society and seeking 'to carve out a space that they define as theirs' (2002a, p. 47), while accommodationist responses may or may not involve accepting dominant definitions of oppressed groups but, either way, feature oppressed individuals being 'determined to seek ways of making the most of their lot within the constraints within which they are embedded' (2002a, p. 47). So, while she notes the existence of lesbians' accommodation of social marginalisation, Dominelli is clear that even apparent acceptance of dominant discourses may well be a strategic act, rather than an internalising of oppression.

Hines' (2012) paper is inspired by Dominelli's discussion of AOP but employs it for quite different purposes and, in so doing, is involved in constructing quite different kinds of lesbian subjects. Hines is writing about social work in a US context, where practitioners may engage in formal psychotherapeutic work as well as the assessment and service co-ordination work that is likely to constitute most local authority social workers' activity in Britain. Consequently, although this isn't explicitly noted in Hines' paper, she is applying Dominelli's approach to AOP to a social work role which is quite different from that imagined by Dominelli. The lesbian identities discussed in Hines' paper are also characterised by very different relationships with homophobia and heterosexism. Hines writes that '[l]esbians can have a deep sense of shame regarding their sexuality' (2012, p. 27). She goes on to discuss how '[t]he pervasiveness of negative messages, violence, and oppression of lesbians is insidious and inescapable throughout their social context. As a result of living in a heterosexist and homophobic society, lesbians may develop internalized heterosexism to one degree or another' (p. 28). Dominelli's and Hines' versions of AOP construct different kinds of lesbian subjectivities which fit the different requirements for the services they are discussing. Hines discusses lesbians who have internalised heterosexism and who can benefit from the psychotherapeutic interventions which social workers provide. Dominelli describes lesbians who either negotiate heterosexism strategically or challenge it head on, and these lesbians make good equal partners to the social workers which her work imagines – practitioners who work with service users on equal terms to resist institutional oppression or to reorient services from within.

While these two AOP texts construct the impact of oppression quite differently, they do not actually contradict each other. Dominelli is not concerned with the ways that oppression is internalised but neither does she deny this possibility, while Hines acknowledges the practical ways in which heterosexism impacts on lesbians, whether or not they have internalised it. However, they each construct oppressed identities which are, in their different ways, also acceptably moral depictions of lesbian identity. Hines stresses that 'practitioners must examine their possible contribution to the problem of oppression through the imposition of a demeaning view of vulnerability' (2012, p. 28). Vulnerability should instead be acknowledged and valued. Meanwhile, the assertive, articulate, challenging lesbians in Dominelli's work appear as such because these are the qualities which are valued in her work. Each account constructs the lesbian that it needs in order to have a moral subject.

So how can we make sense of these apparently disparate takes on both lesbian identity and anti-oppressive practice? In my view they are not simply unrelated, instead they each connect to the different stages of the gay shame/pride discourse which is so pervasive in AOP literature. Both Hines and Dominelli's work raise important points, but they are also each limited to the extent that neither seeks to deconstruct this binarism or consider other experiences of lesbian identity that are not encompassed by either pride or shame. In addition, neither questions the idea of a united lesbian community even though, for Hines, membership is the end goal of intervention while, for Dominelli, lesbians are assumed to have already achieved it.

AOP constructs morally acceptable subjects, so it doesn't deal with the problem of service users who are positioned as outside of morality or outside of humanity. While it questions the positioning of the boundaries between moral and immoral, human and its others, it doesn't question the role of these distinctions themselves. It also doesn't question the identificatory pleasures involved in positioning oneself as an anti-oppressive practitioner – as caring or as radical – which are powerful reasons for AOP's continued currency in social work education and at least certain areas of social work practice. Neither does it acknowledge the function of this kind of work in producing social workers themselves as moral, humane and, therefore, credible practitioners in their practice more generally, a crucial consideration if we are to understand which behaviours or groups of people are seen as beyond the remit of AOP. Deconstruction can help us to identify these kinds of limitations and arrive at a more reflexive understanding of our engagement with AOP as social work practitioners or educators.

Key Ideas for Practice

1. Social workers need to examine the language which is used in accounts which are presented to them and in their own talk and written accounts. Even apparently self-evident terms such as 'human', 'child' and 'minority' are constructs with particular histories which work to open up certain ways of understanding the world and the specific situation in question, while shutting down others.

2. Sexuality is currently represented in social work in a range of different ways: as a question of personal choice, a private matter, an issue that is only relevant for minority groups, a question of vulnerability to emotional or mental health problems or a political matter. These conceptions might seem diverse and can even be presented as challenges to each other, but they often reproduce the same basic assumptions about sexuality and sexual difference. Deconstruction provides ways to identify these assumptions and start to find other ways of knowing and articulating such matters. It enables us to identify repetitions and returns to older ways of understanding, whilst also making apparent the cracks in these structures of meaning and the inconsistencies which point to other, profoundly different, ways of knowing which might be available.

3. Social workers can engage with deconstruction in different ways. It can enable a more critical approach to the ways in which people's experiences and troubles are presented in accounts such as referrals and assessments. Social workers can also employ deconstruction in direct work with individual service users, groups and communities and colleagues, working with others to identify new ways of understanding people's experiences.

Glossary of Terms

Ableism is a network of beliefs, processes and practices in society that produces a particular assumption that we all desire a 'normal' self and body, against which disability is seen to fall short and needs to be overcome. Ableism is a powerful label that has the capacity to ameliorate the use of negative stereotypes and facilitate cultural change by focusing attention on the discriminator rather than the person who is viewed as having an 'impairment'.

Agency is the capacity of a person to act in the world and encompasses both unconscious, involuntary behaviour and purposeful goal directed activity that enables the person to realise and gain a kind of direct control or guidance over their own behaviour. The term is used in social work to recognise the capacity of individuals or collective groups to act independently to make personal choices and to recognise how social structures can limit or influence these opportunities.

Anthology is a collection of literary works or pieces such as poems, short stories or plays and can also be a catalogue or assortment of complaints, comments or ideas. When **anthologising**, we are putting something together or compiling a list.

Anti-discriminatory practice describes the action taken to prevent or curb any form of discrimination against individuals, groups and communities and is mostly associated with legal actions as a result of equality legislation on the grounds of race, class, gender, disability, religious belief, sexual orientation and age.

Anti-oppressive practice is a term used within social work to acknowledge oppression in societies, economies, cultures and groups and is used to develop practice that actively seeks to reduce, remove or negate the influence of that oppression. **Empowerment** is one of the strategies used, which strives to enable service users to take action to improve their own lives through relocating or rebalancing the power inherent in the social worker's role.

Anthropology is the study of humankind, past and present that draws and builds upon knowledge from social and biological sciences as well as the humanities and the natural sciences. It emphasises cross-cultural comparisons, long-term in-depth examination of context and often uses participant observation as a method where the researcher immerses themself in the community or context in order to frame its critique.

Binaries are often used in critical theory to describe a pair of related terms of concepts that are opposite in meaning and set against each other to highlight the dominance of one over the other or devaluing it. Binaries are used in political critiques to argue how power is perpetuated and legitimised and to find ways of deconstructing and undermining positions. These critiques can be seen in third wave feminism and critical race theory.

Biopower was a term coined by Foucault to refer to practices of regulatory mechanisms to subjugate bodies and control of populations. For Foucault, biopower is a technology of power which is a way of managing people as a group. Biopower is literally having power over bodies who are the object of a political strategy, or a general strategy of power using scientific knowledge and methods. Looking at human nature through a series of different mirrors such as biological phenomena, rather than historical phenomena, with sociological and sociocultural characteristics gives rise to different interpretations from which to critique power.

Bureaucracy is a system of government in which most of the important decisions are taken by state officials rather than more democratically and involves excessively complicated administrative procedures. It has negative connotations within social work because of its association with complexity, inefficiency, inflexibility and the dehumanisation of practice. However, sociologists such as Weber argued that bureaucracy constitutes the most efficient and rational way to organise humans and that systematic processes and organised hierarchies were necessary to maintain order, maximise efficiency and eliminate favouritism.

Capitalism is an economic system based on the principle of individual rights. Politically, it is the system of laissez-faire (freedom) and legally, it is a system of objective laws. In economic terms, when such freedom is applied to the sphere of production its result is the free market and you can see this in many areas of care where there is free or private enterprise/private ownership of the means of production, distribution and exchange and is also referred to free or private enterprise in which providers of care make a profit in a market economy.

Convergence is where a concurrence of opinions, ideas or results may come together, perhaps from previously different sources such as in science and philosophy.

Deconstruction is an analytical method and theory used in the study of literature or philosophy which says that a piece of writing does not have just one meaning and that the meaning depends on the reader and the purpose of deconstruction is to reveal inadequacies and render instability.

Discourse refers to communication of thoughts by words, talk, conversation and the treatment of the subject through the ability of reason or the reasoning process. Analysis of discourse is used in social theory to investigate and determine the relations among its language, structure and agency and to reveal how it does not exist in isolation but is a way of thinking about a specific topic that is linked to different theories of power and the State.

Disciplinary rules are commonly known as rules and procedures which say what is acceptable and unacceptable and are used to deal with performance and conduct.

Disciplinary power means a form of power that is stable, unwavering, invisible and internalised. According to Foucault, disciplinary power often leads to an individual inadvertently checking and changing their own behaviour because of fear and to avoid being caught breaking the rules.

Discrimination is the prejudicial and/or distinguishing treatment of an individual based on their actual or perceived membership in a certain group or category.

Divergence means departing or deviating from a norm or the act of difference such as in developing a different opinion.

Diversity is a concept which encompasses acceptance and respect rather than just people being diverse. It means understanding that each individual is unique and actively recognises differences along the dimensions of race, ethnicity, gender, sexual orientation, socioeconomic status, age, physical abilities, religious beliefs, political beliefs and other ideologies. Diversity intends to move beyond simple tolerance to embracing and celebrating its rich dimensions.

Dividing practices are practices used to make a distinction between the 'insiders' and the 'outsiders' in society and was a term used by Foucault which described how people are objectified and excluded when they are seen as a threat to the community, for example between the mad and the sane.

Empowerment – see anti oppressive practice.

Equality is the state of being equal, especially in status, rights or opportunities, and is referred to in social work in relation to individuals or groups in society as a means of promoting fairness, justice and even-handedness, particularly in relation to human rights.

Globalisation is a tem applied to how modern society has become integrated internationally as a result of the interchange of world views, which produces ideas and other aspects of culture as a result of advances in technology, capitalism and migration.

Governmentality is a term coined by Foucault to refer to the way in which the State exercises control over, or governs, its population and to the way in which people are taught to govern themselves by shaping their views through emphasis on individual responsibility and control.

Habitus refers to lifestyle, the values, the dispositions and expectations of a particular social group that are acquired through the activities and experiences of everyday life and are influenced by social structures such as gender, race and class discrimination, which are then reproduced.

Heteronormative asserts that heterosexuality is the norm in society from which other sexual orientations are defined, and in mainstream society creates a hierarchy that places reproductive, monogamous sex between committed heterosexuals as good and places any others in a social deviancy role.

Infrahuman is a tacitly held belief that one's ingroup is more human than an outgroup and where the latter is of a lower order or not yet at the level of understanding of a human being.

Intersectionality is a concept often used in critical theories to describe the ways in which oppressive institutions (racism, sexism, homophobia, transphobia, ableism, xenophobia, classism, etc.) are interconnected and cannot be examined separately from one another.

Intersex is a general term used to describe a variety of conditions in which a person is born with a reproductive or sexual anatomy that doesn't seem to fit the typical definitions of female or male. It has been known as hermaphroditism in the past, which is now thought to be an insensitive term. Although it is typically seen as a condition someone is born with, sometimes this is not discovered until later on in life or perhaps never at all. Intersex is also a socially constructed category that reflects real biological variation.

LGBT are the initials for lesbian, gay, bisexual and transgender, which was adopted from the 1990s and is intended to emphasise a diversity of sexuality and gender identity cultures as well as sometimes used to refer to anyone who is non-heterosexual or without a clear gender. A popular variant adds the letter **Q** for those who identify as queer and who are questioning their sexual identity.

Marketisation is a restructuring process that enables state enterprises to respond to market pressures by changing the legal environment in which they operate as an alternative to administrative means of providing services. This is achieved by reducing state subsidies and partial or wholesale privatisation.

Microcosm denotes a community, place or situation regarded as encapsulating in miniature the characteristics of something much larger.

Neo-colonisation is a policy whereby a major power uses economic and political means to perpetuate or extend its influence over nations or areas that are defined by the coloniser as 'underdeveloped'.

Neo-liberalism is a political movement that blends traditional liberal concerns for social justice with an emphasis on economic growth.

Oppression is the exercise of authority or power in an unjust manner, usually through the exercise of authority and power to subjugate through force and which can be physical or emotional, or both.

Othering is a psychological tactic whereby actions are taken to classify an individual or group as not being 'one of us' and dismissing them as being in some way less human, and less worthy of respect and dignity. This can often be expressed as a relation of power, for example, between professionals and service users or between different professional groups themselves.

Paradigm is a distinct concept or thought pattern within which typical models or preconceived ideas are observed and subjected to conditioning and the collection of further evidence to reinforce it, without questioning.

Performativity is an interdisciplinary term often used to name the capacity of speech and gestures to act or to construct and perform an identity and this is produced culturally and enforced by discursive power and is situated within larger social contexts.

Political correctness refers to a stance taken which is perceived as being over-concerned with the use of language or behaviour in a way that could offend a group of people, sometimes to the exclusion of other genuine debates. It places emphasis on the need to conform to language and practices which could offend political sensibilities and, whilst it is often referred to negatively, the expression originally came about in the 1970s and was intended to mean 'inclusive'.

Poststructuralism is used to describe a range of theories or methods of analysis, including deconstruction and some psychoanalytic theories that deny binary opposition. It argues that there is no one true reading of a text, which can be subject to an unlimited range of interpretations because meanings and intellectual categories are always shifting and unstable.

Queer was originally a derogatory term for 'gay' but has since been reclaimed and re-appropriated by some lesbians, gay men, bisexuals and transgendered persons in the 1990s as a self-affirming umbrella term which established 'community' and asserts a political identity. In academic disciplines, queer theory has used the term to denote a general opposition to binary thinking and to reject traditional gender and sexual identities and by those who see themselves as oppressed by the heteronormativity of the larger culture.

Rationalisation is the process of making something seem consistent with or based on reason and is often used to describe reduction or restructuring of public services in scientific or business terms.

Racism is a set of actions, practices or beliefs that attribute shared traits, abilities or qualities of one group and ranks them as inherently inferior to justify treating that group of people differently. It is often used to describe discrimination which is based on an ethnic or cultural basis, and recognises that assumptions based on stereotypes can occur at both the individual and institutional level.

Reflexivity refers to how a person's values, beliefs, acquaintances and interests influence his or her research or work and seeks to create a circular relationship between cause and effect. In sociological terms, reflexivity refers to the capacity of an agent to recognise forces of socialisation and alter their place in the social structure, so the reflexive social work practitioner would seek to shape their own norms, politics and notion of autonomy.

Relationality refers to the state or condition of being relational and being able to engage with approaches or models that specify the fundamental basis of connectedness as a way of understanding the world.

Rhetoric is the art or study of using language effectively and persuasively and involves discourse as a means of attempting to inform, persuade or motivate particular audiences.

Sectarianism involves bigotry, discrimination or hatred arising from attaching importance to perceived differences between subdivisions within a group, such as between different denominations of a religion, class, region or factions of a political movement. It may be used to express a group's nationalistic or cultural ambitions or to expel those who do not subscribe to orthodoxy.

Selfhood is the quality that makes a person or thing different from others and is used to describe individuality, a distinct identity through the fully developed self.

Service user is used to describe anyone who uses health or social care services and can include carers. There is a lot of debate about how this term has emerged and how it embodies ideologies about consumerism and choice. Similarly, it has been rejected by those who say that it implies passiveness in receiving services, whereas we should see the person first and foremost.

Subjectivity is the condition of being a subject and the quality of a subject's perspective, experiences, feelings, beliefs and desires. The term is used to talk about a person or thing who is existing only as perceived and not as a thing in itself.

Universalism refers to religious, theological and philosophical concepts with universal application or applicability. It is a term used to identify particular doctrines and claims that religion is a universal human quality in which devotional and ritual observances ensure the moral code needed to govern human affairs.

Well-being is a term frequently used in policy terms to describe a dynamic process and holistic outlook which promises to connect mind, body and spirit, that is centred in the person and his/her own priorities and perspective. The person's external circumstances interact with their psychological resources to satisfy, to a greater or lesser extent, their psychological needs and to give rise to positive feelings of happiness and satisfaction. Measuring well-being is the subject of great debate given that it involves a range of subjective indicators and is technically limited.

Worldview is the overall perspective from which one sees and interprets the world and represents a collection of beliefs about life and the universe held by an individual or group.

References

Acker, J. (2006) 'Inequality regimes', *Gender & Society*, vol. 20, no. 4, pp. 441–464.

Adams, R., Dominelli, L. and Payne, M. (2009) *Social Work: Themes, Issues and Critical Debates* (3rd edition), Basingstoke: Palgrave Macmillan

Adkins, L. (2009) 'Feminism after measure', *Feminist Theory*, vol. 10, no. 3, pp. 323–339.

Adlam, D., Henriques, J., Rose, N., Salfield, A., Venn, C. and Walkerdine, V. (1976) 'Psychology, ideology and the human subject', *Ideology and Consciousness*, vol. 1, pp. 1–26.

Ahmad, B. (1990) *Black Perspectives in Social Work*, Birmingham: Venture Press.

Ahmad, W., Atkin, K. and Chamba, R. (2000) '"Causing havoc among their children": parental and professional perspectives on consanguinity and childhood disability', in W. I. U. Ahmad (ed.), *Ethnicity, Disability and Chronic Illness*, Buckingham: Open University Press, pp. 28–44.

Ahmed, S. (1994) 'Anti-racist social work: a black perspective', in C. Hanvey and T. Philpot (eds.), *Practising Social Work*, London: Routledge.

Ahmed, S. (2000) *Strange Encounters: Embodied Others in Post-Coloniality*, London: Routledge.

Ahmed, S. (2012) *On Being Included: Racism and Diversity in Institutional Life*, Durham, NC: Duke University Press.

Aldred, R. (2004) 'In perspective: Judith Butler', *International Socialism Journal*, Issue 103, pp. 1–12.

Ali, S. (2003) *Mixed-Race, Post-Race: Gender, New Ethnicities and Cultural Practices*, Oxford: Berg.

Allen, A. (2006) 'Dependency, subordination and recognition: on Judith Butler's theory of subjection', *Continental Philosophy Review*, vol. 38, pp. 199–222.

Almond, B. (2006) *The Fragmenting Family*, Oxford: Clarendon Press.

Althusser, L. (1971) 'Ideology and ideological state apparatuses', in L. Althusser, Lenin and Philosophy and Other Essays, London: New Left Books, pp. 121–173.

Angrosino, M. V. and May de Perez, K. A. (2003) 'Rethinking observation: from method to context', in N. K. Denzin and Y. S. Lincoln (eds.), *Collecting and Interpreting Qualitative Materials* (2nd edition), London: Sage, pp. 107–154.

Arnold, S. (2012) *State Sanctioned Child Poverty and Exclusion: The Case of Children in State Accommodation for Asylum Seekers*, Dublin: Irish Refugee Council. Available at: http://www.irishrefugeecouncil.ie/wp-content/uploads/2012/09/State-sanctioned-child-poverty-and-exclusion.pdf (accessed 5 February 2014).

Ashencaen S., Crabtree, F. H. and Spalek, B. (2008) *Islam and Social Work: Debating Values, Transforming Practice*, Bristol: Policy Press.

Athey, S. (1996) 'Black feminism', in E. Cashmore (ed.), *The Dictionary of Race and Ethnic Relations*, (4th edition), London: Routledge, pp. 50–51.

Auterman, B. (2011) 'Structural ableism: disability, institutionalized discrimination and denied citizenship', MA Thesis, Sarah Lawrence College, Bronxville, New York.

Ayim, M. (1997) 'Crimes against the deaf: the politics of ableism', *Canadian Journal of Education*, vol. 22, no. 3, pp. 330–335.

Aymer, C. (2002) 'The dilemmas for black social work professionals: therapeutic implications', *Journal of Social Work Practice*, vol. 16, no. 1, pp. 15–21.

Baba, T., Mahina, O., Williams, N. and Nabobo-Baba, U. (eds.) (2004) *Researching the Pacific and Indigenous Peoples,* Auckland: University of Auckland.

Back, L. and Sinha, S. (2010) 'The UK: imperial spectres, new migrations and the 'state of permanent emergency', in K. Fangen, A. Mossan and F. Mohn (eds.), *Inclusion and Exclusion of Young Adult Migrants in Europe: Barriers and Bridges,* Surrey: Ashgate, pp. 5–180.

Badiou, A. (2003) *Saint Paul,* Stanford: University of California Press. (Published in France in 1997.)

Badiou, A. (2008) *The Meaning of Sarkozy,* London: Verso.

Bagilhole, B. (2009) *Understanding Equal Opportunities and Diversity: The Social Differentiations and Intersections of Inequality*, Bristol: Policy Press.

Baines, D. (ed.) (2007) *Doing Anti-Oppresive Practice: Building Transformative Politicized Social Work*, Halifax, NS: Fernwood.

Baistow, K. (1994) 'Liberation and regulation? Some paradoxes of empowerment', *Critical Social Policy*, vol. 14, no. 42, pp. 34–46.

Baker, B. and Campbell, F. (2006) 'Transgressing noncrossable borders: disability, law, schooling and nations', in S. Danforth and S. Gabel (eds.), *Vital Questions Facing Disability Studies in Education,* New York: Peter Lang, pp. 319–347.

Balibar, E. (1994) 'Subjection and subjectivation', in J. Copjec (ed.), *Supposing the Subject*, London: Verso.

Barker, I. and Peck, E. (1996) 'User empowerment – a decade of experience', *The Mental Health Review*, vol. 1, no. 4, pp. 5–13.

Barking and Dagenham Safeguarding Children Board (2011) *Serious Case Review: Services Provided for Child T and Child R August 1997–February 2010 Executive Summary*, London: Barking and Dagenham Safeguarding Children Board.

Barn, R., Sinclair, R. and Ferdinand, D. (1997) *Acting on Principle: An Examination of Race and Ethnicity in Social Services Provision for Children and Families*, London: British Agencies for Adoption and Fostering.

Bar-On, A. (2002) 'Restoring power to social work practice', *British Journal of Social Work*, vol. 32, no. 8, pp. 997–1014.

Barrett, M. and McIntosh, M. (1982) *The Anti-Social Family,* London: Verso.

Barry, A. (2001) *Political Machines: Governing a Technological Society*, London: Athlone Press.

Battiste, M. (2008) 'Research ethics for protecting indigenous knowledge and heritage: institutional and researcher responsibilities', in N. K. Denzin, Y. S. Lincoln and L. T. Smith (eds.), *Handbook of Critical and Indigenous Methodologies*, Los Angeles: Sage, pp. 497–509.

Bauman, Z. (2003) *Liquid Love: On the Frailty of Human Bonds,* Cambridge: Polity Press.

Bauman, Z. (2004) *Wasted lives: Modernity and its outcasts*, Cambridge: Polity Press.

BBC (2012) 'NHS hospital trusts invited to expand abroad', *BBC Online*, 21 August 2012. Available at http://www.bbc.co.uk/news/health-19328105 (accessed 10 February 2014).

The Belfast Agreement (1988) Belfast: Northern Ireland Office.

Bell, M., Shaw, I., Sinclair, I., Sloper, P. and Rafferty, J. (2007) *The Integrated Children's System: An Evaluation of the Practice, Process and Consequences of the ICS in Councils with Social Services Responsibilities*, Department of Social Policy and Social Work, York: University of York.

Bell, V. (2010) 'New scenes of vulnerability, agency and plurality: an interview with Judith Butler', *Theory, Culture and Society*, vol. 27, pp. 130–152.

Belsey, C. (2002) *Critical Practice* (2nd edition), London: Routledge.

Bennett, T., Grossberg, L. and Morris, M. (2005) *New Keywords: A Revised Vocabulary of Culture and Society*, Oxford: Blackwell.

Benson, A. L., Silverstein, L. B. and Auerbach, C. F. (2005) 'From the margins to the center: gay fathers reconstruct the fathering role', *Journal of GLBT Family Studies*, vol. 1, no. 3, pp. 1–29.

Beresford, P. (2003) *It's Our Lives: A Short Theory of Knowledge, Distance and Experience*, London: OSP for Citizen Press

Beresford, P. (2009) *Compass Think Piece 47: Whose Personalisation?*, London: Compass.

Beresford, P. and Holden, C. (2000) 'We have choices: globalisation and welfare user movements', *Disability and Society*, vol. 15, no. 7, pp. 973–989.

Berger, P. and Luckmann, T. (1967) *The Social Construction of Reality: A Treatise in the Sociology of Knowledge*, London: Allen Lane.

Berlant, L. and Warner, M. (1998) 'Sex in public. Intimacy', *Critical Inquiry*, vol. 24, no. 2, pp. 547–566.

Besthorn, F. and Canda, E. (2002) 'Revisioning environment: deep ecology for education and teaching in social work', *Journal of Teaching in Social Work*, vol. 22, no. 1, pp. 79–101.

Bhakta, P., Katbamna, S. and Parker, G. (2000) 'South Asian carers' experiences of primary health care teams', in W. I. U. Ahmad (ed.), *Ethnicity, Disability and Chronic Illness*, Buckingham: Open University Press, pp. 123–138.

Bhattacharyya, G. (2008) *Dangerous Brown Men: Exploiting Sex, Violence and Terrorism in the War on Terror*, London: Zed Books.

Bhatti-Sinclair, K. (2011) *Anti-Racist Practice in Social Work*, London: Palgrave Macmillan.

Bilge, S. (2010) 'Recent feminist outlooks on intersectionality', *Diogenes*, vol. 57, pp. 58–72.

Birch, D. (1989) *Language, Literature and Critical Practice: Ways of Analysing Text*, Routledge: London.

Bishop, R. (1996) 'Addressing issues of self-determination and ligitimation in Kaupapa Maori research', in B. Webber (ed.), *He paepae korero*, Wellington: New Zealand Council of Education Research.

Blackenhorn, D. (2009) *The Future of Marriage*, New York: Encounter.

Boler, M. and Zembylas, M. (2003) 'Discomforting truths: the emotional terrain of understanding difference', in P. Trifonas (ed.), *Pedagogies of Difference: Rethinking Education for Social Change*, London: RoutledgeFalmer, pp. 110–136.

Boltanski, L. and Chiapello, E. (2005) *The New Spirit of Capitalism*, London: Verso.

Bolton, G. (2010) *Reflective Practice: Writing and Professional Development* (3rd edition), London: Sage.

Bourdieu, P. and Wacquant, L. (1992) *An Invitation to Reflexive Sociology*, Chicago: University of Chicago Press.

Bourdieu, P. and Wacquant, L. (2001) 'NewLiberalSpeak: notes on the new planetary vulgate', *Radical Philosophy*, Jan/Feb, vol. 105, pp. 2–6.

Bourdieu, P., Accardo, A., Balazas, G., Beaud, S., Bonvin, F., Bourdieu, E. et al. (2002) *The Weight of the World: Social Suffering in Contemporary Society*, Cambridge: Polity Press.

Bowker, G. C. and Star, S. L. (1999) *Sorting Things Out: Classification and its Consequences*, Cambridge, MA: MIT Press.

Branfield, F. (2009) *Developing User Involvement in Social Work Education*, SCIE Workforce Development Report 29. Available at: http://www.scie.org.uk/publications/reports/report29.pdf (accessed 5 January 2013).

Brewer, J. (1991) 'The parallels between sectarianism and racism: the Northern Ireland experience', in *One Small Step Towards Racial Justice: the teaching of Antiracism in Diploma in Social Work Programmes*, Improving Social Work Education and Training, Eight, London: CCETSW.

Brewer, J. and Higgins, G. I. (1999) 'Understanding anti-Catholicism in Northern Ireland', *Sociology*, vol. 33, no. 2, pp. 235–255.

Brighter Futures (2011) *Flowers that Grow from Concrete: How Support Services Determine a Young Refugee's Life Opportunities*, London: Brighter Futures.

British Medical Association (2002) *Asylum Seekers: Meeting their Healthcare Needs*, London: BMA.

Broadhurst, K., Wastell, D., White, S., Hall, C., Peckover, S. Thompson, K. et al. (2010) 'Performing 'initial assessment': identifying the latent conditions for error at the front-door of local authority children's services', *British Journal of Social Work*, vol. 40, pp. 352–370.

Broese van Groenou, M., Glaser, K., Tomassini, C. and Jacobs, T. (2006) 'Socio-economic status differences in older people's use of informal and formal help: a comparison of four European countries', *Ageing & Society*, vol. 26, no. 5, pp. 745–766.

Brooks, R. (2013) 'Social workers raise concern over care cuts', *Age UK*, 24 June 2013. Available at http://www.helptheaged.org.uk/latest-news/archive/social-workers-raise-concern-over-care-cuts/ (accessed on 10 February 2014).

Brooks, D., Barth, B. P., Bussiere, A. and Patterson, G. (1999) 'Adoption and race: implementing the Multiethnic Placement Act and interethnic adoption provisions', *Social Work*, vol. 44, no. 2, pp. 167–179.

Brown, H. C. (1998) *Social Work and Sexuality: Working with Lesbians and Gay Men*, Basingstoke: Palgrave Macmillan.

Brown, C. G. (2012) 'Anti-oppression through a postmodern lens: dismantling the Master's conceptual tools in discursive social work practice', *Critical Social Work*, vol. 13, no. 1, pp. 34–65.

Brown, H. C. and Cocker, C. (2011) *Social Work with Lesbians and Gay Men*, London: Sage.

Brune, J. and Wilson, D. (2013) *Disability and Passing: Blurring the Lives of Identity*, Philadelphia: Temple University Press.

Bryan, B., Dadsie, S. and Scafe, S. (1985) *The Heart of the Race*, London: Virago.

Burgdorf, R. (1997) '"Substantially limited": protection from disability discrimination: the special treatment model and misconceptions of the definition of disability', *Villanova Law Review* vol. 42, pp. 409–585.

Burkitt, I. (1994) 'The shifting concept of the self', *History of the Human Sciences*, vol. 7, pp. 7–28.

Burman, E., Smailers, S. L. and Chantler, K. (2004) '"Culture" as a barrier to service provision and delivery: domestic violence service for minoritized women', *Critical Social Policy*, vol. 24, no. 3, pp. 332–357.

Burnett, A. and Fassil, Y. (2002) *Meeting the Health Needs of Refugee and Asylum Seekers in the UK; an Information and Resource Pack for Health Workers*, London: Directorate of Health and Social Care for London.

Burr, R. (2006) *Vietnam's Children in a Changing World*, New Jersey: Rutgers University Press.

Butler, J. (1990) *Gender Trouble: Feminism and the Subversion of Identity*, London: Routledge.

Butler, J. (1993) *Bodies That Matter: On the Discursive Limits of 'Sex'*, London: Routledge.

Butler, J. (1997a) *Excitable Speech: A Politics of the Performative*, London: Routledge.

Butler, J. (1997b) *The Psychic Life of Power: Theories in Subjection*, Stanford: Stanford University Press.

Butler, J. (2000) *Antigone's Claim: Kinship Between Life and Death,* New York: Columbia University Press.

Butler, J. (2001) 'Doing justice to someone: sex reassignment and allegories of transsexuality', *GLQ,* vol. 7, no. 4, pp. 621–636.

Butler, J. (2002) 'Is kinship always already heterosexual?', *Differences: A Journal of Feminist Cultural Studies,* vol. 15, no. 1, pp. 14–44.

Butler, J. (2003) 'No it's not anti-semitic', *London Review of Books,* vol. 25, no. 16, pp. 19–21, 21 August 2003.

Butler, J. (2004a) *Precarious Life: The Powers of Mourning and Violence,* London: Verso.

Butler, J. (2004b) *Undoing Gender,* London: Routledge.

Butler, J. (2005) *Giving An Account of Oneself,* New York: Fordham University Press.

Butler, J. (2009) *Frames of War: When Is Life Grievable,* London: Verso.

Callon, M., Méadel, C. and Rabéharisoa, V. (2002) 'The economy of qualities', *Economy and Society,* vol. 31, no. 2, pp. 194–217.

Callon, M. and Muniesa, F. (2003) 'Les marchés économiques comme dispositifs collectifs de calcul', *Réseaux,* vol. 21, no. 122, pp. 189–233.

Cameron, D. (2011) *PM's speech at Munich Security Conference.* 5 February 2011. Available at: http://www.number10.gov.uk/news/pms-speech-at-munich-security-conference/ (accessed on 5 February 2014.

Campbell, F. K. (2001) 'Inciting legal fictions: disability's date with ontology and the ableist body of the law', *Griffith Law Review,* vol. 10, pp. 42–62.

Campbell, F. K. (2004) 'Sensing disability in Buddhism', Paper for *Bridges to Understanding: Multi-Faith Perspectives on Spirituality and Disability,* 22–25 November 2004, Novotel Homebush Bay, Sydney, Australia.

Campbell, F. K. (2005) 'Legislating disability: negative ontologies and the government of legal identities', in S. Tremain (ed.), *Foucault and the Government of Disability,* Ann Arbor: University of Michigan Press, pp. 108–130.

Campbell, F. K. (2008a) 'Refusing able(ness): a preliminary conversation about ableism', *Media and Culture,* vol. 11, no. 3, available at http://journal.media-culture.org.au/index.php/mcjournal/article/view/46 (accessed on 5 February 2014).

Campbell, F. K. (2008b) 'Exploring internalised ableism using critical race theory', *Disability and Society,* vol. 23, no. 2, pp. 151–162.

Campbell, F. K. (2009) *Contours of Ableism: The Production of Disability and Abledness,* Basingstoke: Palgrave Macmillan.

Campbell, F. K. (2011) 'Geodisability knowledge production and international norms: a Sri Lankan case study', *Third World Quarterly,* vol. 32, no. 8, pp. 1425–1444.

Campbell, F. K. (2012) 'Taking back our temples!', *Groundviews Journalism for Citizens.* Available at http://groundviews.org/2012/06/29/taking-back-our-temples/ (accessed 5 February 2014).

Campbell, F. K. (2013) 'Re-cognising disability: cross-examining social inclusion through the prism of queer anti-sociality', *Jindal Global Law Review: Special Issue Law, Culture and Queer Politics in Neoliberal Times,* vol. 4, no. 1, available at http://www.jgls.edu.in/JindalGlobalLawReview/PDF1/Fiona_Kumari_Campbell_(Chapter-9).pdf (accessed on 5 February 2014).

Campbell, F. K. (2014) 'The terrain of disability law in Sri Lanka: obstacles and possibilities for change', in S. Rao and M. Kalyanpur (eds.), *South Asia and Disability Studies: Redefining Boundaries and Extending Horizons,* New York: Peter Lang.

Campbell, J. (2007) 'Social work, political violence and historical change', *Social Work and Society,* vol. 5, available at http://www.fh-kaernten.at/uploads/media/Reflecting_from_Ireland_Campbell.pdf (accessed 5 February 2014).

Campbell, J. (2013) 'A journey from Belfast to London', in V. Cree (ed.), *Becoming a Social Worker: Global Narratives*, Abingdon: Routledge, pp. 29–36.

Campbell, J. and Duffy, J. (2008) 'Social work, political violence and citizenship in Northern Ireland', in S. Ramon (ed.) *Social Work in the Context of Political Conflict*, Birmingham: Venture/BASW, pp. 57–76.

Campbell, J. and Healey, A. (1999) '"Whatever you say, say something": the education, training and practice of mental health social workers in Northern Ireland', *Social Work Education*, vol. 18, no. 4, pp. 389–400.

Campbell, J. and Oliver, M. (1996) *Disability Politics: Understanding our Past, Changing our Future*, London: Routledge.

Campinha-Bocate, J. (2003) *The Process of Cultural Competence in the Delivery of Health Services: A Culturally Competent Model of Care*, Cincinnati: Transcultural Care Associates.

Canvin, K., Jones, C., Marttila, A., Burström, B. and Whitehead, M. (2007) 'Can I risk using public services? Perceived consequences of seeking help and health care among households living in poverty: qualitative study', *Journal of Epidemiology and Community Health*, vol. 61, no. 11, pp. 984–989.

Carballeira, N. (1996) 'The LIVE and learn model for culturally competent family services', *The Source*, vol. 6, no. 2, pp. 4–12.

Care Quality Commission (2011) *Our Reports on Castlebeck*, 28 July 2011. Accessible at http://www.cqc.org.uk/public/news/our-reports-castlebeck (accessed 5 February 2014).

Carey, M. (2008) 'Everything must go? The privatisation of state social work', *British Journal of Social Work*, vol. 38, no. 5, pp. 918–935.

Carlson, L. (2001) 'Cognitive ableism and disability studies: feminist reflections on the history of mental retardation', *Hypatia*, vol. 16, no. 4, pp. 124–146.

Carr, S. (2007) 'Participation, power, conflict and change: theorizing social care system of England and Wales', *Critical Social Policy*, vol. 27, no. 2, pp. 266–276.

Carr, S. (2010) 'Seldom heard or frequently ignored? Lesbian, gay and bisexual (LGB) perspectives on mental health services', *Ethnicity and Inequalities in Health and Social Care*, vol. 3, no. 3, pp. 14–25.

Carr, S. (2011a) '"A chance to cut is a chance to cure": self-harm and self-protection – a gay perspective', in P. Dunk-West and T. Hafford-Letchfield (eds.), *Sexual Identities and Sexuality in Social Work*, Farnham: Ashgate.

Carr, S. (2011b) 'Uniformity or equality? Integration, equity and the challenge of personalisation', *Journal of Integrated Care*, vol. 19, no. 3, pp. 41–47.

Carr, S. (2012) *Personalisation: A Rough Guide* (3rd edition), London: SCIE.

Carroll, L. (1872) *Through the Looking-Glass*, Published by Penguin Popular Classics (2007), London: Penguin Books.

Central Council for Education and Training in Social Work (1995) *Assuring Quality in the Diploma in Social Work 1. Rules and Requirements for the DipSW*, London: CCETSW.

Central Council for Education and Training in Social Work (1999) *Getting Off the Fence: Challenging Sectarianism in Personal Social Services*, London: CCETSW.

Central Intelligence Agency (2008) *CIA World Factbook*, Washington DC: Skyhorse.

Centre for Contemporary Cultural Studies (1982) *The Empire Strikes Back: Race and Racism in 70s Britain*, London: Hutchinson.

Chambers, D. (2012) *A Sociology of Family Life: Change and Diversity in Intimate Relations*, Cambridge: Polity Press.

Chambon, A., Irving, A. and Epstein, A. (eds.) (1999) *Reading Foucault for Social Work*, New York: Columbia University Press.

Cheal, D. (2008) *Families in Today's World: A Comparative Approach*, London: Routledge.

Chen, M. (2012) *Animacies: Biopolitics, Racial Mattering, and Queer Affect*, Durham, NC: Duke University Press.

Children Act (1989) London, HMSO.

Children Act (2004) London, HMSO.

Chouinard, V. (1997) 'Making space for disabling differences: changing ableist geographies, guest editorials', *Environment and Planning D: Society and Space*, vol. 15, pp. 379–390.

Clarke, J. (2004) *Changing Welfare, Changing States*, London: Sage.

Clarke, J. and Newman, J. (2012) 'Brave new world? Anglo-American challenges to universalism', in A. Anttonen, L. Häikiö and K. Stefánsson (eds.), *Welfare State, Universalism and Diversity*, Cheltenham: Edward Elgar, pp. 90–105.

Clarke, J., Gewirtz, S. and McLaughlin, E. (eds.) (2000) *New Managerialism, New Welfare?*, London: Sage.

Clear, M. (1999) 'The "normal" and the monstrous in disability research', *Disability and Society*, vol. 14, no. 4, pp. 435–448.

Clifford, D. and Burke, B. (2009) *Anti-Oppressive Ethics and Values in Social Work*, Basingstoke: Palgrave Macmillan.

Cocker, C. and Brown, H. C. (2010) 'Sex, sexuality and relationships: developing confidence and discernment when assessing lesbian and gay prospective adopters', *Adoption & Fostering*, vol. 34, no. 1, pp. 20–32.

Cocker, C. and Hafford-Letchfield, T. (2010) 'Critical commentary: out and proud? Social work's relationship with lesbian and gay equality', *British Journal of Social Work*, vol. 40, no. 6, pp. 1996–2008.

Coles, C. (2007) 'The question of power and authority in gender performance: Judith Butler's drag strategy', *eSharp: Special Issue on Gender, Power and Authority*, issue 9, pp. 1–18.

The College of Social Work (2012) *Mapping of the PCF against the SoPs – June 2012*. Accessed at http://www.tcsw.org.uk/pcf.aspx (accessed 5 February 2014).

Collier, A. (1977) *R.D. Laing: The Philosophy and Politics of Psychotherapy*, New York: Pantheon.

Collingwood, R. G. (1924) *Speculum Mentis*, Oxford: Clarendon Press.

Collins, P. H. (1986) 'Learning from the outsider within: the sociological significance of black feminist thought', *Social Problems*, vol. 33, no. 6, pp. S14–S32.

Collins, P. H. (2000) *Black Feminist Thought: Knowledge, Consciousness and the Politics of Empowerment*, New York and London: Routledge.

Commission of Investigation (2009) *Report into the Catholic Archdiocese of Dublin*, Dublin: Department of Justice, Equality and Law Reform.

Commission of Investigation (2010) *Report into the Catholic Diocese of Cloyne*, Dublin: Department of Justice, Equality and Law Reform.

Commission to Inquire into Child Abuse (2009) *Commission to Inquire into Child Abuse Report*, Dublin: Stationery Office.

Commissioner for Human Rights (2013) 'Irresponsible media reporting on Roma propagates negative myths', Council of Europe Press Release, 24 October 2013.

Community Care (2006) 'Forced marriage: whose shame', *Community Care*, vol. 16, pp. 28–29. Available at http://www.communitycare.co.uk/2006/11/16/forced-marriage-and-honour-killings (accessed on 6 February 2014).

Community Care (2012) 'Four in ten social workers say homophobia is a problem in the profession', *Community Care*, 31 July 2012, Available at http://www.community care.co.uk/articles/02/08/2012/118416/four-in-ten-social-workers-say-homophobia-is-problem-in-the-profession.htm (accessed 6 February 2014).

Conference of Socialist Economists (1980) *In and Against the State*, London: Pluto Press.

Connell, R. (2007) *Southern Theory: The Global Dynamics of Knowledge in Social Science*, Crows Nest, NSW: Allen & Unwin.

Cooper, D. (1995) *Power in Struggle: Feminism, Sexuality and the State*, Buckingham: Open University Press.

Coulter, S., Campbell, J., Duffy, J. and Reilly, I. (2013) 'Enabling social work students to deal with the consequences of political conflict: engaging with victim/survivor service users and a "pedagogy of discomfort"', *Social Work Education*, vol. 32, no. 4, pp. 439–452.

Council of Europe (2013) *Advisory Committee on the Framework Convention for the Protection of National Minorities: Third Opinion on Ireland adopted on 10 October 2012*. Available at http://www.coe.int/t/dghl/monitoring/minorities/3_FCNMdocs/PDF_3rd_OP_Ireland_en.pdf (accessed on 11 February 2014).

Cournoyer, B. (2010) *The Social Work Skills Workbook*, Florence: Cengage Learning Inc.

Cowden, S. and Singh, G. (2007) 'The "user": friend, foe or fetish? A critical exploration of user involvement in health and social care', *Critical Social Policy*, vol. 27, no. 1, pp. 5–23.

Craig, G. (2013) 'Invisibilizing "race" in public policy', Critical Social Policy, vol. 33, no. 4, pp. 712–721.

Cram, F. (2001) 'Rangahau Maori: Tona tika, tona pono – the validity and integrity of Maori research', in M. Tolich (ed.), *Research Ethics in Aotearoa New Zealand*, Auckland: Pearson Education New Zealand Ltd, pp. 35–52.

Crenshaw, K. (1993) 'Mapping the margins: intersectionality, identity politics, and violence against women of color', *Stanford Law Review*, vol. 43, no. 6, pp. 1241–1279.

Creswell, J. W. (2009) *Research Design: Qualitative, Quantitative, and Mixed Methods Approaches* (3rd edition), Thousand Oaks, CA: Sage .

Cronin, A., Ward, R., Pugh, S., King, A. and Price, E. (2011) 'Categories and their consequences: understanding and supporting the caring relationships of older lesbian, gay and bisexual people', *International Social Work*, vol. 54, no. 3, pp. 421–435.

Culler, J. (2008) *On Deconstruction: Theory and Criticism After Structuralism* (2nd edition), London: Routledge.

Dallmayr, F. (2009) 'Hermeneutics and inter-cultural dialogue: linking theory and practice', *Ethics and Global Politics*, vol. 2, no. 1, pp. 23–39.

Dalrymple, J. and Burke, B. (1995) *Anti-Oppressive Practice: Social Care and the Law*, Maidenhead: Open University Press and McGraw Hill.

Dalrymple, J. and Burke, B. (2006) *Anti-Oppressive Practice: Social Care and the Law* (2nd edition), Maidenhead: Open University Press.

Danaher, G., Schirato, T. and Webb, J. (2000) *Understanding Foucalt*, London: Sage.

Danso, R. (2009) 'Emancipating and empowering devalued skilled immigrants: what hope does anti-oppressive social work practice offer?', *British Journal of Social Work*, vol. 39, pp. 539–555.

Davies, B. (2000) *A Body of Writing*, Walnut Creek, CA: Altamira Press.

D'Cruz, H., Gillingham, P. and Melendez, S. (2007) 'Reflexivity, its meanings and relevance for social work: a critical review of the literature', *British Journal of Social Work*, vol. 37, no. 1, pp. 73–90.

De Alwis, M. (2008) 'Motherhood as a space of protest: women's political participation in contemporary Sri Lanka', in P. Banerjee (ed.), *Women in Peace Politics*, New Delhi: Sage, pp. 152–174.

de Mel, N. (2007) *Militarizing Sri Lanka: Popular Culture, Memory and Narrative in the Armed Conflict*, New Delhi: Sage.

de Mel, N. (2009) 'Gendering the new security paradigm in Sri Lanka', *IDS Bulletin*, vol. 40, no. 2, pp. 36–43.

de Silva, J. (2005) *Globalisation, Terror and the Shaming of a Nation: Constructing Local Masculinities in a Sri Lankan Village*, Victoria, BC: Trafford.

de Silva, J. (2009) 'Researching masculinity and violence in Sri Lankan politics: subject construction as methodology', *IDS Bulletin*, vol. 40, no. 3, pp. 86–93.

Deliovsky, K. and Kitossa, T. (2013) 'Beyond black and white: when going beyond black may take us out of bounds', *Journal of Black Studies*, vol. 44, no. 2, pp. 158–181.

Delphy, C. and Leonard, D. (1992) *Familiar Exploitation: A New Analysis of Marriage in Contemporary Western Societies*, Cambridge: Polity Press.

Deluze, G. (1990) *Negotiations*, New York: Columbia University Press.

Department of Health (2000) *Assessing Children in Need and Their Families: Practice Guidance*, London: The Stationery Office.

Department of Health (2001) *Responding to Diversity: A Study of the Commissioning of Services for People of Black and Minority Ethnic Origin with Physical Disabilities and/or Sensory Impairments, Aged 18–64 Years*, London: The Stationery Office.

Department of Health (2002) *Requirements for Social Work Training*, London: The Stationery Office.

Department of Health (2007) *Putting People First: A Shared Vision and Commitment to the Transformation of Adult Social Care*, London: The Stationery Office.

Department of Health (2012) *Investment in Mental Health: Working Age Adult and Older Adult Reports*, London: The Stationery Office.

Derrida, J. (1976[1967]) *Of Grammatology* (translated by G. Chakravorty Spivak), Baltimore, ML: Johns Hopkins University Press.

Derrida, J. (1981) *Dissemination* (translated by B. Johnson), London: Athlone Press.

Derrida, J. (1982) *Margins of Philosophy* (translated by A. Bass), Chicago: Chicago University Press.

Derrida, J. (1987) *Positions* (translated by A. Bass), London: Athlone Press.

Derrida, J. (2002) 'The animal that therefore I am (more to follow)', *Critical Inquiry*, vol. 28, no. 2, pp. 369–418.

Descombes, V. (2004) *Le Complément de sujet: enquête sur le fait d'agir de soi-même*, Paris: Éditions Gallimard.

Dhamoon, R. K. (2011) 'Considerations on mainstreaming intersectionality', *Political Research Quarterly*, vol. 64, no. 1, pp. 230–243.

Doel, M. and Marsh, P. (1992) *Task-Centred Social Work*, Aldershot: Ashgate.

Dominelli, L. (1988) *Anti-Racist Social Work* (2nd edition), Basingstoke: Macmillan.

Dominelli, L. (1996) 'Deprofessionalising social work: anti-oppressive practice, competencies and postmodernism', *British Journal of Social Work*, vol. 26, pp. 153–175.

Dominelli, L. (1997) *Anti-Racist Social Work*, Basingstoke: Macmillan.

Dominelli, L. (2002a) *Anti-Oppressive Social Work Theory and Practice*, Basingstoke: Palgrave.

Dominelli, L. (2002b) *Feminist Social Work Theory and Practice*, Basingstoke: Palgrave Macmillan.

Dominelli, L. (2008) *Anti-Racist Social Work* (3rd edition), Basingstoke: Palgrave Macmillan.

Dominelli, L. (2009) 'Anti-oppressive practice: the challenges of the twenty-first century', in R. Adams, L. Dominelli and M. Payne (eds.), *Social Work: Themes, Issues and Critical Debates* (3rd edition), Basingstoke: Palgrave Macmillan, pp. 49–64.

Dominelli, L. (2010) 'Anti-oppressive practice', in M. Gray and S. A. Webb (eds.), *Ethics and Value Perspectives in Social Work*, Basingstoke: Palgrave Macmillan, pp. 160–182.

Duggan, L. (2003) *The Twilight of Equality: Neoliberalism, Cultural Politics and the Attack on Democracy*, Boston, MA: Beacon Press.

Dunk-West, P. (2011) 'Everyday sexuality and identity: de-differentiating the sexual self in social work', in P. Dunk-West and T. Hafford-Letchfield (eds.), *Sexual Identities and Sexuality in Social Work: Research and Reflections from Women in the Field*, Farnham: Ashgate.

Dunk-West, P. (2013a) 'Gender, agency and the sexual self: a theoretical model for social work', *Advances in Social Work and Welfare Education*, vol. 15, no. 1, pp. 32–47.

Dunk-West, P. (2013b) *How to be a Social Worker: A Critical Guide for Students*, Basingstoke: Palgrave Macmillan.

Dunk-West, P. and Verity, F. (2013) *Sociological Social Work*, Farnham: Ashgate.

Durie, M. (2004) 'Understanding health and illness: research at the interface between science and indigenous knowledge', *International Journal of Epidemiology*, vol. 33, no. 5, pp. 1138–1143.

Dutt, R. (2003) 'Evidence given to the public inquiry into the death of Victoria Climbié', in H. Laming *The Victoria Climbié Inquiry: Report of an Inquiry*, London: HMSO, p. 345.

Eborall, C. and Griffiths, D. (2008) *The State of the Adult Social Care Workforce in England*, Leeds: Skills for Care

Eby, M. (2000) 'Understanding professional development', in A. Brechin, H. Brown and M. Eby (eds.), *Critical Practice in Health and Social Care*, London: Sage in association with The Open University, pp. 48–69.

ECPAT UK (2011) *Protecting Children Everywhere*. Available at: http://www. ecpat.org.uk/media/ecpat-uk-gives-evidence-education-select-committee (accessed 6 February 2014).

Edwards, R. and Gillies, V. (2012a) 'Farewell to family? Notes on an argument for retaining the concept', *Families, Relationships and Societies*, vol. 1, no. 1, pp. 63–69.

Edwards, R. and Gillies, V. (2012b) 'Farewell to family? A reply', *Families, Relationships and Societies*, vol. 1, no. 3, pp. 431–434.

Edwards, R., Ribbens McCarthy, J. and Gillies, V. (2012) 'The politics of concepts: family and its (putative) replacements', *British Journal of Sociology*, vol. 63, no. 4, pp. 730–746.

Eisenhauer, J. (2007) 'Just looking and staring back: challenging ableism through disability performance art', *Studies in Art Education: A Journal of Issues and Research*, vol. 49, no. 1, pp. 7–22.

El-Lahib, Y. and Wehbi, S. (2011) 'Immigration and disability: ableism in the policies of the Canadian state', *International Social Work*, vol. 55, no. 1, pp. 95–108.

Ellman, L. (2012) 'Opening eyes to the blind: a unit plan that confronts ableism in a standards based general education classroom', *The Clearinghouse: A Journal of Educational Strategies, Issues and Ideas*, vol. 85, no. 1, pp. 15–22.

Equality and Human Rights Commission (2011) *Equality Act 2010 Code of Practice: Services, Public Functions and Associations: Statutory Code of Practice*, London: The Stationery Office.

Ettelbrick, P. L. (1989) 'Since when was marriage a path to liberation?', *Out/look*, vol. 9, pp. 14–16.

Family Diversity Projects (2004–2008) *Love Makes a Family*, Amherst, MA: Family Diversity Projects. Available at: http://www.familydiv.org/lovemakesafamily.php (accessed on 6 February 2014).

Fannin, A., Fenge, L., Hicks, C., Lavin, N. and Brown, K. (2008) *Social Work Practice with Older Lesbians and Gay Men*, Exeter: Learning Matters.

Fanon, F. (1986) *Black Skin, White Mask*, (translated by Charles Lam Markmann), London: Pluto Press.

Fanshawe, S. and Sriskandarajah, D. (2010) *You Can't Put me in a Box: Super-Diversity and the End of Identity Politics in Britain*, London: IPPR.

Fay, M. T., Morrissey, M. and Smyth, M. (1999) *The Cost of the Troubles Study*, London: Pluto Press.

Fazil, Q., Bywaters, P., Ali, Z., Wallace, L. and Singh, G. (2002) 'Disadvantage and discrimination compounded: the experience of Pakistani and Bangladeshi parents of disabled children in the UK', *Disability and Society*, vol. 17, no. 3, pp. 237–253.

Featherstone, B. (2001) 'Where to for feminist social work?', *Critical Social Work*, vol. 2, no. 1. Available at http://www.uwindsor.ca/criticalsocialwork/where-to-for-feminist-social-work (accessed on 6 February 2014).

Featherstone, B. (2004) *Family Life and Family Support*, Basingstoke: Palgrave Macmillan

Featherstone, B. and Green, L. (2009) 'Judith Butler', in M. Gray and S. A. Webb (eds.), *Social Work Theories and Methods*, London: Sage, pp. 53–62.

Featherstone, B. and Green, L. (2010) 'Judith Butler', in M. Gray and S. Webb (eds.) *Social Work Theories and Methods* (2nd edition), London: Sage.

Featherstone, B. and Lancaster, E. (1997) 'Contemplating the unthinkable: men who sexually abuse', *Critical Social Policy*, vol. 17, pp. 51–71.

Featherstone, B., White, S. and Morris, K. (2014) *Re-imagining Child Protection: Towards humane social work with families*, Bristol: Policy Press.

Fejes, A. and Nicoll, K. (eds.) (2008) *Foucault and Lifelong Learning: Governing the Subject*, Oxon: Routledge, pp. 1–18.

Fenge, L. A. (2012) 'Economic well-being and ageing: the need for financial education for social workers', *Social Work Education*, vol. 31, no. 4, pp. 498–511.

Ferguson, I. (2007a) *Reclaiming Social Work: Challenging Neo-Liberalism and Promoting Social Justice*, London: Sage.

Ferguson, I. (2007b) 'Increasing user choice or privatising risk? The antinomies of personalisation', *British Journal of Social Work*, vol. 37, no. 3, pp. 367–403.

Ferguson, H. and Hogan, F. (2004) *Strengthening Families Thorough Fathers*, Dublin: Family Support Agency.

Ferguson, I. and Woodward, R. (2009) *Radical Social Work in Practice: Making a Difference*, Bristol: Policy Press.

Fernando, J. (2009) 'Reflections on demilitarising the Sri Lankan society', *South Asia Citizens Web*. Available at http://www.sacw.net/article1308.html (accessed on 6 February 2014).

Ferry, F., Bolton, D., Bunting, B., Devine, B., McCann, S. and Murphy, S. (2008) *Trauma, Health and Conflict in Northern Ireland: A Study of the Epidemiology of Trauma Related Disorders and Qualitative Investigation of the Impact of Trauma on the Individual*, Derry: NICTT and UUJ.

Fillingham, L. A. (1993) *Foucalt: For Beginners*, New York: Writers and Readers Publishing.

Finkelstein, V. (1991) 'Disability: an administrative challenge?', in M. Oliver (ed.), *Social Work: Disabled People and Disabling Environments*, London: Jessica Kingsley, pp. 19–39.

Finkelstein, V. (1993) 'Disability: a social challenge or an administrative responsibility', in J. Swain, S. French, C. Barnes and C. Thomas (eds.), *Disabling Barriers – Enabling Environments*, London: Sage, pp. 34–43.

Finkelstein, V. (1996) 'Yesterday's model', in V. Finkelstein (ed.), *Modelling Disability: A Kit Based on a Presentation at the Workshop Organised for the 'Breaking The Moulds' Conference, Dunfermline Scotland 16–17 May 1996*, Leeds: The Disability Press, pp. 6–9.

Fish, J. (2006) *Heterosexism in Health and Social Care*, Houndmills: Palgrave Macmillan.

Fish, J. (2008) 'Navigating queer street: researching the intersections of lesbian, gay, bisexual and trans (LGBT) identities in health research', *Sociological Research Online*, vol. 13, no. 1. Available at http://www.socresonline.org.uk/13/1/12.html (accessed 6 February 2014).

Fisher, M. (2009) *Capitalist Realism: Is there no Alternative?*, London: Sero.

Fook, J. (1996) *The Reflective Researcher: Social Workers' Theories of Practice Research*, Sydney: Allen & Unwin.

Fook, J. (1999) 'Reflexivity as method', *Health Sociology Review*, vol. 9, no. 1, pp. 11–20.

Fook, J. (2000) 'The lone crusader: constructing enemies and allies in the workplace', in L. Napier and J. Fook (eds.), *Breakthroughs in Practice: Theorising Critical Moments in Social Work*, London: Whiting & Birch.

Fook, J. (2002) *Social Work: Critical Theory and Practice*, London: Sage.

Fook, J. and Askeland, G. (2007) 'Challenges of critical reflection: "nothing ventured, nothing gained"', *Social Work Education*, vol. 26, no. 5, pp. 520–533.

Fook, J. and Gardner, F. (2007) *Practising Critical Reflection: A Resource Handbook*, Maidenhead: Open University Press and McGraw-Hill Education.

Foucault, M. (1972[1969]) *The Archaeology of Knowledge*, London: Routledge.

Foucault, M. (1975) *The Birth of the Clinic: An Archaeology of Medical Perception*, (translated by A. M. Sheridan-Smith), New York: Vintage.

Foucault, M. (1977) *Discipline and Punish: The Birth of the Prison*, New York: Pantheon.

Foucault, M. (1980) *Power/Knowledge: Selected Interviews and Other Writing 1972–1977*, (edited by C. Gordon), New York: Pantheon.

Foucault, M. (1981a) *The History of Sexuality, Volume 1: An Introduction*, Harmondsworth: Penguin.

Foucault, M. (1981b) 'The order of discourse', in R. Young (ed.), *Untying the Text: A Post-Structuralist Reader*, London: Routledge and Kegan Paul.

Foucault, M. (1982) 'Afterword: the subject and power', Afterword to H. L. Dreyfus and P. Rabinow (eds.), *Michael Foucault: Beyond Structuralism and Hermeneutics*, Chicago: University of Chicago Press, pp. 208–226.

Foucault, M. (1983) 'Afterword: the subject and power', in H. Dreyfus and P. Rabinow (eds.), *Michel Foucault: Beyond Structuralism and Hermeneutics*, Hemel Hempstead: Harvester Wheatsheaf.

Foucault, M. (1986a). *The History of Sexuality, Vol. 2: The Use of Pleasure*, Harmondsworth: Penguin.

Foucault, M. (1986b). *The History of Sexuality, Vol. 3: The Care of the Self*, Harmondsworth: Penguin.

Foucault, M. (1986c) *The Order of Things*, London: Tavistock.

Foucault, M. (1988a) *The Care of the Self: The History of Sexuality*, New York: Random House.

Foucault, M. (1988b) Technologies of the Self: A Seminar with Michel Foucault, Amherst, MA: University of Massachusetts Press.

Foucault, M. (1990[1976]) *The History of Sexuality, Vol. 1: An Introduction*, London: Penguin.

Foucault, M. (1991) 'Governmentality', (translated by Rosi Braidotti and revised by Colin Gordon), in G. Burchell, C. Gordon and P. Miller (eds.), *The Foucault Effect: Studies in Governmentality*, Chicago, IL: University of Chicago Press.

Foucault, M. (1993) 'About the beginning of the hermeneutics of the self (transcription of two lectures in Darthmouth on Nov. 17 and 24, 1980)', ed. By M. Blasius, *Political Theory*, vol. 21, no. 2, pp. 198–227.

Foucault, M. (1997) 'The birth of biopolitics', in M. Foucault, *Ethics: Subjectivity and Truth*, ed. by Paul Rabinow, New York: The New Press, pp. 73–79.

Foucault, M. (2003) *'Society Must be Defended': Lectures at the College de France 1974–1975*, London: Allen Lane.

Foucault, M. (2006[2003]) *Psychiatric Power: Lectures at the Collège de France 1973–1974*, Basingstoke: Palgrave Macmillan.

Fowler, B. (2009) 'The recognition/redistribution debate and Bourdieu's theory of practice', *Theory, Culture and Society*, vol. 26, no. 1, pp. 144–156.

Fox, A. (2012) *Personalisation: Lessons from Social Care*, London: RSA.

Fraser, N. (1989) *Unruly Practices: Power, Discourse and Gender in Contemporary Social Theory*, Cambridge: Polity.

Fraser, N. (1997) *Justice Interruptus: Critical Reflections on the Post-Socialist Condition*, London: Routledge.

Fraser, N. (2000) 'Rethinking recognition', *New Left Review*, vol. 3, pp. 107–120.

Fraser, N. (2003) 'Social justice in an age of identity politics: redistribution, recognition and participation', in N. Fraser and A. Honneth, *Redistribution or Recognition?*, London: Verso.

Fraser, N. and Honneth, A. (2003a) 'Introduction: redistribution or recognition?', in N. Fraser and A. Honneth, *Redistribution or Recognition?*, London: Verso.

Fraser, N. and Honneth, A. (2003b) *Redistribution Of Recognition: A Politico-Philosophical Exchange*, London: Verso.

Freeman, H. (2013) 'Check your privilege! Whatever that means', *The Guardian*, 5 June 2013. Available at http://www.guardian.co.uk/society/2013/jun/05/check-your-privilege-means (accessed on 6 February 2014).

Freire, P. (2007) *Pedagogy of the Oppressed*, New York: Continuum.

Froggett, L. (2004) 'Holistic practice, art, creativity and the politics of recognition', *Social Work & Social Science Review*, vol. 11, no. 3, pp. 29–51.

Frost, P. and Hoggett, P. (2008) 'Human agency and social suffering', *Critical Social Policy*, vol. 28, no. 4, pp. 438–460.

Furedi, F. (2004) *Therapy Culture: Cultivating Vulnerability in an Uncertain Age*, London: Routledge.

Furness, S. and Gilligan, P. (2010) *Religion, Belief and Social Work*, Bristol: Policy Press.

Furness, S. and Gilligan, P. (2012) '"It never came up": encouragements and discouragements to addressing religion and belief in professional practice – what do social work students have to say?', *British Journal of Social Work*, published online 11 October 2012, doi: 10.1093/bjsw/bcs140.

Gallagher, M. (2008) '"Power is not an evil": rethinking power in participatory methods', *Children's Geographies*, vol. 6, pp. 137–150.

Garrett, P. M. (1998) 'Notes from the Diaspora: anti-discriminatory social work practice, Irish people and the practice curriculum', *Social Work Education*, vol. 17, no. 4, pp. 435–448

Garrett, P. M. (2000) 'Responding to Irish "invisibility": anti-discriminatory social work practice and the placement of Irish children in Britain', *Adoption and Fostering*, vol. 24, no. 1, pp. 23–34.

Garrett, P. M. (2001) 'Interrogating "Home Alone": the critical deconstruction of media representations in social work education', *Social Work Education*, vol. 20, no. 6, pp. 643–658.

Garrett, P. M. (2002a) 'Social work and the "just society": diversity, difference and the sequestration of poverty', *The Journal of Social Work*, vol. 2, no. 2, pp. 187–210.

Garrett, P. M. (2002b) '"No Irish need apply": social work in Britain and the history and politics of exclusionary paradigms and practices', *British Journal of Social Work*, vol. 32, no. 4, pp. 477–494.

Garrett, P. M. (2004) *Social Work and Irish People in Britain: Historical and Contemporary Responses to Irish Children and Families*, Bristol: Policy Press.

Garrett, P. M. (2009) *'Transforming' Children's Services? Social Work, Neoliberalism and the 'Modern' World*, Maidenhead: Open University/McGraw Hill.

Garrett, P. M. (2010) 'Recognizing the limitations of recognition theory: Axel Honneth, Nancy Fraser and social work', *British Journal of Social Work*, vol. 40, no. 5, pp. 1517–1533.

Garrett, P. M. (2012) 'Adjusting "our notions of the nature of the State": a political reading of Ireland's child protection crisis', *Capital & Class*, vol. 36, no. 2, pp. 263–281.

Garrett, P. M. (2013) *Social Work and Social Theory: Making Connections*, Bristol: Policy Press.

Garrity, Z. (2010) 'Discourse analysis, Foucault and social work research: identifying some methodological complexities', *Journal of Social Work*, vol. 10, pp. 193–210.

Gates, H. L. (ed.) (1986) *"Race", Writing and Difference*, Chicago, IL: University of Chicago Press.

Gavriel-Fried, B., Shilo, G. and Cohen, O. (2012) 'How do social workers define the concept of family?', *British Journal of Social Work*, published online 20 November 2012, doi: 10.1093/bjsw/bcs176.

Geertz, C. (1973) *The Interpretation of Cultures*, New York: Basic Books.

Gegeo, D. W. (2008) 'Shifting paradigms in Pacific scholarship: towards island-based methodologies, epistemologies and pedagogies', Paper presented at the Building Pacific Research Capacity and Scholarship 2008, Fale Pasifika, Auckland.

Gegeo, D. W. and Watson-Gegeo, K. (2001) 'How we know: Kwara'ae rural villagers doing indigenous epistemology', *The Contemporary Pacific*, vol. 13, no. 1, pp. 55–88.

Gell, A. (1998) *Art and Agency: An Anthropological Theory*, Oxford: Oxford University Press.

General Social Care Council (2010) *Raising Standards: Social Work Education in England 2008–2009*, London: General Social Care Council.

Gent, P. (2011) 'Service-learning and the culture of ableism', in T. Stewart and N. Webster (eds.), *Problematising Service-Learning*, Charlotte,NC: Information Age, pp. 223–243.

George, L. (2010) 'Tradition, innovation and invention: multiple reflections of an urban marae', Unpublished doctoral thesis in Social Anthropology, Auckland, Massey University.

Giddens, A. (1991) *Modernity and Self-Identity: Self and Society in the Late Modern Age*, Cambridge: Polity Press.

Giddens, A. (1992) *The Transformation of Intimacy: Sexuality, Love and Eroticism in Modern Societies*, Cambridge: Polity Press.

Giddens, A. (1993) *The Transformation of Intimacy*, Cambridge: Polity Press.

Gilroy, P. (2004) *After Empire: Melancholia or Convivial Culture?*, London: Routledge.

Gledhill, A. (1989) *Who Cares?* London: Centre for Policy Studies.

Goldman, R. and Papson, S. (2011) *Landscapes of Capital*, Cambridge: Polity Press.

Goldstein, B. P. (2002) '"Catch 22" – black workers' role in equal opportunities for black service users', *British Journal of Social Work*, vol. 29, no. 2, pp. 285–301.

Goodley, D. (2013) 'Dis/entangling critical disability studies', *Disability and Society*, vol. 28, no. 5, pp. 631–644.

Gove, M. (2012) 'The failure of child protection and the need for a fresh start', Education Secretary speech on child protection on 19 November 2012 at the Institute of Public Policy Research. Available at http://www.education.gov.uk/inthenews/speeches/a00217075/gove-speech-on-child-protection (accessed on 6 February 2014).

Graham, M. (2000) 'Honouring social work principles – exploring the connections between anti-racist social work and African-centred worldviews', *Social Work Education*, vol. 19, no. 5, pp. 423–436.

Graham, M. (2007a) 'Knowledge representation in social work education', *The International Journal of the Humanities*, vol. 3, no. 10, pp. 9–14.

Graham, M. (2007b) *Black Issues in Social Work and Social Care*, Bristol: Policy Press.

Graham, M. (2009) 'Reframing black perspectives in social work: new directions', *Social Work Education*, vol. 28, no. 3, pp. 268–280.

Graham, M. and Schiele, J. (2010) 'Anti-discriminatory and equality of oppressions models in social work: reflections from the UK and the USA', *European Journal of Social Work*, vol. 13, no. 2, pp. 231–244.

Grant, C. and Zwier, E. (2011) 'Intersectionality and student outcomes: sharpening the struggle against racism, sexism, classism, ableism, heterosexism, nationalism and linguistic, religious and geographical discrimination', *Teaching and Learning, Multicultural Perspectives*, vol. 13, no. 4, pp. 181–188.

Gray, A. (2010) *Working with Lesbian, Gay, Bisexual and Transgendered People – People with Mental Health Needs: Alison's Story*, Social Care TV, Social Care Institute for Excellence.

Gray, J. (2011) *At Home in the Hills: Sense of Place in the Scottish Borders*, New York: Berghahn Books.

Gray, M. and Webb, S. A. (eds.) (2013) *The New Politics of Social Work*, Houndsmill: Palgrave Macmillan.

Guha, R. (1989) 'The prose of counter-insurgency', in R. Guha and G. Spivak (eds.), *Selected Subaltern Studies*, New York: Oxford University Press, pp. 45–84.

Gula, R. M. (1998) *Reason Informed by Faith*, New York: Paulist Press.

Gunawardena, N. (2010) 'Subverted heroes: narrative experiences of disabled veterans in post-war Sri Lanka', Master of Arts in Disability and Gender, School of Sociology and Social Policy, The University of Leeds. Online at: http://www.academia.edu/3586407/Subverted_Heroes_Narrative_Experiences_of_Disabled_Veterans_in_Post-War_Sri_Lanka (accessed 6 February 2014).

Guru, S. (2010) 'Social work and the "war on terror"', *British Journal of Social Work*, vol. 40, no. 1, pp. 272–289.

Gutting, G. (ed.) (1994) *The Cambridge Companion to Foucault*. Cambridge: Cambridge University Press.

Hafford-Letchfield, T. (2011) 'Grey matter really matters: a study of the learning opportunities and learning experiences of older people using social care services', *International Journal of Education and Ageing*, vol. 2, no. 1, pp. 23–40.

Hafford Letchfield, T. (2013) 'Social work, class and later life', in M. Formosa and P. Higgs (eds.), *Social Class in Later Life: Power, Identity and Lifestyle*, Bristol: Policy Press.

Halperin, D. (1995) *Saint Foucault: Towards a Gay Hagiography*, New York: Oxford University Press.

Hammerton, C. (2006) *Black and Minority Ethnic and Learning Disabilities Research*, Suffolk: Learning Disability Partnership Board and REALISE.

Hankivsky, O. and Cormier, R. (2011) 'Intersectionality and public policy: some lessons from existing models', *Political Research Quarterly*, vol. 64, no. 1, pp. 217–229.

Haraway, D. (1991) 'A cyborg manifesto: science, technology and socialist feminism in the late twentieth century', in D. Haraway, *Simians, Cyborgs, and Women: The Reinvention of Nature*, London: Free Association Books, pp. 149–181.

Haraway, D. (2003) *The Companion Species Manifesto*. Chicago: Prickly Paradigm Press.

Hardest Hit (2012) 'The tipping point: the human and economic costs of cutting disabled people's support', *Hardest Hit Coalition*. Available at: http://thehardesthit.wordpress.com/our-message/the-tipping-point/comment-page-2/ (accessed on 6 February 2014).

Harlow, E. (2003) 'New managerialism, social service departments and social work practice today', *Practice: Social Work in Action*, vol. 15, no. 2, pp. 29–44.

Harpur, P. (2009) 'Sexism and racism; why not ableism-calling for a cultural shift in the approach to disability discrimination', *Alternative Law Journal*, vol. 34, pp. 163–167.

Harpur, P. (2012) 'From disability to ability: changing the phrasing of the debate', *Disability and Society*, vol. 27, no. 3, pp. 325–337.

Harris, J. (2003) *The Social Work Business*, London: Routledge.

Harvey, D. (2007) *A Brief History of Neoliberalism*, Oxford: Oxford University Press.

Hasan, M. (2011) 'How the fear of being criminalised has forced Muslims into silence', *The Guardian*, 8 September 2011. Available at http://www.theguardian.com/commentis-free/2011/sep/08/fear-criminalisation-forces-muslim-silence (accessed 6 February 2014).

Hatton, C., Akram, Y., Shah, R., Robertson, J. and Emerson, E. (2004) *Supporting South Asian Families with a Child with Severe Disabilities*, London: Jessica Kingsley.

Hau'ofa, E. (1994) 'Our sea of islands', *The Contemporary Pacific: A Journal of Pacific Island Affairs*, vol. 6, no. 1, pp. 148–161.

Hau'ofa, E. (2000) 'The ocean in us', in D. N. Hanlon and G. M. White (eds.), *Voyaging Through Contemporary Pacific*, Oxford: Rowman & Littlefield.

Health and Care Professions Council (2012b) *Standards of Proficiency – Social Workers in England*, London: HCPC. Available at http://www.hpc-uk.org/publications/standards/index.asp?id=569 (accessed 6 February 2014).

Healy, K. (1998) 'Participation and child protection: the importance of context,' *The British Journal of Social Work*, vol. 28, no. 6, pp. 897–914.

Healy, K. (2000) *Social Work Practices: Contemporary Perspectives on Change*, London: Sage.

Healy, K. (2005) *Social Work in Context: Creating Frameworks for Practice*, Basingstoke: Palgrave. (Translated into Chinese in 2006 and into Danish in 2008.)

Healy, K. (2007) *Writing Skills for Social Workers*, London: Sage.

Heaphy, B. (2009) 'The storied, complex lives of older GLBT adults', *Journal of GLBT Family Studies*, vol. 5, pp. 119–138.

Hehir, T. (2002) 'Eliminating ableism in education', *Harvard Educational Review*, vol. 72, pp. 1–32.

Hek, R., Hughes, N. and Ozman, R. (2012) 'Safeguarding the needs of children and young people seeking asylum in the UK: addressing past failings and meeting future challenges', *Child Abuse Review*, vol. 21, no. 5, pp. 335–348.

Hendry, E. (2012) 'How does foster care work? Evidence of outcomes', *Child Abuse Review*, vol. 21, no. 1, pp. 72–73.

Henriques, J., Hollway, W., Urwin, C., Venn, C. and Walkerdine, V. (1984) *Changing the Subject: Psychology, Social Regulation and Subjectivity*, London: Routledge.

Hequembourg, A. (2007) *Lesbian Motherhood: Stories of Becoming*, New York: Harrington Park Press.

Heydt, M. J. and Sherman, E. (2005) 'Conscious use of self: tuning the instrument of social work practice with cultural competence', *The Journal of Baccalaureate Social Work*, vol. 10, no. 2, pp. 25–40.

Heyes, S. (1993) 'A critique of the ideology, power relations and language of user involvement'. Unpublished essay.

Hicks, S. (2008a) 'Gender role models … who needs 'em?!', *Qualitative Social Work*, vol. 7, no. 1, pp. 43–59.

Hicks, S. (2008b) 'Thinking through sexuality', *Journal of Social Work*, vol. 8, no. 1, pp. 65–82.

Hicks, S. (2009) 'Sexuality', in R. Adams, L. Dominelli and M. Payne (eds.), *Practising Social Work in a Complex World*, Basingstoke: Palgrave Macmillan.

Hicks, S. (2011) *Lesbian, Gay and Queer Parenting: Families, Intimacies, Genealogies*, Basingstoke: Palgrave Macmillan.

Hicks, S. (2013) 'Lesbian, Gay, Bisexual, and Transgender Parents and the Question of Gender', in A. E. Goldberg and K. R. Allen (eds.), *LGBT-Parent Families: Innovations in Research and Implications for Practice*, New York: Springer.

Hiley, D. R., Bohman, J. R. and Shusterman, R. (eds.) (1991) *The Interpretive Turn: Philosophy, Science and Culture*, Ithaca: Cornell University Press.

Hill, A. (2007) 'Social work crisis puts children at risk', *The Observer*, 7 October 2007. Available at http://www.theguardian.com/society/2007/oct/07/childrensservices. socialcare (accessed 11 February 2014).

Hill Collins, P. (1990) *Black Feminist Thought*, Winchester, MA: Unwin Hyman.

Hines, J. M. (2012) 'Using an anti-oppressive framework in practice with lesbians', *Gay & Lesbian Social Services*, vol. 24, no. 1, pp. 23–39.

HM Government (2007) *Putting People First: A Shared Vision and Commitment to the Transformation of Adult Social Care*, London: HM Government.

Ho, A. (2008) 'The individualist's model of autonomy and the challenge of disability', *Journal of Bioethic Inquiry*, vol. 5, pp. 193–207.

Hodge, N. and Runswick-Cole, K. (2013) '"They never pass me the ball": exposing ableism through the leisure experiences of disabled children, young people and the families', *Children's Geography*, vol. 11, no. 3, pp. 311–325.

Holland, S. (2010) *Child and Family Assessment in Social Work Practice* (2nd Edition), London: Sage.

Holloway, M. and Moss, B. (2010) *Spirituality and Social Work*, Houndmills: Macmillan.

hooks, b. (1984) *Feminist Theory: From Margin to Centre*, Boston, MA: South End Press.

hooks, b. (1989) *Talking Back: Thinking Feminist – Thinking Black*, London: Sheba.

Hoskins, R. (2012) *The Boy in the River: A Shocking True Story of Murder and Sacrifice in the Heart of London*, Basingstoke: Pan Books.

Houston, S. (2008) 'Transcending ethnoreligious identities in Northern Ireland: social work's role in the struggle for recognition', *Australian Journal of Social Work*, vol. 61, no. 1, pp. 25–41.

Howarth, G. (2000) 'Dismantling the boundaries between life and death', *Mortality*, vol. 5, no. 2, pp. 127–138.

Hughes, B. (2008) 'Being disabled: towards a critical social ontology for disability studies', *Disability and Society*, vol. 22, no. 7, pp. 673–684.

Hugman, R. (2009) 'But is it social work? Some reflections on mistaken identities', *British Journal of Social Work*, vol. 39, pp. 1138–1153.

Human Rights Watch (2014) *The World Report*, HRW. Available at http://www.hrw.org/reports/2014/01/21/world-report-2014 (accessed 6 February 2014).

Humphries, B. (1997) 'Reading social work: competing discourses in the Rules and Requirements for the Diploma in Social Work', *British Journal of Social Work*, vol. 27, no. 5, pp. 641–658.

Humphries B (2004) 'An unacceptable role for social work: implementing immigration policy', *British Journal of Social Work*, vol. 34, no. 1, pp. 93–107.

Hussain, Y. (2005) 'South Asian disabled women: negotiating identities', *The Sociological Review*, vol. 53, no. 3, pp. 522–538.

Ife, J. (1997) *Rethinking Social Work: Towards a Critical Practice*, Longman: Melbourne.

Immigrant Council of Northern Ireland (2013) 'Racial profiling assurances urgently needed', Press Release, 23 October 2013. Available at http://www.immigrantcouncil.ie/media/press-releases/743-racial-profiling-assurances-urgently-needed (accessed on 11 February 2014).

Ingold, T. (2000) *The Perception of the Environment: Essays on Livelihood, Dwelling and Skill*, London: Routledge.

The Integration Centre (TIC) (2013) *Annual Monitoring Report on Integration 2012*. Available at http://www.integrationcentre.ie/getattachment/eda7574b-b459-4045-be11-123b74 bcdb0d/Annual-Monitoring-Report-on-Integration-2012.aspx (accessed 11 February 2014).

International Association of Schools of Social Work/International Federation of Social Workers (2001) *Definition of Social Work Jointly Agreed 27 June 2001 Copenhagen*. Available at http://www.iassw-aiets.org/international-definition-of-social-work (accessed 6 February 2014).

Irving, A. (1999) 'Waiting for Foucault: social work and the multitudinous truth(s) of life', in A. Chambon, A. Irving and L. Epstein (eds.), *Reading Foucault for Social Work*, New York: Columbia University Press.

Ives, P. (2004) *Language and Hegemony in Gramsci*, London: Pluto Press.

Iwasaki, Y. and Mactavish, J. (2005) 'Ubiquitous yet unique: perspectives of people with disabilities on stress', *Rehabilitation Counselling Bulletin*, vol. 48, no. 4, pp. 194–208.

Ixer, G. (1999) 'There's no such thing as reflection', *British Journal of Social Work*, vol. 29, no. 4, pp. 513–527.

Jack, G. (1997) 'Discourses of child protection and child welfare', *British Journal of Social Work*, vol. 27, no. 5, pp. 659–678.

Jagose, A. (2002) *Inconsequence: Lesbian Representation and the Logic of Sexual Sequence*, Ithaca: Cornell University Press.

Jameson, F. (1991) *Postmodernism, or, the Cultural Logic of Late Capitalism*, Durham, NC: Duke University Press.

Jayasekara, R. (2007) 'Health status, trends and issues in Sri Lanka', *Nursing and Health Sciences*, vol. 9, pp. 228–233.

Jayasuriya, J. (2010) 'Over 14,000 soldiers disabled in Sri Lankan Civil War', *China Radio International English*. Available at http://english.cri.cn/6966/2010/03/19/189s5 57666.htm (accessed on 10 February 2014).

Jeganathan, P. (2001) 'A space for violence: anthropology, politics and the location of a Sinhala practices of masculinity', *Subaltern Stud*ies, vol. 11, pp. 37–65.

Jeyasingham, D. (2008) 'Knowledge/ignorance and the construction of sexuality in social work education', *Social Work Education*, vol. 27, no. 2, pp. 138–151.

Joas, H. (1998) 'The autonomy of the self: the Meadian heritage and its postmodern challenge', *European Journal of Social Theory*, vol. 1, pp. 7–18.

Johnson, B. (1980) *The Critical Difference: Essays in the Contemporary Rhetoric of Reading*, Baltimore: Johns Hopkins University Press.

Johnson, B. (1987) *A World of Difference*, Baltimore: Johns Hopkins University Press.

Johnson, B. (1998) *The Feminist Difference: Literature, Psychoanalysis, Race, and Gender*, Cambridge, MA: Harvard University Press.

Jones, C. (1983) *State Social Work and the Working Class*, Basingstoke: Macmillan.

Jones, C. and Hackett, S. (2011) 'The role of "family practices" and "displays of family" in the creation of adoptive kinship', *British Journal of Social Work*, vol. 41, no. 1, pp. 40–56.

Jones, C. and Hackett, S. (2012) 'Redefining family relationships following adoption: adoptive parents' perspectives on the changing nature of kinship between adoptees and birth relatives', *British Journal of Social Work*, vol. 42, no. 2, pp. 283–299.

Jung, T. (2010) 'Review essay: citizens, co-producers, clients, captives? A critical review of consumerism and public services', *Public Management Review*, vol. 12, no. 3, pp. 439–446

Kaeser, G. (photographs) and Gillespie, P. (ed.) (1999) *Love Makes a Family: Portraits of Lesbian, Gay, Bisexual, and Transgender Parents and Their Families*, Amherst: University of Massachusetts Press.

Kafer, A. (2003) 'Compulsory bodies: reflections on heterosexuality and ablebodiedness', *Journal of Women's History*, vol. 15, no. 30, pp. 77–88.

Kane, E. W. (2012) *The Gender Trap: Parents and the Pitfalls of Raising Boys and Girls*, New York, New York University Press.

Kane, E. W. (2013) *Rethinking Gender and Sexuality in Childhood*, London: Bloomsbury.

Kapur, R. and Campbell, J. (2005) *The Troubled Mind of Northern Ireland*, London: Karnac.

KC, NNC v City of Westminster Social and Community Services Department [2008] EWCA Civ198.

Keating, F. (2000) 'Anti-racist perspectives: what are the gains for social work?', *Social Work Education*, vol. 19, no. 1, pp. 77–87.

Kelly, N. and Stevenson, J. (2006) *First Do No Harm: Denying Healthcare to People Whose Asylum Claims Have Failed*, London: Refugee Council.

Kenney, C. M. (2009) '*Me aro ki te ha o hine ahuone*: women, miscarriage stories and midwifery: Towards a contextually relevant research methodology'. Doctor of Philosophy in Midwifery PhD, Palmerston North, Massey University.

Kenney, C. M. (2011) 'Maori women, maternity services and the Treaty of Waitangi', in V. M. Tawhai and K. Gray-Sharp (eds.), *Always Speaking: The Treaty of Waitangi and Public Policy*, Wellington: Huia Publishers.

King, D. (1988) 'Multiple jeopardy, multiple consciousness: the context of black feminist ideology', *Signs: Journal of Women in Culture and Society*, vol. 14, no. 1, pp. 42–72.

Kirkpatrick, I. (2006) 'Taking stock of the new managerialism in English social services', *Social Work and Society*, vol. 4, no. 1, pp. 14–24.

Klein, D. (1999) 'The humiliation dynamic: an overview', *The Journal of Primary Prevention*, vol. 12, no. 2, pp. 93–121.

Knott, C. and Scragg, T. (eds.) (2010) *Reflective Practice in Social Work* (2nd edition), Exeter: Learning Matters.

Kohli, R. (2006) 'The comfort of strangers – social work practice with unaccompanied asylum-seeking children and young people in the UK', *Child and Family Social Work*, vol. 11, no. 1, pp. 1–91.

Kohli, R. (2013) 'The sound of silence: listening to what unaccompanied asylum-seeking children say and do not say', *British Journal of Social Work*, vo. 36, no. 5, pp. 707–721.

Koppelman, K. and Goodhardt, L. (2011) 'Ableism: disability does not mean inability', in K. Koppelman, *Understanding Human Difference: Multicultural Education for a Diverse America* (3rd edition), Boston: Pearson, pp. 285–307.

Kress-White, M. (2009) 'The quest of inclusion: understanding ableism, pedagogy, and the right to belong', Master of Education Thesis, Department of Educational Foundations, University of Saskatchewan.

Krumer-Nevo, M. (2008) 'From "noise" to "voice": how can social work benefit from knowledge of people living in poverty', *International Social Work*, vol. 51, no. 4, pp. 556–565.

Kumar, A., Sonpal, D. and Hiranandani, V. (2012) 'Trapped between ableism and neoliberalism: critical reflections on disability and employment in India', *Disability Studies Quarterly*, vol. 32, no. 3. Available at http://dsq-sds.org/article/view/3235/3109 (accessed on 6 February 2014).

La Com, C. (2012) 'Ableist colonizations reframing disability studies in multicultural studies', in S. Pinder (ed.), *American Multicultural Studies: Diversity of Race, Ethnicity, Gender, and Sexuality*, Thousand Oaks: Sage, pp. 53–68.

Laing, R. D. (1960) *The Divided Self: An Existential Study in Sanity and Madness*, Harmondsworth: Penguin.

Laird, S. E. (2008) *Anti-Oppressive Social Work: A Guide for Developing Cultural Competence*, London, Sage.

Laird, S. E. (2010) *Practical Social Work Law: Analysing Court Cases and Inquiries*, London: Pearson Education.

Laird, S. E. (2013) *Child Protection: Managing Conflict, Hostility and Aggression*, Bristol: Policy Press.

Laming, H. (2003) *The Victoria Climbié Inquiry: Report of an Inquiry by Lord Laming*, Cmnd. 5730, London: HMSO.

Landmine and Cluster Munitions Monitor Report for Sri Lanka (2009) *Landmine Monitor Report 2009 Annual Report, Special Ten-Year Review of the Mine Ban Treaty*, Mines Action Canada, pp. 1101–1121. Available at http://www.the-monitor.org/ lm/2009/countries/pdf/sri_lanka.pdf (accessed 7 February 2014).

Langan, M. (1992) *Women, Oppression and Social Work*, London: Routledge.

Lasch, C. (1979) *The Culture of Narcissism: American Life in an Age of Diminishing Expectations*, New York: W. W. Norton.

Lash, S. (2001) 'Technological forms of life', *Theory, Culture & Society*, vol. 18, pp. 105–120.

Latour, B. (1993) *We Have Never Been Modern*, Cambridge, MA: Harvard University Press.

Latour, B. (2007) *Reassembling the Social: An Introduction to Actor-Network Theory*, Oxford: Oxford University Press.

Law, J. (2004) *After Method: Mess in Social Science Research*, London: Routledge.

Law, J. and Mol, A. (2008) 'The actor-enacted: Cumbrian sheep in 2001', in C. Knappett and L. Malafouris (eds.), *Material Agency: Towards a Non-Anthropocentric Approach*, New York: Springer.

Law, J. and Moser, I. (2011) 'Contexts and culling', *Science, Technology, Human Values*, vol. 37, no. 4, pp. 332–354.

Lawrence, C. R. (1987) 'The id, the ego, and equal protection: reckoning with unconscious racism', *Stanford Law Review*, vol. 39, pp. 317–388.

Lawson, A. (2008) *Disability and Equality Law in Britain: The Role of Reasonable Adjustment*, Oxford: Hart.

Lefebvre, H. (2000) *Critique of Everyday Life*, London: Verso.

Leininger, M. (2002a) 'The theory of cultural care and the ethnonursing research method', in M. Leininger and M. R. McFarland (eds.), *Transcultural Nursing*, New York: McGraw-Hill, pp. 71–98.

Leininger, M. (2002b) 'Transcultural nursing and globalization of health care: importance, focus and historical aspects', in M. Leininger and M. R. McFarland (eds.), *Transcultural Nursing*, New York: McGraw-Hill, pp. 3–43.

Levitas, R. (1996) 'The concept of social exclusion and the new Durkheimian hegemony', *Critical Social Policy*, vol. 16, no. 1, pp. 5–21.

Lewis, G. (1998) 'Coming apart at the seams: the crisis of the welfare state', in G. Hughes and G. Lewis (eds.), *Unsettling Welfare: The Reconstruction of Social Policy*, London: Routledge/Open University, pp. 38–79.

Lewis, G. (2000) *Race, Gender and Social Welfare: Encounters in a Postcolonial Society*, Cambridge: Polity Press.

Loja, E., Costa, M., Hughes, B. and Menezes, I. (2013) 'Disability, embodiment and ableism: stories of resistance', *Disability and Society*, vol. 28, no. 2, pp. 190–203.

Lovell, J. (2013) 'This profession should be challenging prejudice, not telling social workers to hide their sexuality', *Community Care*, 18 July 2013. Available at http://www.communitycare.co.uk/blogs/mental-health/2013/07/this-profession-should-be-challenging-prejudice-not-telling-social-workers-to-hide-their-sexuality/ (accessed 7 February 2014).

Lymberry, M. (2010) 'A new vision for adult social care? Continuities and change in the care of older people', *Critical Social Policy*, vol. 30, no. 1, pp. 5–26.

MacConnell, E. (2013) 'Boy taken into care by HSE reunited with his parents', *The Irish Times*, 24 October 2013, p. 5.

Macey, M. (1995) 'Towards racial justice? A re-evaluation of anti-racism', *Critical Social Policy*, vol. 15, no. 44–45, pp. 126–146.

Macey, D. (2009) 'Rethinking biopolitics, race and power in the wake of Foucault', *Theory, Culture and Society*, vol. 26, pp. 186–205.

Macey, M. and Moxon, E. (1996) 'An examination of anti-racist and anti-oppressive theory and practice in social work education', *British Journal of Social Work*, vol. 26, no. 3, pp. 297–314.

Mafile'o, T. (2008) 'Tongan social work practice', in M. Gray, J. Coates and M. Yellow Bird (eds.), *Indigenous Social Work Around the World*, Farnham: Ashgate, pp. 117–127.

Marvasti, A. (2004) *Qualitative Research in Sociology*, London: Sage.

Marx, K. (1964[1857–1858]) *Pre-Capitalist Economic Formations*, (translated by Jack Cohen, edited and with an Introduction by Eric Hobsbawm), London: Lawrence & Wishart.

May, V. (2012) 'Are we really saying farewell to family? A response to Edwards and Gillies' "Farewell to family?"', *Families, Relationships and Societies*, vol. 1, no. 3, pp. 415–421.

Mbembe, A. (2008) 'Necropolitics', in A. Mbembe, S. Morton and S. Bygrave (eds.), *Foucault in and Age of Terror: Essays on Biopolitics and the Defence of Society*, Basingstoke: Palgrave Macmillan, pp. 152–182.

McCarry, M. (2007) 'Masculinity studies and male violence: critique or collusion', *Women's Studies International Forum*, vol. 30, pp. 404–415.

McClintock, A. (1995) *Imperial Leather: Race, Gender and Sexuality in the Colonial Conquest*, New York: Routledge.

McDonald, C. (2006) *Challenging Social Work: The Context of Practice*, Basingstoke: Palgrave Macmillan.

McLaren, M. (1997a) 'Foucault and the subject of feminism', *Social Theory and Practice*, vol. 21, pp. 109–128.

McLaren, P. (1997b) *Revolutionary Multiculturalism: Pedagogies of Dissent for the New Millennium*, Boulder, CO: Westview.

McLaughlin, K. (2005) 'From ridicule to institutionalization: anti-oppression, the state and social work', *Critical Social Policy*, vol. 25, no. 3, pp. 283–305.

McLaughlin, K. (2008) *Social Work, Politics and Society: From Radicalism to Orthodoxy*, Bristol: Policy Press.

McLaughlin, H. (2009) 'What's in a name: "client", "patient", "customer", "consumer", "expert by experience", "service user" – what's next?', *British Journal of Social Work*, vol. 39, pp. 1101–1117.

McNay, L. (2008) *Against Recognition*, Cambridge: Polity Press.

McNulty, A., Richardson, D. and Monro, S. (2010) *Lesbian, Gay, Bisexual and Trans (LGBT) Equalities and Local Governance Research Report for Practitioners and Policy Makers*, Newcastle: Newcastle University.

McRuer, R. (2006) *Crip Theory: Cultural Signs of Queerness and Disability*, New York: New York University Press.

McVeigh, R. (1997) 'Cherishing the children of the nation unequally; sectarianism in Ireland', in P. Clancy, S. Drudy, K. Lynch and L. O'Dowd (eds.), *Irish Society: Sociological Perspectives*, Dublin: IPA, pp. 620–651.

McVeigh, R. (2007) '"Ethnicity denial" and racism: the case of the government of Ireland against Travellers', *Translocations*, vol. 2, no. 1, pp. 90–133.

McVeigh, R. and Roulston, B. (2007) 'From Good Friday to good relations: sectarianism, racism and the Northern Ireland State', *Race and Class*, vol. 48, no. 4, pp. 1–23.

Mead, G. H. (1913[2011]) 'The social self', in F. C. Da Silva (ed.), *G. H. Mead: A Reader*, Abingdon: Routledge, pp. 58–62.

Mead, G. H. (1922[2011]) 'A behavioristic account of the significant symbol', in F. C. Da Silva (ed.), *G. H. Mead: A Reader*, Abingdon: Routledge, pp. 65–69.

Mead, G. H. (1925[2011]) 'The genesis of the self and social control', in F. C. Da Silva (ed.), *G. H. Mead: A Reader*, Abingdon: Routledge, pp. 70–85.

Mead, G. H. (1926[2011]) 'The objective reality of perspectives', in F. C. Da Silva (ed.), *G. H. Mead: A Reader*, Abingdon: Routledge, pp. 195–203.

Mead, G. H. (1934) *Mind, Self and Society from the Standpoint of a Social Behaviourist*, Chicago: Chicago University Press.

Mendes, P. (2009) 'Tracing the origins of critical social work practice', in J. Allan, L. Briskman and B. Pease (eds.), *Critical Social Work: Theories and Practices for a Socially Just World*, Crows Nest: Allen & Unwin.

Mendoza-Denton, N. (1995) 'Pregnant pauses: silence and authority in the Anita Hill-Clarence Thomas Hearings', in K. Hall and M. Bucholtz (eds.), *Gender Articulated: Language and the Socially Constructed Self*, London: Routledge.

Meo-Sewabu, L. (2012) 'Ethics and ethnography as an Indigenous researcher: a Fijian perspective', Paper presented at the Development Studies Seminar Series, Massey University, Palmerston North, New Zealand.

Michael, M. (1996) *Constructing Identities*, London: Sage.

Miehls, D. and Moffatt, K. (2000) 'Constructing social work identity based on the reflexive self', *British Journal of Social Work*, vol. 30, pp. 339–348.

Mila-Schaaf, K. (2009) 'Pacific health research guidelines: the cartography of an ethical relationship', *International Social Science Journal*, vol. 60, no. 195, pp. 134–143.

Millar, M. (2008) '"Anti oppressiveness": critical comments on a discourse and its context', *British Journal of Social Work*, vol. 38, pp. 362–375.

Mills, C. W. (1959) *The Sociological Imagination*, New York: Oxford University Press.

Mir, G., Andrew, N., Ahmad, W. and Jones, L. (2001) *Learning Difficulties and Ethnicity*, London: Department of Health.

Mitchell, W. (2007) 'The role of grandparents in intergenerational support for families with disabled children: a review of the literature', *Child and Family Social Work*, vol. 12, no. 1, pp. 94–101.

Moi, T. (1985) *Sexual/Textual Politics: Feminist Literary Theory*, London: Methuen.

Moore, S. (2013) 'I don't care if you were born a woman or became one', *The Guardian*, 10 January 2013. Available at http://www.guardian.co.uk/commentisfree/2013/jan/09/dont-care-if-born-woman (accessed on 7 February 2014).

Moran, M. (2006) 'Social inclusion and the limits of pragmatic liberalism: the Irish case', *Irish Political Studies*, vol. 21, no. 2, pp. 181–201.

Morgan, D. H. J. (1996) *Family Connections: An Introduction to Family Studies*, Cambridge: Polity Press.

Morgan, P. (2002) *Children as Trophies? Examining the Evidence on Same-Sex Parenting*, Newcastle-upon-Tyne: The Christian Institute.

Morgan, P. (2007) *The War Between the State and the Family: How Government Divides and Impoverishes*, London: Institute of Economic Affairs.

Morgan, D. H. J. (2011) *Rethinking Family Practices*, Basingstoke: Palgrave Macmillan.

Morgan, H. (2012) 'The social model of disability as a threshold concept: troublesome knowledge and liminal spaces in social work education', *Social Work Education: The International Journal*, vol. 31, no. 20, pp. 215–226.

Morris, K. (2012) 'Thinking family? The complexities for family engagement in care and protection', *British Journal of Social Work*, vol. 42, no. 5, pp. 906–920.

Morris, K. (2013) 'Troubled families: vulnerable families' experiences of multiple service use', *Child & Family Social Work*, vol. 18, no. 2, pp. 198–206.

Morton, T. (2011) 'Here comes everything: the promise of object-oriented ontology', *Qui Parle*, vol. 19, no. 2, pp. 163–190.

Mullaly, B. (1997) *Structural Social Work, Ideology, Theory and Practice*, (2nd edition), Oxford: Oxford University Press.

Mullaly, U. (2013) 'Questions to ask now the Roma hysteria is over', *The Irish Times*, 25 Octiober 2013, p. 14.

Mullaly, B. (2007) *The New Structural Social Work: Ideology, Theory and Practice*, Oxford: Oxford University Press.

Munck, R. (2011) 'Ireland in the world, the world in Ireland', in B. Fanning and R. Munck (eds.), *Globalization, Migration and Social Transformation*, Farnham: Ashgate.

Munro, E. (2011) *The Munro Review of Child Protection. Final Report: A Child-Centred System*, London: Department for Education.

Murphy, F. D., Buckley, H. and Joyce, L. (2005) *The Ferns Report*, Dublin: Stationery Office.

Nabobo-Baba, U. (2006) *Knowing Learning: An Indigenous Fijian Approach*, Suva: IPS Publications/University of the South Pacific.

Nabobo-Baba, U. (2008) 'Decolonising framings in Pacific research: Indigenous Fijian Vanua research framework as an organic response', *Alter Native Journal: Nga Pae o te Maramatanga*, vol. 4, no. 2, pp. 140–154.

National Working Group on Child Abuse Linked to Faith or Belief (2012) *National Action Plan for Tackling Child Abuse Linked to Faith or Belief*, London: The National Working Group on Child Abuse Linked to Faith or Belief.

Needham, C. (2011) 'Personalisation: from storyline to practice', *Social Policy & Administration*, vol. 45, no. 1, pp. 54–68.

Needham, C. and Carr, S. (2009) *SCIE Research Briefing 31: Co-Production: An Emerging Evidence Base for Adult Social Care Transformation*, London: SCIE.

Neely Barnes, S., Graff, G., Roberts, R., Hall, H. and Hankins, J. (2010) '"It's our job": qualitative study of family responses to ableism', *Intellectual and Developmental Disabilities*, vol. 48, no. 4, pp. 245–258.

Nickels, H. C., Thomas, L., Hickman, M. J. and Silvestri, S. (2012) 'De/constructing "suspect" communities', *Journalism Studies*, vol. 13, no. 3, pp. 340–355.

Nicoll, K. and Fejes, A. (2008) 'Mobilizing Foucault in studies of lifelong learning', in A. Fejes and K. Nicoll (eds.), *Foucault and Lifelong Learning: Governing the Subject*, Oxford: Routledge, pp. 1–18.

Norris, C. (1987) *Derrida*, Fontana: London.

Norris, C. (2002) *Deconstruction: Theory and Practice*, (3rd edition), London and New York: Routledge.

Northern Ireland Office (2012) *Census 2011 Key Statistics*. Available at http://www.northernireland.gov.uk/news-dfp-111212-census-2011-key (accessed on 7 February 2014).

Nosek, M., Hughes, R., Swedland, N., Taylor, H. and Swank, P. (2003) 'Self- esteem and women with disabilities', *Social Sciences and Medicine*, vol. 56, no. 8, pp. 1737–1747.

Nzira, V. (2011) *Social Care with African Families in the UK*, London: Routledge.

Oakes, W. (2005) *Perspectives on Disability, Discrimination, Accommodations and Law*, New York: LFB Scholarly.

Obeyesekere, G. (1981) *Medusa's Hair: An Essay on Personal Symbols and Religious Experience*, Chicago: University of Chicago Press.

O'Connell, K. (2011) 'From black box to pen brain: law, neuroimaging and disability discrimination', *Griffith Law Review*, vol. 20, no. 4, pp. 883–904.

Office of First and Deputy First Minister (2009) *Strategy for Victims and Survivors*, Belfast: OFDFM.

Office of the Minister for Integration (2008) *Migration Nation*. Available at http://www.integration.ie/website/omi/omiwebv6.nsf/page/AXBN-7SQDF91044205-en/$File/migration %20Nation.pdf (accessed on 11 February 2014).

Office of National Statistics (2006) *Focus on Ethnicity and Religion*, Houndmills: Palgrave Macmillan.

Ofsted, Healthcare Commission and HM Inspectorate of Constabulary (2008) *Joint Area Review: Haringey Children's Services Authority Area*. Available at http://www.minutes.haringey.gov.uk/Published/C00000127/M00002933/AI00014912/JARreport11208.pdf (accessed 7 February 2014).

O'Neale, V. (2000) *Excellence Not Excuses: Inspection of Services for Ethnic Minority Children and Families*, London: Department of Health.

Orjuela, C. (2005) 'Civil society in civil war: the case of Sri Lanka', *Civil Wars*, vol. 7, no. 2, pp. 120–137.

O'Rourke, L. (2010) *Recording in Social Work: Not Just an Administrative Task*, Bristol: Policy Press.

Otsuka, S. (2005) 'Talanoa research: culturally appropriate research design in Fiji', *Proceedings of the Australian Association for Research in Education (AARE) 2005 International Education Research Conference: Creative Dissent-Constructive Solutions*, Melbourne: AARE. Available at http://www.aare.edu.au/data/publications/2005/ots05506.pdf (accessed on 10 February 2014).

Overboe, J. (2007) 'Vitalism: subjectivity exceeding racism, sexism and (psychiatric) ableism', *Wag.a.du: A Journal of Transnational Women's and Gender Studies*, vol. 4, pp. 23–34.

Painter, N. (2010) *The History of White People*, New York: W.W. Norton.

Paludi, M. (2011) 'Women with disabilities: mental health impact of disabilities and ableism', in P. Lundberg-Love, K. Nadal and M. Paludi (eds.), *Women and Mental Disorders*, Santa Barbara: ABC-CLIO, pp. 55–80.

Parrott, B., MacIver, A. and Thoburn, J. (2007) *Independent Inquiry into the Circumstances of Child Sexual Abuse by Two Foster Carers in Wakefield*, Wakefield: Wakefield County Council.

Parton, N. (1994) '"Problematics of government", (post) modernity and social work', *British Journal of Social Work*, vol. 24, pp. 9–32.

Parton, N. (1999) 'The "social construction of child maltreatment": some political, research and practice implications', in A. Jokinen, K. Juhila and T. Pösö (eds.), *Constructing Social Work Practices*, Aldershot: Ashgate, pp. 153–172.

Parton, N. (2012) 'Thinking and acting constructively in child protection', in S. L. Witkin (ed.), *Social Construction and Social Work Practice: Interpretations and Innovations*, New York: Columbia University Press.

Pavee Point Traveller and Roma Centre (2013) 'Pavee Point response to child protection case in Tallaght', Press Release, 22 October 2013. Available at http://www.paveepoint.ie/pavee-point-response-to-child-protection-case-in-tallaght/ (accessed on 11 February 2014).

Payne, M. (2006) *What is Professional Social Work?*, (2nd edition), Bristol: Policy Press.

Pease, B. (2002) 'Rethinking empowerment: a postmodern reappraisal for emancipatory practice', *British Journal of Social Work*, vol. 32, pp. 135–147.

Pease, B. and Fook, J. (eds.) (1999) *Transforming Social Work Practice: Postmodern Critical Perspectives*, Sydney: Allen & Unwin.

Penketh, L. (2000) *Tackling Institutional Racism: Anti-Rascist Policies and Social Work Education and Training*, Bristol: Policy Press.

Perera, S. (2007) 'The construction of masculinity and bravery in the context of combat in southern Sri Lanka', conference paper, South Asian Travelling Seminar on Masculinities, 30–31 March 2007, Hyderabad, CIEFL/Anveshi/Aakar, unpublished, cited with kind permission of the author.

Perlman, H. H. (1957) *Social Casework: A Problem-Solving Process,* Chicago: University of Chicago Press.

Phillips, M. (1999) *The Sex-Change Society: Feminised Britain and the Neutered Male*, London: Social Market Foundation.

Pinkerton, J. and Campbell, J. (2002) 'Social work and social justice in Northern Ireland: towards a new occupational space', *British Journal of Social Work*, vol. 32, no. 6, pp. 723–737.

Pithouse, A. (1987) *Social Work: The Organisation of an Invisible Trade*, Aldershot: Avebury.

Ploesser, M. and Mecheril, P. (2012) 'Neglect – recognition – deconstruction: approaches to otherness in social work', *International Social Work*, vol. 55, no. 6, pp. 794–808.

Polikoff, N. D. (2008) *Beyond (Straight and Gay) Marriage: Valuing All Families Under the Law*, Boston, MA: Beacon Press.

Pollard, A. J. and Savulescu, J. (2004) 'Eligibility of overseas visitors and people of uncertain residential status for NHS treatment', *British Medical Journal*, vol. 329, no. 7461, pp. 346–349.

Popke, E. J. (2003) 'Poststructuralist ethics: subjectivity, responsibility and the space of community', *Progress in Human Geography*, vol. 27, no. 3, pp. 298–316.

Powell, J. (2000) *Managing Old Age: The Disciplinary Web of Power, Surveillance and Normalization*, New York: Springer.

Powell, F. (2001) *The Politics of Social Work*, London: Sage.

Powell, J. (2011) 'Michel Foucault', in M. Gray and S. Webb (eds.), *Social Work Theories and Methods*, (2nd edition), London: Sage, pp. 46–62.

Powell, J. (2012) 'Social work and elder abuse: a Foucauldian analysis', *Social Work and Society*, vol. 10, no. 1, pp. 1–10.

Prado, C. G. (1995) *Starting with Foucault: An Introduction to Genealogy*, Boulder, CO: Westview.

Prince, K. (1996) *Boring Records? Communication, Speech and Writing in Social Work*, London: Jessica Kingsley.

Prinz, J. (2009) 'Mind and body', in D. Papineau (ed.), *Philosophy*, (2nd edition), London: Duncan Baird, pp. 42–71.

Puar, J. K. (2007) *Terrorist Assemblages: Homonationalism in Queer Times*, Durham, NC: Duke University Press.

Pullen-Sansfacon, A. and Cowden, S. (2012) *The Ethical Foundations of Social Work*, Harlow: Pearson-Longman.

Purnell, L. D. and Paulanka, B. J. (1998) *Transcultural Health Care*, Philadelphia: F.A. Davis.

Rabinow, P. (ed.) (1984) *The Foucault Reader*, New York: Pantheon.

Rai, L. (2006) 'Owning (up to) reflective writing in social work education', *Social Work Education*, vol. 25, no. 8, pp. 785–797.

Ratuva, S. (2007) 'Na kilaka a vaka-Viti ni veikabula: Indigenous knowledge and the Fijian cosmos: implications on bio-prospecting', in A. T. P. Mead and S. Ratuva (eds.), Pacific Genes and Life Patents: Pacific Indigenous Experience and Analysis of

Commodification and Ownership of Life, (1st edition),Wellington: Call of Earth Llamado de la Tierra and the United Nations University of Advanced Studies, pp. 90–101.

Rauscher, L. and McClintock, N. (1997) 'Ableism curriculum design', in M. Adams, L. A. Bell and P. Griffin (eds.), *Teaching for Diversity and Social Justice: A Sourcebook*, New York: Routledge, pp. 198–229.

Ravuvu, A. (1987) *The Fijian Ethos*, Suva: Institute of Pacific Studies, University of the South Pacific.

Razak, S. (1998) 'Race, space and prostitution: the making of the bourgeois subject', *Canadian Journal of Women and Law*, vol. 10, pp. 338–376.

Reiff, P. (1966) *The Triumph of the Therapeutic: Uses of Faith after Freud*, New York: Harper and Row.

Reupert, A. (2007) 'Social worker's use of self', *Clinical Social Work Journal,* vol. 35, pp. 107–116.

Ribbens McCarthy, J., Doolittle, M. and Day Sclater, S. (2012) *Understanding Family Meanings: A Reflective Text,* Bristol: Policy Press.

Richardson, D. (2004) 'Locating sexualities: from here to normality', *Sexualities*, vol. 7, no. 4, pp. 391–411.

Richardson, G. and Maltby, M. (1995) 'Reflection-on-practice: enhancing student learning', *Journal of Advanced Nursing*, vol. 22, no. 2, pp. 235–242.

Ricoeur, P. (1981) *Hermeneutics and the Human Sciences: Essays on language, action and interpretation,* (edited and translated by J. Thompson), Cambridge: Cambridge University Press.

Riessman, C. (2004) 'Exporting ethics: a narrative about narrative research in South India', *Health,* Special Issue of Informed Consent, Ethics and Narrative, vol. 9, no. 4, pp. 473–490.

Rigby, P. (2011) 'Separated and trafficked children: the challenges for child protection social workers', *Child Abuse Review*, vol. 20, no. 5, pp. 324–340.

Riggs, D. W. (2006) *Priscilla, (White) Queen of the Desert: Queer Rights/Race Privilege*, New York: Peter Lang.

Roberts, M. (1994) 'The cultured gentleman: the appropriation of manners by the middle class in British Ceylon', *Anthropological Forum*, vol. 7, no. 1, pp. 55–74.

Roberts, A. (2008) 'A crusade for dignity – Andrew Roberts recalls his involvement in the foundation of the Mental Patients Union', *The Guardian*, 3 September 2008. Available at http://www.guardian.co.uk/society/2008/sep/03/mentalhealth.health (accessed 6 February 2014).

Robinson, L. (2009) *Psychology for Social Workers: Black Perspectives on Human Development and Behaviour*, (2nd edition), London: Routledge.

Rogers, C. (1951) *Client Centred Therapy,* Boston, MA: Houghton.

Rojek, C., Peacock, G. and Collins, S. (1988) *Social Work and Received Ideas,* London and New York: Routledge.

Runswick-Cole, K. (2011) 'Time to end the bias towards inclusive education?', *British Journal of Special Education*, vol. 38, no. 3, pp. 112–119.

Rush, M. and Keenan, M. (2013) 'The social politics of social work: anti-oppressive social work dilemmas in twenty-first-century welfare regimes', *British Journal of Social Work*, published online 28 February 2013, doi:10.1093/bjsw/bct014.

Rutter, L. and Brown, K. (2012) *Critical Thinking and Professional Judgement for Social Work,* (3rd edition), Exeter: Learning Matters.

Ryan, W. (1971) *Blaming the Victim*, New York: Random House.

Sage Publications (no date) 'Patricia Hill Collins: intersecting oppressions'. Available at http://www.uk.sagepub.com/upm-data/13299_Chapter_16_Web_Byte_Patricia_Hill_Collins.pdf (accessed 10 February 2014).

Said, E. W. (2002) 'Conversation with Neeladri Bhattacharya, Suvir Kaul;, and Ania Loomba', in D. T. Goldberg and A. Quayson (eds.), *Relocating Postcolonialism*, Oxford: Blackwell.

Sakamoto, I. and Pitner, R. O. (2005) 'Use of critical consciousness in anti-oppressive social work practice: disentangling power dynamics at personal and structural', *British Journal of Social Work*, vol. 35, no. 4, pp. 435–452.

Saltiel, D. (2013) 'Understanding complexity in families' lives: the usefulness of "family practices" as an aid to decision-making', *Child and Family Social Work*, vol. 18, no. 1, pp. 15–24.

Sampson, E. E. (1983) *Justice and the Critique of Pure Psychology*, New York: Plenum Press.

Sandahl, C. (2003) 'Queering the crip or cripping the queer? Intersections of queer and crip identities in solo autobiography and performance', *GLQ*, vol. 9, no. 1–2, pp. 25–56.

Schalk, S. (2011) 'Expanding our theoretical toolbox: the politics of (dis)ability in black feminist scholarship', Society for Disability Studies Paper, San Jose, USA, June 15–18, 2011, unpublished.

Schwartz, W. (1974) 'Private troubles and public issues: one social work job or two?', in R. W. Klenk and R. W. Ryan (eds.), *The Practice of Social Work*, (2nd edition), Belmont, CA: Wadsworth.

Secretary of State for Health and the Secretary of State for the Home Department (2003) *The Victoria Climbié Inquiry – Report of an Inquiry by Lord Laming*, London: HMSO, Cm 5730.

Sedgwick, E. K. (1990) *Epistemology of the Closet*, Berkeley and Los Angeles: University of California Press.

Segal, L. (ed.) (1983) *What is to Be Done About the Family?* Harmondsworth: Penguin.

Seidman, S. (2003) *Beyond the Closet: The Transformation of Gay and Lesbian Life*, New York: Routledge.

Seidman, S. (2010) *The Social Construction of Sexuality*, London: W. W. Norton.

Selwyn, J., Quinton, D., Sturgess, W. and Baxter, C. (2006) *Costs and Outcomes of Non-Infant Adoptions*, London: BAAF.

Seva Vanitha Branch [SVB] (2009) *Wellness Project Brave Hearts*. Available at: http://www.army.lk/sevavanitha/videogal.php?galid=2 (accessed 7 February 2014).

Shulman, G. (2011) 'On vulnerability as Judith Butler's language of politics. from excitable speech to precarious life', *Women's Studies Quarterly*, vol. 39, no. 1–2, pp. 227–235.

Silverman, D. (2006) *Interpretative Qualitative Data*, (3rd edition), London: Sage.

Sinclair, R. and Albert, J. (2008) 'Social work and the anti-oppressive stance: does the emperor really have new clothes?', *Critical Social Work*, vol. 9, no. 1.

Singh, G. (1996) 'promoting anti-racist and black perspectives in social work education and practice teaching', *Social Work Education*, vol. 15, no. 2, pp. 35–56.

Singh, G. and Cowden, S. (2013) 'Is cultural sensitivity always a good thing? Arguments for a universal social work', in M. Carey (ed.) *Practical Social Work Ethics: Complex Dilemmas within Applied Social Care*, London: Ashgate.

Sinha, S. (2008) 'Seeking sanctuary: exploring the changing postcolonial and racialised politics of belonging in East London', *Sociological Research Online*, vol. 13, no. 5. Available at www.socresonline.org.uk/13/5/6.html (accessed 7 February 2014).

Sinha, S. and Uppal, S. (2009) 'Lesser youth? Particular universalisms and young separated migrants in East London', *Journal of Youth Studies*, vol. 2, no. 3, pp. 257–273.

Sissons, J. (ed.) (2007) *Ethnography*, (2nd edition), Auckland: Pearson Education.

Skeggs, B. (1997) *Formations of Class and Gender: Becoming Respectable*, London: Sage.

Skehill, C. (2000) 'An examination of the transition from philanthropy to professional social work in Ireland', *Research on Social Work Practice*, vol. 10, no. 6, pp. 688–704.

Slack, J. (2011) 'Human rights gives perverts chance to have names taken off sex register (costing taxpayers £1m every year)', *Daily Mail*, 15 June 2011, Available at: http://www.dailymail.co.uk/news/article-2003408/Human-rights-gives-sex-offenders-chance-names-taken-register.html (accessed 7 February 2014).

Slater, J. (2012) 'Youth for sale using critical disability perspectives to examine the embodiment of youth', *Societies*, vol. 2, pp. 195–209.

Small, J. (1982) 'New black families', *Adoption & Fostering*, vol. 6, no. 3, pp. 35–40.

Small, J. with Prevatt Goldstein, B. (2000) 'Ethnicity and placement: beginning the debate', *Adoption & Fostering*, vol. 24, no. 1, pp. 9–15.

Smart, C. (2007) *Personal Life: New Directions in Sociological Thinking*, Cambridge: Polity Press.

Smith, D. E. (1999) *Writing the Social: Critique, Theory, and Investigations*, Toronto: University of Toronto Press.

Smith, M., Foley, P. and Chaney, M. (2008) 'Addressing classicism, ableism and heterosexism in counsellor education', *Journal of Counselling and Development*, vol. 86, pp. 303–309.

Smyth, M. and Campbell, J. (1996) 'Social Work, sectarianism and anti-sectarian practice in Northern Ireland', *British Journal of Social Work*, vol. 26, no. 1, pp. 77–92.

Solas, J. (1995) 'Deconstruction and clinical social work', *Clinical Social Work Journal*, vol. 23, no. 2, pp. 151–158.

Solomos, J. and Back, L. (2000) *Theories of Race and Racism*, London: Routledge.

Spiker, P. (2013) 'Personalisation falls short', *British Journal of Social Work*, vol. 43, pp. 1259–1275.

Spoonley, P. (2001) 'Transnational Pacific communities: transforming the politics of place and identity', in C. McPherson, P. Spoonley and M. Anae (eds.), *Tangata o te moana nui: The Evolving Identities of Pacific Peoples in Aotearoa/New Zealand*, Palmerston North: Dunmore Press, pp. 81–96.

Stacey, J. (1996) *In the Name of the Family: Rethinking Family Values in the Postmodern Age*, Boston, MA: Beacon Press.

Stack, C. (1997[1974]) *All Our Kin: Strategies for Survival in a Black Community*, New York: Basic Books.

Steven, B. (2011) 'Interrogating Transability: A Catalyst to View Disability as Body Art', *Disability Studies Quarterly*, 31 (4). Available at http://dsq-sds.org/article/view/ 1705

St Guillaume, L. (2011) 'Critical race and disability framework: a new paradigm for understanding discrimination against people from non-English speaking backgrounds and indigenous people with disability', *Critical Race and Whiteness Studies ejournal*, vol. 7. Available at http://www.acrawsa.org.au/files/ejournalfiles/162CRAWSGuillaume 714.pdf (accessed 7 February 2014).

Stobart, E. (2006) *Child Abuse Linked to Accusations of 'Possession' and 'Witchcraft'*, London: Department of Education and Skills.

Stoller, E. P. and Gibson, R. C. (2000) *Worlds of Difference: Inequality in the Aging Experience*, (3rd edition), London: Sage.

Storey, K. (2007) 'Combating ableism in schools', *Preventing School Failures in Alternative Education for Children and Youth*, vol. 52, no. 1, pp. 56–58.

Strega, S. and Carrière, J. (eds.) (2009) *Walking This Path Together: Anti-Racist and Anti-Oppressive Child Welfare Practice*, Halifax, NS: Fernwood.

Strier, R. (2009) 'Class-sensitive social work: a preliminary definition', *International Journal of Social Welfare*, vol. 18, no. 3, pp. 237–242.

Strier, R. and Binyamin, C. (2013) 'Introducing anti-oppressive social work practices in public services: rhetoric to practice', *British Journal of Social Work*, published online 24 April 2013, doi: 10.1093/bjsw/bct014.

Stubblefield, A. (2009) 'Race, disability, and the social contract', *The Southern Journal of Philosophy*, vol. 47, pp. 104–111.

Subramani (2001) 'The oceanic imaginary', *The Contemporary Pacific*, vol. 13, no. 1, pp. 149–162.

Sue, D. W. (2001) 'Multidimensional facets of cultural competence', *The Counselling Psychologist*, vol. 29, no. 6, pp. 790–821.

Sundar, P. and Ly, M. (2013) 'Multiculturalism', in M. Gray and S. Webb (eds.), *Social Work Theories and Methods*, (2nd edition), London: Sage.

Swift, K. (1995) *Manufacturing 'Bad Mothers': A Critical Perspective on Child Neglect*, Toronto: University of Toronto Press.

Szasz, T. S. (1961) *The Myth of Mental Illness: Foundations of a Theory of Personal Conduct*, New York: Harper & Row.

Szasz, T. S. (1970) *The Manufacture of Madness?: A Comparative Study of the Inquisition and the Mental Health Movement*, New York: Harper & Row.

Taylor, C. (1989) *Sources of the Self*, Cambridge, MA: Harvard University Press.

Taylor, C. (1992) *Multiculturalism and 'The Politics of Recognition'*, Princeton: Princeton University Press.

Taylor, C. (2003) 'Narrative practice: reflective accounts and the textual construction of reality', *Journal of Advanced Nursing*, vol. 42, no. 3, pp. 244–251.

Taylor, C. and White, S. (2000) *Practising Reflexivity in Health and Welfare: Making Knowledge*, Buckingham: Open University Press.

Tew, J., Gould, N., Abankwa, D., Barnes, H., Beresford, P., Carr, S. et al. (2006) *Values and Methodologies for Social Research in Mental Health*, London: NIMHE/SCIE/SPN.

Thalagala, N. I. (2000) 'Attempted suicides in Sri Lanka: antecedents and consequences', unpublished MD Thesis, Institute of Medicine, University of Colombo.

Thaman, K. H. (2003) 'Decolonizing Pacific studies: Indigenous perspectives, knowledge, and wisdom in higher education', *The Contemporary Pacific*, vol. 15, no. 1, pp. 1–17.

Thaman, K. H. (2007) 'Research and Indigenous knowledge in Oceania', in L. Meek and C. Suwanwela (eds.), *Higher Education, Research and Knowledge in the Asia Pacific Region*, New York: Palgrave Macmillan.

The Rainbow Project/Age NI (2011) *Making this Home my Home*, Belfast: Age NI.

Think Local Act Personal (2011) *Think Local Act Personal: A Sector-Wide Commitment to Moving Forward with Personalisation and Community-Based Support*, London: TLAP.

Thomas, M. and Pierson, J. (eds.) (1995) *Dictionary of Social Work*, London: Collins.

Thomas, S., Thomas, S., Nafees, D. and Bhugra, D. (2004) '"I was running away from death" – the pre-flight experiences of unaccompanied asylum seeking children in the UK', *Child: Care, Health & Development*, vol. 30, no. 2, pp. 113–122.

Thompson, N. (1993) *Anti-Discriminatory Practice*, Basingstoke: Palgrave Macmillan.

Thompson, N. (2001) *Anti-Discriminatory Practice*, (3rd edition), Basingstoke: Palgrave MacMillan.

Thompson, J. (2002) 'Ugly, unglamorous and dirty: theatre of relief/reconciliation/liberation in places of war', *Research in Drama Education: The Journal of Applied Theatre and Performance*, vol. 7, no. 1, pp. 108–114.

Thompson, N. (2003) *Promoting Equality: Challenging Discrimination and Oppression*, (2nd edition), Basingstoke: Palgrave Macmillan

Thompson, S. (2004) 'Operation "special" interrogating the queer production of everyday myths in special education', in J. McNinch and M. Cronin (eds.), *I Could Not Speak My Heart: Education and Social Justice for Gay and Lesbian Youth*, Plain Rivers Research Center, Saskatchewan: University of Regina, pp. 273–288.

Thompson, N. (2006) *Anti-Discriminatory Practice*, (4th edition), Basingstoke: Palgrave Macmillan.

Thompson, N. (2008) 'Anti-discriminatory practice', in M. Davis (ed.), *The Blackwell Companion to Social Work*, (3rd edition), Oxford: Blackwell.

Thompson, N. (2012) *Anti-Discriminatory Practice: Equality, Diversity and Social Justice*, (5th edition), Basingstoke: Palgrave Macmillan.

Thompson, S. and Thompson, N. (2008) *The Critically Reflective Practitioner*, Basingstoke: Palgrave Macmillan.

Thorne, B. (1993) *Gender Play: Girls and Boys in School*, Buckingham: Open University Press.

Trevithick, P. (2004) *Social Work Skills: A Practice Handbook*, Milton Keynes: Open University Press.

Tuhiwai-Smith, L. (1999) *Decolonizing Methodologies: Research and Indigenous People*, Dunedin: Otago University Press.

Turner, B. (1992) *Regulating Bodies: Essays in Medical Sociology*, London: Routledge.

Turney, D. (1996) 'The language on anti-racism in social work: towards a deconstructive reading', *Critical Urban Studies: Occasional Paper*, London: Goldsmiths University of London.

Turney, D. (1997) 'Hearing voices, talking difference: a dialogic approach to anti-oppressive practice', *Journal of Social Work Practice*, vol. 11, no. 2, pp. 115–125.

Tuwere, I. S. (2002) *Vanua. Towards a Fijian Theology of Place*, Suva: Institute of Pacific Studies, USP

Union of the Physically Impaired Against Segregation (UPIAS) (1975) *Fundamental Principles of Disability*, London: UPIAS.

United Nations (1989) *United Nations Convention on the Rights of the Child*, New York: United Nations.

United Nations High Commissioner for Refugees (2004) *Trends in Unaccompanied and Separated Children Seeking Asylum in Industrialized Countries 2001–2003*, Geneva: UNHCR.

Urry, J. (2005) 'The complexities of the global', *Theory, Culture & Society*, vol. 22, pp. 235–254.

Vaioleti, T. (2006) 'Talanoa research methodology: a developing position on Pacific research', *Waikato Journal of Education*, vol. 12, pp. 23–31.

Verloo, M. (2006) 'Multiple inequalities, intersectionality and the European Union', *European Journal of Women's Studies*, vol. 13, no. 3, pp. 211–228.

Vertovec, S. (2009) *Transnationalism*, London: Routledge.

Wacquant, L. (2004) 'Critical thought as solvent of *doxa*', *Constellations*, vol. 11, no. 1, pp. 97–102.

Wade, J., Sirriyeh, A., Kohli, R. K. S. and Simmonds, J. (2013) *Fostering Unaccompanied Refugee and Asylum Seeking Young People in the UK*, London: BAAF.

Walsh, F. (2009) 'Human-animal bonds II: the role of pets in family systems and family therapy', *Family Processes*, vol. 48, no. 4, pp. 481–499.

Walsh, T., Wilson, G. and O'Connor, E. (2010) 'Local, European and global: an exploration of migration patterns of social workers into Ireland', *British Journal of Social Work*, vol. 40, no. 6, pp. 1978–1995.

Wardhaugh, J. and Wilding, P. (1993) 'Towards an explanation of the corruption of care', *Critical Social Policy*, vol. 13, no. 1, pp. 4–32.

Wardle, L. D. (1997) 'The potential impact of homosexual parenting on children', *University of Illinois Law Review*, vol. 3, pp. 833–920.

Webb, D. (2006) *Social Work in a Risk Society: Social and Political Perspectives*, Houndsmill: Palgrave.

Webb, S. (2009) 'Against difference and diversity in social work: the case of human rights', *International Journal of Social Welfare*, vol. 18, pp. 307–316.

Webb, S. (2010) '(Re)assembling the left: the politics of redistribution and recognition in social work', *British Journal of Social Work*, vol. 40, no. 8, pp. 2364–2379.

Webb, S. A. and McBeath, G. B. (1989) 'A political critique of Kantian ethics in social work', *British Journal of Social Work*, vol. 20, no. 1, pp. 491–506.

Weber, B. (2006) 'Negative autonomy and the intuitions of democracy', *Philosophy Social Criticism*, vol. 32, no. 3, pp. 325–346.

Weerasuriya, N. and Jayasinghe, S. (2005) 'A preliminary study of the hospital admitted older patients in a Sri Lankan tertiary care hospital', *Ceylon Medical Journal*, vol. 50, pp. 18–19.

Werbner, P. (2000) 'Who sets the terms of the debate? Heterotopic intellectuals and the clash of discourses', *Theory, Culture & Society*, vol. 17, no. 1, pp. 147–156.

Westwood, J. (2012) 'Social work and the media', in A. Worsley and T. Mann (eds.), *Concepts in Social Work*, London: Sage.

Whan, M. (1986) 'On the nature of practice', *British Journal of Social Work*, vol. 16, no. 2, pp. 243–250.

White, V. (2006) *The State of Feminist Social Work*, London: Routledge.

Wickman, K. (2007) '"I do not compete in disability": how wheelchair athletes change the discourse of able-ism through action and resistance', *European Journal for Sport and Society*, vol. 4, no. 2, pp. 151–167.

Wickramasinghe, N. (2006) *Sri Lanka in the Modern Age: A History of Contested Identities*, Colombo: Vijitha Yapa.

Wilkinson, E. and Bell, D. (2012) 'Ties that blind: on not seeing (or looking) beyond "the family"', *Families, Relationships and Societies*, vol. 1, no. 3, pp. 423–429.

Wilkinson, R. and Pickett, K. (2009) *The Spirit Level: Why Equality is Better for Everyone*, London: Penguin.

Williams, R. (1983) *Keywords: A Vocabulary of Culture and Society*, (2nd edition), New York: Oxford University Press.

Williams, C. (1999) 'Connecting anti-racist and anti-oppressive theory and practice: retrenchment or reapprasial?', *British Journal of Social Work*, vol. 29, pp. 211–230.

Williams, C. (2010) *Race Equality and 'Cultural Competency' in Qualifying Social Work education and Training in Wales*, Keele: Wales Ethnicity Research Collaboration.

Williams, J. and Mavin, S. (2012) 'Disability as constructed difference: a literature review and research agenda for management and organisation studies', *International Journal of Management Reviews*, vol. 14, pp. 159–179.

Williams, C. and Parrott, L. (2012) 'Anti-racism and predominantly 'white areas': local and national referents in the search for race equality in social work education', *British Journal of Social Work*, published online 24 July 2012, doi: 10.1093/bjsw/bcs113.

Williams Institute (2012) 'Gallup special report: the U.S. adult LGBT population', The Williams Institute, October 2012. Available at http://williamsinstitute. law.ucla.edu/research/census-lgbt-demographics-studies/gallup-special-report-18oct-2012/ (accessed on 7 February 2014).

Wilson, A. and Beresford, P. (2000) '"Anti-oppressive practice": emancipation or appropriation?', *British Journal of Social Work*, vol. 30, no. 5, pp. 553–573.

Winker, G. and Degele, N. (2011) 'Intersectionality as multi-level analysis: dealing with social inequality', *European Journal of Women's Studies*, vol. 18, no. 1, pp. 51–66.

Wittig, M. (1980) 'The straight mind', *Gender Issues*, vol. 1, no. 1, pp. 103–111.

Wolbring, G. (2007) *The Triangle of new emerging technologies, Disabled People and the World Council of Churches: Able-ism: A Prerequisite for Transhumanism*, WWC, Ebook.

Wolbring, G. (2012a) 'Ableism and energy security and insecurity', *Studies in Ethics, Law and Technology*, vol. 5, no. 1, pp. 1–17.

Wolbring, G. (2012b) 'Expanding ableism: taking down the ghettoization of impact of disability studies scholars', *Societies*, vol. 2, pp. 75–83.

Woolham, J., Daly, G. and Hughes, E. (2013) 'Loneliness amongst older people: findings from a survey in Coventry, UK', *Quality in Aging and Older Adults*, vol. 14, no. 3, pp. 192–204.

World Health Organization (2009) *Women and Health: Today's Evidence Tomorrow's Agenda*, Geneva: WHO.

XXY (2007) directed by L. Puenzo (film), Argentina, Distribution Company (Argentina)/ Pyramide Distribution (France).

Yosso, T. J. (2005) 'Whose culture has capital? A critical race theory discussion of community cultural wealth', *Race, Ethnicity and Education*, vol. 8, no. 1, pp. 69–91.

Young, I.J (1990) *Justice and the Politics of Difference*, Princeton University Press.

Young, M. and Wilmott, P. (2007[1957]) *Family and Kinship in East London*, London: Penguin.

Yuval-Davis, N. (2006) 'Intersectionality and feminist politics', *European Journal of Women's studies*, vol.13, pp. 193–209.

Yuval-Davis, N. (2011) *The Politics of Belonging: Intersectional Contestations*, London: Sage.

Zizek, S. (2002) *Revolution at the Gates: Selected Writing of Lenin from 1917*, London: Verso.

Index

Numbers in **bold** refer to Glossary entries